Service-oriented Software System Engineering

Service-oriented Software System Engineering

Editor:

Dr. Jovan Pehcevski, Ph.D.

ArclerPress

www.arclerpress.com

Service-oriented Software System Engineering

Editor: Dr. Jovan Pehcevski, Ph.D.

708 3rd Avenue, 6th Floor
New York
NY 10017
United States of America
www.arclerpress.com

ISBN: 978-1-68094-461-7

Library of Congress Control Number: 2016951155

About the Editor

Dr. Jovan Pehcevski, Ph.D.

Jovan obtained his PhD in Computer Science from RMIT University in Melbourne, Australia in 2007. His research interests include big data, business intelligence and predictive analytics, data and information science, information retrieval, XML, web services and service-oriented architectures, and relational and NoSQL database systems. He has published over 30 journal and conference papers and he also serves as a journal and conference reviewer. He is currently working as a Dean and Associate Professor at European University in Skopje, Macedonia.

Contents

List of Contributors

Claus Pahl
School of Computing, Dublin City University

Ronan Barrett
School of Computing, Dublin City University

Ghadeer Ghazal
Department of Computer Information Systems, Faculty of King Abdullah II, The University of Jordan, Jordan

Amjad. Hudaib
Department of Computer Information Systems, Faculty of King Abdullah II, The University of Jordan, Jordan

Waffa Maitah
Department of Computer Science, Faculty of Information Technology, Al al-Bayt University, Jordan

Vishnuvardhan Mannava
Department of Computer Science and Engineering, K L University, Vaddeswaram, 522502, A.P., India

T. Ramesh
Department of Computer Science and Engineering, National Institute of Technology, Warangal, 506004, A.P., India

Luigi Coppolino
Centro Direzionale di Napoli, Dipartimento per le Tecnologie, Università degli Studi di Napoli "Parthenope", Napoli, Italy

Luigi Romano
Centro Direzionale di Napoli, Dipartimento per le Tecnologie, Università degli Studi di Napoli "Parthenope", Napoli, Italy

Valerio Vianello
Centro Direzionale di Napoli, Dipartimento per le Tecnologie, Università degli Studi di Napoli "Parthenope", Napoli, Italy

Marcos Kalinowski
Federal University of Juiz de Fora, Rua José Kelmer s/n, Juiz de Fora 36.036-330, Brazil

Stefan Biffl
Institute of Software Technology and Interactive Systems, CDL-Flex-, Vienna University of Technology, Favoritenstr. 9/188, Vienna 1040, Austria

Rodrigo Oliveira Spínola
University of Salvador, Rua Doutor José Peroba 251, Salvador 41.770-235, Brazil

Sheila Reinehr
Catholic University of the State of Paraná, Rua Imaculada Conceição 1155, Curitiba 80.215-901, Brazil

Amanda S Nascimento
Institute of Exact Sciences and Biology, Federal University of Ouro Preto, Ouro Preto, MG, Brazil

Cecília MF Rubira
Institute of Computing, University of Campinas, Campinas, SP, Brazil

Rachel Burrows
Department of Computer Science, University of Bath, Bath, UK

Fernando Castor
Informatics Center, Federal University of Pernambuco, Recife, PE, Brazil

Patrick HS Brito
Institute of Computing, University of Campinas, Campinas, SP, Brazil
Institute of Computing, Federal University of Alagoas, Maceió, AL, Brazil

Zulqarnain Abdul Jabbar
Department of Computer Science, Muhammad Ali Jinnah University, Karachi, Pakistan

Manoj Kumar
Department of Computer Science, Muhammad Ali Jinnah University, Karachi, Pakistan

Asia Samreen
Department of Computer Science, Bahria University, Karachi, Pakistan

Tao Xu
College of Computer Science and Technology, Civil Aviation University of China, Tianjin, China

Chunxiao Yi
College of Computer Science and Technology, Civil Aviation University of China, Tianjin, China

Eman El-Sheikh
Department of Computer Science, University of West Florida, Pensacola, USA

Thomas Reichherzer
Department of Computer Science, University of West Florida, Pensacola, USA

Laura White
Department of Computer Science, University of West Florida, Pensacola, USA

Norman Wilde
Department of Computer Science, University of West Florida, Pensacola, USA

John Coffey
Department of Computer Science, University of West Florida, Pensacola, USA

Sikha Bagui
Department of Computer Science, University of West Florida, Pensacola, USA

George Goehring
Department of Computer Science, University of West Florida, Pensacola, USA

Arthur Baskin
Intelligent Information Technologies Corporation, Indianapolis, USA

Derya Birant
Dokuz Eylul University, Turkey

Yifang Liu
School of Engineering, Design and Technology, University of Bradford United Kingdom

Yongqiang Cheng
School of Engineering, Design and Technology, University of Bradford United Kingdom

Yim Fun Hu
School of Engineering, Design and Technology, University of Bradford United Kingdom

Prashant Pillai
School of Engineering, Design and Technology, University of Bradford United Kingdom

Vincenzo Esposito
SELEX Sistemi Integrati S.p.A. Italy

Tanko Ishaya
The University of Hull, Scarborough Campus United Kingdom

Musiliudeen Folarin
The University of Hull, Scarborough Campus United Kingdom

Rich C. Lee
System Technology Group, IBM, Taipei, Chinese Taipei
Department of Information Management, National Sun Yat-Sen University, Taipei, Chinese Taipei

Harekrishna Misra
Institute of Rural Management Anand India

Adomas Svirskas
Eurecom Sophia-Antipolis, France
Vilnius University Vilnius, Lithuania

Jelena Isačenkova
Eurecom Sophia-Antipolis, France

Refik Molva
Eurecom Sophia-Antipolis, France

Jorge Torres
The Distributed and Adaptive Systems Lab for Learning Technologies Development Tecnológico de Monterrey, Mexico

César Cárdenas
The Distributed and Adaptive Systems Lab for Learning Technologies Development Tecnológico de Monterrey, Mexico

Juan Manuel Dodero
Computer Science Department Universidad de Cádiz, Spain

Eduardo Juárez
The Distributed and Adaptive Systems Lab for Learning Technologies Development Tecnológico de Monterrey, Mexico

Mazanai Musara
University of Fort Hare South Africa

Preface

Service Oriented Architecture (SOA) is a type of an integrated information environment of a business system, which is characterized by publishing and usage of distributed functions, so called services. It provides the basis for the concept of uniform posting, discovery, communication, and usage of individual business functions in order to achieve desired goals. SOA represents a set of principles that define a new concept of designing corporate information systems, by using loosely coupled business services and a unified view of the business processes that is supported by a granular business system architecture, whose implementation is independent of the technologies used by the different underlying vendor modules.

SOA can be viewed as a perspective of the global IT environment, in the sense that it allows for development, supply and use of independent, third-party software services that support individual requirements of the business processes and the users. In the SOA environment, services are available to business processes and users without control and coordination mechanisms; instead, they are invoked by a predefined infrastructure framework. SOA is neutral from the technology standards and protocols, i.e., it does not involve the use of specific technology and can be implemented by any interoperability standards, such as RPC, DCOM, ORB, or SOAP. The main focus of the SOA concept is the modeling and implementation of the business, not the technical infrastructure. Each service represents a set of business functions within a business environment. Technical services, such as transactions, data persistence, etc., which are necessary for the technical implementation of business services, are not relevant to the strategic modeling and development of the SOA environment. In this sense, the technical implementation details should not have any impact on the SOA structure's higher levels, especially when it comes to the interdependence of different business services or their components. In this edition we cover topics about SOA-based software engineering, the design and the communication aspects of service-oriented systems, as well as different use-case scenarios and usage of the SOA in the public sector. Section 1 focuses on SOA-based software engineering, describing pattern-based software architecture for service-oriented software systems, software architectural patterns for service composition, feature-oriented service injection and composition of web services for distributed computing systems, security engineering of SOA applications via reliability patterns, and an industrial experience for service-oriented software development. Section 2 focuses on design and communication aspects of service-oriented systems, describing designing fault-tolerant SOA based on design diversity, conceptual framework for aligning service oriented architecture with business process, SOAP-based security interaction of web service in heterogeneous platforms, and enhanced program comprehension for service-oriented architectures. Section 3 focuses on different SOA use-case scenarios, describing distributed e-learning based on SOA, service-oriented data mining, SOA-based aeronautical service integration, business intelligence in telecoms industry, and service oriented analytics framework for multi-level marketing. Section 4 focuses on usage of SOA in the public sector, describing SOA perspective of e-governance in the Indian context, lightweight SOA-based collaboration framework for European public sector, educational modelling languages and service-oriented learning process, and the usage of SOA in the financial services sector in South Africa.

Editor
Dr. Jovan Pehcevski, Ph.D.

INTRODUCTION

Service-oriented Software Engineering (SOSE) is a software engineering methodology focused on the development of software systems by composition of reusable services (service-orientation) often provided by other service providers. Since it involves composition, it shares many characteristics of component-based software engineering, the composition of software systems from reusable components, but it adds the ability to dynamically locate necessary services at run-time. These services may be provided by others as web services, but the essential element is the dynamic nature of the connection between the service users and the service providers.

Service-oriented interaction pattern

There are three types of actors in a service-oriented interaction: service providers, service users and service registries. They participate in a dynamic collaboration which can vary from time to time. Service providers are software services that publish their capabilities and availability with service registries. Service users are software systems (which may be services themselves) that accomplish some task through the use of services provided by service providers. Service users use service registries to discover and locate the service providers they can use. This discovery and location occurs dynamically when the service user requests them from a service registry.

Component-Based and Service-Oriented Software Engineering: Key Concepts and Principles

Today, designing and implementing a large scale and complex system has been a challenging task. Two of the most well recognized software engineering paradigms coping with this challenge are: component based software engineering and service-oriented software engineering. Component-based software engineering (CBSE) provides support for building systems through the composition and assembly of software components. It is an established approach in many engineering domains, such as distributed and web based systems, desktop and graphical applications and recently in embedded systems domains. CBSE technologies facilitate effective management of complexity, significantly increase reusability and shorten time to market. On the other hand, the growing demands for Internet computing and emerging network-based business applications and systems are the driving forces for the evolvement of service-oriented software engineering (SOSE). Service-oriented design utilizes services as fundamental elements for developing applications and software solutions. Service-oriented design technologies offer great feasibility of integrating distributed systems that are built on various platforms and technologies and further push focus on reusability and software development efficiency. SOSE has evolved from CBSE frameworks and object oriented computing to face the challenges of open environments. Therefore, CBSE and SOSE are similar to each other in many senses. Both use similar approaches and technologies. Both have software architecture as the common source and base. Meanwhile, both paradigms have continued with their development tracks in parallel and have different focus. Consequently, the mixture of similarities and specialized utilization of concepts in CBSE and SOSE have also resulted in confusion in understanding and applying concepts in a correct way. This may lead to less efficient utilization and combination of these paradigms. Furthermore, since both CBSE and SOSE can co-exist in enterprise systems and complement each other, any divided understanding and different interpretation of the terminologies would lead to less efficient combination and adaptation of these paradigms in future software development. For these reasons, it is important to clarify the concepts, principles and characteristics of CBSE and SOSE, shorten the gap between them and bring these worlds together so that researchers and practitioners can become aware of both sides. This clarification may serve as inputs to the subsequent investigation in how to take advantages of the strengths of these two paradigms, how to adapt and integrate the component based and service-oriented technologies, concepts and their strengths so that both component-base and service-oriented software engineering can complement each other to the ultimate extent. The goal of this paper is to provide a clarification framework of the component-based and service oriented software engineering to avoid any misunderstandings and misuses. A brief discussion of reasonable utilization, combination and adaptation of the two paradigms is also outlined through looking into a set of research studies in how they have been used. These studies have exampled the benefits of improved quality attributes of software solutions through combining CBSE and SOSE. Since both paradigms are evolving rapidly, there exists increasing research interest in further exploration of their combination potentials.

Overview of component-based and service-oriented software engineering

Component-based software engineering (CBSE) is a software engineering paradigm that aims to accelerate software development and promote software reusability and maintenance through assembling components to software systems that meet certain business requirements. The prerequisite requirements that enable components to be integrated and work together are component models and component framework. Component models specify the standards and conventions that components need to follow during component composition and interaction. Component framework provides design time and run time infrastructure. Numerous component models exist nowadays. Some examples are COM/DCOM/COM+, .Net component model, JavaBeans, Enterprise JavaBeans and CORBA component model. Examples of component models that have been developed specifically for applications to embedded systems include Koala, Rubus, PECOS. Important areas of research within CBSE include, but not limited to, determination and specification of QoS (Quality of Service), predictability of nonfunctional properties, component interference and process related activities such as component classification, identification and selection, component adaptation, testing and deployment techniques. Although CBSE has proved to be successful for software reuse and maintainability, it does not address all of the complexities software developers are facing today, such as varying platforms, varying protocols, various devices, the Internet, etc. Service-oriented software engineering paradigm has emerged to address these issues. Service-oriented software engineering (SOSE) is a software engineering paradigm that aims to support the development of rapid, low-cost and easy composition of distributed applications even in heterogeneous environments. It utilizes services as fundamental elements for developing applications and solutions. Important areas of research within SOSE include service foundations, service composition, service management and monitoring and service-oriented engineering. Service foundations provide service oriented communication technologies to support run time service-oriented infrastructure and connect heterogeneous systems and applications. These communication technologies provide the communication mechanisms between service providers and service requesters; they differ with respect to service description techniques and messaging functions. Service composition encompasses necessary roles and functionality to support service composition. The dynamic composition feature in SOSE makes QoS a major challenge. Different initiatives have emerged such as orchestration and choreography. Service management encompasses the control and monitoring of SOA-based applications throughout life cycle. A key element in SOSE is the service-oriented interaction pattern, i.e. service-oriented architecture (SOA), which enables a collection of services to communicate with each other. SOA is a way of designing a software system to provide services to applications or other services through published and discoverable interfaces.

The basic elements of service oriented architecture are illustrated in Figure 1.

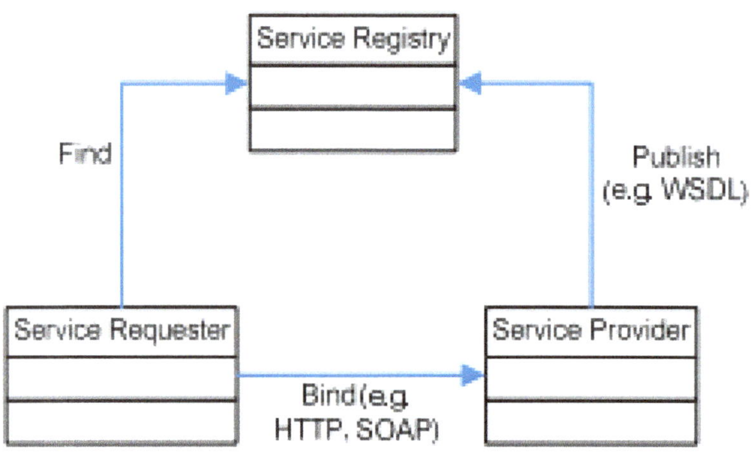

Figure 1 Service-oriented interaction pattern.

As shown in Figure 1, SOA has three main actors: a service provider, a service requester and a service registry. The service provider defines service descriptions of a collection of services, supplies services with functionalities and publishes the descriptions of the services so as to make the services discoverable. The service registry contains service descriptions and references to service providers and provides mechanisms for service publishing and discovery, e.g. Universal Description, Discovery and Integration (UDDI). The service requester is a client that calls a service provider. It can be an end-user application or other services. A service requester searches in the service registry for a specific service via the service interface description. When the service interfaces match with the criteria of the service requester, the service requester will use the service description and make a dynamic binding with the service provider, invoke the service and interact directly with the service.

Classification of component-based and service-oriented software engineering

The main concepts and principles of CBSE and SOSE may look similar at the first sight, but differences exist in mechanisms, approaches and implementations. Therefore, we group particular characteristics that have similar concerns to describe the same or related aspects of CBSE and SOSE. The categories in the comparison framework that we are going to address are: key concepts and principles, process concerns, technology concerns, quality and composition

Key concepts

Table 1 Comparison of key concepts in CBSE and SOSE

Concepts	CBSE	SOSE
Module	Component	Service
Specification	Component contract	Service description
Interface	Component interface	Service interface
Assembly	Component composition	Service composition

Module

In CBSE, components are the building blocks that can be deployed independently and are subject to composition by third party. Based on the formulation by Clemens Szyperski, a software component is a unit of composition with contractually specified interfaces and explicit context dependencies only. It can be both fine-grained providing specific functionality and coarse-grained encompassing complicated logics. In SOSE, services are the building blocks that can be reused and offer particular functionalities. They are generally implemented as coarse-grained discoverable software entities [2], operating on larger data sets, encapsulating business functionality and exposing the functionality to any source that requests the functionality through well-defined interfaces. Thus, the services can be reused and accessed at various levels of the enterprise application and even across enterprises boundaries.

Specification

In CBSE, the component specification provides for the clients the definition of the component's interface, i.e. the operations and context dependencies. Furthermore, an abstract definition of the component's internal structure is specified for the component providers. In SOSE, the service description is a service contract that advertises the following information: (i) service capabilities - stating the conceptual purpose and expected results of the service; (ii) interface - describing the service signatures of a set of operations that are available to the service requester for invocation; (iii) behavior - describing the expected behavior of a service during its execution; and (iv) quality - describing important functional and nonfunctional service quality attributes

Interface

Although both CBSE and SOSE are interface-based in the sense that interfaces are the specifications of access points, the separation between service descriptions and service implementation is more explicit than the separation between component specification and implementation

Assembly

In CBSE, component composition is the process of assembling components using connectors or glue code to form an assembly, a larger component or an application. The components are assembled through the component interfaces and the composition is made out of several component instances that are connected and interact together. In SOSE, the composite services are built by composing service descriptions. The realization of the service composition is during run time when the service providers are discovered and bound.

Key principles

A summary of the key principles of implementation in CBSE and SOSE is listed in Table2.

Table 2 Comparison of key principles of implementation in CBSE and SOSE

PRINCIPLES	CBSE	SOSE
Coupling	Loose and tight coupling	Loose coupling
Self describing	Component specification	Service descriptions
Self contained	yes	yes
State	Stateless/stateful	Stateless/stateful
Location transparency	In some component models e.g. DCOM	yes

Coupling

CBSE enables both loose coupling and tight coupling. As a component is used within the scope of a component model, it needs to conform to the rules specified by the component model. A component model often uses one particular interaction style, such as broadcasting, asynchronous connection and connection-oriented style. All these interaction styles imply some kind of coupling between components, such as referential coupling and temporal coupling. In contrast to CBSE, SOSE enables only loose coupling, with minimized dependencies between service providers and service requesters. The service providers need not to know anything about the service requesters or any other services. They have great flexibility in choosing their design and deployment environment to offer their services. Likewise, the service requesters or calling applications need not to know anything about underlying logic of the service implementation and service deployment except the service descriptions. The service descriptions are the only communication channel between service requesters and service providers. Service loose coupling is enabled through the use of service descriptions that allow services to interact within predefined parameters.

Self-describing

Both CBSE and SOSE share the same self-describing characteristic with their own specialization. In CBSE, the component specification is the key to the component's self-describing characteristic and specifies the rules that the components must conform to. In SOSE, the service description is the key to the service's self-describing characteristic. The service provides its clients with all the relevant information in the service descriptions, which contain combinations of syntactic, semantic and behavioral information.

Self-contained

In CBSE, components can be self-contained. For example, for CCM, a component is 'a self-contained unit of software code consisting of its own data and logic, with well-defined connections or interfaces exposed for communication. It is designed for repeated use in developing applications; either with or without customization'. In SOSE, services are self-contained. The services provide the same functionality regardless of the other services, even if any other services may fail for some reason

Stateless

Both components and services can be stateful or stateless. In SOSE, stateless services are used to meet the performance requirements and in some circumstances, the stateless property is optimal for services' reusability. As a result, the services should minimize the amount of state information they manage and the duration for holding the message information. Otherwise, the services would not be able to timely correspond to other service requesters. On the other hand, there are circumstances when stateful services are necessary so as to maintain states across several method calls by the same service requester. The service object creation policy determines whether a stateful service can be returned.

Location transparency

In CBSE, some component models can provide location transparency, e.g. DCOM allows component-based applications to be distributed across memory spaces or physical machines using proxies and stubs. In SOSE, since services have their descriptions and location information stored in the service registry through e.g. UDDI, which is accessible to a variety of service requesters, services can be invoked by service requesters from different locations.

Development process concerns

Three aspects related to development process are identified for further comparison.

Building from pre-existing entities (components or services). The main idea for CBSE is to build systems from pre-existing components. This feature applies in the same way for SOSE in the sense that systems can be built from composing appropriate pre-existing services to meet certain business functionality.

Separation of development process of system and entities (components or services). In CBSE, the development process of component-based systems is separated from the development process of components. This feature applies in the same way for SOSE in the sense that services can be developed by various service providers across organizational boundaries and the service requesters need only to discover and invoke the services.

Development process. In CBSE, engineering a component-based software system is a process of finding components, evaluating and selecting proper components, testing, adapting if necessary and integrating the components into the software system, e.g. in the COTS-based development process. In SOSE, engineering a service-oriented computing system is a process of discovering and composing the appropriate services to satisfy a specification. The process of service discovering, matching, planning and composing is essential. Service-oriented engineering process focuses more on run-time activities, such as dynamically adding, discovering and composing services illustrated in Figure 2

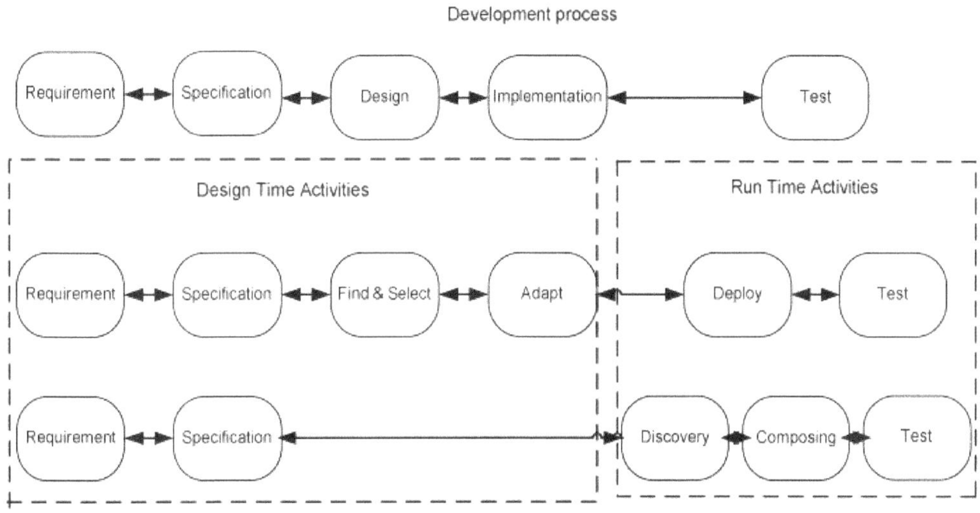

Figure 2 Comparison of typical activities during development process in CBSE and SOSE

Technology concerns

Three aspects are identified for further comparison: technology neutrality, encapsulation and static or dynamic behavior.

Technology neutrality

In CBSE, components need to conform and follow the rules that are set up by a specific component model. As a result, the feasibility to compose components of different component models is relatively limited. On the other hand, compliance to a certain technology may also lead to advantages in the sense that many solutions can be optimized since they can be directly supported by the specific technology. In contrast to CBSE, SOSE provides the feasibility for services to be implemented in diverse technologies and for multiple applications running on different platforms to communicate with each other. This feasibility is enabled through applying commonly accepted message standards for interface descriptions to the services. Hence, the enterprise applications or solutions can cut across technology and platform boundaries, performing business functionalities by composing services from different sources of service providers.

Encapsulation

Encapsulation means that the business logic and implementation are shielded from the outside world. CBSE supports a variety of encapsulation types, ranging from white box exposing all the implementation, or gray box exposing parts of component implementation to black box. In the cases of white box and gray box, the component clients have the flexibility to make modifications to the component in order to meet specific needs in their solutions. In contrast to CBSE, SOSE supports only black box encapsulation. The logical view of a service consists of one or a set of service interfaces and service implementation. A service can be regarded as a business logic entity which can be accessed and executed through the well-defined and formal interfaces by any service requester that wants to use the service. This is called the service interface level abstraction, which enables the services to act as black boxes, leading to the inflexibility of service requesters to modify services.

Static vs. dynamic

Two aspects are concerned:

(1) Binding: There are two types of binding: early binding and late binding. Early binding allows clients to obtain compile-time type information from the component's type library. Late binding allows clients to bind to components at run time and the compiler has no clue during build time about the method calls that are to be made at run time. CBSE allows static early binding and supports dynamic late binding in some component models. An example is early and late binding to COM components. In early binding, the components are instantiated as needed and invocations of operations are based on the interface definitions, statically checked and bound to by the compiler. In late binding, components are bound by invoking IDispatch methods in COM that redirects dynamically to the sought interface. The choice of static or dynamic binding has both pros and cons, and consequently need to be taken into consideration during design. Static binding between components may lead to the disadvantage of less flexibility in facilitating changes, but it allows for stronger type checking during compile time and is much faster than the late binding approach. SOSE allows only dynamic binding. The service requesters make targeted named calls and search in the service registry for a specific service. When the service requesters find the services that match certain criteria, the service requester will use the service description to make a dynamic binding with the service provider.

(2) Dynamic discovery and availability:Discovery implies the ability that an entity (component or service) is discovered for use. Availability is the ability that an entity (component or service) is operational or accessible when required for use. In CBSE, dynamic discovery and dynamic availability of components are not the major concerns. In SOSE, services exhibit the feature of dynamic availability, since they can be added or removed from the service registry at any time. Consequently, services are readily available running entities and need to be dynamically discovered and composed in run time.

Quality concerns

Quality attributes can be classified into life cycle properties and run time properties. Hundreds of quality properties exist and we cannot analyze all of them. Therefore, we choose only quality attributes that are of common or related interest to CBSE and SOSE.

Reusability as life cycle property

CBSE emerged to accelerate reusability of software. However, there are some constraints in achieving component reusability, such as component specification should be explicit, no architectural mismatches among composed components, etc. Similar to CBSE, services can be reused to construct applications. In SOSE, the concern in having similar architecture needs not to be taken into consideration because of the technology neutrality, platform independence and interoperability characteristics of SOSE. On the other hand, extra emphasis is put on having explicit service descriptions. There are several factors that contribute to the reusability of components and services. Firstly, both components and services are compostable. This implies that the level of granularity of components and services need to be considered when taking reusability into account. The design of operations should be in a standardized manner and with appropriate level of granularity so that the components or services can be reused and composed. Secondly, the separations between component/service development and applications also promote component and service reusability. Recently, researchers have been active in investigating the possibilities of enhancing service reusability with service-oriented architectures. One study is presented by Zhu in, where he proposed the idea that services are new types of components and service-oriented architectures may provide more chances for the development of reusable components.

Substitutability as life cycle property

Substitutability means that alterative entity (component or service) implementation may be used with the constraints that the system can still meet the requirements on functional level and non-functional level. According to, white box and gray box reuse very likely prevents the component substitutability. In such cases, explicit conventions about the implementation information and changes that are made in components are required to achieve substitutability. In SOSE, since the service-oriented interaction pattern enables the loose coupling characteristic between a service requester and service providers, services can be substituted with new services as long as the service descriptions fulfill the criteria from service requesters.

Interoperability as runtime property

The main idea in CBSE is to assemble components together to perform certain functionality. However, each component conforms to a certain component model that specifies different rules from another component model. Therefore, interoperability between heterogeneous components is still a challenging issue in CBSE. Although in some circumstances, interoperability can be achieved through implementing wrapper class or proxies. On the other hand, broad interoperability among different vendors' applications and solutions can be achieved in SOSE through the use of well accepted standards. For instance, WSDL, UDDI, SOAP, XML. These descriptions are independent of underlying platform, programming languages and implementation details and therefore promote interoperability.

Section I - SOA-based Software Engineering

CHAPTER 1

PATTERN-BASED SOFTWARE ARCHITECTURE FOR SERVICE-ORIENTED SOFTWARE SYSTEMS

Claus Pahl and Ronan Barrett

INTRODUCTION

The development of distributed software systems based on service architectures is rapidly gaining momentum. Service-oriented architecture (SOA) is emerging as a new design paradigm and conceptual framework for distributed service-centric software systems, supported by platforms such as the Web Services Framework (WSF) [2]. Services are reusable software components that are explicitly described, published and provided at fixed locations. Due to the ubiquity of the Web, the WSF platform and SOA paradigm play a major role for software systems.

In service-centric distributed environments such as the Web services platform that allows services to be invoked using Internet protocols, a notion of workflow processes is central to capture service composition and interaction between services. We present techniques to support, firstly, modelling of services and service-oriented processes and, secondly, property-preserving transformations of service-oriented architectures. In contrast to a variety of architecture approaches that focus primarily on static, structural properties, we concentrate on dynamic dependencies in the form of interaction processes between services. Our solution is an approach to the architectural transformation of services, supporting the evolution of service-oriented architectures. Three aspects characterise our approach:

- Architecture modelling using hierarchical patterns. A three-layered architecture model addresses different levels of abstraction. Each layer is supported by a pattern-based modelling approach for service processes. A service-oriented architectural configuration notation that combines patterns and process behaviour in architectures forms the backbone. Patterns enhance reuse in SOA.
- Property-preserving architectural transformation. Based on the configuration notation as the abstract description language for source and target architectures, a transformation technique is developed. Patterns are considered as characteristics of a service architecture that are, due to the implied reliability and maintainability, worth being preserved in transformations.
- Distribution and quality-of-service. We investigate the role of distribution for modelling and look at functional and non-functional service properties. The integration of quality aspects into modelling is important for the services platform, where providers and users are usually from different organisations.

We address the lack of behaviour and quality aspects in service-oriented architectural transformations. Our patterns capture essential behavioural service dependencies in the form of interaction process patterns and link these to quality properties. We utilise patterns to capture these properties and allow these properties to be preserved in transformations by identifying patterns as invariants. Formality is required to obtain unambiguous models of process-based service architectures and to complement modelling by analysis and reasoning facilities. Architectural change and integration require a technique for process-oriented property-preserving transformations.

We introduce our architecture model and transformation technique in Section 2. Pattern-based architecture modelling and specification, supported by the architecture configuration notation, is addressed in Section 3. Architectural transformations are defined in Section 4. Finally, we discuss related work and end with conclusions.

Citation: Claus Pahl, Ronan Barrett, Pattern-Based Software Architecture for Service-Oriented Software Systems, http://www.e-informatyka.pl/attach/e-Informatica_-_Volume_4/eInformatica2010Art3.pdf

ARCHITECTURE MODEL AND SPECIFICATION

Based on background definitions of service and software architecture, we now define the principles of our architecture model and the core notation.

Service-oriented Architecture

The objective of software architecture is the separation of computation and communication. Architectures are about components (i.e. loci of computation) and connectors (i.e. loci of communication). Various architecture description languages (ADL) and modelling techniques have been proposed [17]. An architectural model captures common concepts in architectural description: components provide computation, interfaces provide access and connectors provide connections between components. In service architecture, the main emphasis is on the composition of services to workflow processes and on the overall configuration of services and service processes. For instance [10], use scenarios – descriptions of interactions of a user with a system – to operationalise requirements and map these to a system architecture. We extend the notion of interaction and also consider system-internal interactions and allow interaction processes to be composite.

We focus on service architectures, i.e. service-oriented software architectures, here. A service is usually defined as a coherent set of operations provided at a certain location [2]. A service provider makes an abstract interface description available, which can be used by potential service users to locate and invoke this service. The Web Service platform provides description languages (WSDL) and invocation protocols (SOAP) for this purpose. Services are often used 'as is' in single request-response interactions. More recently, research has focused on the composition of services to processes [2]. Orchestration is the prevalent form of service composition. Existing services can be reused to form business or workflow processes. The principle of architectural composition that we look at here is process assembly.

An Architectural Configuration Notation

At the core of our architecture modelling and transformation technique is a conceptual architecture model. The objective of this conceptual architecture model is to capture the core layering and structuring principles of service-oriented architectures. The conceptual service architecture model (SAM), tailored towards the needs of service- and process-oriented platforms, shall address the different abstraction levels and perspectives in service-oriented architectures:

- Reference architectures are high-level specifications representing common structures of architectures specific to a particular domain or platform.
- Architectural design patterns are medium-scale patterns – usually referred to as design patterns or architectural frameworks.
- Workflow patterns are process-oriented patterns that represent common data exchange-oriented workflow processes in an application domain.

Based on the architecture model, we define a notation for architectural specification – the service-oriented architectural configuration notation (SAC) – that has features of an abstract architectural description language (ADL). Two elements define our transformation technique: a description notation to capture architectural properties and rules and techniques for transformation.

Various formal approaches to the representation of processes have been suggested in the past, e.g. [6] using Petri nets. Process calculi such as the π-calculus [15, 13] are suitable frameworks for architectural configurations of service- and process-centric systems, i.e. support of modelling and transformation, due to their abstraction from service implementation and their focus on interaction processes. The π-calculus, a calculus for mobile processes, is particularly useful due to a similarity between mobility and evolution – both are about changes of a service in relation to its neighbourhood – which helps us to support architectural transformations. Our notation is defined in terms of the π-calculus [15], but we want to firstly provide a less mathematical syntax and, secondly, allow the addition of further combinators to express workflow and design patterns. A simulation notion captures property-preservation and permitted structure and behaviour variations during transformation.

Actions:

π	$::=$	$\textbf{inv}\ x(y)$	Invocation
		$\textbf{rcv}\ x(a)$	Activation – Receive
		$\textbf{rep}\ x(b)$	Activation – Reply

Processes – workflow combinators:

P	$::=$	π	Action
		$P_1; P2$	Sequential Composition
		$\textbf{par}\ (P_1, P_2)$	Parallel Composition
		$\textbf{repeat}\ (P)$	Iteration
		$\textbf{choice}\ (P_1, P_2)$	Exclusive Choice
		$\textbf{mchoice}\ (P_1, P_2)$	Multi-Choice

Processes – other constructs:

P	$::=$	$\textbf{let}\ x = \pi\ \textbf{in}$	Variable
		0	Inaction

Abstraction:

$$A(a_1, \ldots, a_n) \quad = \quad P_A \quad \text{with } a_1, \ldots, a_n \text{ are free in } P_A$$

Figure 1. Syntactical Definition of the SAC Notation.

Our notation consists of process activities, combinators and abstractions, which are summarised in Fig. 1. The basic element describing process activity is an action. Actions π are combined to service process expressions. Actions of a service are primitive processes divided into invocations and activations. Invocations inv x(y) by a client of a service via channel x connects to the remote service, passing y as a parameter. Activations receive rcv x(a) from a provider from other services and the dual reply rep x(b), with channel x and parameters a and b. Based on actions, process combinators are basic forms of workflow patterns. Sequences are represented as P_1; P_2 – process P_1 is executed and the system transfers to P_2 where the next action is executed. Exclusive choice means that one P_i (i = 1, . . . , n) from choice P_1, . . ., P_n is chosen, Multi-choice mchoice P_1, . . ., P_n allows any number of the processes P_i (i = 1, . . . , n) to be chosen and executed in parallel. Iteration repeat P executes process P an arbitrary number of times. Parallel composition par (P_1, . . ., P_n) executes processes P_i concurrently. A(a_1, . . . , a_n) = P_A is a process abstraction, where P is a process expression and the a_i are free variables in P. A variable is introduced using let x = π in P. Inaction is denoted by 0.

The semantics is defined in terms of the π-calculus [15], by mapping constructs directly to π-calculus constructs. The actions are de- fined in terms of send $\overline{x}\langle y\rangle$ (for invocation inv and reply rep) and receive x(y) (for receive rcv) of the π-calculus. Combinators are defined through their π-calculus counterparts, except multichoice mchoice P_1, P_2, which is defined as choice (A, B, par (A, B)) – essentially a parallel composition of all elements of the powerset of the mchoice argument list. The abstraction is the π-calculus abstraction.

PATTERN-BASED SERVICE ARCHITECTURE MODELLING

The architectural configuration notation SAC enables the modelling of pattern-based service architecture configurations.

Patterns and Abstraction Levels

Architectural and design patterns are recurring solutions to software design problems [7]. Although originally proposed for object-oriented development, their applicability for service-based architectures has been demonstrated [18]. These patterns are about structure and interaction and provide reusable solutions to commonly encountered design problems. We use patterns at different levels of abstraction – reference architectures, architectural design patterns, and workflow patterns. We cover the three layers of the architecture model SAM. Work- flow operators for service processes are directly integrated as operators. Architectural design patterns expressing service interaction patterns can be formulated as a number of concurrently executing processes. Reference architectures can be modelled at the level of abstractions.

Reference architectures, often emerge in an abstracted and standardised form from successful architectural assemblies. Reference architectures define accepted structures that help us to built maintainable and interoperable systems. Besides domain-specific architectures, which we will illustrate in the case study section, platform-specific reference architecture are important. Examples of classical Web-based architectures are client-server architectures or three-tiered architectures.

Design patterns are recognised as important building blocks in the development of software systems [7]. Their purpose is the identification of common structural and behavioural patterns. A rich set of design patterns has been described, which can be used to structure a software design at an intermediate level of abstraction. Usually, architectural patterns (such as model-view-controller) are distinguished from design patterns (such as factory, composite, or iterator) as the former are linked to component frameworks. We see both forms as intermediate-level constraints on a system architecture, i.e on services and on their interaction patterns.

Design patterns also play a role in the design of Web services architectures [18]. An example of an architectural design pattern in the Web services context is the client-dispatcher-server pattern [18]. The pattern architecture with its interactions is visualised in Fig. 2. The SAC notation adds behaviour specification to the static view of UML class diagrams. It is a textual description, similar to UML activity and interaction diagrams in purpose. We have used a UML class diagram to present the abstract service interface and the service connectivity. Pattern definitions such as client-dispatcher-server can act as building blocks of complex architectures. Patterns are defined as process expressions and made available as process abstractions. These macro-style building blocks can also form a pattern repository.

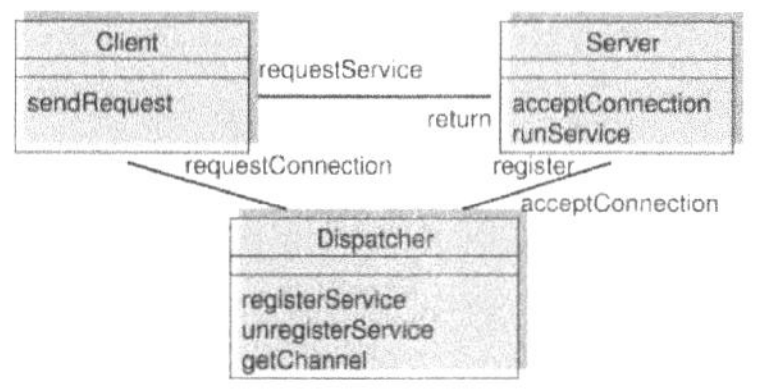


```
Client     = repeat (let requestServ = inv requestConnection()
                      in inv requestServ(resId))
Server     = inv registerServ(id):
              repeat (rcv acceptConnection(c): rcv requestServ(s):
                       rep requestServ(runService(s)))
Dispatcher = choice (
              choice (rcv registerServ(id). rcv unregisterServ(id)).
              repeat (rcv requestConnection():
                let c = getChannel()
                in  inv acceptConnection(c): rep requestConnection(c)))
```

Figure 2. Pattern – the Client-Dispatcher-Server Architectural Design Pattern

Workflow patterns are small-scale process patterns [19] – often at the same level of abstraction as design patterns, but more focussed on data exchange. Workflow patterns relate to connector types that are used in the composition of services – we provide them as built-in operators. An example of a workflow pattern is the sequencing workflow pattern. Workflow patterns are small compositions of activities. Workflow patterns for Web services architectures are described in [20].

To identify workflow patterns in an architecture specification is important since often not all patterns are supported by the implementation language.

choice(A, B, C, par(A, B), par(A, C), par(B, C), par(A, B, C))

is an equivalent workaround to the multichoice workflow, needed if the implementation language does not support the multichoice pattern mchoice(A, B, C) – which is the case with some WS-BPEL implementations [20].

Patterns and Quality

Patterns can influence a system's quality characteristics such as understandability or maintainability. For service-centric software systems specific properties arising from the often distributed and cross-organisational context are of central importance. The reliability of a system, the availability of services, and the individual service and overall system performance are often crucial.

- The qualtiy benefits of the client-dispatcher-server pattern are: composition is easy to maintain, as composition logic is contained at a single participant, the central dispatcher. Low deployment overhead as only the dispatcher manages the composition. Composition can consume participant services that are externally controlled. Web service technology enables the reuse of services.
- The main disadvantages are: a single point of failure at the dispatcher provides for poor reliability/availability. Communication bottlenecks at the dispatcher result in restricted scalability. Messages have considerable overhead for deserialisation and serialisation. A high number of often verbose messages between dispatcher and clients/servers is sub-optimal and results in poor performance.

All patterns have their advantages and disadvantages. Often, the qualities mutually affect each other negatively such as maintainability and performance. What is, however, important here is that the qualities associated to a given pattern are preserved during a transformation. The client-dispatcher-server pattern is typical for learning technology systems, for which maintainability and interoperability are central. Failure is not a highly critical problem and the number of users is predictable – which allows us to neglect two of the major disadvantages. Note, that these characteristics are associated to pattersn, but not part of our notation. For instance distribution is not part of our notation. We can use an annotation for the composition operators to indicate a distributed implementation if an extension is considered.

Case Study – Modelling Service Architectures

Our case study system is a learning environment called IDLE – the Interactive Database Learning Environment [14], which is based on object technology with a Web-based access interface. IDLE is a multimedia system that uses different mechanisms to provide access to learning content, e.g. Web server and a (synchronised) audio server. It is an interactive system that integrates components of a database development environment (a design editor, a programming interface, and an analysis tool) into a teaching and learning context. Learners can develop database applications, supported by shared storage and workspace.

IDLE has been developed since 1996 in several stages. The consequence of this growth is a system without a designed architecture – an architecture that is even not explicitly captured and documented. However, the existing architecture is service-oriented (although not fully Web Service-based) and, consequently, is a suitable starting point for transformations. Evolving Internet technologies and frequently changing software developers are only two of the contributors to difficult maintenance. Besides achieving maintainability, interoperability and componentisation were reasons to choose a fully service-based architecture as the target.

Architecture modelling starts with the proposed three-layered approach. In the context of our case study domain, the IEEE-defined Learning Technology System Architecture (LTSA) provides a domain-specific service-oriented reference architecture [9], visualised in the UML-style class diagram in Fig. 3. Six central components such as Delivery or Coach are identified. These components provide services, e.g. the Delivery component provides a Multimedia delivery service to the LearnerEntity. These services are usually related to processing multimedia data. We use the LTSA reference architecture as a starting point for the re-engineering of IDLE.

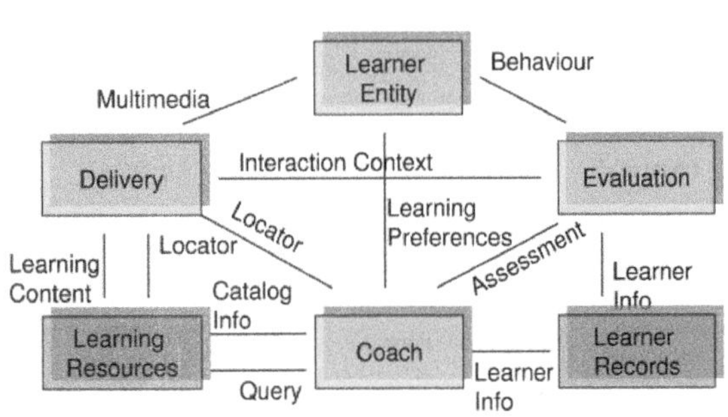

Figure 3. Overview of the LTSA Reference Architecture

In IDLE, a learner requests content from a resources server. The IDLE specification in SAC, Fig. 4, is based on the client-dispatcher-server design pattern, Fig. 2, with the learner (as client), a coach (as dispatcher), and the resources and delivery subsystem (as server). This specification captures a central behavioural property of IDLE, captured using the pattern. It is an extension of the pattern in terms of the IDLE application context that adds interaction with the Resources server to the Delivery component. Servers register their services with the dispatcher and clients request connection channels to servers in order to use the services. The learner is a client invoking services of the delivery (request a connection and an educational service). The coach is a broker and mediator that handles the service registration (from the delivery) and forwards the delivery channel (provided by the delivery component) to the learner. Passing channel names over channels, as in the example, is typical for the notation's ability to model dynamic infrastructures. A learner uses the provided channel to access the delivery's educational service.

```
Learner  = repeat (let requestEducServ = inv requestConnection()
                   in   inv requestEducServ(resId))
Delivery = inv registerEducServ(id);
            repeat (rcv acceptConnection(c); rcv requestEducServ(s);
                    rep requestEducServ(run(s)); rcv locator(uri);
                    let learnResource = inv retrieveResource(uri)
                    in  rep multimedia(learnResource))
Coach    = choice (
            choice (rcv registerEducServ(id), rcv unregisterEducServ(id)),
            repeat (rcv requestConnection();
              let c = getChannel()
              in  inv acceptConnection(c); rep requestConnection(c)))
```

Figure 4. Specification – Educational Service (EducServ) Registration and Provision in IDLE directly based on the Client-Dispatcher-Server Design Pattern

Another example of a design pattern is the factory method pattern – a creational pattern [7] that provides an interface for creating related objects without specifying their concrete classes. This pattern can be applied in IDLE for manipulating a variety of related persistent stores such as the learners records or adding/retrieving objects to/from a database such as a workspace feature.

Workflow patterns are the final architectural aspect. The multichoice operator denotes a process composition pattern. mchoice(Lecture, Tutorial, Lab) expresses that any selection of the IDLE services Lecture, Tutorial, and Lab can be used concurrently. We have realised the storage and workspace function, which could have been integrated into either learning resources or learner records, as a separate service. This IDLE feature can be specified as a complex service workflow process, see Fig. 5. The workspace service deals with incoming retrieval or storage requests.

Our service modelling notation needs a methodological context that covers modelling existing systems and transformations. Service-oriented architecture usually starts with the identification of services. Two cases can be distinguished:

- Some system components will exhibit service character – an SQL execution element, part of the IDLE lab resources and delivery subsystem, is an example.
- Some components could easily be wrapped up as services, if required. An example of this category is the IDLE storage and workspace feature.

Once all services have been identified, the connections and interactions between services have to be modelled. In our case study, the problem is re-engineering of a legacy system into a service-based system. The existing architecture – even though not adequately designed and documented – provides a starting point for service identification. The LTSA also determines the service-based modelling of IDLE due to the LTSA's SOA character. We have used a top-down approach to service identification as the first step of the transformation part.

The need to change, adapt and extend makes it clear that the original architecture cannot be fully preserved. An abstraction mechanism – in the form of patterns – answers the need to focus on essential, but not all architectural properties that should be preserved. Patterns not only identify common functional structures; they also have typical quality attributes associated with them. A central difficulty arises: how to identify suitable patterns. The collection of frequent patterns is often domain-specific, as our investigation indicates. Examples of frequently occurring design patterns in IDLE, other learning technology systems, and also the LTSA include the client-dispatcher-server pattern, but also the factory, proxy, observer, composite, and serialiser patterns [7]. Other, less frequent patterns include the iterator and the strategy pattern. These common patterns could result in a domain-specific formulation of patterns and a repository of domain-specific patterns, which would help software architects in identifying invariants of the transformation.

```
WorkSpace  =  choice (
                  repeat (rcv retrieve(resId); inv provide(res)),
                  repeat (rcv store(resId, res)))
```

Figure 5. Specification – Specification of the IDLE Storage and Workspace Service

TRANSFORMATION

Software architecture addresses more than the high-level system design. Software change resulting from maintenance requirements and integration problems is equally important. We focus on architecture transformations as a central software change technique. A number of reasons might require transformations:

- Interoperability can be a transformation objective.
- A reference architecture might need to be adopted.
- Changes in interface and interaction of services need to be addressed.

Architectures are often transformed if implementation restrictions have to be dealt with. An objective of architecture transformation is to implement changes, but also to preserve properties. Existing service connectivity and interaction is often worth being preserved, i.e. act as invariants of the transformation. Our patterns express processes at different levels of abstraction. Preserving patterns is desirable since patterns represent architectural configurations that are easy to understand and implement and describe structures that are often easy to maintain and reliable.

While the idea of preserving patterns at all architecture layers is therefore obvious, a verifiable transformation technique is needed. A generic constructive mapping rule is at the centre of our transformation technique. A notion of simulation captures the notions of equivalence and refinement of services and service processes.

A prerequisite for transformations is the explicit architecture specification of an existing system. A complete specification is not necessary; accuracy and level of preservation of the transformation, however, depend on the degree of detail and number of patterns identified. In IDLE, we have for instance analysed an inadequately documented system to extract structures and patterns.

Simulation and Transformation Rules

Our transformation technique is based on a notion of simulation and on simulation-based transformation rules. It has to address the needs of the three pattern-based architecture layers and the focus on patterns as transformation invariants. Each of the three architecture models might create its own requirements:

- Reference architectures. Each service abstraction is mapped to a service abstraction in the new architecture. The transformation objective determines whether the service process definition has to be changed. The transformation is subject to invariants, i.e. pattern preservation.
- Architectural design patterns. Often, interaction processes need to be changed to accommodate new or modified service functionality. Ideally, newly emerging patterns that a service participates in will simulate the original patterns.
- Workflow patterns. Workflow pattern transformations can often be handled automatically in architecture implementations.

Property preservation is the goal of our architecture transformations. A simulation notion shall capture service process pattern preservation in the transformation technique. A simulation definition, adopted from the π-calculus, satisfies the pattern preservation requirement for the processes that we envisage:

Process Q simulates process P if there exists a binary relation S over the set of processes such that if whenever PSQ and $P \xrightarrow{m} P'$ then there exists Q' such that $Q \xrightarrow{n} Q'$ and $P'SQ'$ for service processes n and m.

This definition expresses when process Q based on service expression n preserves, or simulates, the behaviour of process P based on service expression m. The services n and m can here be unrelated, as this definition is about observable behaviour only.

In order to automate transformation support based on this definition, a constructive theorem supporting simulation is needed. This theorem is the basis of a transformation rule which allows the verification of preservation and the automation of transformation. In [12], we have developed a constructive simulation test based on the construction of transition graphs for SAC process expressions.

Since usually not the entire specified behaviour should be preserved, we have introduced the notion of patterns to capture common behavioural aspects that need to be preserved. Patterns at different levels of abstraction identify reliable and maintainable interaction patterns between services. Central to our transformation technique is a transformation rule, which associates patterns and simulation:

Given an architecture specification S in SAC, create an architecture specification S' as follows. For each abstraction A in S (apply this rule recursively from top to bottom), map A to A' where A' is another abstraction such that for any pattern P that A participates in, A' simulates P' with P' = P[A/A'], i.e. A' substitutes A and P is replaced by P' to cater for renaming of abstractions.

This produces pattern-preserving target architectures, if no further modification are made. We, however, argue that further modifications of the initial architecture in terms of additional or modified functionality are typical for transformations in evaluation and integration contexts. In this case, the invariant pattern preservation needs to be demonstrated. Pattern-preserving transformation rules can aid here. These are based on standard simulation relationships discussed in the process algebra literature [15], such as:

- A; B simulates A: only transitions of B are added that do not affect A.
- repeat(A) simulates A: a single repetition corresponds to A.
- choice(A; B) simulates A: the selection of A corresponds to A.
- par(A; B) simulates A: A is always executed in the parallel composition.

From this constructive rule set, pattern-preserving transformations that even include structural and behavioural changes can be formulated.

The determination of an invariant, here the pattern P, is a common, but often non-trivial problem, which can be alleviated through domain-specific patterns.

Case Study – Pattern-Preserving Transformations

We demonstrate the adoption of the LTSA reference architecture on the highest level of abstraction for the IDLE system. The transformation aim is interoperability of IDLE services and components with other LTSA-specified components. This interoperability objective, however, can have an impact on all levels of abstraction. Other learning technology standards, for instance, prescribe interfaces for learning technology objects, which would have to be reflected in service interfaces here.

The starting point for the transformation is the architecture specification of an existing system – in our case IDLE in its original form. IDLE on the highest level of abstraction is a parallel composition of composite processes

IDLE = par(Learner, Delivery, StudentModel, PedagogyModel, Workspace, Evaluation, . . .)

where each top-level service is an abstraction of a process expression based on other, more basic services. Some of these are already similar to LTSA components – we have indicated this fact by using the similar names. Other existing IDLE components such as StudentModel and PedagogyModel have no direct counterpart in the LTSA, but can be abstracted by e.g. the Coach. Several different combinations of individual services can form patterns; these might actually overlap.

The first transformation step is to describe IDLE's architectural characteristics – ideally in LTSA terminology to simplify the transformation, see Fig. 3. The client-server-dispatcher pattern, see Fig. 2, is not identical to the structure that can be found in the IDLE system, see Fig. 4, since interactions with the resources server are added. The pattern itself as an identifiable pattern is nonetheless worth preserving and is, thus, one of the invariants. In our case, the client-dispatcher-server pattern par (Client, Dispatcher, Server) is therefore simulated by the composite IDLE process par (LearnerEntity, Coach, Delivery), resulting from the composition of learner, coach, and resources and delivery subsystems of the IDLE reformulation in LTSA terminology. This property is in our case easy to verify, since the IDLE specification in Fig. 4 describes only the service requests and connections that establish functionality defined in the pattern.

LTSA is a high-level system specification, to which we add functionality in IDLE in the form of new services not covered by LTSA. Architectural changes are necessary due to the workspace service integration into IDLE. The explicit storage and workspace service, see Fig. 5, requires the services LearnerEntity and Delivery to be modified in their interaction behaviour. Again, the pattern shall be the invariant of the transformation, but some refinements – constrained by the simulation definition – need to be made to accommodate the added service within the system.

Workflow patterns to be preserved can be identified due to their implementation as operators in the notation. The specification of the IDLE educational service system based on the client-dispatcher-server architectural design pattern in Fig. 4 based on Fig. 2 is defined in terms of workflow patterns. The Learner is based on a sequence of activities. The Coach is based on choice in the first part, and a concurrent split and merge in the second part. These are candidates for invariants.

The reconstructed IDLE architecture is the transformation basis. The integration of specifications of the identified existing or created services forms the transformed architecture. The transformation task is to transform IDLE into LTSA-IDLE – an architectural variant of IDLE with LTSA-conform service interfaces and interaction processes. In the transformation, we need to consider the source, the invariant, the target construction, and the preservation proof.

Source. The starting point of the transformation is the original IDLE specification. Since in our case a full specification did not exist, we analysed the system and extracted its current structural, behavioural and quality properties based on existing documentation and system tests. The high-level architecture was given earlier and some detailed excerpts are presented in Figs. 4 and 5.

Invariant. The invariant is determined by patterns on different levels of abstraction. The LTSA determines the high-level architecture. We focus here on the client-dispatcher-server pattern as the architectural pattern invariant. The identification of patterns as invariants is a crucial and difficult step that depends on the expertise of the software architect – domain-specific patterns with common behaviour or qualities provide a starting point for invariant identification. The central pattern that we have identified and chosen to be an invariant captures the interactions between three of the central components of IDLE, i.e. learner, coach and delivery. It is one of the patterns that we found frequently in learning technology systems, and that we considered suitable to capture common interaction behaviour between central system components.

Target Construction. The LTSA-based architecture specification of some IDLE services – which is the transformation result –can be found in Fig. 6. It is constructed based on our transformation rule as follows.

- At the reference architecture level, IDLE is mapped to LTSA-IDLE where the merger of StudentModel and PedagogyModel simulates the Coach. This requires a reformulation of the IDLE process (parallel composition of composite processes, e.g. Delivery) as LTSA-IDLE by renaming abstractions and introducing Coach as a new element on the highest level.
- At the architectural design pattern level, the composition is changed at the subcomponent level. Coach is defined to reflect the merger of the two model components as a parallel composition of StudentModel and PedagogyModel.

```
LearnerEntity  =  repeat (let requestEducServ = inv requestConnection()
                            in inv requestEducServ(resId);
                               let preferencesInfo = inv getPreferences();
                                   learnResource = inv multimedia()
                               in inv setPreferences(alter(preferencesInfo)))
Delivery       =  inv registerEducServ(id);
                  repeat (rcv acceptConnection(c); rcv requestEducServ(s);
                          rep requestEducServ(run(s)); rcv locator(uri);
                          let learnResource = inv retrieveResource(uri)
                          in rep multimedia(learnResource))
Coach'         =  choice (
                  choice (rcv registerEducServ(id), rcv unregisterEducServ(id)),
                  repeat (rcv requestConnection();
                    let c = getChannel()
                    in  inv acceptConnection(c); rep requestConnection(c);
                      repeat (
                        choice (
                          rcv getPreferences(); rep getPreferences(prefInfo),
                          rcv setPreferences(preferencesInfo),
                          rcv getLearnerInfo(id); rep getLearnerInfo(info),
                          let uri = inv locator(resource) in 0))))
LearningRes    =  rcv retrieveResource(uri); rep retrieveResource(retrieve(uri))
LearnerRec     =  rcv getLearnerInfo(id); rep getLearnerInfo(info(id))
```

Figure 6. Transformation – Resulting Adaptive Delivery in IDLE Architecture (selected components and services) based on the LTSA

Simulation and Preservation. The invariants – LTSA and client-dispatcher-server – are two patterns that have to be simulated by the new architecture. We have adapted our terminology to LTSA. For instance, Learner becomes LearnerEntity. Renaming does not affect the simulation property. The two components StudentModel and PedagogyModel are merged into Coach, i.e. the model components were abstracted by a single Coach interface, which results in the LTSA pattern being simulated. In this case, Coach is only introduced as an abstraction for behaviour that already existed in the source system. Simulation is therefore also guaranteed. The new Coach' service handles the interaction with the learner and pedagogy model components. The original Coach specification from Fig. 4 has been extended to reflect this fact, which is presented in Fig. 6. The structural and behavioural properties of the client-dispatcher-server pattern P := par(Client, Dispatcher, Server) are still intact, i.e. the pattern is preserved according to the transformation with pattern P and the original Coach adapted to Coach'. The three pattern components are still present and the externally visible interaction behaviour is the same[1].

[1] The formal proof is based on a constructive simulation test developed in [12], which is beyond the scope of this paper.

The specification in Fig. 6 describes a more complete range of interactions than the initial focus of Fig. 4 on educational service request and connection establishment. Fig. 6 adds the adaptive delivery of resources. After updating preferences by interacting with the coach, the learner entity requests and receives learning resources via a multimedia channel from the delivery service. The learning resources service retrieves the actual content for the delivery service, which in turn delivers it to the learner entity. Adding functionality or significantly modifying the original architecture is common in evolution and integration situations. This is also the primary motivation for introducing invariants that are abstractions of the original architecture. The original architecture can due to these modifications in practice rarely be fully preserved – only well-chosen abstractions can be suitable invariants.

Verifying the preservation of the client-dispatcher-server invariant in the resulting architecture is a non-trival task. We can demonstrate for each affected service, i.e. LearnerEntity, Coach' and Delivery, that each simulates the original component:

- LearnerEntity simulates the Client through the first process elements (the repeat expression with the first two invocations) in the sequence of four subprocess expressions. In general, repeat(A; B) simulates repeat(A) because for each state transition in A there is a corresponding one in A; B.
- Delivery (which is unchanged) simulates the Server since, similar to the first case, only basic activities such as receive-reply interactions and invocations with the Resources component are added within the repeat loop.
- Coach' simulates the Dispatcher as the Dispatcher functionality becomes the outer process structure of the Coach to which preferences and learner initialisation and the location retrieval aspects are added. A; B simulates A because transitions in A are also part of A; B.

Constructive rules are important in discharging the simulation proof obligation.

In our method, design patterns that can be identified in an existing system such as the original IDLE, should be invariants of the architectural transformation. This method can be supported by transformation tools. The architect provides the source system model and identifies preservable patterns from the model patterns and, if necessary, renamings and non-standard transformations. More involvement from the software architect is required if in the context of the transformation process, architectural features are also changed or extended. In this case, which is actually the standard situation in application integration and software migration, a fully automated approach is not feasible and the software architect needs to apply the provided constructive transformation rules to guarantee pattern preservation.

RELATED WORK

Some ADLs are similar to SAC in terms of their focus on processes. Darwin [11] is a π-calculus based ADL. Darwin focuses on component-oriented development approach, addressing behaviour and interfaces. Restrictions based on the declarative nature of Darwin make it rather unsuitable for the design of service-based architectures, where flexibility and change demands such as both binding and unbinding on demand are required features. Wright [1] is an ADL based on CSP as the process calculus. Wright supports compatibility and deadlock checks through formalised specifications, based on explicit connector types. This is an aspect that we have neglected here, but that could enable further analysis techniques, if we introduced typed channels. In [5], the formal foundations of a notion of behaviour conformance are explored, based on the π-calculus bisimilarity relation. We chose the π-calculus as our basis, since it caters for mobility, and, consequently, allows us to address transformation in the context of architecture evolution. Mobility allows us to deal with changes in the interaction infrastructure. The client-dispatcher-server pattern is an example where a new channel is dynamically formed. Architecture transformation also means controlled changes of architectural structures.

Patterns have recently been discussed in the context of Web service architectures [18, 19, 20, 4]. In [19, 20], collections of workflow patterns are compiled. We have based our catalog on these collections. The client-dispatcher-server pattern is also discussed in [18]. Other patterns that we have mentioned mainly originate from [7]. Grønmo et al. [16] consider the modelling and building of compositions from existing Web services using model-driven development. The authors consider two modelling aspects, service (interface and operations) and workflow models (control and data flow concerns). These efforts embed patterns into a methodological framework, similar to our objectives. Our consideration of distribution as a further dimension in service patterns, however, goes beyond those approaches.

A recent software architecture approach for service-based systems is model-driven development (MDD). MDD emphasises the importance of modelling and transformations. The latter are, in contrast to our framework, part of the modelling process between modelling levels of abstraction. Our framework addresses the transformation of architecture specifications, for instance to support software change and evolution. While MDD is vertically oriented, i.e. mapping from abstract domain models to more concrete platform models, we follow a more horizontal transformation approach on the level of architectures. We have focused on hierarchical pattern-based process modelling and architectural configuration – two aspects that can complement and extend MDD by providing higher levels of abstraction and architectural transformation. The formality of our approach satisfies the automation requirements of model-driven development and even adds reasoning support.

CONCLUSIONS

A new architectural design paradigm such as service-oriented architecture (SOA) requires adequate methodological support for design, maintenance, and evolution. While an underlying deployment platform exists in the form of Web Services, an engineering methodology and techniques are still largely missing. We have presented a layered architecture model that captures behavioural aspects and associates quality of architectural structures at different levels of abstraction through patterns. A modelling notation allows interaction behaviour in architectures and architectural configurations to be captured and distribution and quality characteristics to be associated. Interaction behaviour and composite processes are essential aspects for the development and maintenance of distributed service-based systems.

Our emphasis here was on the applicability of the method by demonstrating the usefulness for a service-based learning technology system. We have investigated the role that hierarchically organised patterns, supported by the architecture model and the transformation technique, can play for service-oriented architecture. Patterns that capture interaction behaviour between services are ideally suited for the service context with its focus on processes. Process patterns provide an abstraction mechanism that captures relevant invariants for architectural transformation.

- Patterns as abstractions greatly improve the possibility to reuse and evolve architectural designs. As architectural abstractions, they capture important behaviour and quality invariants.
- Pattern-based modelling has implications for functional and quality characteristics of a service-centric software system. Pattern-based transformation focuses on functional properties, but also preserves the quality characteristics.

The novelty of our architecture transformation technique is to use patterns to capture behaviour and quality invariants in a layered architectural modelling approach to service-based architecture evolution and change.

We have applied the presented techniques in the ongoing design, maintenance and evolution of the IDLE system. It is an extensive system with a range of interactive, distributed features, characterised by complex a information architecture, that has been developed by more than 20 people and maintained for more than ten years – which indicates the scalability of the transformation technique. The technique was described in its principles and illustrated using the case study. Our tool implementation for distribution pattern architecture demonstrates the positive effect of pattern-based transformations on architectures in terms of quality. However, the pragmatics of modelling with formal notations need to be addressed further. While in the case study, architects were familiar with the notation, a closer integration with UML activity diagrams is envisaged to improve acceptance and usability.

A critical aspect of the approach is the reliance on the quality of the architectural description of the original system and the adequacy of the identified patterns – particularly obvious is migration and legacy integration projects. Transformations depend on the detail of the input architecture and the patterns that define the transformation invariant. The extraction of a system's architecture and the correct identification of intended patterns for undocumented systems is a difficult aspect that, although essential for the success, has been addressed only through the idea of domain-specific patterns here. Re-engineering and migration approaches for the architectural level can provide further solutions here.

REFERENCES

1. R. Allen and D. Garlan. A formal basis for architectural connection. ACM Transactions on Software Engineering and Methodology (TOSEM), 6(3):249, 1997.

2. G. Alonso, F. Casati, H. Kuno, and V. Machiraju. Web services: concepts, architectures and applications. Springer Verlag, 2004.
3. R. Barrett, L. M. Patcas, C. Pahl, and J. Murphy. Model driven distribution pattern design for dynamic web service compositions. In Proceedings of the 6th international conference on Web engineering, page 136, 2006.
4. F. Buschmann, K. Henney, and D. C. Schmidt. Pattern-Oriented Software Architecture Volume 4: A Pattern Language for Distributed Computing. Wiley, May 2007.
5. C. Canal, E. Pimentel, and J. M. Troya. Compatibility and inheritance in software architectures. Science of Computer Programming, 41(2):105–138, 2001.
6. R. Dijkman and M. Dumas. Service-oriented design: A multi-viewpoint approach. International journal of cooperative information systems, 13(4):337–368, 2004.
7. E. Gamma, R. Helm, R. Johnson, and J. Vlissides. Design patterns: elements of reusable object-oriented software. Addison-wesley Reading, MA, 1995.
8. D. Garlan and B. Schmerl. Architecture-driven modelling and analysis. In T. Cant, editor, Proceedings of the eleventh Australian workshop on Safety critical systems and software, page 17, 2007.
9. IEEE P1484.1/D8. Draft standard for learning technology – learning technology systems architecture LTSA, 2001.
10. R. Kazman, S. J. Carri`ere, and S. G. Woods. Toward a discipline of scenario-based architectural engineering. Annals of software engineering, 9(1–4):5–33, 2000.
11. J. Magee, N. Dulay, S. Eisenbach, and J. Kramer. Specifying distributed software architectures. Software Engineering—ESEC'95, pages 137–153.
12. C. Pahl. An ontology for software component matching. Fundamental Approaches to Software Engineering, pages 6–21.
13. C. Pahl. A Pi-calculus based framework for the composition and replacement of components. In SAVCBS 2001 Proceedings, page 97, 2001.
14. C. Pahl, R. Barrett, and C. Kenny. Supporting active database learning and training through interactive multimedia. ACM SIGCSE Bulletin, 36(3):31, 2004.
15. D. Sangiorgi and D. Walker. The pi-calculus: a Theory of Mobile Processes. Cambridge University Press, 2003.
16. D. Skogan, R. Grønmo, and I. Solheim. Web service composition in UML. In Eighth IEEE International Enterprise Distributed Object Computing Conference, 2004. EDOC 2004. Proceedings, pages 47–57, 2004.
17. R. N. Taylor, N. Medvidovic, and E. M. Dashofy. Software architecture: Foundations, theory, and practice. 2009.
18. N. Y. Topaloglu and R. Capilla. Modeling the variability of web services from a pattern point of view. Web Services, pages 128–138.
19. W. van der Aalst, A. ter Hofstede, B. Kiepuszewski, and A. Barros. Workflow patterns. Distributed and Parallel Databases, 14(1):5–51, July 2003.
20. M. Vasko and S. Dustdar. An analysis of web services workflow patterns in collaxa. Web Services, pages 1–14.

CHAPTER 2

SOFTWARE ARCHITECTURAL PATTERNS FOR SERVICE COMPOSITION

Ghadeer Ghazal, Amjad. Hudaib and Waffa Maitah

Keywords: Services, Services Composition, Architectural Pattern, Services Composition Model (SCM)

INTRODUCTION

Services offered online are defined as a loosely coupled, reusable software component that encapsulates discrete functionality. One essential characteristic of such services is the ability to be described, published, discovered and invoked dynamically in a distributed computing environment. These services can range from simple calculations and data retrievals to complex business applications (Sommerville, 2007), (Agarwl, et al., 2008).

In this research, we attempt to enhance the performance of Service Composition, which aims at increasing reusability, flexibility and maintainability by breaking down the functionalities into services running platform-independently and exhibiting their interface with a description of functionality and the domain of objects employed.

Another significant point of services composition is that composite services must not be arranged at design time. The final functionalities of services working together are defined by the service request and must not be specified beforehand. When composing services, a composition only needs to include a reference that identifies what service will be invoked, the dynamic binding takes place as late as possible when the service is actually invoked.

There are situations in which a client request cannot be satisfied by any single available service, but a composite service obtained by combining some available services might fulfill such a request. The services used to form a composite service are referred to as component services.

Citation: Ghazal, Amjad. Hudaib, Waffa Maitah, Software Architectural Patterns for Service Composition, DOI:10.5121/ijcsit.2014.6403

Services

Services provide a new way of distributed computing that achieves the interoperability between heterogonous application through platform and language independent interfaces. The creation of a value which has added services by composition of the already existing ones is gaining a significant momentum. (Guoping, et al., 2008) t (Rao, et al., 2005).

ARCHITECTURAL PATTERNS

Software architectural pattern is a description of the architectural design problem and the essence of its solution, (Hudaib and Montangero, 2002), (Cooper, 1998) and (Tut and Edmond, 2002). Software architectural pattern has the following essential elements (Gamma, et al., 1998).

- Pattern Name: A meaningful name to refer to the pattern, typically a single word or short phrase.
- A description of the problem: with a concrete example and its context, (Al-Masri,et al., 2008). It also describes a solution to the concrete example and when to use the pattern.
- General solution: describes the elements of a design, their relationships, responsibilities and collaborations.
- Consequences: good and bad of using the given solution. It describes the results and trade-off of applying the pattern.
- Related patterns: naming patterns that are closely related (Buschmann, et al, 2007).

Automated Web Service Composition

Automated distributed Service Composition denotes a method to integrate services at runtime. The complete service runs by composing components based on a service request. The service request specifies the requested service, which does not exist before issuing the request. (Gekas, et al., 2005).

LITERATUE REVIEW

SOA Structure

Keen, et al. (2004) interested in SOA; the basic assumption of SOA is that there are many consumers that require services. Consumers are also referred to as clients or customers; there are many providers that provide services on the network. These two groups have to be linked together in a dynamic way.

Service providers register their services at the broker (Chmielowiec, et al., 2008); service consumers request a service from the service broker, which returns a known provider for the requested service. Consumer and provider agree on the semantics. The consumer then binds himself to the service provider and uses the service.

Services Composition Models

Stein, et al. (2009) defined the workflow of the service model and the services that it can provision in order to execute these workflows and describe the lifecycle Figure (2.2) shows the Workflow Lifecycle for the service model.

- Workflow Selection. a general workflow is chosen to suit the consumer's current objectives. This is generally created either manually by domain experts or automatically by a planner.
- Matching. Once a general workflow has been selected, abstract tasks are mapped to candidate service instances via a matching process. Here, the consumer searches a public service registry or requests matching services from a broker.
- Provisioning. Given lists of matching services, the consumer provisions individual service instances for each task of the workflow.
- Invocation. When appropriate services have been provisioned, the consumer starts to invoke the chosen services as dictated by the ordering constraints of the workflow. If services fail to complete their tasks, the consumer may provision other services, until the workflow is successfully completed.

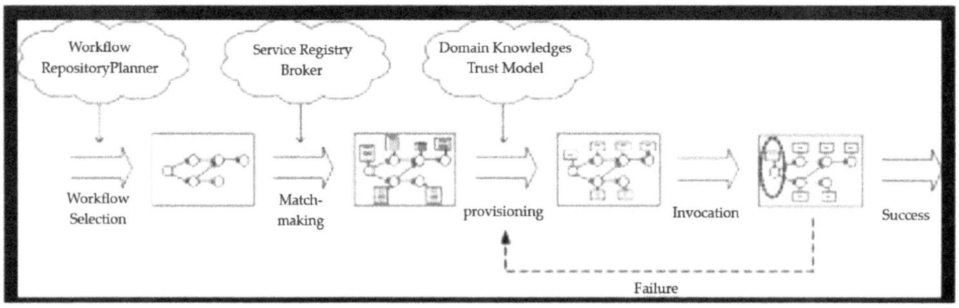

Figure (2.2): Lifecycle of Service Model (Stein, et al., 2009)

Patterns used in Service Composition

Barrett, et al. (2006) provided a subtle difference between two of the modelling aspect within the service composition, namely workflow and distribution patterns. They considered workflows as compositional services, whereby the internal and external messages to and from services are modelled. In contrast, distribution patterns are considered composition where only the external messages between services are modelled. This approach considers the basic four distributed patterns: Centralized, Decentralized or peer-to-peer, Ring, Hierarchical.

Zirpins, et al. (2004) addressed using the patterns through the interaction composition. This approach aimed to gather generic interaction patterns in a catalogue, this catalogue contains the concrete generic interaction patterns, coordination policies and coordination idioms and their relationships with the services to refines the service based on analysis of its interaction patterns.

MODEL AND DESIGN

Services Composition Model Overview

Services Composition Model (SCM) aims to provide a general solution for the services composition problem by realizing the requirements of a new service using the requirements of the existing service and to automate the steps of the composition process; services discovery, services selection, services invoking and services integration.

Although the SCM is not bounded to one particular algorithm, we generate an example to test the SCM.

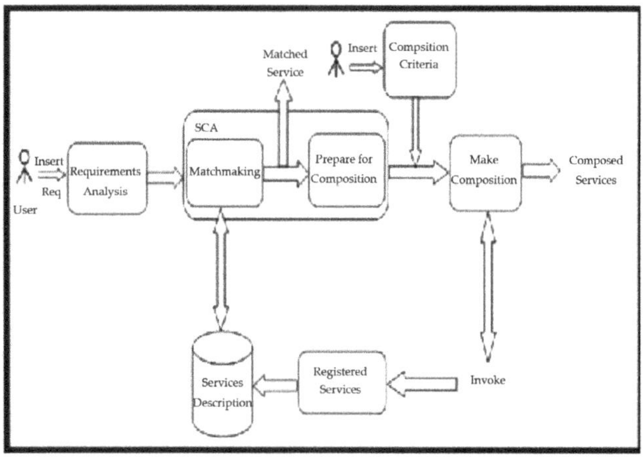

Figure (3.1) shows a brief description of the stages of the services composition model

Users: A user may compose some distributed services that may belong to different administrative domains. Each user inserts the request of service using the service composition language as an input language, the requirements of the requested service may be satisfied by one of the following cases:

- *Matched service*: there is one service that satisfies the user request, or
- *Composed services*: the request could be satisfied by composing more than one service.

In this case we need the service composition algorithm to discover, select and compose these services.

Requirements Analysis: We introduce a new algorithm (Parsing Algorithm) to analyze the inserted request from the user to specify the name of the services that satisfy the user's request.

Services Descriptions: The description of each service generated and stored in the database; this database will be used to discover and select the desired service.

Service Composition Algorithm (SCA): Services Composition Algorithm discovers and selects the most suitable services to be integrated; this selection will be according to the inserted requirements and composition criterion from the user, the SCA work in three steps:

- *Matchmaking*: Once the requirements analyzed; the services composition algorithm discovers the services by matchmaking between inserted requirements and the description of the available services, this will generate abstract services.
- *Prepare for composition*: Contains the entire abstract services that are chosen to suit the consumer's requirements; there are many services which may satisfy one requirement. This is generally created automatically allowing the consumer to retrieve services from a repository then according to the inserted composition's criterion from the user, the composition algorithm will select the actual services from the abstract services.
- *Make composition*: According to the inserted composition's criterion from the user, the composition algorithm will select the actual services from the abstract services to be invoked and integrated based on WSDL. This step will invoke and integrate the selected services from the previous ste..

Registered Services: Each provider can register his service by implementing the DLL and each service contains the Web Services Description Language file (WSDL) as an indicator for the services methods and functionalities.

In The following sections, we will discuss the stages of the Services Composition Model in details.

Services Registry

Services registry is a searchable directory that contains a specification about the available services from the provider. We suggest classifying these service's specifications to be stored in different categories in the centralized repository; each category contains all the services that provide the same function.

Classified Repository pattern

In the following section we propose a new pattern to classify the registered services.

The structure of the classified repository pattern includes four participants as depicted in Figure (3.2):

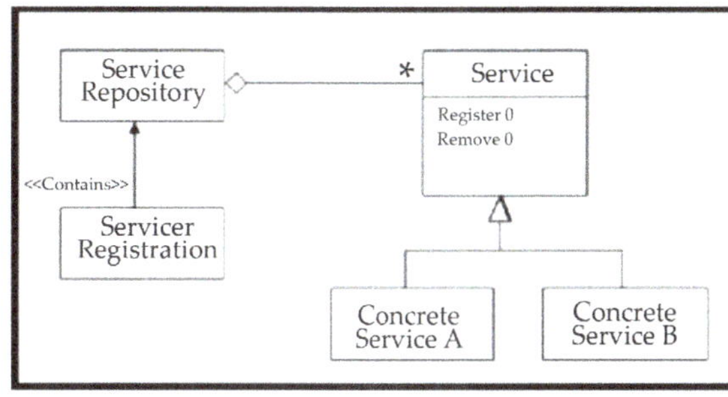

Figure (3.2): components of Classified Repository Pattern

Dynamic Link Language

We also suggest the idea of using the Dynamic Link Language (DLL) as an abstract interface. It defines a unique service name, function name parameters and return value as follows:

```
Public interface service name
Function name (parameters of the function)
Return value
End interface
```

One DLL will be implemented by all the services which provide the same function and stored in the same category, for example the {S11, S12, S13 … S1n} are the services that stored in (category 1) and provides the same function, these services were implemented from the same DLL (DLL1) and stored in one layer as depicted in Figure (3.3).

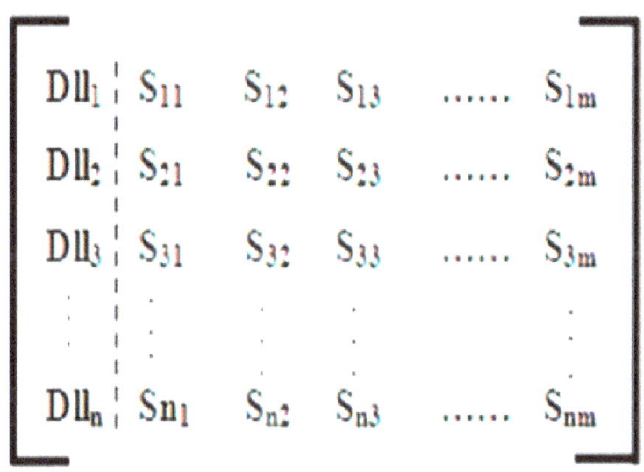

Figure (3.3): DLL and related services.

Service Composition Language (SCL)

We propose a new Service Composition language (SCL) for the composition purpose, which allows the user to express his service request in a simple way using the SCL notations.

Service Composition language is a simple text-based language. It absorbs most of the syntax from VB.net and deals with the services that should be requested to be composed. The SCL is considered a simpler composition language than the available composition BPEL language.

The main aim of the SCL is to automate the processes of the services selection and invoking. BPEL is a powerful XML used in services composition, but the selection and the invoking of the services in this language is static, so we generate the SCL which is able to select and invoke the services dynamically.

Requirements Analysis

The inserted requirements (service composition program) will be analyzed by the parsing algorithm. This algorithm is able to analyze the inserted program to generate the name of the requested services and determine how the services will be composed. The pseudo code of the parsing algorithm is depicted in Figure (3.4).

```
Input: composition program
Instruction = first line
While instruction ≠ final line
Get next line
    If instruction contains (if statement)
    Parse if statement
    Else if it contains (while statement)
      Parse while statement
    Else if it contains (variable, and assignment operator)
    Parse variable statement
    Else if it contains (service calling)
    Invoke the services composition algorithm
    End if
End while
```

Figure (3.4): Parsing Algorithm Pseudo code

The parsing algorithm contains the following two major functions:

- Parse Function parses each line of the inserted composition language and determines if the instruction contains a variable, a return message, a service calling, or an if statement.
- Resolve Variable trims all the external notations such that ($, $$, $$$) and invokes the Services Composition algorithm.

Services Description

The services description is a description for registered service. Such a description would be inserted in the database to allow the user to discover and select the desired services. The description for each service is stated in Figure (3.5).

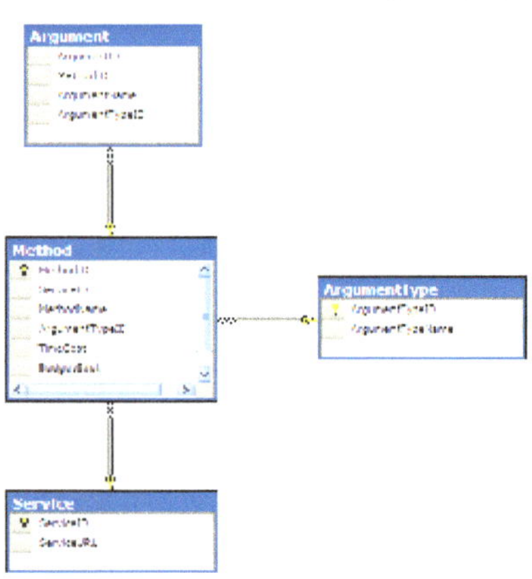

Figure (3.5): Attributes to describe the services.

This description of the registered web services will be as the follow:

- Information about services: Services ID and service URL.
- Information about functions (methods) in the service: method ID, method name, Criteria of the method (budget cost, time cost).
- Information about the arguments in the method: argument ID, argument type.

Services Composition Algorithm

Services Composition Algorithm is the actual algorithm performing composition upon the user's request. The SCA composes the services thorough many steps as shown in Figure (3.6); (1) matchmaking stage: the requirements are matched to the service's description, (2) preparation stage: the most suitable services from the matched services are selected relying on the composition criterion and then prepared for the next stage known as composition, (3) composition stage: the matched services are finally integrated and composed.

The Services Composition Algorithm depends on runtime discovery and selection for the registered services.

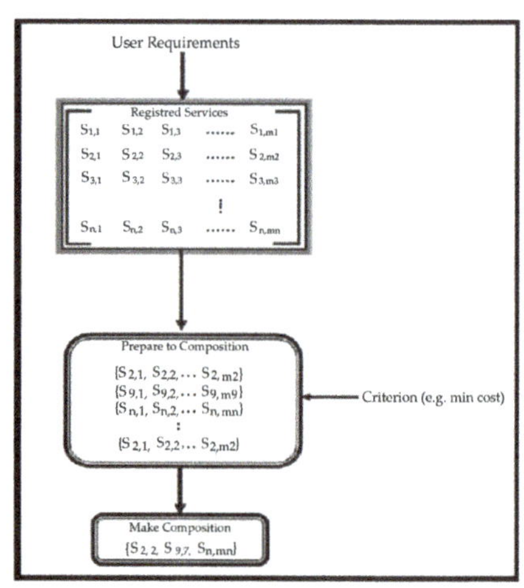

Figure (3.6): Composition process

Matchmaking

Matchmaking is the process of services discovery of the registered services (Al-Masri, et al., 2008); the description of the desired service and the description of the available services which have to be compared. If the available services match, the required service is proved to be successfully discovered.

The matchmaking step generates all the services that match the inserted requirements as abstract services to prepare for composition; for example ,the abstract services for two requested services are the following services {(S11, S12... S1n) and (S91, S92...S9n)}, these services generated from the available services.

Prepare for Composition

This phase enables the selection of the services from the abstract services according to the preferred composition criterion; the non functional requirements which inserted by the user (e.g. cost) compared with the values of the abstract services to generate the concrete services to make the composition, these services are really invoked and integrated e.g. {S11, S49, Snm}.

Services Composition Criteria

Multiple distributed services may provide similar functionalities with different non-functional property values (e.g., different prices). To select the services that will be invoked, we suppose many criteria for the composition.

In our example, we consider three generic quality criteria for composition process (1) execution price, (2) execution duration and (3) reliability.

- Execution price (cost): the execution price is the amount of money that a service requester has to pay for executing the operation.
- Execution duration: the execution duration measures the expected delay in seconds between the moment when a request is sent and the moment when the results are received.
- Reliability is the probability that a request is correctly responded within a maximum expected time frame (which is published in the service description) (Zeng, et al. 2003).

Make Composition

This step invokes and integrates the selected services from the previous step. The composition algorithm will invoke the selected services based on the WSDL.

IMPLEMENTATION

We develop (6) services in our Application; Banking service, Police service, Average Calculation Service, Grade Point Average (GPA) Service, File Search Service and Get File Attributes Service. The first step is to develop these Web Services and deploy them. The actual code is written in VB.Net classes.

The description and deployment of the Web Services are accomplished with WSDL documents.

- Banking Service allows the client of the bank who has an account to interact with the service to carry out certain transactions online, such a withdraw transaction is given in Figure (4.1).

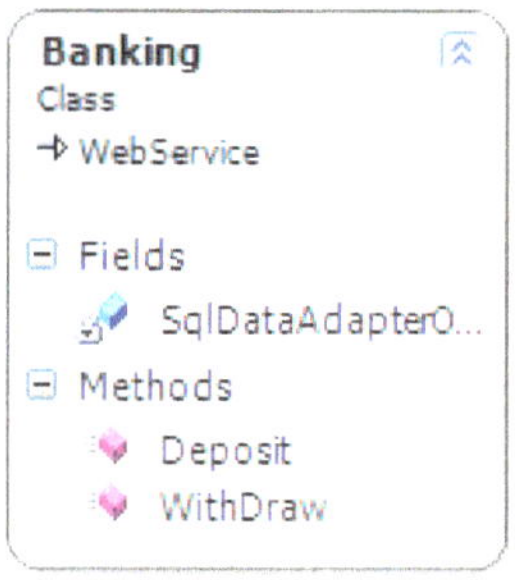

Figure (4.1): Banking Service

- Police service: this service examines if the credit card of the user is blocked or not. The Police Service has one main function called IsBlackListed

  IsBlackListed as shown in Figure (4.2).

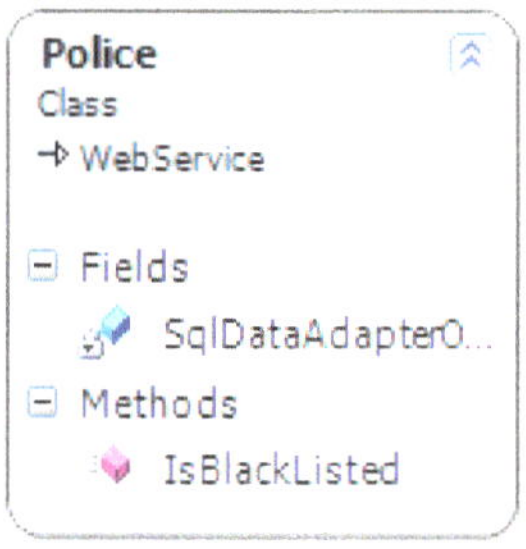

Figure (4.2): Police Service

- Average Calculate Service: calculate the average of the student marks using the following formula:

  Mean = sum of marks / number of marks

  The Average Calculate Service has one function named with Calculate as shown in Figure (4.3)

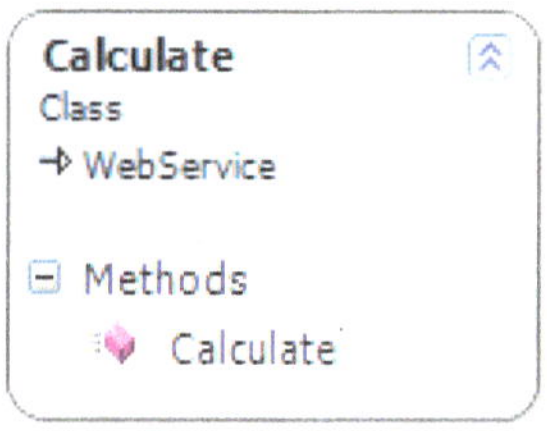

Figure (4.3): Average calculate service

- GPA Service calculates the Grade Point Average according to the shown standard provided in Figure (4.4).

Percentage	GPA value
90-100	3.5-4.0
80-89	2.5-3.49
70-79	1.5-2.49
60-69	1.0-1.49
0 - 59	0.0

Figure (4.4): GPA Standard.

The GPA service has one function named with GetGPA as shown in Figure (4.5).

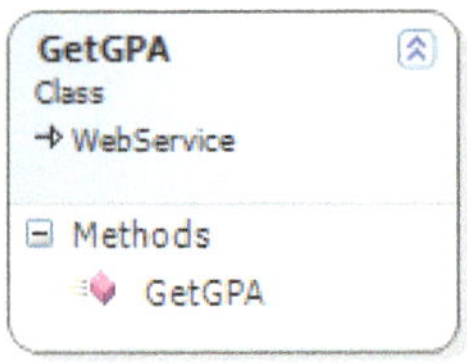

Figure (4.5): GPA Service

- File Search service: search for file at specific location on the server based on name and extension of the file (e.g. c:\com.doc), the File Search service has one function named with Search File as shown in Figure (4.6).

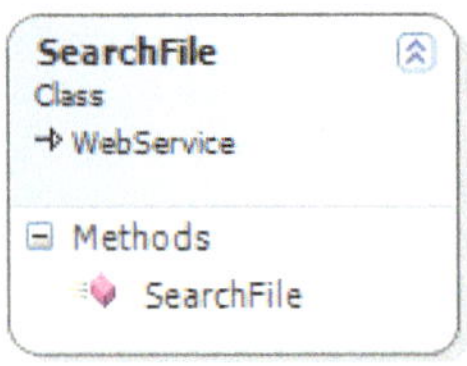

Figure (4.6): File Search Service

- Get file attributes service retrieves the information about a specific file; this service retrieves the file name, file extension, creation time and size of the file. The Get file attributes service has one function known as GetFileAttributes as shown in Figure (4.7).

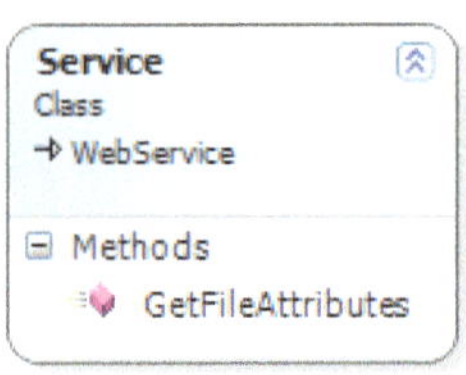

Figure (4.7): Get File Attributes service

Case Study1 (Payment Scenario)

The following payment example illustrates a possible application for Web Service Composition. A customer consults a web page of online payment service.

The payment service has many business processes; such as (1) check the information of the Credit Card then (2) check if the credit card is black (3) withdraw the inserted amount of the money if the information is correct (4) or deny the process if there is any error in the inserted information.

Payment service is basically composed of two services; the Banking Service and IsBlackListedCreditCard Service as shown in Figure (4.8).

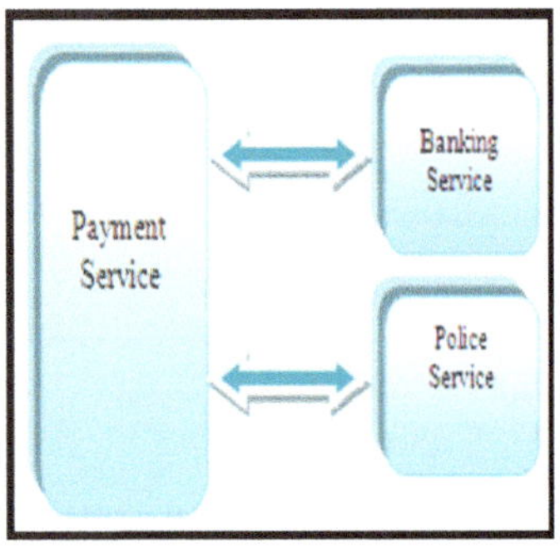

Figure (4.8): Payment Service.

- The user writes a services request using the composition language, The user uses the (if) statement to compose withdraws function with the is blacklisted service.
- Parse and analyze the inserted program line by line to specify the requested services using the parsing algorithm.
- Discover all the services that matched the inserted one by matchmaking between the requested services in composition program and the registered services, the discovery will generate an abstract work flow contains all the payments and is blacklisted services (e.g. payment1, payment2, islacklisted1).
- Select the most suitable services from the generated workflow according the selected criterion (e.g. payment1 and isblacklisted1). This step will generate the concrete workflow using the GetSuitableClass function.
- Invoke the selected services based on the WSDL using the WebClient Object; these services will be composed.
- Integrate the invoked services and return the result for the user.

Case Study (2)

Another scenario works with two similar Web Services representing composition process use the while composition style.

The file discovery service Figure (4.9) has many services; (1) file search, this service will not stop until it finds the requested file, (2) return the information about the found file.

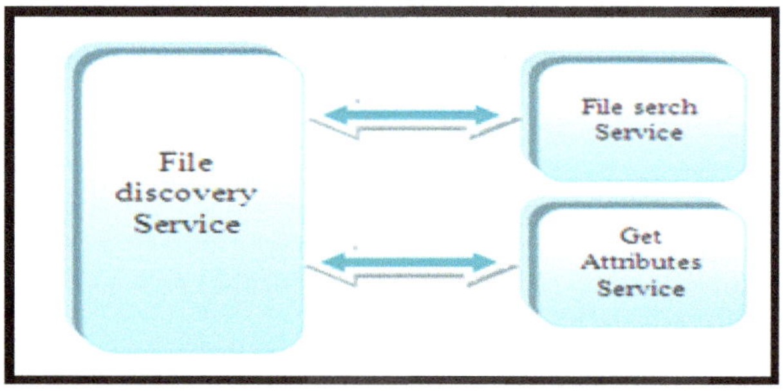

Figure (4.9): File Discovery Service.

The user writes a services request using the composition language. The user used the (while) statement to compose search file service with get file attributes service.

The file search service takes the name, location and extension of a file as input, then search for the file at the specified location. This service will search for the file (while loop) the file is found. After that it invokes the get file attributes to return the information about the file.

COMPARISON BETWEEN SCMVIA ANOTHER COMPOSITIONMODELS

This section aims at providing a comparison between many of the presented models in the related work chapter. This comparison is achieved by creating a table, listing many of the Models and listing some of the most important features that were identified to categorize the composition Models.

The comparison between the presented models will be according to the following categories:

- Composition strategy: Static and dynamic composition strategies concern the time when web services are composed; the Static composition takes place during design-time, while the dynamic composition takes place during run-time. Another composition strategy is the declarative way. The declarative approach consists of two phases: the first phase takes an initial situation and the desired goal as starting point and constructs generic plans to reach the goal; the latter one chooses one generic plan, discovers appropriate services and builds a workflow out of them.
- Execution monitor: The central scheduler controls the execution of the components of the composite service.
- Dynamic Conversation selection: allows the user to select the conversation within a service node at run-time, which may be useful when services are also discovered at runtime.
- QoS Modeling: service discovery in UDDI is not limited to the functional requirements only, but it also considers the nonfunctional requirements QoS to discover and select the services.
- WSDL Language: uses the Web Services Description Language to describe the services functionalities.
- Graph support: Composite services are modeled by a graph defining the flow of service invocations similar to UML activity diagrams.
- Service Composition Language is used by the user to express his requirements for services composition.

Table (5.1): Comparison between Web Services Composition Models

Categories / Models	Composition Strategy	Execution Monitor	Dynamic conversation selection	QoS Modeling	WSDL Language	Graph Support	Service Composition Language
SCM	Dynamic Composition	Yes	Yes	Yes	Yes	No	Yes
PAMCS	Dynamic Composition	Yes	Yes	No	No	No	No
SELF-SERV	Declarative Composition	No	No	No	No	Yes	No
E-Flow	Dynamic Composition	Yes	Yes	No	No	Yes	No
FAWSS	Dynamic Composition	No	No	Yes	Yes	No	No

Summary and Conclusion

Service composition enables flexible process of new application from reuse available services by composing and integrating services.

This paper presents many results:

- Develop a new model for the service composition problem.
- Generate a composition language to express the user request and an algorithm (Parsing Algorithm) which is able to analyze the composition program.
- Generate a new composition algorithm; this algorithm able to discover, select and invoke the services based on WSDL.
- Generate a new architectural pattern (classified repository pattern) as suggestion to store the registered services.
- Applying and executing services composition process by providing many case studies as examples; these cases based on the provided services composition approach.
- Providing solutions for many of the difficulties in the services composition process.
- Provide a formal description for the services registration process and for the composition process using the Z-Language.
- Explain the Services Composition Architecture with the Composition Process.
- Comparison between the Business Process Execution Language (BPEL) and the provided approach.

This research also discussed in details the stages of the services composition model:

- Services registration: the providers implements the DLL for services registration process, the registered services will be stored in the classified repository pattern.
- Services description; Web Services Description Language (WSDL) and the description in the database.
- Services discovery: matchmaking between the inserted requirement and the description of the services.
- Services selection, matchmaking between the inserted criterion the most suitable services.
- Services invoking based on the WSDL and the integration of these services.

REFERENCES

1. Sommerville, I. (2007), Software Engineering, 8th edition, united State of America, Pearson Education Limited.
2. Guoping, Z. Huijuan, Z. Zhibin, W (2009), A QoS-based web services selection method for dynamic web service composition, First International Workshop on Education

Technology and Computer Science, vol. 3, Wuhan, Hubei, China, 832-835.

3. Hudaib, A. and Montanero, C. (2002), A UML Profile to Support the Formal Presentation of Software Architecture, Proceeding of the 26th IEEE international Computer Software and Application conference on prolonging software life : Development and Redevelopment (COMPSAC'02), 217-223.

4. Cooper, J.W. (1998), The Design Patterns Java Companion, (1st ed.), James W. Cooper.

5. Gamma, E. Helm, R. Johnson, R. and Vlissides, J. (1998), Design Patterns: Elements of Reusable Object-Oriented Software, (1st ed.), Addison-Wesley, Baarn, Holland.

6. Tut, M.T and Edmond, D. (2002), The use of Patterns in Service Composition, Revised Papers from the International Workshop on Web Services, E-Business and the Semantic Web, Vol. 2512, London, UK, 28 - 40 .

7. Agarwl, V. Chafle, G. Mittal, S. and Srivastava, B. (2008), Understanding approaches for web service composition and execution, Proceedings of the 1st Bangalore annual Compute conference, Article No. 1 Bangalore, India.

8. Al-Masri, E. and Mahmoud, Q.H. (2008), Investigating Web Services on the World Wide Web, Proceeding of the 17th international conference on World Wide Web, Beijing, China, April 21–25, 2008, 795-804.

9. Rao, J. and Su, X. (2005), A Survey of Automated Web Service Composition Methods. Proceedings of the First International Workshop on Semantic Web Services and Web Process Composition, San Diego, California, USA, Volume: 3387, 43-54.

10. Buschmann, F. Henney, K. and C.Schidt, D. (2007), pattern – Oriented Software Architecture on Patterns and Pattern Language, Vol.5.

11. Gekas, J. and Fasli, M. (2005), Automatic Web Service Composition Using Web Connectivity Analysis Techniques, W3C Workshop on Frameworks for Semantics in Web Services 2005 Position Paper.

12. Keen, M. Acharya, A. Bishop, S. Hopkins, A. Milinski, S. Nott, C. Robinson, R. Adams, J. Verschueren, P. (2004), Patterns: Implementing an SOA Using an Enterprise Service Bus SOA Steps, (1st edition), IBM Corp.

13. Chmielowiec, A. Pierre, G. Gordijn, J. (2008), Technical challenges in market-driven automated service provisioning, Proceedings of the 3rd workshop on Middleware for service oriented computing, Leuven, Belgium, 25-30.

14. Stein, S. Payne, T.R. Jennings, N.R. (2009), Flexible provisioning of web service workflows, Proceedings of the 17th European Conference on Artificial Intelligence, ACM Transactions on Internet Technology, Volume 9, United Kingdom, 295–299.

15. Barrett, R. Pahl, C. M.Patcas, L. and Murphy, J. (2006), Model driven distribution pattern design for dynamic web service compositions, Proceedings of the 6th international conference on Web engineering, Palo Alto, California, USA, July 11-14, 2006, 129 – 136.

16. Zirpins, C. Lamersdorf, W. and Baier,T. (2004), Flexible Coordination of Service Interaction Patterns, Proceedings of the 2nd international conference on Service oriented computing, New York, USA, 49-56.

CHAPTER 3 DISTRIBUTED COMPUTING SYSTEMS WITH SERVICE ORIENTED ARCHITECTURE

Vishnuvardhan Mannava and T. Ramesh

Keywords: Design Patterns, Distributed Computing, Feature-Oriented Programming (FOP), Service Oriented Architecture (SOA), Web Services, Web Service Description Language (WSDL)

INTRODUCTION

Patterns are reusable good-quality design practices that have proven useful in the design of software applications. A large number of software design patterns have been described, catalogued and included in software tools. Design patterns yields better-quality software within reduced time frames. When designing software two or more patterns are to be composed to solve a bigger problem. Pattern composition has been shown as a challenge to applying design patterns in real software systems [4]. Composite patterns represent micro architectures that when glued together could create an entire software architecture. Thus pattern composition can lead to readymade architectures from which only instantiation would be required to build robust implementations. A composite design patterns shows a synergy that makes the composition more than just the sum of its parts. As far as we know, there are no studies on composition of design patterns for self adaptive distributed computing domain.

Composition of web services is the most important technique that the developers are now a day's most interested in providing the web services with. So in order to achieve the composition in our paper we are adopting to the Service Oriented Architecture (SOA). SOA provides composition of the services provided by the different servers to fulfil the complex service requests of the clients. The requester's of the web services will request a functionality that cannot be fulfilled by a single service provider. In many cases the web services are having limited functionality. So when a client requests for a complex service, he many not find a WSDL that provides the perfect execution of the service. In that case in order to fulfil the users request that require multiple tasks may fail due to unavailability of suitable Web services WSDL xml file. In such scenario there is a requirement to compose the web services to satisfy the requester's complex request.

We can use either Java or .Net platform to develop the SOA with web services. Even if you use any one of them it's the web services that make the SOA compatible with the composition of the services in any platform. When using the web services, interface definitions are provided using the WSDL. Each service at the server is associated with a WSDL document. WSDL is expressed using XML. It defines the input and output parameters of a Web service in terms of XML Schema. So with the help of the Simple Object Access Protocol (SOAP) is used as XML-based protocol for exchanging information in a distributed environment. SOAP provides a common message format for exchanging data between clients and services. The SOAP messages can be exchanged with the help of HTTP GET, POST, PUT requests. The HTTP GET is used to request the WSDL messages. The HTTP POST used for the service request/ response.

A web service is defined as an interface which implements the business logic through a set of operations that can be accessed with the help of standard Internet protocols [7]. In this paper we will propose a design pattern that is an amalgamation of the Visitor pattern [6] and Case-Based Reasoning pattern [11]. A design pattern is a particular form of recording information about a design such that the same pattern can be applied in future, if same situation is repeated to solve problem . So the design patterns are accepted in wide range of object-oriented designs. Collections of design patterns can be found in numerous publications.

We will use the case-based reasoning pattern for the purpose of decision making at the client side. When the client asks for a service, this pattern is helpful in deciding which among the available Web Service Description Language

Citation: Vishnuvardhan Mannava and T. Ramesh, Distributed Computing Systems with Service Oriented Architecture, DOI: 10.5121/ijwest.2012.3305

(WSDL) will be helpful to perform the required task. Initially the client will request all the web service providers to send the WSDLs of their respective services. Then the pattern in the client will decide the best WSDL of a service provider to be selected according to the case based selection of the service with respect to the WSDL that can be used. The visitor pattern at the server side will provide the services to the clients request by either just invocation of the service or by the composition of the services at different servers. In this proposal we have also emphasized the Feature-Oriented Programming (FOP) based Service injection into the current service provider[8]. The FOP [2] has been the most popular programming model that has showed a vast degree of enhancements in the field of Software Product-Lines (SPL). So using the feature based functional module insertion we can include the new services by maintaining transparency to the user of the services in run time.

RELATED WORK

In this section we present some works that deal with different Design patterns oriented work. There are number of publications reporting the reusability features of the design patterns when the same problem occurs in the future.

Demian Antony D'Mellon, V.S. Ananthanarayana, and Supriya Salian in paper [3] proposed the review of Web Services composition Architectures and techniques used to generate new services.

V.S.Prasad Vasireddy, Vishnuvardhan Mannava, and T. Ramesh paper [10] discuss applying an Autonomic Design Pattern which is an amalgamation of chain of responsibility and visitor patterns that can be used to analyze or design self-adaptive systems. They harvested this pattern and applied it on unstructured peer to peer networks and Web services environments.

Olivier Aubert, Antoine Beugnard [9] they proposed an Adaptive Strategy Design Pattern that can be used to analyze or design self-adaptive systems. It makes the significant components usually involved in a self-adaptive system explicit, and studies their interactions. They show how the components participate in the adaptation process, and characterize some of their properties. Don Batory, Jacob Neal Sarvela, and Axel Rauschmayer [2] in this work they have explained that Step-wise refinement is a powerful paradigm for developing a complex program from a simple program by adding features incrementally. They presented the AHEAD (Algebraic Hierarchical Equations for Application Design) model that shows how step-wise refinement scales to synthesize multiple programs and multiple noncode representations.

In Vishnuvardhan Mannava, and T. Ramesh paper [13] they have proposed a design pattern for Autonomic Computing System which is designed with Aspect-oriented design patterns and they have also focused on the amalgamation of the Feature-oriented and Aspect-oriented software development methodology and its usage in developing a self-reconfigurable adaptive system.

In Vishnuvardhan Mannava, and T. Ramesh paper [14] they have proposed a system for dynamically configuring communication services. Server will invoke and manage services based on time stamp of service. The system will reduce work load of sever all services in executed by different threads based on time services are executed, suspended and resumed. In Vishnuvardhan Mannava, and T. Ramesh paper [15] they have proposed an adaptive reconfiguration compliance pattern for autonomic computing systems that can propose the reconfiguration rules and can learn new rules at runtime.

Because of the previous proposed works as described above, we got the inspiration to apply the aspect oriented design patterns along with inclusion of the feature-oriented software development capability to autonomic systems.

PROPOSED AUTONOMIC DESIGN PATTERN

In this paper we have proposed a design pattern that provides the composition of the web services by the support of service Oriented Architecture (SOA) [7]. Here we are using two design patterns both of them results to an amalgamation of our proposed design pattern. Initially when the user requests for the service the client machine will generate the HTTP GET request to all the service providing servers in the network to send the respective WSDL (Web Service Description Language). Then after that the Case-Based Reasoning Design Pattern [11] at the Client side machine will use the WSDLs that it have received from different servers in the network and also the service request that was given as input to the client by the user to decide the Best perfect matched web Service provider to the user's request. All the above steps of decision making will be performed on the bases of some cases or statement based decision making, so that the WSDL that matched the service request that is requested by the user can be used to fulfil the service. Then once a perfect WSDL has been selected based on the condition that the input parameters of the service requested have to match the input parameters in the WSDL XML file, then the SOAP message is used to send the request to the Server.

On the other hand that is at the server side the request for the service is received in the form of SOAP Message by the server. Then it will use the Visitor Design Pattern [6] to handle the request. If the requested service is available at the server, then it will provide service without any problem. If the service is a complex service then the server will take help of other servers that provide the service which is not available by itself. So in order to provide the Composition of the services at different servers the current server that knows where the service is available will send the service request to the peer server. The current server have to know the access reference to the operation at the other server to invoke that service and perform the clients requested complex task. For this purpose we have used the Visitor pattern in order to get the reference to access the other server's services and to invoke the service operation in the peer server.

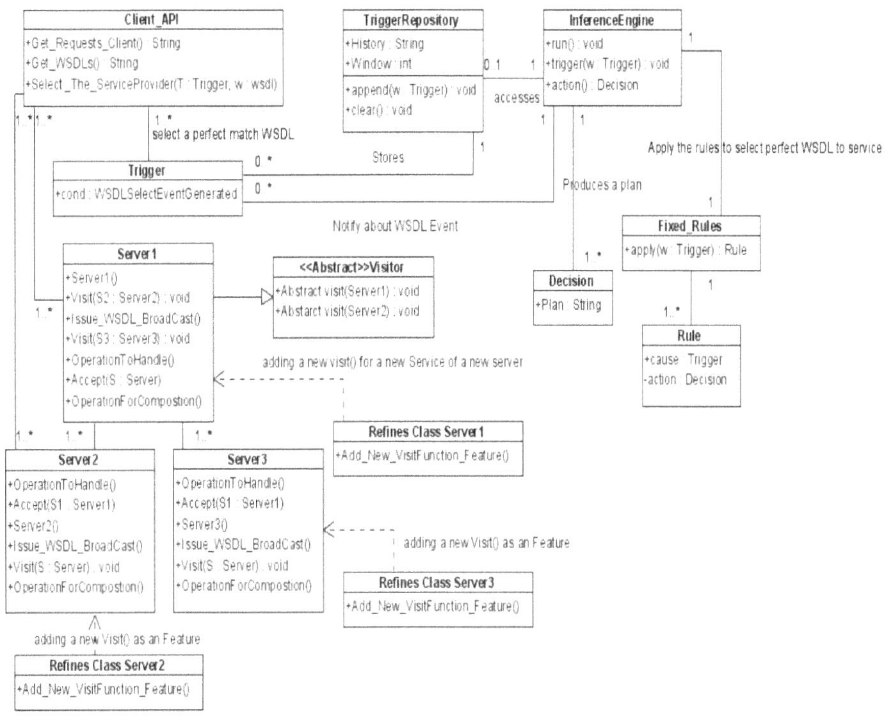

Figure 1: Applying Design Pattern for the Distributed Computing System

In this way the server that is only having the worth to serve the two functionalities out of three in the requested task at that situation will take help of the other peer servers to fulfill the job it has accepted from the client. Here the server can handle multiple clients in the same time using the thread based processing of the requests. Server can allocate a separate thread for each and every client to handle the requests concurrently.

We have provided a capability to our proposed design pattern that, it can add a new service operation to a server by just including the new service as a Feature Module with the help of Feature-Oriented Programming (FOP). Here the injection of the new service is done without disturbing the already existing code or writing again from starch is to develop the application is eliminated [8].

So in our design pattern we have provided the capabilities of Web Services Composition, Service Invocation, and Inclusion of the new Service Operation as a Feature Module, all the three are provided in each and every server in a Distributed Application.

DESIGN PATTERN TEMPLATE

To facilitate the organization, understanding, and application of the proposed design patterns, this paper uses a template similar in style to that used in [11]. Likewise, the Implementation and Sample Code fields are too application-specific for the Design Patterns presented in this paper.

Pattern Name

Feature-Oriented Service Injection and Composition of Web Services with SOA

Classification

Structural –Decision Making

Intent

Systematically applies the Design Patterns to a distributed Computing System to provide the Web Services Composition and service injection with a Refinement class for providing new service in the servers in terms of a Feature Module.

Context

Our design pattern may be used when:

- The service requested is a complex service and need to be executed with the help of collaboration of different servers in the network
- To include the new service operations into servers as a Feature Modules [2].
- When the service in the other server need to be accessed, and for that purpose we can use the use this pattern to provide the Invocation capability to our distributed Application.
- In order to provide the Composition of the services, we may use this pattern which provides the SOA (Service Oriented Architecture) based composition with the JWS (Java Web Services)[7].

Proposed Design Pattern Structure

A UML class diagram for the proposed design Pattern can be found in Figure 1.

Participants

a) ***ClientAPI***: It is Responsible for the purpose of accepting the requests from the Client and then requesting the servers in the network that are responsible for providing the services will send the WSDLs of the respective Web Service providers. Once the above two tasks are completed then it will generate a Trigger Event to find the perfect WSDL that can serve the user requested service.

b) ***Trigger***: It is responsible for the purpose of accepting the events that are generated by the clientAPI to check whether the selected WSDL of a web service provider is suitable to handle the client's request.

c) ***Inference Engine***: It is responsible for accepting the events from the Trigger and then checking the WSDL with respect to the service that is requested by the client based on the some case based Reasoning statements or rules provided in the FixedRules class.

d) ***FixedRules***: This will take the WSDL and then it will apply some rules to get some inference results from the operation to check whether the WSDL can handle the service requested by the client.

e) ***Decision***: Here based upon the results from the FixedRules class it will help the InferenceEngine to select a perfect WSDL by applying or checking the Service requested by client and results to take decision whether it can handle the request or not.

f) ***TriggerRepository***: it will look after the backup storage or just for storing the cause, situation, and results of the particular Event for the future based analysis and enquire.

g) ***ServerN(N=1 or 2 or 3)***: It is the web service provider which will look after providing the services to the clients who have requested them. Here we are using the visitor design pattern, which is very important aspect in our whole paper. Because it is responsible for invoking the services at the servers and also if a service is not available for current instance of a situation and the server need that service to complete the complex task of a client, so for that purpose it can invoke the service that is provided by the neighbouring server with the help of visitor pattern. Visitor pattern will get the reference of the peer server to access or invoke the service in the peer server and then retrieve the result from it to fulfil the client's request. The web service composition is provided with the help of Service Oriented Architecture (SOA).

h) ***Refines Class ServerN(N=1 or 2 or 3)***: It is responsible for the purpose injection of the new service providing servers Visit() as a Feature Module using the Feature-Oriented Programming (FOP)[1].

The view of our proposed design pattern for the Distributed Computing System can be seen in the form of a class diagram see Figure 1.

The flow of control in the Distributed Computing System can be shown with a sequence diagram in Figure 2.

Consequences

- With the help of the Web Service Description Language (WSDL) all the clients can get information about the services that are currently provided by the peer servers.
- We use the Feature-Oriented Programming [2][1] to insert the new service providers visit (Reference Object) into current running server as a feature into the current executing services code.
- With the help of Service Oriented Architecture (SOA) for the purpose of web service composition using the JWS (java web services) we can provide the composition of the service in a distributed application environment.
- Invocation of the service can be done with the help of the visitor design pattern.

Related Design Patterns

a) ***Worker Object Pattern [12]:*** The worker object pattern is an instance of a class that encapsulates a worker method. A worker object can be passed around, stored, and invoked. The worker object pattern offers a new opportunity to deal with otherwise complex problems. It will provide the server with the facility to handle the service request form different clients in a separate per client connection. We may use this pattern in different situations like, implementing thread safety in swing applications and improving the responsiveness of the UI applications to performing authorization and transaction management.

b) ***Strategy Design Pattern [4]:*** This pattern can be used to define a family of algorithms, encapsulate each one, and make them interchangeable. Strategy lets the algorithm vary independently from the clients that use it.

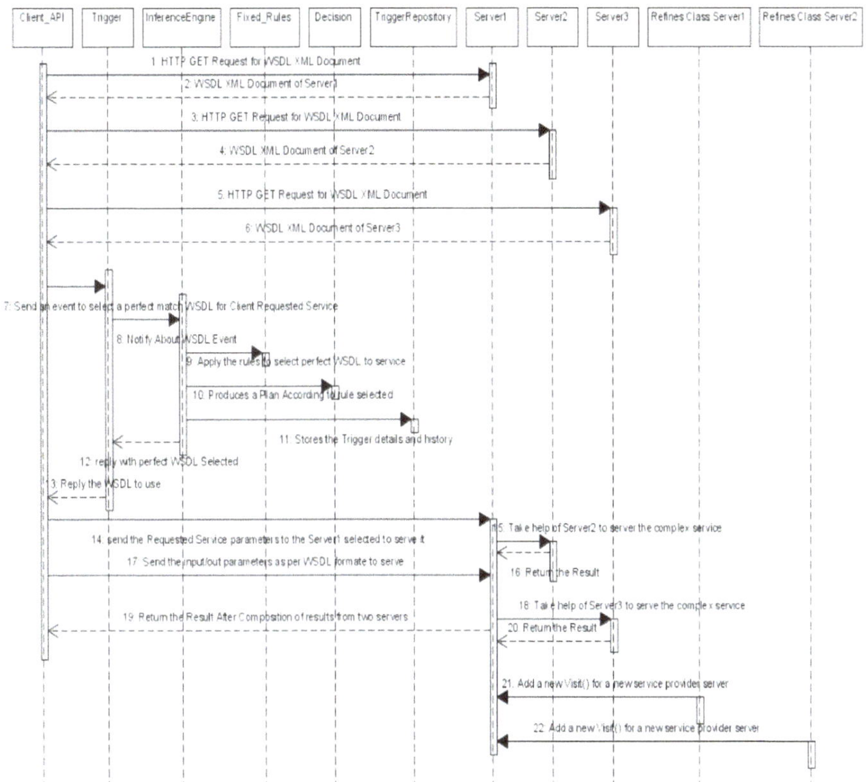

Figure 2: Sequence Diagram for the proposed Design Pattern

Role of Our Design Pattern in Autonomic Computing System

Case-Based Reasoning Design Pattern [11]: The Case-Based Reasoning Design Pattern in will apply the rule based decision making mechanism to determine a correct reconfiguration plan. This design pattern will separate the decision-making logic from the functional logic of the Application. In our proposed pattern we will use this pattern for the decision making purpose to decide which WSDL among the received WSDLs from the service providers can fulfill the clients request in accordance to the service requested by the client.

Visitor Design Pattern [5]: The visitor pattern turns the tables on OO model and creates an external class to act on data in other classes. We use this pattern when we want to perform an operation on the data contained in a number of objects that have different interfaces.

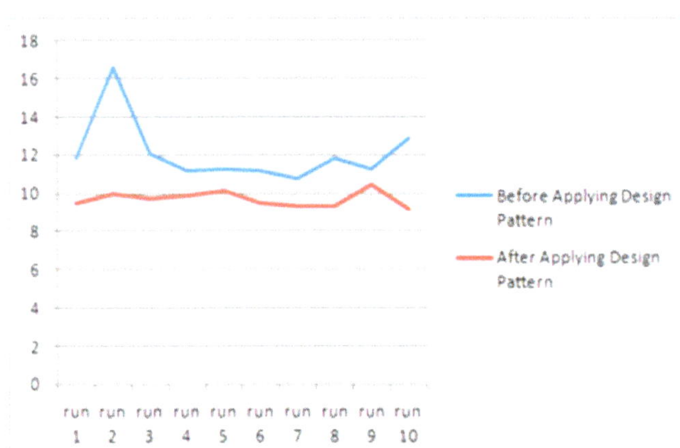

Figure 3: Profiling data after applying proposed AOP pattern and before applying with OOP pattern

PROFILING RESULTS

We are presenting the profiling results taken for ten runs without applying this pattern and after applying this pattern using the profiling facility available in the Netbeans IDE. The graph is plotted taking the time of execution in milliseconds on Y-axis and the run count on the X-axis. The graph has shown good results while executing the code with patterns and is shown in Figure 3.This can confirm the efficiency of the proposed pattern.

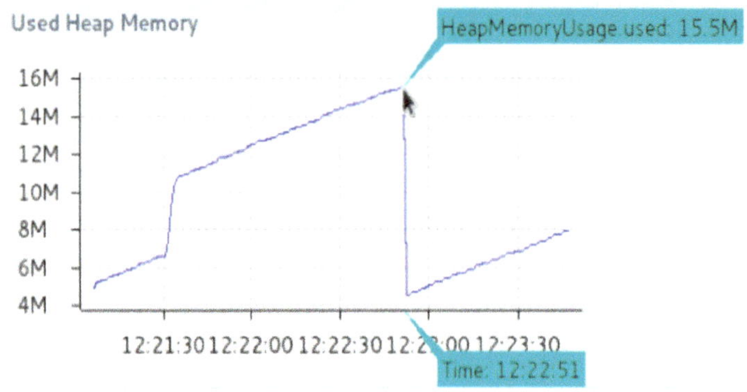

Figure 4: The Heap Memory usage after applying Aspect-Oriented Programming Techniques to Visitor pattern

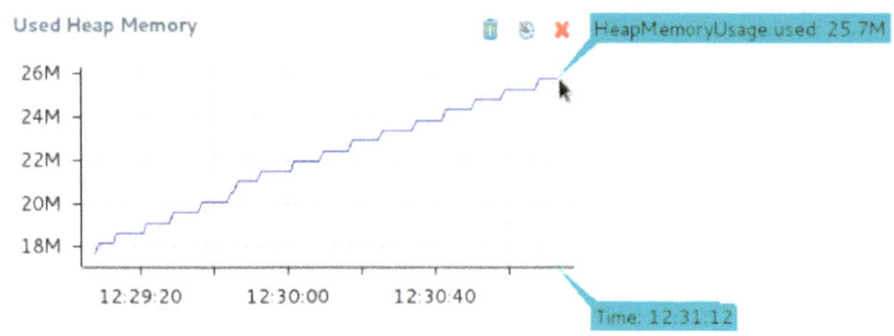

Figure 5: The Heap Memory usage after applying Object Oriented Visitor Design Pattern

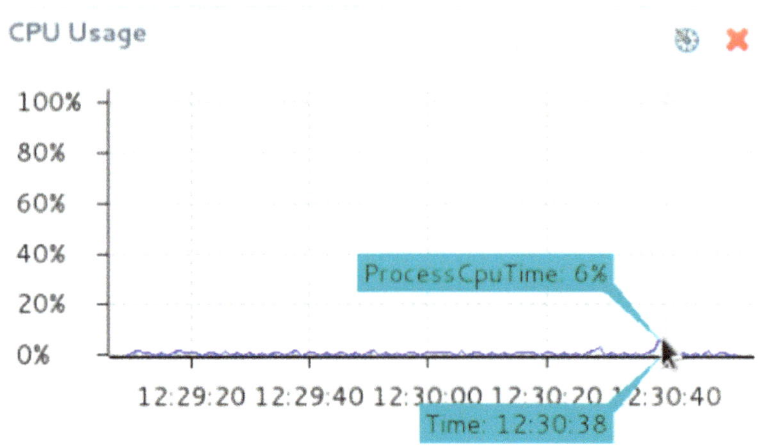

Figure 6: The CPU usage time after applying Aspect-Oriented Programming Techniques to Visitor pattern

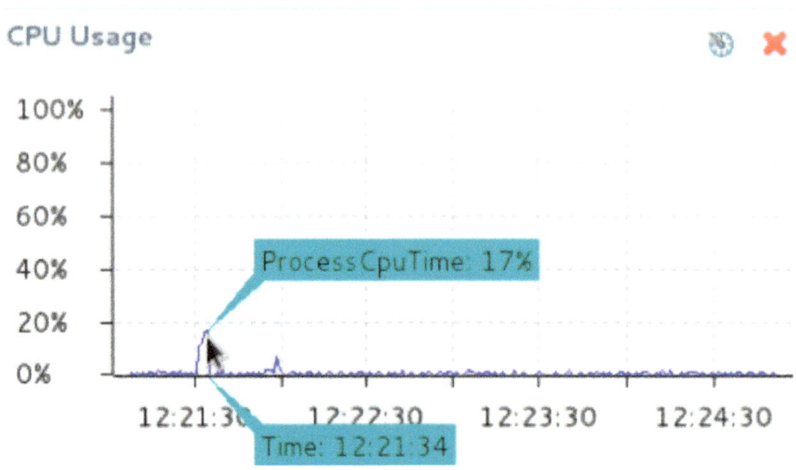

Figure 7: The CPU usage time after applying Object Oriented Visitor Design Pattern

Simulation Results after Visitor Pattern

In our implementation we can evaluate the effectiveness of our implemented case-study with SOA and Socket Programming. In order to make our proposal clear we have successfully developed some critical parts of our system i.e., implementation of visitor pattern integrated with SOA with the help of Aspect-Oriented Programming (AOP) and new service injection as a Feature with the help of Feature-Oriented Programming (FOP), and at the same time we have implemented the same pattern with Object-Oriented visitor design pattern with pure socket programming.

The simulation results for the code developed to prove the benefits of Aspect Oriented Programming features are collected with respect to:

- Used Heap memory
- Process CPU Time

Discussion

From the Figure 4 and Figure 5 we can evaluate that the amount of Heap Memory used by applying Object Oriented Programming Visitor pattern is 51492 kbytes and where as for the amount of Heap Memory used with AOP Visitor pattern along with SOA is 10,691 kbytes. It's clear that the application developed using Aspect-Oriented Programming along with SOA takes less heap memory when compared to implementation with respect to Object Oriented Visitor design pattern.

From the Figures 6 and Figure 7 we can evaluate that the amount of CPU Time used by applying AOP Visitor pattern along with SOA is 7.350sec and where as for the amount of CPU Time used by applying Object Oriented Programming Visitor pattern is 10.270 sec. It's clear that the application developed using Aspect-Oriented Programming takes less CPU Time when compared to implementation with respect to OOP based Visitor design pattern.

CONCLUSION

In this paper we have proposed a pattern to facilitate the ease of Design Pattern for FeatureOriented Service Injection and Composition of Web Services with SOA. So with the help of our proposed design pattern named Service Injection Design pattern for Distributed computing systems, provide services to clients with the help of Object-Oriented design patterns. So with this pattern we can handle the service-request of the clients and inject the new services into server's code as feature modules. We have also focused on how we have achieved the Composition of the Web services through Service Oriented Architecture (SOA). The Several future directions of work are possible. We are examining how the SOA Oriented Design patterns can be used to provide much powerful application developments in distributed environments.

REFERENCES

1. Apel, S. Leich, T. Saake, G. (2008) `Aspectual Feature Modules', IEEE Transactions on Software Engineering, Vol. 34, No. 2, pp.162--180.
2. Don Batory, Jacob Neal Sarvela, Axel Rauschmayer (2004) `Scaling Step-Wise Refinement', IEEE Transactions on Software Engineering, Vol. 30, No. 6, pp.187--197.
3. Demian Antony, D'Mello, Ananthanarayana, V. S., Salian, Supriya (2011) `A Review of Dynamic Web Service Composition Techniques', Communications in Computer and Information Science, Springer Berlin Heidelberg, Vol. 133, pp.85--97.
4. Gamma, E., Helm, R., Johnson, R., Vlissides, J (1995) `Design Patterns: Elements of Reusable ObjectOriented Software', Addison-Wesley.
5. Hannemann, Jan and Kiczales, Gregor (2002) `Design pattern implementation in Java and aspectJ', Proceedings of the 17th ACM SIGPLAN conference on Object-oriented programming, systems, languages, and applications, Vol. 37, No. 11, pp.161--173.
6. James W. Cooper (2007) `Java Design Patterns, A Tutorial', Pearson Education, Inc.
7. Mark D. Hansen (2007) `SOA Using Java Web Services', Pearson Education, Inc.
8. Martin Kuhlemann, Marko Rosenmuller, Sven Apel, Thomas Leich (2007) `On the duality of aspectoriented and feature-oriented design patterns', Proceedings of the 6th workshop on Aspects, components, and patterns for infrastructure software, ACM, ACP4IS '07, New York, NY, USA.
9. Olivier Aubert, Antoine Beugnard, June 25, (2001) `Adaptive Strategy Design Pattern', d'Informatique des Telecommunications, ENST Bretagne, France.
10. Prasad Vasireddy, V.S., Vishnuvardhan, M., Ramesh, T. (2011) `A Novel Autonomic Design Pattern for Invocation OF Services', Communications in Computer and Information Science, Springer-Verlag Berlin Heidelberg, Vol. 196, Part. 2, pp.545--551.
11. Ramirez, Andres J. and Cheng, Betty H. C. (2010) `Design patterns for developing dynamically adaptive systems', Proceedings of the 2010 ICSE Workshop on Software Engineering for Adaptive and Self-Managing Systems, ACM, SEAMS '10, New York, NY, USA, pp.49--58.
12. Ramnivas Laddad (2010) `AspectJ in Action 2nd Edition', Chapter 12, Manning.
13. Vishnuvardhan, M., Ramesh, T. (2012) `An Aspectual Feature Module Based Adaptive Design Pattern for Autonomic Computing Systems', Intelligent Information and Database Systems - 4th Asian Conference, ACIIDS 2012, Proceedings, Part III, Springer, Lecture Notes in Computer Science, Vol. 7198/2012, pp.130--140.
14. Vishnuvardhan, M., Ramesh, T. (2012) `A Service Administration Design Pattern for Dynamically Configuring Communication Services in Autonomic Computing Systems', Intelligent Information and Database Systems - 4th Asian Conference, ACIIDS 2012,Proceedings, Part I, Springer, Lecture Notes in Computer Science, Vol. 7196/2012, pp.53--63.
15. Vishnuvardhan, M., Ramesh, T. (2012) `A novel adaptive re-configuration compliance design pattern for autonomic computing systems', Procedia Engineering, International Conference on Communication Technology and System Design 2011, Vol. 30, pp.1129-1137.

CHAPTER 4

SECURITY ENGINEERING OF SOA APPLICATIONS VIA RELIABILITY PATTERNS

Luigi Coppolino Luigi Romano and Valerio Vianello

Keywords: Reliability of Security Services, Reliability Patterns, Workflow Systems, SOA Applications, Web Services Technology

RATIONALE AND CONTRIBUTION

Web Services can be combined in complex composite services achieving new functionalities [1]. Composition may aggregate services developed and exposed within a certain organization. More interestingly, the composed Web Services can be the result of an orchestration of services exposed by different organizations. Benefits of composition have been long discussed in the past few years highlighting and demonstrating the advantages coming from the achievement of new functionality by composing autonomous services [2]. Nevertheless it is widely accepted that web applications are easy to fail as confirmed by a U.S. Government study [3] and for Web Services the situation is also worst since a number of application layers are built on top of classical web servers. As pointed out in [4], failures are inevitable in the modern Internet-Connected environments and, when dealing with composite services, assuming the failure of any individual Web Service will cause the failure of the composite service, even if all the other Web Services are reliable, one unreliable Web Service could decrease the overall reliability to a very low level. This evidence related to the reliability of the composite Web Service rises up a doubt with respect to the actual adoption of this distributed model of developing complex services [5]. Since the reliability engineer designing the workflow has no chance to modify the simple services at all, especially while dealing with services composed across organization boundaries, the only way to ensure the reliability of the composite service is increasing the reliability of the workflow by appropriately planning its architecture, i.e. properly adopting diversity and redundancy. This requires the development of appropriate methodologies for a quick and early evaluation of the composite service reliability and the development of tools which can be easily adopted to compare multiple architectural choices for the orchestration of a service. In this paper, we propose a formal approach that allows a workflow architect to perform reliability analysis of a SOA-based service. The approach exploits the concept of reliability patterns to derive an aggregate reliability function and it is suited for a wide class of workflow processes. The approach is implemented in a tool (more precisely, as a plug-in for Active BPEL Designer). The tool allows the system architect to evaluate the impact—in terms of reliability—of possible workflow alternatives, as early as in the first steps of the design. The effectiveness of the approach and the operation of the tool are demonstrated with respect to a case study of a business security infrastructure realized by orchestrating simple security services. The rest of the paper is organized as follows. Section 2 provides an overview of the related work. Section 3 presents the concept of workflow patterns, while in Section 4 reliability patterns are derived and their reliability formulas evaluated. Section 5 discusses the assumptions and limitations of the model. Section 6 presents a typical case study of a business security infrastructure. In Section 7 it is described the implementation of the plug-in for ActiveBPEL and its operation is demonstrated with respect to the case study at hand. Finally, Section 8 concludes the paper with final remarks.

RELATED WORK

Web Services based systems are typically composed by orchestrating a number of simpler services (generally Web Services themselves) in a common workflow. In such a case it is widely accepted that the reliability function of the workflow must be derived based on the reliability functions of individual tasks in the workflow. A mature work in this field is [6], where the authors propose a set of workflow patterns with related reliability expressions. A workflow engine named METEOR, which allows combining such patterns to build a more

Citation: Luigi Coppolino, Luigi Romano, Valerio Vianello, Security Engineering of SOA Applications Via Reliability Patterns, doi:10.4236/jsea.2011.41001

complex workflow, is also presented. Based on the reliability expression of the elementary patterns METEOR permits to derive the aggregate reliability expression of the composed workflow. The main limitation of this approach lies in the possibility of getting the reliability expression only for those workflows that can be obtained by composing the patterns described in [6]. To overcome such limitation, we start from results presented in [7] where the authors present, by extending results reported in [8], a set of 43 workflow patterns whose combinations can provide pretty every workflow. Starting from this set of patterns, we identify the combinations of them that are meaningful from a reliability point of view and derive for them a reliability expression. We refer such combinations as "reliability patterns". Since virtually any workflow can be obtained by combining the workflow patterns in [7], "reliability patterns" can also be applied to obtain the reliability formula for any workflow. We demonstrate our approach to the patterns defined in [8], similarly it is possible to derive new reliability patterns from the remaining patterns defined in [7]. By doing so we verify that, not only all the patterns defined in [6] are also obtained as reliability patterns, but new patterns, not considered in [6], such as the "Multi-Merge Parallel", are also identified and considered for reliability evaluation. Since our approach can be applied to retrieve the reliability expression of virtually any workflow, it can be applied to already existing workflow designing tools, instead of needing the design of new ones, as it was for METEOR. This is verified by applying the concept of reliability patterns to a popular commercial workflow designing tool, namely Active BPEL Designer [9], and enabling an early evaluation of reliability formulas for designed workflows. Even more interestingly, the proposed plug-in can be easy adapted to any WS-BPEL [10] compliant designer. Finally it is worth noting that the estimation of such formulas is not intended at exactly measuring the reliability of a composed service, but at allowing a what-if analysis of alternative architectural solutions at design time. This means that the simplicity of reliability expressions should be preferred to their precision.

WORKFLOW PATTERNS

E. Gamma et al. defined a pattern as "The abstraction from a concrete form which keeps recurring in specific non arbitrary contexts" [11]. When dealing with Web Services composition it is worth considering workflow patterns that are defined in [12] as "An abstract description of a recurrent class of interactions based on activation dependencies". Workflow patterns can be considered from multiple perspectives, namely a control-flow perspective, a data perspective, a resource perspective, an operational perspective. In particular control-flow perspective refers the execution order of a set of activities. With respect to the control-flow perspective of workflow, W. M. P van der Aalst et al. identifies a set of twenty basic control-flow patterns (in the following referred as patterns), which can be combined to generate virtually any control flow. While analyzing the patterns provided in [8], some observations are due: 1) Since we are only interested in the reliability of the workflow from an architectural point of view, not all the patterns are relevant for our purposes. As an example, the pattern Cancel Case relates to the workflow management system and is therefore not relevant for the composition process. 2) From a reliability point of view some patterns are equivalent. As an example the Multiple Instances pattern provides the same reliability of a Parallel Split or of a Multiple Choice depending on the necessity of completing or not all the activated instances. 3) Combinations of patterns are often needed—in order to address reliability—instead of individual patterns. This is the case of the Parallel Split, for which deriving reliability requires knowing if the following task is a Synchronization or a Multi-Merge. 4) Finally, not all pattern combinations yield valid workflows, as one example the sequence of a XOR-Split and an AND-Join is not allowed since it refers to a scenario, where only one in a set of tasks is activated but the end of all of them is waited before the workflow can terminate. In the next sections, we first describe an algorithm which derives the aggregate reliability function through a workflow graph reduction, then we discuss the derived reliability patterns and their reliability formulas, finally we present an example showing how the algorithm works.

WORKFLOW RELIABILITY PATTERNS

Starting from the resulting presented in [8] and considering the definitions provided in Section 3, we define the concept of reliability pattern as: "An elementary combination of patterns which itself behaves as a pattern from a reliability perspective". The previous definition yields that 1) for a reliability pattern, a reliability formula can be defined starting from the reliability formula of each activity in the pattern, 2) for any subset of patterns in the reliability pattern, a related reliability formula cannot be defined. As an example the sequence of an AND-SPLIT pattern and a MULTI-MERGE JOIN pattern matches an m-out-of-n reliability structure so it can be uniquely characterized from a reliability point of view. On the other hand it is not possible to characterize the reliability of neither the AND-SPLIT pattern nor the MULTI-MERGE JOIN pattern if they are considered separately. In the following sections, first is defined a reduction algorithm exploiting the concept of reliability patterns to characterize the reliability of a workflow, then reliability patterns are identified and their reliability formulas are obtained.

Reduction Algorithm

When dealing with a workflow, we are assuming that Web Services are composed in an orchestration. We assume a workflow described as

$$W = (t,a,fr,fp,fc) \tag{1}$$

Where: t is a set of tasks (each represented by a circle); a is a set of transitions (each represented by an arrow); fr is a function which associates to every task ti in t its reliability function; fp is a function which associates to every transition aij (connecting the task i to the task j) a probability pij, representing the probability that once task ti terminates task tj is activated. In other words pij represents the probability of activation of the transition aij. Every time the task ti is unambiguously identified, the index "i" will be omitted and pij substituted with pj; and fc is a function which for every task ti in t associates a value ci in [0, 1] representing the probability that a failure of task ti does not lead to a failure of the workflow. Hence ci represents a coverage factor, and can be expressed as:

$$ci = \sum_{g \in G} \phi(g) P(g) \quad (2)$$

Where:

- g is a failure mode for the task i
- G is the fault dictionary for the task i
- f ( ) g = 1 if the failure g can be tolerated, 0 otherwise
- P(g) is the occurrence probability of the failure g

This implies that the reliability for the single task is increased by a factor representing the probability that the component will fail without leading to a workflow failure, that is:

$$R_i = R_i' + \left((1 - R_i')c_i\right) \quad (3)$$

Where R_i' represents the reliability of the task ti and represents the reliability of the task ti as perceived by the workflow engine. The latter equals the former when c is zero, i.e. the workflow cannot tolerate a fault in one of the orchestrated services. If c equals 1 the formula returns 1 meaning that the component is optional from a reliability point of view. In the next two sub-sections we will always use the term reliability with reference to the meaning it assumes in (3). A start task and an end task must be identified into the set of the tasks. The start task does not have any incoming transition and represents the invocation of the orchestrated service by an external client. The end task does not have any outgoing transition and represents the end of the orchestration. Once the graph representing the Web Services orchestration is defined, the reduction algorithm is performed by going backward through the graph (from the end task to the start one) and each time an individual reliability pattern is found its component tasks are collapsed in a single task whose reliability is defined by the pattern reliability formula. The process is than iterated until the whole workflow is collapsed in a single task whose reliability depends on the reliability of the individual tasks, the probabilities pij and the coverage factors c_i.

Reliability Patterns

The authors described the identified reliability patterns in a previous work [13], in Table 1 are reported the formulas of these patterns.

ASSUMPTIONS AND LIMITS OF THE MODEL

The main hypothesis underling the analysis proposed in the previous section, and of course the proposed approach, is the independence of events Ai = 'time to first failure of activity i'∈t and Aj = 'time to first failure of activity j'∈t , for each I ¹ j. This means, for example, that if two services are offered by the same provider it is assumed that they are deployed on physically independent servers. A further simplification in this approach lies in the absence from the model of the communication channel reliability. Actually the communication channel may itself introduce faults, as an example by dropping packets, or modifying them or just delaying their delivery beyond timeout expiration. Anyway such a kind of behavior can be embedded into the model of the single service. Finally it is worth noting that the obtained model provides the reliability of the services orchestration without considering the reliability of the service that performs the orchestration. As an example let us consider a service which by means of an orchestration engine (e.g. BPEL) coordinate the invocation of other services by following a predefined workflow. In this case the reliability of the orchestration service, of the server hosting such a service and of the orchestration engine, should be modeled and in case of hypothesis of independence it should be multiplied by the reliability of the entire workflow.

Table 1. Reliability pattern expressions.

Reliability Pattern Name	Reliability Pattern Expression
Sequence	$R = R_A x R_B$
Synchronizing Parallel	$R = R_A R_B \sum_{i_1=0}^{2} \ldots \sum_{i_N=0}^{2} u\left(\sum_{j=1}^{n} \partial(i_j - 1) - k\right) \times$ $\times \prod_{j=1}^{n} \left[\partial(i_j - 1)R_j p_j + \partial(i_j)(1 - R_j)p_j + \partial(i_j - 2)(1 - p_j)\right]$ Where u(n) = 1 if n ≥ 0, 0 otherwise ∂ (n) = 1 if n = 0, 0 otherwise And $\sum_{j=1}^{n} \partial(i_j - 1) > k \Leftrightarrow \sum_{j=1}^{n} \partial(i_j - 1) - k > 0$
Multi-merge Parallel	$R = R_A \sum_{i_1}^{2} \ldots \sum_{i_n=0}^{2} u\left(\sum_{j=1}^{n} \partial(i_j - 1) - k\right) \times$ $\times \prod_{j=1}^{n} \left[\partial(i_j - 1)R_j p_j R_B + \partial(i_j)(1 - R_j)p_j + \partial(i_j - 2)(1 - p_j)\right]$
XOR Parallel	$R = R_A R_B \sum_{i=1}^{n} p_{Ai} R_i$ Where … $\sum_i p_{Ai} = 1$
Loop	$R_l = \frac{R(1-p)}{1-pR}$ Where p is the probability of running the loop.
Discriminator Parallel	$R = R_A R_B \sum_{i=1}^{n} p_{iB} R_i$ Where $\sum_{i=1}^{n} p_i = 1$

CASE STUDY

This section considers a realistic case study to show how the proposed approach can be applied in the field of reliable workflow development. The case study considers a company with four branches each with its IT department [14]. The four branches are federated in a trusted domain [15]. So that a user which logs at one of the federated entities, in order to access a service, obtains a SAML [16] token which can be used at a later time to log in at any of the other federated entities without the need of being authenticated again. In the presented scenario the user, holding the SAML token, sends a request to access a service provided by the company (Figure 1). The request is intercepted by the Access Manager of one federated entity which picks the SAML token up and tries to validate it. Two alternatives are possible:

- The SAML token was actually released by that entity (branch 1 of the company): in this case, the Access Manager requests the Identity Manager to retrieve the appropriate authorization profile for the user holding the token. The Identity Manager will do it by means of the Directory Server which provides an abstraction of the data repositories in the company.
- The SAML token is not recognized as a valid token by the branch 1 of the company: the Access Manager charges the Federation Manager in its domain with

managing the SAML token. The Federation Manager will ask other Federation Managers in the same trusted domain to check for the SAML token. Each of the Federation Manager will provide its Access Manager with a copy of the token. These in turn will repeat the same steps of the validation procedure as operated by the Access Manager in the branch 1. Finally the required service will be accessed with the authorization profile provided by the federated entity which actually issued the SAML token.

Assuming, that each of such functionalities is provided as a service, the whole procedure can be described by the workflow graph of Figure 2. A workflow architect can study the workflow in order to make a reliability prediction of the orchestrated service. Further the designer can study the workflow even to modify the architecture of the service itself; if, for example, the four federated entities are distributed in Europe but two of them are both in Italy, the workflow architect could compare the reliability of an architecture where the four entities are seen as four branches of the company, with an architecture where the two entities in Italy are connected through a virtual dedicated LAN resulting in a company with only three branches for a reliability point of view. The workflow architect can take the best decision based on a trade-off analysis in terms of total reliability of the service versus implementation cost for the chosen solution. While, to evaluate the cost of an architectural solution could be a simple task, to compute the total reliability function of a complex workflow is not straightforward. In the next section we present a useful tool that can help the workflow architect performing a reliability prediction analysis.

IMPLEMENTATION

In this section we first show the main capability of the proposed reliability prediction tool and then we have demonstrated the usage of the tool with respect to the case study presented in the previous section.

The Plug-in

The proposed algorithm was developed as a plug-in for Active BPEL Designer in [9] which is a widely used workflow designing tool. Once installed the plugin allows the workflow designer to perform a reliability analysis for a BPEL Web Services orchestration. More precisely it allows to:

- Retrieve the reliability function for the workflow under design;
- Evaluate the reliability of the workflow at a specific point in time, that is the probability that the workflow will not fail until the specified time;
- Plot the resulting reliability function with respect to the time;
- Obtain usual reliability metrics, such as the MTTF (Mean Time To Failure), for the analyzed workflow.

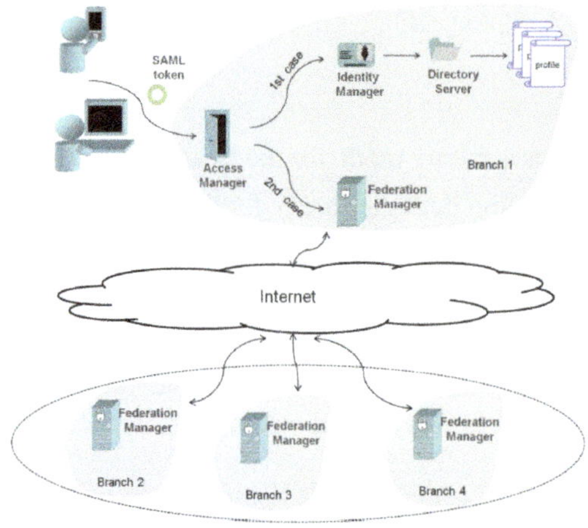

Figure 1. The case study scenario: A company with four branches federated in a trusted domain.

In order to perform the above described analysis the designer has to provide the workflow with the information required by the model (such as the symbolic expression of the reliability function of each activity, and the transition probabilities). Such information is directly embedded in the BPEL description of the workflow by exploiting the standard WS-BPEL [10] extensibility. This allows the tool to remain compliant with any WS-BPEL orchestration despite the specific editor adopted for its design. Moreover the plug-in extends the Active BPEL Designer interface to simplify the provisioning of reliability related data. Then, in order to compute the total workflow reliability function, the plug-in uses an XSLT stylesheet to convert the workflow BPEL/XML based representation to an internal representation that only includes the workflow dependability attributes and the recognized reliability patterns. After this transformation has been done, the plug-in calls a class that calculates the global reliability function as described in the reduction algorithm. The desired analysis estimates are then obtained by evaluating the retrieved reliability function. Symbolic operations are made possible by the adoption of the MathEclipse plug-in [17].

Experiment

With respect to the case study workflow depicted in the previous section in Figure 2, Figure 3 shows the steps made by the reduction algorithm in order to obtain the workflow reliability function. Each step is represented by a numbered box in which the patterns recognized by the algorithm are highlighted. In the first and third steps sequence patterns are recognized and reduced (dotted boxes). In the second and fifth steps XOR parallel patterns are matched and reduced (dashed boxes). In the fourth step an AND-SPLIT configuration is found (dotdashed boxes). Even though pencil and paper calculation is possible, this is for sure an error prone process, as well as a time consuming one, since the most complex is the workflow graph the toughest is to evaluate the reliability function by hand. As an alternative the reliability function for the workflow can be automatically evaluated by using the proposed plug-in. Figure 4 shows the workflow as it could be implemented with the Active BPEL Designer tool. To make possible the evaluation of the reliability estimates it was required specifying the reliability function of each activity as well as the transition probabilities. In our case study, for the sake of simplicity, we assumed all the non-empty activities to have reliability functions exponentially distributed with the same failure rate value. We explicitly note that evaluating the failure rate of Web Services is beyond the scope of this paper, we instead use a realistic value of 0.005 failures/second as resulting from the experiments conducted in [18]. The transition probabilities were assumed to be p = 50% and q = 0.37%, and the value of k for the Synchronizing Parallel pattern is always equals to the number of branches of the pattern. Once fixed those values the tool can infer the desired reliability evaluations. For example using the plug-in we can easily compare the reliability of the two architectural solutions presented in the previous section. Figure 5 depicts the final reliability expressions in the two cases and Figure 6 illustrates a screenshot which shows the workspace with the charts of R1(t) (4 branches) and R2(t) (3 branches), obtained running the plot reliability function command.

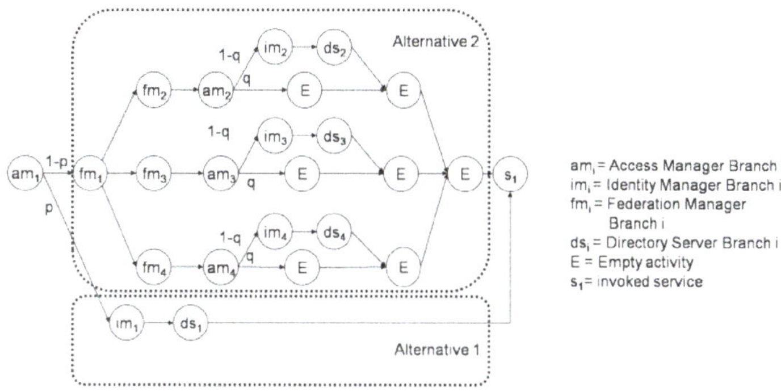

Figure 2. The workflow graph of the case study scenario.

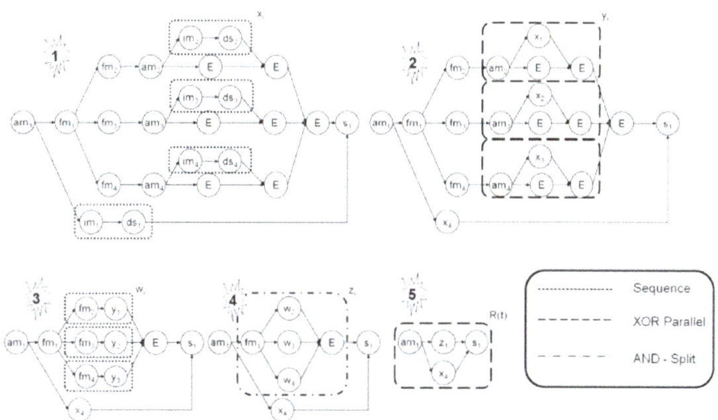

Figure 3. The workflow of the case study scenario and the related reduction process.

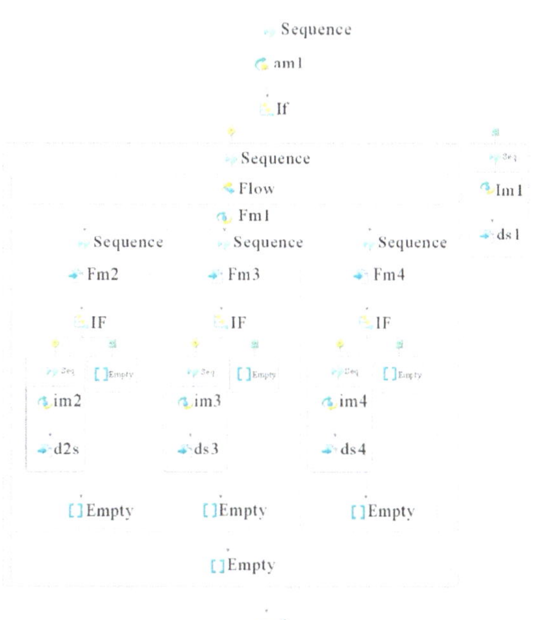

Figure 4. The schematic of the case study workflow in Active BPEL Designer.

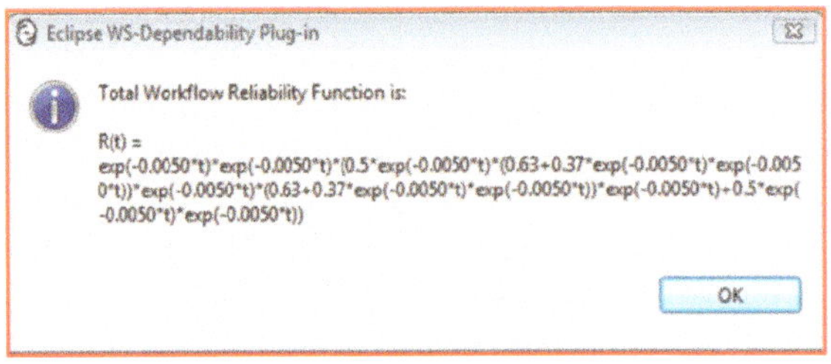

(a) Company with four federated entities

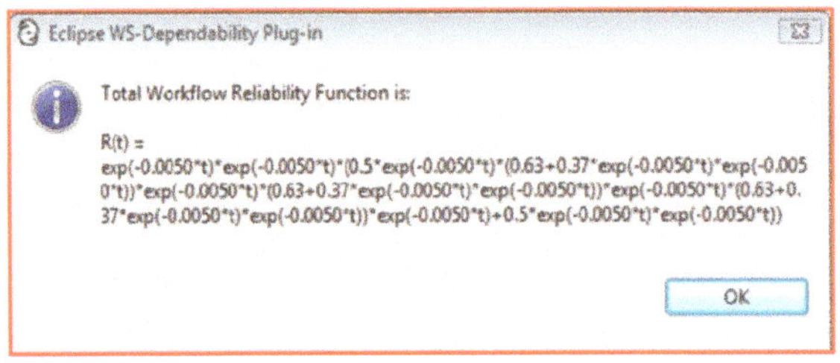

(b) Company with three federated entities

Figure 5. Total workflow reliability function.

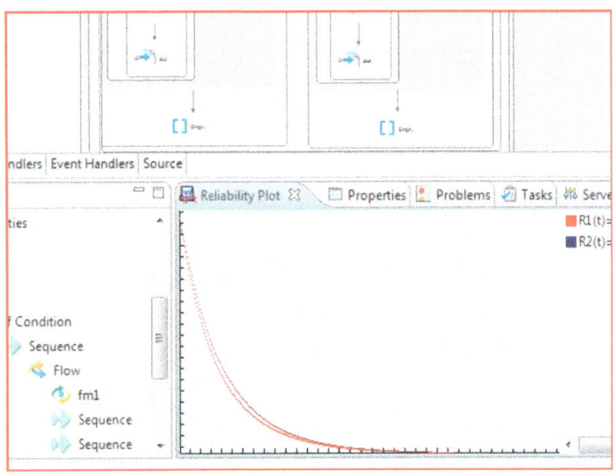

Figure 6. A screenshot of the ActiveBPEL workspace showing the plot reliability function.

CONCLUSIONS

In this paper we have proposed a formal approach that allows a workflow architect to perform reliability analysis of a SOA-based service. The approach exploits the concept of reliability patterns to evaluate the reliability function of a wide class of workflows. We have integrated our reduction process into an orchestration engine so to provide a useful plug-in, which can be used to perform a reliability analysis for a planned workflow, as well as to compare the reliability of alternative solutions in a what-if analysis.

ACKNOWLEDGEMENTS

This work has been partially supported by the Italian Ministry for Education, University, and Research (MIUR) in the framework of the Project of National Research Interest (PRIN) DOTS-LCCI: Dependable Off-The-Shelf based middleware systems for Large-scale Complex Critical Infrastructures, by the Italian Ministry of Industry in the framework of funding INDUSTRIA 2015 (SISTEMA project). This work received funding from the European Community's Seventh Framework Programme (FP7/2007-2013) under grant agreement No. 225553 (INSPIRE Project).

REFERENCES

1. L. Cherbakov, G. Galambos, R. Harishankar, S. Kalyana, and G. Rackham, "Impact of Service Orientation at the Business Level," IBM Systems Journal, Vol. 44, No. 4, 2005, pp. 653-668. doi:10.1147/sj.444.0653
2. L. Zeng, B. Benatallah, A. Ngu, M. Dumas, J. Kalagnanam and H. Chang, "QoS-Aware Middleware for Web Services Composition," IEEE Transactions on Software Engineering, Vol. 30, No. 5, May 2004, pp. 311-327. doi: 10.1109/TSE.2004.11
3. BIGSF, "Government Web Application Integrity," The Business Internet Group, San Francisco, 2003.
4. S. Bhiri, O. Perrin and C. Godart, "Ensuring Required Failure Atomicity of Composite Web Services," Proceedings of the International World Wide Web Conference (WWW'05), Chiba, 2005, pp. 138-147.
5. "Will Reliability Kill the Web Service Composition?" 2010. http://www.cs.rutgers.edu/rmartin/teaching/spring04/cs553/papers/009.pdf
6. J. Cardoso, A. Sheth, J. Miller, J. Arnold and K. Kochut, "Quality of Service for Workflows and Web Service

Processes," Web Semantics: Science, Services and Agents on the World Wide Web, Vol. 1, No. 3, April 2004, pp. 281-308. doi:10.1016/j.websem.2004.03.001

7. N. Russell, A. H. ter Hofstede, W. M. van der Aalst and N. Mulyar, "Workflow Control-Flow Patterns: A Revised View," BPM Center Report BPM-06-22, BPMcenter.org, 2006.

8. W. M. P van der Aalst, A. H. M. ter Hofstede, B. KiePuszewski and A. P. Barros, "Workflow Patterns," Distribuited and Parallel Database, Vol. 14, No. 3, 2003, pp. 5-51.

9. Y. Qian, Y. Xu, Z. Wang, G. Pu, H. Zhu and C. Cai, "Tool Support for BPEL Verification in ActiveBPEL Engine," Proceeding of 18th Australian Software Engineering Conference (ASWEC 2007), Australia, 2007, pp. 90-100. doi:10.1109/ASWEC.2007.50

10. "WS-BPEL Specification," http://www.oasis-open.org/committees/tchome.php?wgab brev=sbpel(lastaccessed30/11/2010)OASISSecurityAssertionMarkupLanguage(SAML), http://www.oasis−open.org/committees/tchome.php?wga bbrev =security(last accessed30/11/2010)

11. E. Gamma, R. Helm, R. Johnson and J. Vlissides, "Design Pattern—Elements of Reusable Object-Oriented Software," Addison-Wesley, Menlo Park, California 1995.

12. S. Bhiri, O. Perrin and C. Godart, "Extending Workflow Patterns with Transactional Dependencies to Define ReLiable Composite Web Services," Proceedings of the Advanced International Conference on Telecommunications and International Conference on Internet and Web Applications and Services, Guadeloupe, 2006.

13. L. Coppolino, L. Romano, N. Mazzocca and S. Salvi, "Web Services Workflow Reliability Estimation Through Reliability Patterns," Proceedings of the 3rd International Conference on Security and Privacy in Communications Networks and the Workshops, (SecureComm'07), 2007, pp.107-115.

14. F. Campanile, L. Coppolino, S. Giordano and L. Romano, "A Business Process Monitor for a Mobile Phone Recharging System," Journal of System Architecture, Vol. 54, No. 9, 2008, pp. 843-848. doi:10.1016/j.sysarc.2008. 02.005

15. "The WS-Federation Specification," 2010, http://msdn2.microsoft.com/enus/library/ms951236.aspx

16. "OASIS Security Assertion Markup Language (SAML)," http://www.oasis-open.org/committees/tc_home.php?wg_ abbrev = security (last accessed 30/11/2010)

17. "MathEclipse Project," 2010, http://sourceforge.net/projects/matheclipse/

18. P. Chan, M. Lyu and M. Malek, "Making Services Fault Tolerant," Lecture Notes in Computer Science, Vol. 4328, pp. 43-61, 2006. doi:10.1007/11955498_4

CHAPTER 5

PROJECT-ORIENTED AND SERVICE-ORIENTED SOFTWARE DEVELOPMENT

Marcos Kalinowski, Stefan Biffl, Rodrigo Oliveira Spínola and Sheila Reinehr

Keywords: Service reference model Software development as a service Software process Software project management Software quality

BACKGROUND

In dynamic organizational environments with software systems in production, it is not always possible to forecast and formalize in a contract the requirements for development that will arise over time (Barney *et al.*[2008]). Collecting upcoming requirements in formal projects can incur significant overhead and delay to evolving the software that supports mission-critical business processes and analyses.

Therefore, it is common for customer organizations to seek for Information Technology (IT) suppliers who can provide services to efficiently and quickly handle demands according to their business needs, respecting the varying volumes and priority of these demands (Khan *et al.*[2011]). However, from the point of view of the supplier, restructuring the software development process to meet such customer expectations is not always an easy task, in particular, if it is not clear whether the supplier software organization process is sufficiently mature to drive towards a service delivery format (Lehman and Sharma [2011]).

Treating a customer demand for software development as a request for an IT service is a promising way for addressing the customer value expectations, in line with the definition of services by ISO/IEC ([2011]), which defines a service as a "means of delivering value to customers by facilitating outcomes customers want to achieve". In practical terms this means migrating software development from a traditional project management format (PMI [2013]) to a continuous service delivery management format (TSO [2011]).

IT service management can be defined along the lines of the ITIL (Information Technology Infrastructure Library), a model conceived by the British government with a view to provide a consensus on the best IT service management practices, as "a set of specialized organizational capabilities for providing value to customers in the form of services" (TSO [2011]).

In the context of providing IT services, it is important to make an effort to establish efficient service management processes (TSO [2011]), preferably based on a reference model that supports the best practices for improving service processes and, consequently, increasing productivity and effectiveness of the services provided.

One of the programs available to meet this type of need is the Brazilian nationwide MPS.BR program (Santos *et al.*[2012]). In Brazil about 73% of the software industry is constituted of small and medium-sized enterprises (SMEs) (MCTI [2013]). Therefore, an effort was made to developed national reference models for software development and IT service delivery, which are compliant to well-established international standards and reference models, in order to provide their suppliers, including SMEs, with more fine-grained steps to define and achieve an appropriate level of software process maturity. Software regulators in other countries with a high share of SME software suppliers can benefit from the lessons learned in Brazil to better support their small-scale software suppliers.

Thus, the main MPS.BR objective is to develop and disseminate reference models that meet the requirements of the Brazilian software and IT services industries, allowing software suppliers, including SMEs, to deliver to customers according to internationally recognized quality standards (Santos *et al.*[2012]). The MPS.BR family of reference models currently consists of the MPS-SW for Software (SOFTEX [2012a]) and the MPS-SV for IT Services (SOFTEX [2012b]). The MPS-SV reference model is a promising basis for establishing service management processes. Another similar and compatible alternative (SOFTEX [2012b]) would be

Citation: Marcos Kalinowski, Stefan Biffl, Rodrigo Oliveira Spínola and Sheila Reinehr, Project-oriented and service-oriented software development, DOI: 10.1186/s40411-014-0010-x

following the guidelines of the international CMMI-SVC (CMMI for Services) reference model (SEI [2010]).

While the MPS-SW has been established in 2003 and has been widely adopted in Brazil, with 548 official assessments (over 70% of them in SMEs) published by April 2014 (SOFTEX [2014]), the MPS-SV model is still very recent and saw its first evaluation published in September 2012. The MPS-SW has already helped on the adoption of good software engineering practices in the Brazilian industry (Kalinowski *et al.*[2010]). There is also objective evidence of positive impacts on the performance of the software suppliers that adopted this model (Kalinowski *et al.*[2008a]) (Travassos and Kalinowski [2013]), which could be transferred to other countries with a similar software development structure. The MPS-SV model has a broader application scope than the MPS-SW model, since MPS-SV can be applied to support the structuring and improvement of IT service processes in general. These services might include Help Desk and support services (SOFTEX [2012b]) or even software development services, as in the experience reported in this paper.

The MPS-SV was developed in conformance to the international standards ISO/IEC 20000:2011 (ISO/IEC [2011]), ISO/IEC 15504 (ISO/IEC [2004]), being compatible with the CMMI-SVC model (SEI [2010]) (SOFTEX [2012b]). Therefore, in the context of this paper the MPS-SV can be seen as a representative for international standards. Similar to the MPS-SW model, the MPS-SV is structured in seven maturity levels for assessment (G to A, where A is the highest maturity level), while the CMMI-SVC reference models is structured in four maturity levels (2 to 5, where 5 is the highest maturity level). The compatibility between the MPS-SV and CMMI-SVC reference models is given by the maturity level mapping shown in Table 1.

Table 1 MPS-SV and CMMI-SVC maturity level compatibility

MPS-SV maturity levels	CMMI-SVC maturity levels
A – In Optimization	5 – In Optimization
B – Quantitatively Managed	4 – Quantitatively Managed
C – Defined	3 – Defined
D – Largely Defined	
E – Partially Defined	
F – Managed	2 – Managed
G – Partially Managed	

Software development as a service (SDaaS) started being discussed recently (Lehman and Sharma [2011]) and the thematic of applying service reference models to software development has been informally presented at the SEPG North America 2011 (Penn [2011]) and SEPG North America 2013 (Penn [2013]). However, to the best of our knowledge, there are no published experience reports available on this topic. Therefore, the lack of published work related to moving from a project-oriented to a service-oriented process, and in particular based on a service reference model, leads to uncertainties concerning feasibility, effects, and success and risk factors (pitfalls). An initial effort to bridge this gap was reported in (Kalinowski and Reinehr [2013]), the paper we are herein extending. Given this scenario, we investigate the following two research issues (RIs) to shed light on applying service reference models to re-structure software development from a project-oriented to a service-oriented management format from an industry perspective.

RI-1. Survey on Perceived Utility of Structuring Software Development Guided By Service Reference Models

Do software engineering consulting experts see significant utility in adopting service delivery practices for software development? Would these experts consider using a service reference model as a basis for adopting service delivery practices?

To address this research issue, a survey was conducted in the MPS-SV context with software engineering consultants (19 certified MPS-SW implementation consultants from 11 different MPS.BR accredited implementation institutions), who work with software development suppliers helping them to organize their production processes (Jordão and Kalinowski [2013]). The survey was structured following the Technology Acceptance Model (TAM) (Davis [1989]) to gather the perception on the utility, ease of adoption and intention to adopt from the point of view of those consultants. In a systematic review concerning the TAM, conducted by Turner *et al.* ([2010]), a correlation between the intention to adopt, as stated in the studies that used the TAM, and actual adoption could be identified, which reinforced the decision of following this model.

Results indicated that the MPS-SW software engineering consultants consider service reference models useful and that they would consider adopting them for providing continuous delivery capabilities to their software industry customers. A summary of these results, which reinforce the motivation for investigating the following research issue, are compiled in the Discussion and Evaluation Section. Further details on the survey planning, operation and limitations are published in a separate paper (Jordão and Kalinowski [2013]).

RI-2. Industry Experience Report on the Feasibility and Results on Restructuring Software Development Guided By a Service Reference Model

What are typical stakeholder needs that trigger software development restructuring? Can a service reference model be helpful to meet restructuring needs in software development? What effort is to be expected? What are the potential effects on quality and productivity? What are the main lessons learned? What are the involved success and risk factors?

To address this research issue a real experience of restructuring software development guided by a service reference model was conducted, analyzed, and an initial report (in Portuguese) was produced (Kalinowski and Reinehr [2013]). Main reported results were: (i) the MPS-SV model was found helpful to guide the restructuring; (ii) restructuring required only modest effort; and (iii) significant benefits were perceived in terms of quality, productivity, and customer satisfaction.

However, this initial report only provided an overview of the restructuring and brief indications on effort and on the produced effects on quality and productivity. Therefore, many questions raised in RI-2, to which answers would provide additional insights into structuring software development as a service, remained unanswered. For instance, stakeholder needs that typically trigger such restructuring and how the MPS-SV can support meeting these needs were not described. Lessons learned were also not discussed in depth to allow further understanding the assumptions for such restructuring and possible improvements. Finally, major success and risk factors were not identified.

This paper extends the initial report (Kalinowski and Reinehr [2013]) by providing further details on the context and on how managerial skills for handling service requests were established aiming at complying to a Service Level Agreement (SLA) with the customer to satisfy his business needs. Contractual aspects of the restructuring and internal controls used to ensure compliance with the SLA, are described in details. Those internal controls encompass the integrated use of managerial spreadsheets, issue-tracking systems and Kanban charts (Anderson [2010]) to monitor the demand prioritization.

Moreover, further analyses of the experience allowed identifying the stakeholder needs and how the MPS-SV supported meeting them. The discussion on lessons learned was extended and success and risk factors were identified. We assume that these additional details, analyses and extensions can provide further insights into the feasibility of applying service reference models to software development, which are relevant for SME software suppliers in Brazil and in comparable international contexts.

The remainder of this paper is organized as follows. Case description describes the case: context of the experience, including the identification of the stakeholder needs, and how the development process was re-structured. Discussion and evaluation presents the discussion and evaluation, including obtained results, lessons learned, success and risk factors. Conclusions concludes and discusses issues for further research.

CASE DESCRIPTION

This section describes the experience related to investigating RI-2 by restructuring the software development process guided by a service reference model. Therefore, the context is described and further details on how the development was structured as a service are provided.

Context and Stakeholder Needs

The experience described herein occurred in the context of the companies Kali Software (KS), as the software supplier, and Tranship Transportes Marítimos (TTM), as the customer.

The supplier, KS, can be characterized as a small-sized Brazilian software supplier (20 employees – including the board of directors) that had worked on custom development for almost a decade, providing services for national and international customers in a range of business areas (e.g., naval industry, health insurances, and financial). Despite of its small size the development followed distributed processes, with the development team and their local management were located in the city of Juiz de Fora (Brazil), and directors and requirement analysts located in the city of Rio de Janeiro (Brazil). The previously adopted development process followed a traditional interactive and incremental development life cycle, where increments were included in plan-driven projects (Boehm and Turner [2003]), with each project negotiated as a separate development contract.

The customer, TTM, is a medium-sized Brazilian sea freight company (about 400 employees) that provides strategic services to the country. These services include coastal transport and naval support to oil rigs working at the pre-salt layer of the continental shelf. TTM had several software suppliers and internal IT support. The internal support was provided by an IT manager (responsible for supplier agreement management and conducting acceptance tests) and an IT support analyst (responsible for the installed server infrastructure and help desk support).

The software development partnership between the two companies was established in February 2011. The main developed software in this context concerned an Enterprise Resource Planning (ERP) system, involving several modules, such as administrative, operations, allocation of ship crew members, finance, and human resources, which were gradually put into production. In total, 87 use cases were implemented in an overall effort of more than 4000 hours, resulting in a management system of around 83,000 lines of Java code and 167 data tables. At the time of the herein reported experience, 10 of KS employees (1 director, 1 project manager, 1 requirements analyst, 6 developers and 1 testing analyst) were involved – not all exclusively –with the TTM ERP project.

With the modules entering production, the stakeholder's needs started to change. TTM's directors (executive, operations, financial, and human resources), for instance, began needing information and new functions very quickly according to their immediate strategic, tactical, and operational business goals. The contractual model for new development requests was previously structured as separate projects (characterized according to the definition of the PMI ([2013]) by having a manageable scope, a beginning and an end), in which a new contract had to be negotiated in order to develop new functions. This contractual approach was not adequate for the new scenario anymore. The main problems of this value-neutral approach (Boehm [2006]) were the effort of negotiating new contracts and not considering added business value for prioritizing individual demands. As a consequence, fast deployment of the most important new system capabilities from a business point of view, was not achieved.

Table 2 shows an overview on the different stakeholder interests after the system entered production. The interests mainly conflicted with the negotiation of demands to be included in a value-neutral project context. This negotiation effort and not sufficiently considering added business value of individual development requests hindered delivering optimal business value to the customer.

Table 2 Stakeholder interests conflicting with the value-neutral project approach

Stakeholder	Stakeholder interests
TTM - Directors, managers and operational level employees of the different business areas.	Simple contract negotiation; fast definition and deployment of system capability changes or increments; delivery priority according to current added business value.
TTM - IT Manager & IT support analyst	Fast, predictable, and high quality deliveries.
KS – Directors and Project Manager	Simple contract negotiation; steady inflow of system capability changes or increments; translate technical productivity into higher net gains; visibility of team productivity.
KS – Developer& Quality Assurance	Quick customer feedback.

Therefore, the directors of both companies met to define a new and more flexible contractual model to satisfy the new stakeholder needs. They decided on a contractual framework based on the provision of services, in which demands were treated as separate requests for services with different priorities and the billing would be linked to compliance with a SLA (in traditional project-oriented development, contracts usually include terms for incremental delivery and related penalties). By considering a SLA based on the customer's business needs, this contractual framework helps integrating value considerations into software development, as suggested by the Value-Based Software Engineering (VBSE) discipline (Biffl *et al.*[2006]).

The decision of establishing a provision-of-services contract meant that the supplier had to adopt a strategy for delivering such services with internal controls to facilitate the management of individual requests in order to comply with the SLA. The following subsection describes this strategy.

Restructuring Software Development as a Service

Although an official assessment was not in the plans of the supplier, it was decided that the structuring of software development as a service should follow the guidelines of the reference model MPS-SV maturity level G (SOFTEX [2012b]). This decision was taken to ensure that service delivery best practices would be incorporated into the new development process. The MPS-SW has contributed to the adoption of good practices by the Brazilian software industry (Kalinowski *et al.*[2010]), and the national experts expect that the MPS-SV can do the same for the IT services sector.

Level G of the MPS-SV reference model (SOFTEX [2012b]) contemplates five processes: Work Management, Requirements Management, Service Delivery, Service Level Management, and Incident Management. During the experience described in this paper, the practices of Work Management and Requirements Management, already in place at KS in the software development context, were complemented with practices of the remaining three processes directly related to service management. A brief description of these three processes (Service Delivery, Service Level Management, and Incident Management) follows.

The Service Delivery process aims to use a strategy for service delivery in line with the established service agreements. Service Level Management process aims to ensure that the customer's SLAs are fulfilled. Finally, the purpose of the Incident Management process involves capabilities for managing incidents and service requests (SOFTEX [2012b]).

MPS-SV's Service Delivery precepts are handled in Contractual aspects Section, in which the contractual aspects that made the service delivery strategy possible and the SLA established in order to meet the customer's needs are described. Service Level Management and Incident Management are addressed in Supplier-side managerial controls Section, in which the internal managerial controls employed for monitoring the SLA and how to operate service requests are detailed.

Contractual Aspects

The contractual model had to undergo changes to enable the new service delivery strategy. In this new model, demands for development came to be treated as service requests. Previously, demands had been grouped into increments handled as development projects, billed accordingly as the projects progressed (20% at the outset, 30% after functional specification, and 50% following final delivery).

With the new desired dynamics, requests would no longer be grouped into development projects, but rather handled as work associated with isolated services that should comply with a SLA. The CMMI-SVC reference model (SEI [2010]) defines work as "a managed set of people and other resources that delivers one or more products or services to a customer or end user". Thus, in the case of this experience, switching from project management to work management would result in a finer granularity of items to manage.

The strategy that was defined to enable service delivery involved dividing the billing of the contract into two parts, one fixed and one variable. The former included the payment of a full-time requirements analyst in charge of receiving requests from users and specifying them as service requests. In addition to the analyst, the fixed part also included a fee for corrective maintenance services (development effort related to fixing system failures). The variable monthly part, on the other hand, was calculated on a fixed day of the month, based on the implemented requests, according to the SLA. Therefore, higher productivity would directly and intuitively result in a higher monthly net gain for the software supplier.

The strategy for satisfying customer requests is outlined in Figure 1. As shown in this figure, the requirements analyst receives business requests from the system's users. These requests get prioritized according to their added business value and written in the form of requirements to be implemented, in order to become service requests. The priorities are defined together with TTM's IT Manager and other appropriate stakeholders.

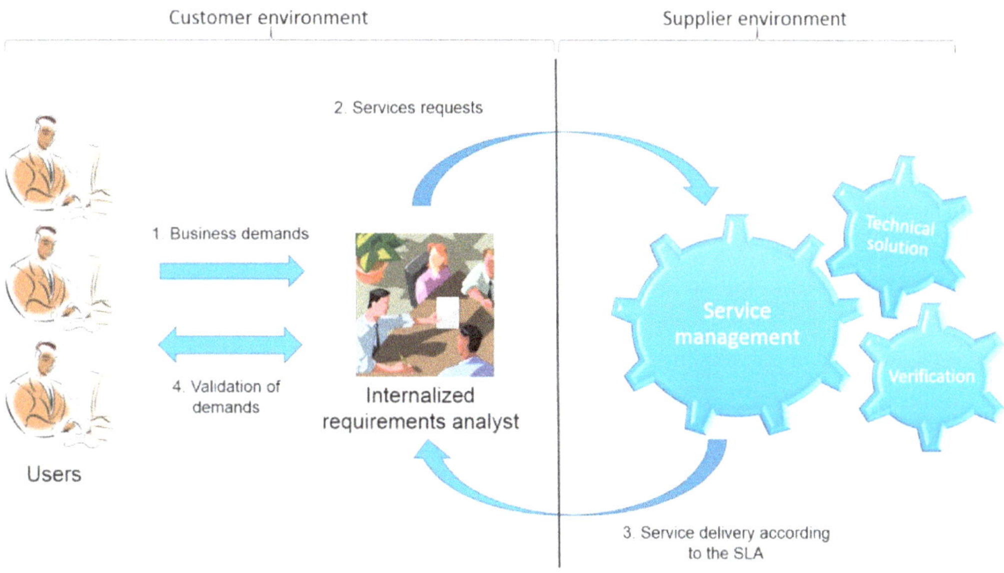

Figure 1 Strategy for Meeting Customer's Demands.

The treatment of the service requests was managed to ensure that each request was attended complying with the established SLA. As soon as the developer concludes the technical solution of a request, before it is considered ready for validation, the solution is sent to a test by an independent team. Finally, the delivered requests get validated with the system's users.

The 'Service Level Agreement and Penalties' subsection shows the SLA part of the contract. In this SLA, requests have different deadlines, defined as numbers of days, according to their priority. The priority should reflect the added business value, so that higher added business value has to be treated faster. The following prioritization criteria was adopted:

- *Critical Requests:* these impede the use of the system for the business activities of some sectors or relate to new functionalities that can significantly improve business results.
- *High Priority Requests:* these do not impede the use of the system for the business activities of entire sectors, but hinder the conclusion of some specific business operations;
- *Medium Priority Requests:* these relate to new functionalities that can allow the speedier execution of some business operations;

Low Priority Requests: these relate to new functionalities that enable features of the system to be improved.

According to this SLA, if a critical request of a new functionality with estimated effort of 40 hours is fully answered on the tenth working day after the request and with a total effort of 80 hours, then only 42 of the 80 worked hours would be billable. This amount corresponds to the maximum billable amount of 60 hours with a penalty of 30%, since it should have been answered at the eights workday and was only answered in the tenth workday. In cases the supplier did not agree with classifying a new functionality as critical, the customer had to explain how the new functionality would improve business results (e.g., avoiding losses or enabling higher gains).

On the other hand, if a critical correction with estimated effort of 40 hours is fully answered on the tenth working day after the request and with a total effort of 80 hours, then 18 billable hours would be deduced from the total monthly billable hours. In this case, corresponding to a 30% penalty for the delay over the 60 maximum billable hours.

Given this scenario, in which delays have direct financial impact, monitoring the request against the SLA becomes of critical importance. Therefore, to monitor compliance with the SLA, requests were recorded on a spreadsheet, one of the internal managerial controls used to facilitate management of services. More information concerning managerial controls is provided in subsection Supplier-side managerial controls.

Service Level Agreement and Penalties

This service level agreement is valid for corrections, as well as for changes and new developments, requested from the entry date of this agreement.

Agreement

The requests will have the following deadlines to be fully met (with no defects)

- Critical Requests

Deadline in hours = (1.5 x estimated effort) Hours.

Deadline in days = (Deadline in hours/8) Working Days.

- High Priority Requests

Deadline in hours = (1.5 x estimated effort) Hours.

Deadline in days = (Deadline in hours/8) + 1 Working Days.

- Medium Priority Requests

Deadline in hours = (1.5 x estimated effort) Hours.

Deadline in days = (Deadline in hours/8) + 2 Working Days.

- Low Priority Requests

Deadline in hours = (1.5 x estimated effort) Hours.

Deadline in days = (Deadline in hours/8) + 4 Working Days.

The deadline in hours will be used as a limit on the number of billable hours. The deadline in days will be used for penalties related to the deadline. Whenever this number is odd it should be rounded up, i.e., a period of 8.32 days should be met within the ninth day.

Penalties

Change requests or new developments that are not answered within the service level agreement will automatically be penalized by 30%.

Correction requests, included in the monthly amount, that are not answered within the service level agreement, will be automatically converted into a penalty of 30% of the deadline in hours, taking into account the hourly cost established in this agreement. This amount will be deduced from the variable cost to be billed monthly.

Supplier-side Managerial Controls

The following three internal managerial controls were used for supporting service management at the software supplier:

- a *request-tracking spreadsheet* for monitoring the requests and their conformance to the SLA;

an *issue-tracking system* (integrated with the version control), in which a ticket is registered for each service request; and

- a *Kanban chart* to show the service status at any time to the whole team involved in providing the overall continuous development service.

Kanban charts have been used in agile development approaches such as Lean and SCRUM, for more information on the use of Kanban charts in the technology business refer to (Anderson [2010]). Figure 2 shows the sequence in which these controls are applied for handling service requests according to the precepts of the MPS-SV Service Level Management and Incident Management processes. This figure also highlights the purpose and facilities offered by each of these controls.

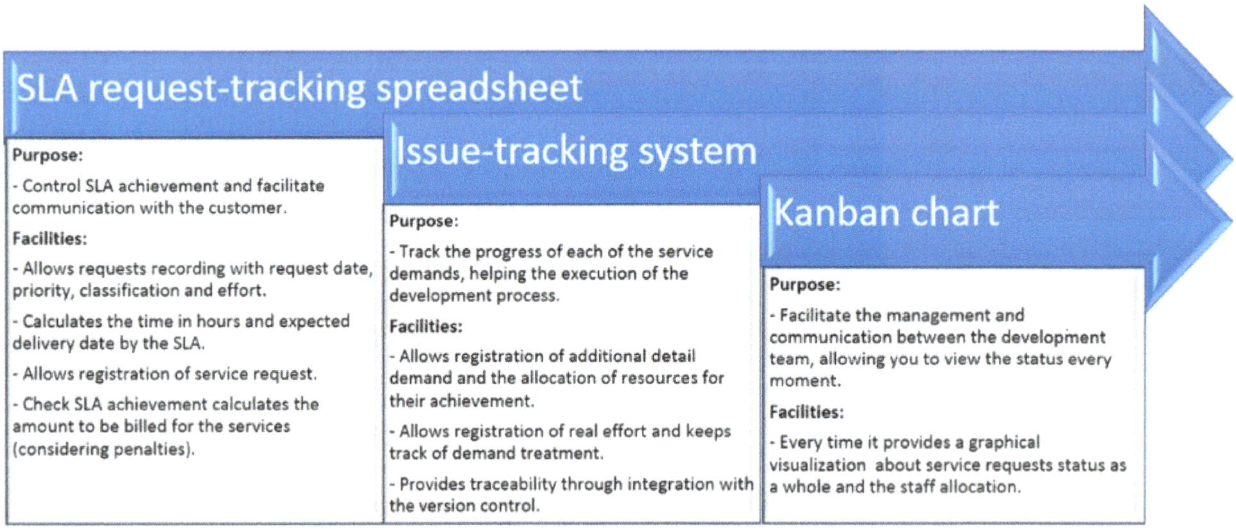

Figure 2 Internal controls for Service Management.

Initially, a new service request is recorded in the request-tracking spreadsheet. The spreadsheet containing the requests made between 01/16/2013 and 01/31/2013 is shown in Figure 3. The columns for the developer and the cost have been deliberately modified to avoid revealing individual performance and cost information. The cost is represented by the number of billable hours rather than the expected cash value of the services. This spreadsheet allows incident management and monitoring the conformance of the provided services to the SLA, as required for compliance with the MPS-SV Incident Management and Service Level Management processes. This enables services delivery according to their business value and priority. It is important to state that this spreadsheet was also shared with the customer for billing purposes, thus communicating the status to the interested stakeholders, as also required by the MPS-SV Service Level Management process, is also achieved. Figures 4 and 5 present a zoomed view of the parts containing data related to registering and processing the new service request.

Legend: Critical; High Priority; Medium Priority; Low Priority; Approved/Met; Not Approved/Met

SLA REQUEST TRACKING SPREADSHEET																	
REQUEST DATA											SERVICE DATA						
STATUS	PRIORITY	REQUEST DATE	REQUEST TYPE	TICKET OPENING DATE	TICKET NUMBER	MODULE	USE CASE / DESCRIPTION	ESTIMATED EFFORT	DEADLINE IN HOURS	DELIVERY DEADLINE	DEVELOPER	REAL EFFORT	DELIVERY DATE	APPROVED	SLA	COST
Delivered	Medium Priority	1/16/2013	Change	1/16/2013	560	MFI	Lançar Despesa	8	12	1/21/2013	A	8	1/20/2013	✓	✓	8
Delivered	Medium Priority	1/16/2013	Change	1/16/2013	561	MFI	Lançar Despesa	8	12	1/21/2013	A	16	1/21/2013	✓	✓	12
Delivered	High Priority	1/17/2013	Correction	1/17/2013	563	MFI	Lançar Despesa	8	12	1/21/2013	B	10	1/21/2013	✓	✓	0
Delivered	Low Priority	1/17/2013	Change	1/18/2013	564	SGI	Todos que cada	8	12	1/24/2013	C	16	2/1/2013	✓	✗	8,4
Delivered	Low Priority	1/17/2013	Change	1/18/2013	565	SGI	Todas que utiliz	16	24	1/28/2013	B	20	1/24/2013	✓	✓	20
Delivered	Low Priority	1/18/2013	Change	1/18/2013	566	SGI	Todas que utiliz	16	24	1/29/2013	D	24	1/30/2013	✓	✗	16,8
Delivered	High Priority	1/18/2013	Correction	1/18/2013	567	MFI	Imprimir Chequ	4	6	1/21/2013	C	6	1/21/2013	✓	✓	0
Delivered	Low Priority	1/18/2013	Correction	1/18/2013	568	MOP	Manter Serviços	16	24	1/29/2013	C	16	1/28/2013	✓	✓	0
Delivered	Low Priority	1/18/2013	Change	1/18/2013	569	MFI	Importar Despe	16	24	1/29/2013	E	8	1/28/2013	✓	✓	8
Cancelled	Critical	1/23/2013	Correction	1/23/2013	570	MOP	Manter Serviços	6	9	1/24/2013	E	8	Not Delivered			
Delivered	Medium Priority	1/23/2013	Correction	1/25/2013	571	MFI	Lançar Despesa	8	12	1/28/2013	A	8	2/4/2013	✓	✗	-2,4
Delivered	Low Priority	1/24/2013	Change	1/25/2013	572	SGI	Banco de Dados	16	24	2/4/2013	B	16	1/30/2013	✓	✓	16
Delivered	Medium Priority	1/24/2013	Change	1/25/2013	573	MALO	Relatório de Alo	16	24	1/31/2013	F	20	1/29/2013	✓	✓	20
Delivered	Low Priority	1/25/2013	Change	1/25/2013	574	MFI	Lançar Despesa	24	36	2/6/2013	A	32	1/31/2013	✓	✓	32
Delivered	Low Priority	1/28/2013	Correction	1/28/2013	575	MOP	Manter Serviços	2	3	2/1/2013	C	2	2/4/2013	✓	✗	-0,6
Delivered	Critical	1/28/2013	Change	1/28/2013	576	MADM	Manter Clientes	8	12	1/29/2013	D	8	1/29/2013	✓	✓	8
Delivered	Low Priority	1/28/2013	Change	1/30/2013	577	MFI	Consultar Despe	6	9	2/4/2013	F	8	2/1/2013	✓	✓	8
0	Medium Priority	1/29/2013	Change	1/29/2013	579	MFI	Importar Despe	16	24	2/5/2013	A					
1	Low Priority	1/29/2013	Correction	1/30/2013	578	MOP	Cadastrar C.T	12	18	2/6/2013	D					
Delivered	Critical	1/31/2013	Change	1/31/2013	580	MFI	Lançar Despesa	8	12	2/1/2013	E	8	2/1/2013	✓	✓	8
3	Low Priority	1/31/2013	Change	1/31/2013	581	SGI	Telas do SGI	12	18	2/8/2013	E					
																162,2

Figure 3 Spreadsheet for controlling SLA.

Figure 4 shows the data registered for each request: (i) the date of the request, (ii) the request type ("correction" or "change" – in this case "change" also includes new development requests), (iii) the opening date of the ticket, (iv) the ticket number (to enable monitoring in the issue-tracking system), (v) the system module (e.g., administrative, financial), (vi) the related use case, and (vii) the estimated effort. Using this information, the deadline in work hours is calculated and the intended delivery date is set in accordance with the SLA. The first column highlights the overall managerial status, showing whether each request has been delivered, cancelled or how many days are left before delivery ought to be accomplished.

REQUEST DATA										
STATUS	PRIORITY	REQUEST DATE	REQUEST TYPE	TICKET OPENING DATE	TICKET NUMBER	MODULE	USE CASE / DESCRIPTION	ESTIMATED EFFORT	DEADLINE IN HOURS	DELIVERY DEADLINE
Delivered	Medium Priority	1/16/2013	Change	1/16/2013	560	MFI	Lançar Despesa	8	12	1/21/2013
Delivered	Medium Priority	1/16/2013	Change	1/16/2013	561	MFI	Lançar Despesa	8	12	1/21/2013
Delivered	High Priority	1/17/2013	Correction	1/17/2013	563	MFI	Lançar Despesa	8	12	1/21/2013

Figure 4 Part of the spreadsheet used for registering new requests.

SERVICE DATA					
DEVELOPER	REAL EFFORT	DELIVERY DATE	APPROVED	SLA	COST
A	8	1/20/2013	✓	✓	8
A	16	1/21/2013	✓	✓	12
B	10	1/21/2013	✓	✓	0

Figure 5 Part of the spreadsheet used for registering the treatment of the requests.

Figure 5 shows the data registered in the spreadsheet for the service being processed for each request, including the chosen developer, real development effort (obtained from the issue-tracking system), actual delivery date and customer approval (validation). With this information, the spreadsheet calculates the extent of compliance of the work performance with the SLA and the amount to be billed for the service, taking into account contractual SLA penalties for late delivery, when applicable. In the fifteen day period shown in Figure 3, for instance, besides the fixed cost (regarding the internalized requirements analyst and the corrections), there are 162.2 billable hours concerning the provided services of implementing changes and eventual penalties.

The issue-tracking system used was *Assembla* (Assembla [2013]), a cloud-based service system, already including the integration of tickets (requests) with version control. The integration with version control provides traceability on how the tickets were handled. For each ticket all the files added or changed for providing the technical solution can be explicitly identified, as well as the modifications done in each file. Therefore, if a change request on a given ticket is received, the files to be modified can be traced, supporting the involved impact analysis and effort estimation.

This system was also used for allocating the developers and registering the real effort. As soon as a developer concludes the technical solution of a request, he registers the effort and passes corresponding ticket to be tested by an independent team. If the ticket passes testing then its status is changed and it is considered ready to be deployed for customer validation, with the support from the internalized requirements analyst at the customer side.

Finally, monitoring the service status for each request was facilitated by the Kanban chart, which was physically displayed in the room where the development team was located. Figures 6 and 7 show a real example of a request in Assembla and a Kanban chart with the progress status of service requests, respectively. In this Kanban chart the status of each ticket can be easily identified. Each ticket becomes a separate post-it, using different colors reflecting the SLA priorities. To illustrate the use of the Kanban chart, Figure 7 highlights the status of ticket #560, shown in Figure 6, as being in the queue for supplier side testing.

Figure 6 Real request in the Assembla issue-tracking system.

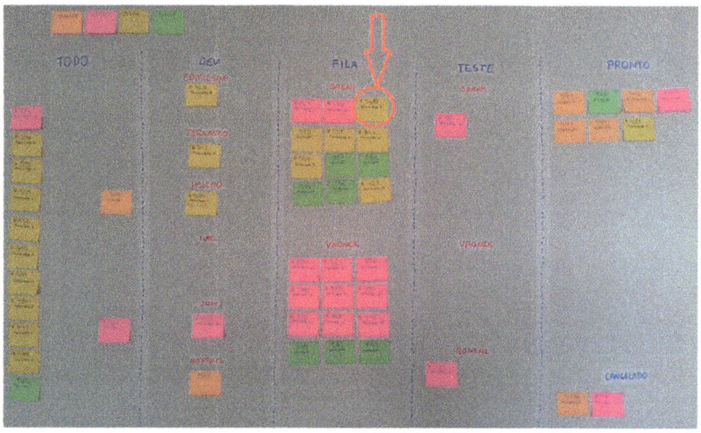

Figure 7 Kanban chart showing the status of requests.

The importance of tests in this context is obvious, since a service request is only accepted for billing if it does not show any failures during validation. Moreover, if an acceptance test fails, the delivery data remains unchanged and the SLA will probably not be met, resulting in penalties. Considering this critical quality issue, requirements inspections (Kalinowski *et al.*[2007]) and code peer reviews (Kemerer and Paulk [2009]) were also adopted.

Having presented the contractual aspects and the internal managerial controls defined in this industrial experience, based on the guidelines of the MPS-SV service reference model, to allow switching from a project-oriented to a service-oriented software development approach, the next section presents the discussion and evaluation of the overall experience.

DISCUSSION AND EVALUATION

Aiming at understanding the feasibility and effects of restructuring software development from a project-oriented to a service-oriented approach guided by a service reference model, two research issues were identified in the Background Section. RI-1, related to the perceived utility, was investigated through a survey reported in detail in (Jordão and Kalinowski [2013]).

Results indicated that the MPS-SW software engineering consultants consider service reference models, such as the MPS-SV, useful for providing continuous delivery capabilities to their software industry customers (93% totally or partially agreed). The consultants also indicated an expected ease of use (76% totally or partially agreed) and intention to adopt (63% totally or partially agreed). The survey's overall confidence level was of 78.5%.

These survey results can be seen as an additional motivation for investigating the second identified research issue, RI-2, which is the main contribution of this article and concerns the feasibility and results or restructuring software development guided by a service reference model. The discussion and evaluation of questions that provide further insights into RI-2, based on the reported experience, follows.

What are Typical Stakeholder Needs That Trigger The Restructuring From A Project-Oriented Approach To A Service-Oriented Approach?

Table 2 provides an overview on the main stakeholders and their interests. From the customer's point of view, the main interests on software development were facilitating contract negotiations and integrating value considerations into the development process. Therefore, allowing faster deployment of new system capabilities prioritized according to the added business value. From the supplier's point of view, on the other hand, the main interests were related to simple contract negotiation, a steady (or growing) inflow of development requests, and translating productivity directly into higher monthly net gains. It is noteworthy that there were no specific expectations regarding changes in the cost of developing individual functionalities. Actually, given the need to comply with the SLA (and potential penalties) the customer and supplier agreed to increase the hourly cost rate.

We assume that the restructuring allowed properly addressing the stakeholder's main interests, by (i) providing a contractual framework that avoids excessive negotiation effort for new development requests, and (ii) allowing the new service requests to be directly addressed according to the added business value, as defined in the SLA. From the supplier's point of view, the variable monthly net gain also accounted for the direct return of investment of efforts to improve productivity.

The general perception from the customer and the supplier was that a more flexible model had been adopted to meet the customer's business needs and to live up to his expectations in terms of supply, as expressed in the SLA. In fact, the contract model considers the business priority of individual requests and does not have to be reconsidered due to a variation in the volume of requests, for instance.

Can a Service Reference Model Be Helpful To Meet Those Needs?

In this experience, the Brazilian MPS-SV service reference model, which is representative for similar international standards, directly supported the restructuring to the service-oriented approach. The resulting process implementation followed the guidelines of MPS-SV maturity level G (SOFTEX [2012b]). The Service Delivery, Service Level Management, and Incident Management reference processes, directly related to providing services, were considered helpful to structure basic service delivery capabilities in order to meet the identified stakeholder needs and to increase the confidence in the provided solutions. The main purpose of each of those processes, their expected results according to the MPS-SV reference model, and how they were implemented during this experience are shown in Table 3. This implementation does also meet (SOFTEX [2012b]) the specific goals of the CMMI-SVC (SEI [2010]) Service Delivery process area (maturity level 2), and of the related ISO/IEC 20000 processes (ISO/IEC [2011]).

Table 3 MPS-SV level G processes and how they were implemented

MPS-SV process purpose and expected results	**How the expected results were implemented**
Service Delivery (SD)	
Purpose:	
The purpose of this process is defining the strategy and establishing the service system to deliver services in conformance with the service agreements.	
Required Results:	
SD 1. A service delivery and operation strategy is established and maintained;	SD 1. The defined service delivery and operation strategy is shown in Figure 1.
SD 2. The availability of the needed elements for providing the service is confirmed;	SD 2. The availability of needed elements was assured by the contractual framework, which included an internalized requirements analyst at the customer side.
SD 3. The service system is put into operation to deliver the agreed services;	SD 3. The service system was put into operation.
SD 4. The service system is maintained to assure continuous service delivery.	SD 4. The service system was maintained operating.
Service Level Management (SLM)	
Purpose:	
The purpose of this process is to assure that the SLA goals for each customer are met.	
Required Results:	
SLM 1. Services and their dependencies are identified;	SLM 1. The identified service was software development, including corrective and evolutionary (new functionalities) maintenance.

SLM 2. Service level goals are defined in an SLA;	SLM 2. The defined SLA is shown in subsection 'Service Level Agreement and Penalties'.
SLM 3. Services are monitored against the SLA;	SLM 3. Monitoring was achieved by defining the service management controls depicted in Figure 2.
SLM 4. Service level performance is communicated to relevant stakeholders;	SLM 4. The request-tracking spreadsheet (Figure 3) was shared with the customer and sent monthly for billing purposes. It provides an overview of the service performance against the SLA.
SLM 5. Changes in service requirements reflect in the SLA.	SLM 5. Those changes did not happen in the context of this experience, but would imply in changing the SLA appendix of the contractual framework and both sides, supplier and customer) were open to discuss such changes.
Incident Management (IM)	
Purpose:	
The purpose of this process is to handle individual incidents and service requests within a SLA.	
Required Results:	
IM 1. A strategy for incident and service request management is established and maintained;	IM 1. The defined strategy involved fine-grained request monitoring by using the internal managerial controls shown in Figure 2.
IM 2. An incident and service request management system is established and maintained;	IM 2. The internal managerial controls were established and maintained.
IM 3. Incidents and service requests are registered and classified;	IM 3. Each request was registered into the request-tracking spreadsheet (Figure 3) and classified as an incident (correction) or a new service request (change or new functionality).
IM 4. Incidents and service requests are prioritized and analyzed;	IM 4. Each request had its priority defined and impact analysis performed, using the traceability provided by the issue-tracking system, to estimate the required effort.
IM 5. Incidents and service requests are resolved and concluded;	IM 5. The request-tracking spreadsheet shows the managerial status of each request, allowing managing them until conclusion.
IM 6. Incidents and service requests that did not progress according the SLA are communicated to higher level management;	IM 6. The request-tracking spreadsheet was shared and monthly sent to directors of both companies. It explicitly identifies the request that did not meet the SLA.
IM 7. Status information on incidents or service requests is communicated to relevant stakeholders.	IM 7. Status communication to higher management and customer stakeholders was achieved through the spreadsheet. Communication to the internal development team by using the Kanban chart.

What is the Effort to be expected?

The restructuring took 160 person hours and happened within the timeframe of one month. As the restructuring included aspects of all processes at Level G of the MPS-SV model, we assert that implementing this model for software development requires only moderate effort, when compared for instance to the average duration of over 12 month for implementing MPS-SW maturity levels (Travassos and Kalinowski [2013]). Especially if work management and requirements management capabilities, including requirements traceability, are previously installed, as in the experience here described. Besides the moderate effort, interesting results were obtained, including increases in the productive capacity, as pointed out in the answer to the next question.

Table 4 Comparison of the project and IT service delivery approaches

Approach	# of use cases	# Failures (Acceptance)	Effort (Person-hours)
Project	12	4	284
IT Service	11	2	232

What are the Potential Effects on Quality and Productivity?

Quantitative data concerning this question was obtained by comparing the deliveries in the new service format to the most recent delivery in the previously established project format. For this comparison, only new use case developments of comparable medium complexity (according to the criteria for counting use case points: from 4 to 7 transactions including alternative steps) were considered. Table 4 summarizes these quantitative results.

Regarding quality, during customer acceptance tests of medium complexity cases, the number of failures was notably lower, falling from 0.33 failures per use case to 0.18 failures per use case. Concerning productivity, the real development effort spent per use case was also slightly lower, falling from 24 person hours per use case to 21 person hours per use case. Note that these productivity improvements directly translate into saved costs as the supplier pays for the overall development effort in person hours.

Of course, these differences are not statistically significant since only 23 medium complex use cases served as the basis for the comparison (12 implemented in the project format and 11 implemented in the IT service format). Moreover, there are several factors that can influence these results (e.g., low precision in measuring use case complexity, inherent variations of individual productivity, learning factor). However, feedback from the customer also allowed observing a perceived improvement in quality (fewer problems during acceptance tests) and productivity, especially regarding the fact that the new service-oriented value-based approach resulted in faster delivery of demands of higher added business value.

An informal causal analysis session (Kalinowski *et al.*[2008b]) (Kalinowski *et al.*[2012]), aiming at investigating the causes of these changes in quality and productivity, was conducted with the suppliers development team and showed that the existence of the SLA and closer management resulted in greater commitment on the part of the developers. Some developers mentioned that, knowing of the individual penalties that the company would be liable to pay in each request, they saw that it was much more important to meet deadlines than they did when the project format was in use, in which the tasks were scheduled but the overall deadline was scoped to the entire project. Indeed, closer management and finer granularity are suggestions included in Humphrey's reflections on efficient team management (Humphrey [2010]).

What are the Main Lessons Learned?

In the reported experience, applying practices of service management to software development resulted in a flexible contractual framework, allowing addressing the customer's business needs according to their priorities without additional contract negotiation delays. New requests could be directly Among the lessons learned, that could be passed on to international SME companies that seek to supply development as an IT service guided by a service reference model, the following stand out:

- • ***Contractual framework.*** In this supply model, it is important to have some headroom in the budget for the fixed monthly part of the contractual framework, compensating for possible variations in the volume of delivered requests to be billed in the variable part. Otherwise, financial constraints may lead to excessive pressure, on management and development levels, at the supplier's side. After all, the development team has to be paid by the supplier anyway, although if the supplier has different customers following similar contractual service frameworks he might be able to allocate developers to his project portfolio according to the individual project's volume of received demands.
- ***Prioritization criteria.*** The priority criteria for customer requests should be very clear, as it might be applied when it comes to avoiding undue financial penalties, as specified in the SLA. After all, ambiguities involving financial aspects may lead to potential relationship problems between the contractor and the supplier.
- ***SLA and team capacity.*** It is important to assess the SLA carefully, checking whether the company has the installed productive capacity of actually satisfying the requested service level. If not, this would result in deliveries not meeting the SLA and the application of penalties with direct impact on the monthly net gain.
- ***Managerial controls.*** The managerial controls were fundamental to allow handling the demands as separate service requests, by facilitate monitoring the compliance with the SLA. Not having such controls established may imply in several request passing the SLA's deadline and, as a consequence, in penalties.
- ***Traceability.*** Traceability plays a key role when handling request as separate services to be provided, by supporting effective impact analysis, effort estimation and risk assessments for handling each new request.
- ***Build, Test and Deployment Automation.*** Aiming at continuous delivery, efficient build, test and deployment automation is strongly desired (Humble and Farley [2010]). In the case of our experience the build and deployment were fully automated. Test automation however could be improved to reduce regression testing effort. So far, only superficial smoke tests had been recorded to allow identifying major side effects of new handled request, by using the Selenium IDE plugin (Selenium [2013]).
- ***Team and individual benefits.*** Some employees felt pressured by the SLA and the close and quantitative monitoring. Therefore, it might be interesting to establish a complementary policy for awarding employees with bonuses for improved productivity. Note that this is feasible, since an improvement in productivity also implies in a higher monthly net gain.
- ***Overall restructuring effort and benefits.*** Around one person month effort was required for the restructuring and benefits were perceived in terms of improved quality, productivity, and customer satisfaction. We take it that the increased customer satisfaction was mainly related to meeting their main interests by considering the integration of added business value into the software engineering practices.

What are the Involved Success and Risk Factors?

Another fruitful consequence of the experience was the opportunity to identify success (and risk) factors related to restructuring software development in the format of service delivery. Based on the lessons learned from the experience report, the main success factors were:

- ***Success factor service reference model.*** The adoption of a service reference model allowed benchmarking the new service format against IT service delivery best practices and improved the confidence in the solutions provided by the restructuring approach. These solutions include the internal managerial controls to facilitate monitoring the compliance with the SLA.

- ***Success factor senior management support.*** The idea of the restructuring addressed specific interests of stakeholders including the directors of both companies. Therefore, direct support from senior management was obtained for the process improvement initiative. We saw on several occasions that this support has considerably facilitated and accelerated the restructuring.
- ***Success factor relationship of trust.*** The previous period of over one year providing development services successfully allowed establishing a relationship of trust between the contractor and the supplier. This relationship provided the basis to discuss the new contractual framework for continuous delivery with varying monthly net payments and gains.
- ***Success factor previously established capabilities.*** Some previously established software engineering capabilities were crucial in the successful transition. Concrete requirement traceability capacity, for instance, helps to handle request separately by allowing effective impact analysis, effort estimation and risk assessments for handling each new request. Moreover, build, test and deployment automation was also extremely helpful for implementing the continuous delivery strategy.

Concerning the risk factors, we see a direct mapping, in the sense that the absence of any of the success factors represents a significant risk. Additional risks can also be identified from not addressing major issues in the the lessons learned.

CONCLUSIONS

This article reported on an experience of restructuring software development in the form of providing IT services in the context of an SME software supplier. The restructuring involved, in addition to the technical changes, important management changes, i.e., establishing a contractual framework and capacities for managing service requests in order to comply with a Service Level Agreement (SLA) made between the supplier and the customer to satisfy the business needs of the latter.

The restructuring project was guided by the MPS-SV service reference model, which is compatible to the CMMI-SVC reference model, complementing already established software engineering practices for the provision of development as a continuous IT service. The contractual aspects and internal managerial controls employed to facilitate the compliance with the SLA were described. Those controls included the integrated use of a managerial spreadsheet, an issue-tracking system, and a Kanban chart to monitor how demands were prioritized to be met.

Further insight into the feasibility and results on such structuring were provided by discussing valuable and experience-grounded answers to the following core questions: What are typical stakeholder needs that trigger such a restructuring? Can a service reference model be helpful to meet those needs? What effort is to be expected? What are the potential effects on development quality and productivity? What are the main lessons learned? What are the involved success and risk factors?

The overall analysis of the experience showed that only moderate effort, around one person month, was required for structuring software development as a service guided by a reference model and that perceived benefits were obtained in terms of quality, productivity, and customer satisfaction. The increased customer satisfaction was mainly related to meeting the customer's business needs by integrating value considerations into software engineering practices. Therefore, using a service reference model for restructuring software development can represent an alternative path towards value-based software engineering. Nevertheless, we would like to reinforce that, as expected in an experience report, the obtained results relate to a specific scenario and industrial environment. However, those results provide preliminary indications into feasibility and potential benefits, further motivating the conduct of more rigorous studies (e.g., case studies or controlled experiments) on the impact of applying service reference models to re-structure software development from a project-oriented to a service-oriented management format.

A key benefit of the Brazilian standards is the provision of smaller steps in the lower range of the process maturity levels, which allows, in particular, small companies with limited resources to systematically define and achieve software and service maturity levels that suit their needs and means. This report and the identified lessons learned can serve as a reference for SME companies that operate in the context of an international software maturity reference model and wish to restructure in order to supply software development in the format of an IT service. These companies can benefit from adopting a service reference model, such as the MPS-SV or CMMI-SVC models, in synergy with their already established software engineering practices.

AUTHORS' INFORMATION

MK holds a MS and PhD in Computer and Systems Engineering from the Federal University of Rio de Janeiro (UFRJ) and is currently professor of Software Engineering at the Federal University of Juiz de Fora (UFJF) in transference to Fluminense Federal University (UFF). He is part of the MPS.BR project team and a certified MPS.BR lead appraiser and process implementation consultant.

SB holds a MS and PhD in Computer Science from the Vienna University of Technology (TUW) and a MS in Social and Economic Sciences from the University of Vienna. He also received a Habilitation degree (Venia Docendi) in "Praktische Informatik" for his contributions on empirical software engineering. Currently he is professor of Software Engineering at TUW and the head of the Christian Doppler research laboratory – Software Engineering Integration for Flexible Automation Systems. He was lead editor for the book "Value-Based Software Engineering" in collaboration with co-editors A. Aurum, B.W. Boehm, H. Erdogmus, and P. Grünbacher.

ROS holds a MS and PhD in Computer and Systems Engineering from the Federal University of Rio de Janeiro (UFRJ) and is currently professor of Software Engineering at the University of Salvador (UNIFACS). He is a certified MPS. BR process implementation consultant.

SR holds a MS in Informatics from the Catholic University of the State of Paraná (PUCPR) and a PhD in Production Engineering from the University of São Paulo (USP) and is currently professor of Software Engineering at PUCPR. She is the coordinator of the service area of the MPS.BR project team and a certified MPS.BR lead appraiser and process implementation consultant.

DECLARATIONS

Acknowledgements

We would like to thank CNPq (Brazilian Research Council) for financial support. Thanks also to everyone at Tranship Transportes Marítimos and Kali Software directly involved in the experience reported in this article, especially Rosiene Dilly (the project manager) and Vagner Lopes (the internalized requirements analyst). This research was in part supported by the Christian Doppler Forschungsgesellschaft and the BMWFJ, Austria.

Authors' Contributions

MK was the executive director of the supplier company and worked directly with the customer on establishing the contractual framework and the service level agreement. He also worked with the supplier team to enable the restructuring in the format of the service-oriented approach. He was the lead author of the initial report and of this extended paper. SB helped to extend the initial report, discussing the overall solution and argumentation line and enriching it with his strong scientific stakeholder analysis and value-based software engineering background. ROS was the operations director of the supplier and helped extending the report with additional details of the overall experience. SR is the main responsible person for the MPS-SV reference model and used her service quality background to help writing the initial report and to support the extension with the argumentation on the international standards and reference models. All authors read and approved the final manuscript.

REFERENCES

1. Anderson DJ: *Kanban: successful evolutionary change for your technology business*. Blue Hole Press, Sequim, WA; 2010.
2. *Assembla task & issue management*. 2013.
3. Barney S, Aurum A, Wohlin C: A product management challenge: creating software product value through requirements selection. *J Syst Architecture* 2008,54(6):576–593. 10.1016/j.sysarc.2007.12.004
4. *Value-based software engineering*. Springer, Heidelberg; 2006.
5. Boehm B: Value-based software engineering: overview and agenda. In *Value-based software engineering*. Edited by: Biffl S, Aurum A, Boehm B, Erdogmus H, Grünbacher P. Springer, Heidelberg; 2006.
6. Boehm B, Turner R: *Balancing agility and discipline: a guide for the perplexed*. Wesley, Addison; 2003.
7. Davis F: Perceived usefulness, perceived ease of use, and user acceptance of information technology. *MIS Quarterly* 1989,13(3):319–340. 10.2307/249008
8. Humble J, Farley D: *Continuous delivery: reliable software releases through build, test, and deployment automation*. Addison-Wesley, Boston, MA; 2010.
9. Humphrey WS: *Reflections on management: How to manage your software projects, your teams, your boss, and yourself*. Addison-Wesley, Boston, MA; 2010.
10. *ISO/IEC 15504–1: information technology - process assessment – part 1 - concepts and vocabulary*. ISO, Geneve; 2004.
11. *ISO/IEC 20000–1:2011 – information technology service management*. ISO, Geneve; 2011.
12. Jordão L, Kalinowski M: Investigando a Aplicabilidade do MPS-SV na Melhoria de Serviços de Desenvolvimento e Manutenção de Software. In *IX Workshop Anual do MPS.BR (WAMPS)*. Brazilian Computer Society (in Portuguese), Campinas, Brazil; 2013.
13. Kalinowski M, Reinehr S: Estruturando Desenvolvimento de Software como um Serviço de TI: Uma Experiência Prática. In *XII Simpósio Brasileiro de Qualidade Software (SBQS)*. Brazilian Computer Society (in Portuguese), Salvador, Brazil; 2013.
14. Kalinowski M, Spínola RO, Dias-Neto AC, Bott A, Travassos GH: Inspeções de requisitos de software em desenvolvimento incremental: Uma experiência prática. In *VI simpósio brasileiro de qualidade software (SBQS)*. Brazilian Computer Society (in Portuguese), Porto de Galinhas, Brazil; 2007.
15. Kalinowski M, Weber KC, Travassos GH: IMPS: an experimentation based investigation of a nationwide software development reference model. In *International symposium on empirical software engineering and measurement (ESEM)*. ACM and IEEE, Kaiserslautern, Germany; 2008a.
16. Kalinowski M, Travassos GH, Card DN: Guidance for efficiently implementing defect causal analysis. In *VII Brazilian symposium on software quality (SBQS)*. Brazilian Computer Society (in Portuguese), Florianópolis, Brazil; 2008b.
17. Kalinowski M, Santos G, Reinehr S, Montoni M, Rocha AR, Weber KC, Travassos GH: MPS.BR: Promovendo a Adoção de Boas Práticas de Engenharia de Software pela Indústria Brasileira. In *XIII Congreso Iberoamericano en "Software Engineering" (CIBSE)*. Universidad del Azuay (in Portuguese), Cuenca, Equador; 2010. ISBN 978–9978–325–10–0 ISBN 978-9978-325-10-0
18. Kalinowski M, Card DN, Travassos GH: Evidence-based guidelines to defect causal analysis. *IEEE Software*2012,29(4):16–18. doi:10.1109/MS.2012.72
19. Kemerer CF, Paulk MC: The impact of design and code reviews on software quality: an empirical study based on PSP data. *IEEE Trans Softw Eng* 2009,35(4):534–550. 10.1109/TSE.2009.27
20. Khan SU, Niazi M, Ahmad R: Factors influencing clients in the selection of offshore software outsourcing vendors: an exploratory study using a systematic literature review. *J Syst Softw* 2011,84(4):686–699. 10.1016/j.jss.2010.12.010

21. Lehman TJ, Sharma A: Software development as a service: agile experiences. In *Annual SRII global conference (SRII)*. IEEE, San Diego, USA; 2011.

22. *Brazilian ministry of science, technology and innovation*. 2013.

23. Penn ML: *Applying CMMI-SVC process areas to CMMI-DEV projects. Presentation at SEPG North America 2011, available via CMMI Institute*. 2011.

24. Penn ML: *Harmonization of CMMI-SVC and CMMI-DEV*. 2013.

25. *A guide to the project management body of knowledge*. Project Management Institute, Newtown Square, PA; 2013.

26. Santos G, Kalinowski M, Rocha AR, Travassos GH, Weber KC, Antonioni JA: MPS.BR program and MPS model: main results, benefits and beneficiaries of software process improvement in Brazil. In *International Conference on the Quality in Information and Communications Technology (QUATIC)*. IEEE, Lisbon, Portugal; 2012.

27. *CMMI for services, version 1.3 (CMU/SEI-2010-TR-034)*. 2010.

28. *Selenium IDE*. 2013.

29. *MR-MPS-SW – guia geral MPS de software*. 2012a.

30. *MR-MPS-SV – guia geral MPS de serviços*. 2012b.

31. *SOFTEX MPS.BR program website*. 2014.

32. Travassos GH, Kalinowski M: *IMPS 2012: evidências sobre o desempenho das empresas que adotaram o modelo MPS-SW desde 2008*. SOFTEX, Campinas; 2013.

33. *ITIL – information technology infrastructure library v2011*. 2011.

34. Turner M, Kitchenham B, Brereton P, Charters S, Budgen D: Does the technology acceptance model predict actual use? a systematic literature review. *Inf Softw Technol* 2010, 52: 463–479. 10.1016/j.infsof.2009.11.005

Section II - Design and Communication Aspects of SOA

CHAPTER 6

DESIGNING FAULT-TOLERANT SOA BASED ON DESIGN DIVERSITY

Amanda S Nascimento, Cecília MF Rubira, Rachel Burrows, Fernando Castor and Patrick HS Brito

Keywords: Software fault tolerance Design diversity Service-oriented architecture Systematic literature review Fault-tolerant service composition

INTRODUCTION

Nowadays, society is highly dependent on systems utilizing Service-Oriented Architectures (SOA) for its basic day-to-day functioning (Huhns and Singh [2005]; Papazoglou et al. [2007]). These systems range from online stores to complex applications, called mashups, that combine their own resources with content retrieved via services from external data sources to create new functionalities (Huhns and Singh [2005]; Papazoglou et al. [2007]; Zheng and Lyu [2010b]). Nevertheless, it is unlikely that services (often controlled by third parties) will ever be completely free of software faults arising from wrong specifications or incorrect coding (Trivedi et al. [2010]). Consequently, SOA-based applications should operate according to their specification in spite of faults from reused services. If faults are not tolerated then undesirable consequences could happen, which may range from mildly annoying to great financial losses (Nascimento et al. [2011]; Papazoglou et al. [2007]; Zheng and Lyu [2010b]).

The adoption of software fault tolerance techniques based on design diversity has been advocated as a means of coping with residual software design faults in operational software (Lee and Anderson [1990]). Design diversity is the provision of software components called variants, which have the same or an equivalent specification but with different designs and implementations (Gärtner [1999]). An assumption of software fault tolerance techniques is that the probability of having the same fault in multiple variant components is lower, meaning that a fault present in a component should be detected and tolerated based on the behaviour of other variants (Lyu [1996]). In the nineties, the use of techniques based on design diversity to tolerate software faults was widely criticised since variant software components used to be developed from scratch, which is very expensive (Anderson et al. [1985]; Vouk et al. [1993]). Therefore these techniques were generally used only in highly critical systems, in which the occurrence of failures would result in large financial losses or even loss of life. Nevertheless, in the context of SOA on the web, there are already many services that provide equivalent functionality, thus making such techniques more practical (Zheng and Lyu [2010b]). These variant services might be simply cost-free and open access, or even offered by external organizations to cope with changes to user quality of services (QoS) requirements (Papazoglou et al. [2007]). Due to the low cost of reusing existing variant services, several diversity-based approaches have been developed to support reliable SOA-based applications. These approaches operate as mediators between clients and variant services. The latter are structured in fault-tolerant composite web services (Nascimento et al. [2011]; Zheng and Lyu [2010b]). Hereafter we refer to fault-tolerant composite web services as FT-compositions. From the clients' viewpoint, an FT-composition works as a single, reliable service.

In order to design reliable SOA applications, important design decisions have to be made by the architect. Such decisions are difficult, especially in the context of mashups, since the architect has to consider many aspects related to both fault tolerance and SOA-specific quality requirements. Regarding fault tolerance, the architect has to consider, for example: the availability of variants, the best fault tolerance technique to be used in a certain context, how the system should fail and scenarios involving error detection and handling (failure modes), the categories of faults to be tolerated (fault latency), assumptions about the environment and components (fault assumptions), etc.

The software architect developing a fault-tolerant SOA application should consider three major design issues when using design diversity: (i) selection of variants, since the

Citation: Amanda S Nascimento, Cecília MF Rubira, Rachel Burrows, Fernando Castor and Patrick HS Brito, Designing fault-tolerant SOA based on design diversity, DOI: 10.1186/s40411-014-0013-7

variants need to be sufficiently diverse and able to tolerate software faults; (ii) selection of an adjudicator to determine the acceptability of the results obtained from the variants (Daniels et al. [1997]; Lee and Anderson [1990]); and (iii) execution strategy that directs the execution of the variants. For each of these design issues, the architect has to choose the specific fault tolerance technique to be used. Guidelines to support this task should also take into account implementations that realize different sets of quality requirements (e.g. memory consumption, financial cost, response time or reliability). The design decisions are also affected by characteristics of the functionality (e.g., allows re-try, allows undo operation). Variants can be executed either sequentially or in parallel and variant outputs can be adjudicated by adopting different voting and acceptance algorithms (Daniels et al. [1997]; Laprie et al. [1990]).

When designing a system, the architect may reuse and adapt existing solutions. Nevertheless, existing work regarding fault-tolerant service compositions is written from different viewpoints and relies on different technical backgrounds. As a result, it is hard to compare them and to choose an appropriate solution to be applied. Thus, it is unclear the extent to which existing solutions support the above mentioned design issues related to software fault tolerance based on design diversity. In order to avoid neglecting important design issues related to fault tolerance, architects should use guidelines to support the identification of which design issues and respective solutions should be used depending on the application's requirements.

In this sense, the contribution of this work is twofold: (i) the proposal of guidelines for supporting the design of fault-tolerant SOA based on a taxonomy for fault tolerance techniques and (ii) a systematic review of existing solutions for designing FT-compositions using design diversity. Results from reviewed solutions are presented to support reuse of existing solutions. The central purpose, which unifies the two contributions, is to support the architect in the design of fault-tolerant compositions. The proposed guidelines utilize an existing taxonomy for fault-tolerant systems (Pullum [2001]) in order to guide architects in their design decisions. Then, the systematic literature review classifies existing solutions according to the same taxonomy, thus providing a basis for comparison and analysis of the solutions according to the architect's specific needs.

Guidelines support different decisions regarding the design of FT-SOA: first, the guidelines address different failure modes. This enables the architect to plan which faults are to be tolerated. Subsequently, the guidelines support the architect in modelling the faults and the behavioural pattern of how these faults should be tolerated. This decision influences the choice of the adjudicator type. For example, intermittent faults can be detected and tolerated utilizing design diversity and majority election design techniques. Also, the number of variants will be directly affected by the number of concurrent failures to be tolerated. The architect can assess the number of variants that are required to achieve the desired level of reliability. This design decision is also affected by the availability of resources as this will place limits on the number of variants that are feasible.

The systematic review compares characteristics of existing solutions in order to support architectural-level decisions regarding software fault tolerance and SOA quality requirements. We followed the literature review method proposed by Kitchenham ([2007]). We first investigated design issues related to the selection and the execution of variants, as well as the adjudication of their outputs. Secondly, we investigated which SOA-specific requirements were addressed by the existing solutions. The proposed guidelines address the three major design issues and their different implementation solutions. Finally, we report our main findings and identify gaps in current approaches in order to suggest opportunities for research on reliable SOA-based applications.

The remainder of the paper is structured as follows. Section 5 presents important concepts related to SOA and software fault-tolerance. These concepts are utilized in the taxonomy for fault-tolerant SOA. Section 5 presents the taxonomy combining elements from the fault-tolerance domain with elements from the SOA domain. Section 5 presents the results and discussion. This includes the guidelines for supporting the SOA architect in designing FT-compositions. It also presents results from the systematic literature review.

Section 5 discusses the threats and the validity of the review. Section 5 presents related work, which also considers related literature reviews of software fault tolerance techniques. Finally, Section 5 presents some concluding remarks and directions for continuing work.

BACKGROUND

Service-Oriented Architecture (SOA)

Many software systems are being implemented following the Service-Oriented Architecture (SOA) approach with the aim of achieving higher levels of interoperability (Huhns and Singh [2005]; Papazoglou et al. [2007]). SOA is focused on creating a design style, technology, and process framework that allow enterprises to develop, interconnect, and maintain enterprise applications and services efficiently and cost-effectively (Huhns and Singh [2005]). A service in SOA is an exposed piece of functionality with three essential properties. Firstly, a service is self-contained in that it maintains its own state. Secondly, a service is platform-independent, implying that the interface contract to the service is limited to platform-independent assertions. Lastly, a service can be dynamically located, invoked and (re)combined (Huhns and Singh [2005]; Papazoglou et al. [2007]). Therefore, multiple services running over heterogeneous systems may then interact and be used as building blocks for new applications (Papazoglou et al. [2007]).

SOA-specific Scenarios

As previously mentioned, software architects can achieve the benefits of both fault-tolerant and service-oriented architectures by structuring variants as FT-compositions. Papazoglou et al. ([2006], [2007], [2007]) list a set of roles and functionalities that a service composition should encompass for the aggregation of multiple services into a single composite service. We use this list to classify elements of our primary studies as described below:

- *Interoperability Capabilities*: Whenever a service composition provides its functionalities by means of interfaces that are platform-independent, a client from any communication device using any computational platform, operating system, or programming language can reuse the solution. That is, the service composition aggregates services provided by other service providers into a distinct value-added service and may itself act as service provider (Papazoglou et al. [2006]).

- *Autonomic composition of services:* service compositions should equip themselves with adaptive service capabilities so that they can continually morph themselves to respond to environmental demands and changes without compromising operational and financial efficiencies (Papazoglou and Heuvel [2007]). Examples of support for autonomic composition of services include automatically discovering new partners to interact with; automatically selecting partners and options that would, for example, maximize benefits and reduce costs (Papazoglou et al. [2006]); and automatically detecting that some business composition requirements are no longer satisfied by the current implementation and react to requirement violations (Papazoglou et al. [2006]).
- *QoS-aware service compositions:* To be successful service compositions need to be QoS-aware. For example, services should be composed in accordance with an extensible set of Quality-of-Service (QoS) properties and high-level policies (e.g. performance levels, security requirements, SLA stipulations, and so forth). QoS encompasses important non-functional service requirements, such as performance metrics (response time, for instance), security attributes, (transactional) integrity, reliability, scalability, and availability (Papazoglou and Heuvel [2007]; Papazoglou et al. [2006]).
- *Business-driven automated compositions:* a service composition at the business-level should pose the requirements, possibly from different stakeholders with conflicting needs, and the boundaries for the automatic composition at the system level. While the service composition at the business level should be supported by user-centered and highly interactive techniques, system level service compositions should be fully automated and hidden to the end users. System level compositions should be QoS-aware, should be generated and monitored automatically, and should also be based on autonomic computing principles (Papazoglou and Heuvel [2007]; Papazoglou et al. [2006]).

Software Fault Tolerance and Design Diversity

A fault is the identified or hypothesized cause of an error (Avizienis et al. [2004]; Trivedi et al. [2010]). An error is part of the system state that is liable to lead to a failure (Avizienis et al. [2004]; Trivedi et al. [2010]). A failure, in turn, occurs when the service delivered by the system deviates from the specified service (Avizienis et al. [2004]). So, with software fault tolerance, we want to prevent failures by tolerating faults whose occurrences are known when errors are detected (Lee and Anderson [1990]). When designing fault tolerance, a first prerequisite is to specify, by means of fault models, the faults that should be tolerated (Gärtner [1999]). The next step is to enrich the system under consideration with components or concepts that provide protection against faults from the fault models (Gärtner [1999]).

For instance, this work specifically addresses software faults According to Pullum ([2001]), '*software faults may be traced to incorrect requirements (where the software matches the requirements, but the behaviour specified in the requirements is not appropriate) or to the implementation (software design and coding) not satisfying the requirements*'. Software faults are also called design faults or bugs (Pullum [2001]).

Software faults cannot be tolerated by simple replication of identical software components since the same mistake will exist in each copy of the components (Lee and Anderson [1990]). A solution to this problem is to introduce diversity into the software replicas (Lee and Anderson [1990]; Lyu [1996]; Wilfredo [2000]). Design diversity is the provision of functionally-equivalent software components, called variants, through different designs and implementations.

Design diversity begins with an initial requirements specification. Each developer or development organization is responsible for a variant and implements the variant according to the specification (Gärtner [1999]; Laprie et al. [1990]; Pullum [2001]). Figure 1 illustrates the basic design diversity concept. Inputs are distributed to variants. The variants execute their operations and produce their results, from which a single correct or acceptable result must be derived, if any (Pullum [2001]). The mechanism responsible for this task is called an *adjudicator*.

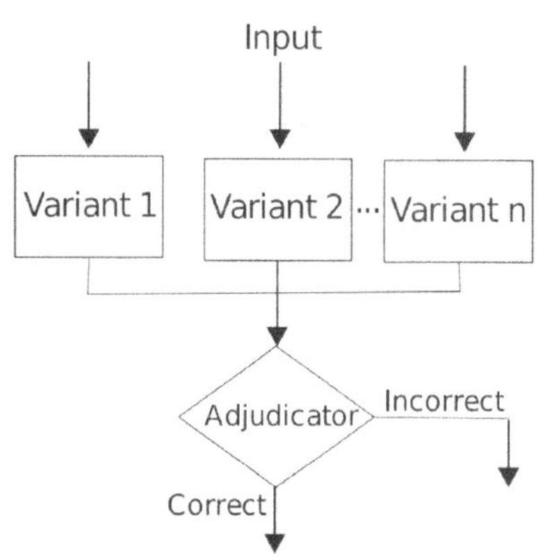

Figure 1 Basic design diversity (Pullum[2001]).

Adjudicators generally come in two flavours, voters and Acceptance Tests (ATs). A brief description of voter characteristics and differences are presented in Section 5, in the context of the proposed taxonomy. We refer to Pullum ([2001]) for a more detailed description about the various types of adjudicators and their operations (pages 269-324). For example, specific adjudicators covered by Pullum ([2001]) are exact majority, consensus, formal consensus, formal majority, median, mean, weighted, and dynamic voters; acceptance tests can be based on satisfaction of requirements, accounting tests, computer run-time acceptance tests and reasonableness acceptance tests.

The philosophy behind design diversity is to decrease the probability that variants fail at the same time for the same input value because this usually makes failures of variants detectable (Lyu [1996]). To illustrate this point with a hypothetical example, Figure 2 presents a diversity-based solution that leverages three variants and a majority voter to tolerate software faults. For instance, two variants present software faults, however these variants do not fail for the same input cases. Consequently, for the provided input, the majority voter is able to tolerate the software fault whose activation has led to failure of one of the variants. Figure 3 illustrates a diversity-based solution that leverages three variant services such that two of them fail on the same input value, leading to a failure of the majority voter as whole.

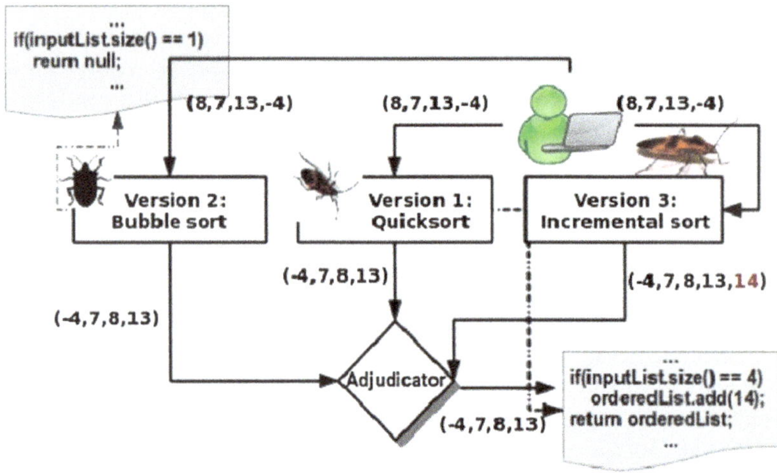

Figure 2 Variants failing on different values of the input space.

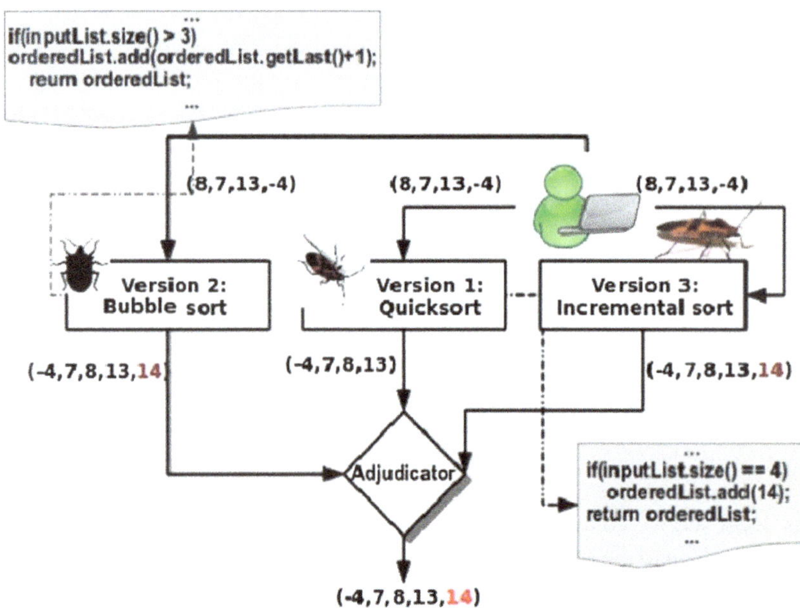

Figure 3 Variants failing on the same values of the input space.

Error Recovery

Error recovery is the process in which the erroneous state is substituted with an error-free state (Lee and Anderson [1990]). Error recovery is performed using either backward recovery or forward recovery. On the one hand, *backward recovery* attempts to return the system to a correct or error-free state by restoring or rolling back the system to a previously saved state, which is assumed to be error-free. On the other hand, *forward recovery* attempts to return the system to a correct or error-free state by finding a new state from which the system can continue operation. Compared to backward error recovery, forward recovery is usually more efficient in terms of the overhead (*e.g.* time and memory) it imposes (Lee and Anderson [1990]). On the other hand, it is usually not possible to design general forward recovery mechanisms.

METHOD

A Taxonomy for Software Fault Tolerance Based on Design Diversity for SOA

We define a taxonomy combining elements from the fault-tolerance domain (Section 5) with elements from the SOA domain (Section 5).

Figure 4 presents the taxonomy, which considers the common design issues and their different design solutions, as well as the specific roles desirable in SOA-based applications. The proposed taxonomy was adopted to classify our primary studies. Both design issues and decisions were derived from the analysis of fault tolerance techniques based on design diversity (*e.g.* *Recovery Blocks*, *N-Version Programming*,

N-Self Checking Programming,Consensus Recovery Block and *Acceptance Voting*) and adjudicators (Elmendorf [1972]; Horning et al. [1974]; Kim [1984]; Laprie et al. [1990]; Lee and Anderson [1990]; Lyu [1996]; Pullum [2001]; Scott et al. [1987]). We also considered the reliable hybrid pattern structure proposed by Kim and Vouk ([1997]). In comparison with their work, our work *(i)* identifies different types of voters and acceptance tests based on the general taxonomy of adjudicators presented by Pullum ([2001]); and *(ii)* explicitly distinguishes the different schemes of variant execution (i.e. sequentially or in parallel). Different design decisions employ different measures of quality requirements (Pullum [2001]). These differences make each design solution suitable for a particular application. In Section 5, we briefly compare the described design solutions and present some general remarks about their effectiveness.

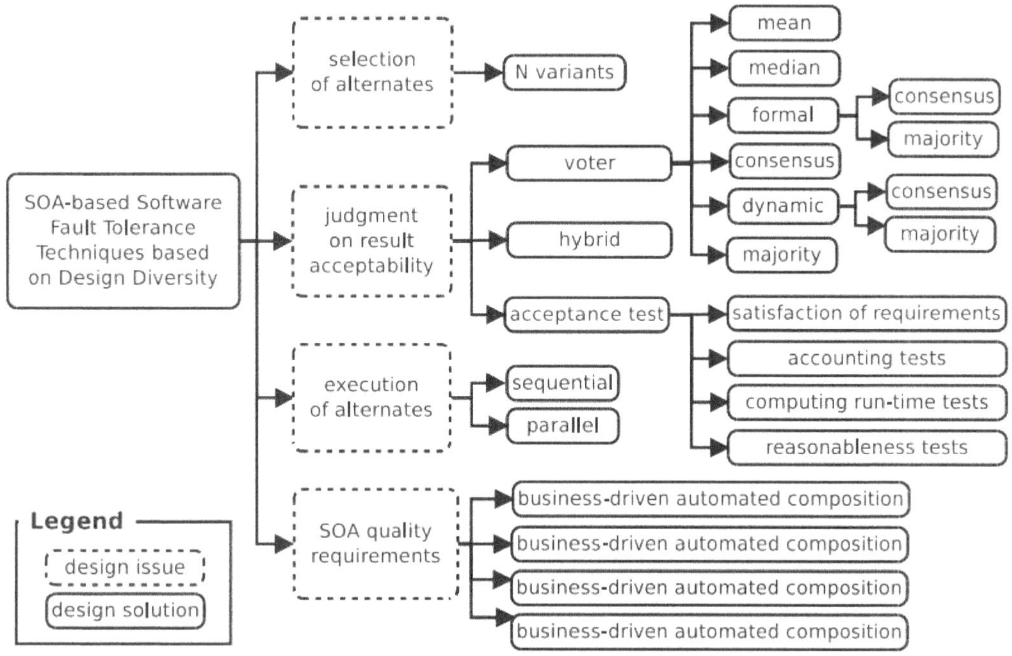

Figure 4 General taxonomy of design issues and solutions.

The elements of the taxonomy are described below.

Design issue I - selection of variants: The number of variant software components (n) must each be provided by components with different software designs and implementations. The main goal of increasing diversity is to detect faults in variant when the variants fail on disjoint subsets of the input space. Even if variants fail on overlapping subsets of the input space, design diversity is still considered a useful measure of reducing the risk from design faults (Laprie et al. [1990]; Lyu [1996]). If variants have minimal overlaps between their failure regions, a reliable configuration may be formed even when variants individually have modest reliability. Finally, variants might be chosen at different points during the software lifecycle.

Design issue II - judgement on result acceptability: Adjudicators, or decision mechanisms, generally come in two flavours, voters and Acceptance Tests (ATs).

Voters: Voters are based on a relative judgement on result acceptability by comparison of variant results (Pullum [2001]). We present an overview of voters that are mostly described in the literature (Lee and Anderson [1990]; Pullum [2001]). We refer to Pullum ([2001]) for further details on voter procedures and pseudocode.

- *Exact majority voter*: The exact majority selects the value of the majority of the variants as its presumably the correct result (McAllister and Vouk [1996]). This voter is also known as the m-out-of-n voter (Pullum [2001]). The agreement number, m, is the number of versions required to match for system success (Eckhardt and Lee [1985]). The total number of alternatives, *i.e.* n, is rarely more than 3. Consequently, the majority voter is generally seen as a 2-out-of-3 voter.
- *Consensus voter:* This voter allows the selection of a consensus or set of matching variant results as the adjudicated result if no majority exists (Pullum [2001]). That is, this voter is a generalization of the majority voter (Vouk et al. [1993]).
- *Formal consensus and Majority voter:* The *Formal Consensus* and *Majority* voters are variations of, respectively, the consensus and the exact majority voters (Pullum [2001]). Basically, the formal voter uses a comparison tolerance indicating the maximum distance allowed between two correct output values for the same input. In this way, variant results that are different, but quite close together, are the adjudicated correct answers.
- *Median voter:* The median voter selects the median of the variant output values as its adjudicated result. Variant outputs must be in an ordered space (Pullum [2001]).
- *Mean and weighted voter:* The mean and weighted voter select, respectively, the mean or weighted average of the variants' output values, which are in an ordered space, as the adjudicated result (Broen [1975]). Additional information related to the trustworthiness of the alternatives might be used to assign weights to the variant outputs, if using the weighted average voter (Pullum [2001]).

- *Dynamic majority and Consensus voters:* Unlike the previously described voters, dynamic voters are not defeated when any variant fails to provide a result (Pullum [2001]). Dynamic majority and consensus voters operate in a way similar to, respectively, majority and consensus voters, with the exception that dynamic voters can handle a varying number of inputs (Pullum [2001]). When the dynamic voter adjudicates upon two results, a comparison takes place. When comparing, if the results match, the matching value will be output as the correct result. Otherwise, no selected output will be returned.

Acceptance Tests (ATs): ATs rely on an absolute judgement with respect to a specification (Lee and Anderson [1990]; Pullum [2001]). With ATs, only one variant is executed at a time. The AT is responsible for checking whether the produced result is correct. In case it is not, another variant is executed until a correct result is obtained, if possible.

- *Acceptance tests based on satisfaction of requirements:* ATs are constructed with conditions that must be met at the completion of variant execution (Pullum [2001]). These conditions might arise from the problem statement of the software specifications.
- *Accounting tests:* Accounting ATs are suitable for transaction-oriented applications with simple mathematical operations (Pullum [2001]). For example, when a large number of records are reordered or transmitted, a tally is made of both the sum over all records and the total number of records of a particular data field. These results can be compared between the source and the destination to implement an accounting check AT (Pullum [2001]).
- *Computer run-time tests:* Run-time tests detect anomalous states such as overflow, undefined operation code, underflow, write-protection violations, or end of file (Pullum [2001]).
- *Reasonableness tests:* These ATs are used to determine if the state of an object in the system is reasonable,*e.g.*, precomputed ranges or expected sequences of program states (Pullum [2001]).
- *Hybrid adjudicators:* A hybrid adjudicator generally incorporates a combination of AT and voter characteristics. For example, variant results are evaluated by an AT, and only accepted results are sent to the voter (Laprie et al. [1990]).

Design issue III - execution of variants: Variants can be executed either sequentially or in parallel. The execution schemes should provide all variants with exactly the same experience of the system state when their respective executions start to ensure consistency of input data (Nascimento et al. [2013]), which be can be achieved by employing backward recovery or forward recovery (*Section* 5). Sequential execution often requires the use of checkpoints (it usually employs backward recovery), and parallel execution often requires the use of algorithms to ensure consistency of input data (it usually employs forward recovery by invoking all the variants and coordinating their execution through a synchronization regime) (Pullum [2001]; Wilfredo [2000]).

- *Sequential:* in implementing a sequential execution scheme the variants are executed one at a time. Generally, in the sequential execution scheme, the most efficient variant, *e.g.* in terms of response time or financial cost, is located first in the series, and is termed *primary variant*. The less efficient variants are placed serially after the primary variant and are referred to as (secondary) variants. Thus, the resulting rank of the variants reflects the graceful degradation in the performance of the variants (Pullum [2001]).
- *Parallel:* in the parallel execution scheme, variants are executed concurrently. The resulting outputs can be provided to the adjudicator in an *asynchronous* fashion as each version completes, or in a *synchronous* manner (Daniels et al. [1997]).

Systematic Literature Review Method

This review has been conducted as a systematic literature review based on guidelines proposed by Kitchenham and Charters ([2007]). The guidelines cover three phases of a systematic review: planning, executing and reporting. In our work, the goal of the review is to provide a better understanding of diversity-based approaches for FT-compositions (Kitchenham and Charters [2007]), in order to support decisions of the software architect in terms of reuse. In the following, Section 5 presents details about the planning of the systematic review, while Section 5 presents details about the execution and results.

Planning

Research Questions

This work aims to answer the following research questions.

RQ1 What design issues and respective design solutions related to the fault tolerance taxonomy of Figure 4 are being addressed?

RQ2 What SOA specific requirements are being addressed?

To address RQ1, we classify existing solutions using the proposed taxonomy of design solutions for fault tolerance based on design diversity (Figure 4). To address RQ2, we consider a list of quality requirements that service compositions should address, presented in Section 5. Related to RQ1 and RQ2, we also describe some important design issues related to general software fault tolerance techniques, and analyze such solutions in terms of preserving important requirements inherent of SOA.

Search Process

Searches for primary studies were performed upon databases of Software Engineering research that met the following criteria (Williams and Carver [2010]):

- Contains peer-reviewed software engineering journals articles, conference proceedings, and book chapters.
- Contains multiple journals and conference proceedings, which include volumes that range from 2000 to 2012.
- Used in other software engineering systematic reviews (e.g. (Cardozo et al. [2010]; Jorgensen and Shepperd [2007]; Kitchenham et al. [2007]; Williams and Carver [2010])).

The resulting list of databases was: *(i)* ACM Digital Library; *(ii)* IEEE Electronic Library; *(iii)* SpringerLink; *(iv)* Scopus; and *(v)* Scirus (Elsevier).

Search String

A search string was created to extract data from each database. We adopted various combinations of terms from *(i)*the main purpose of this review; *(ii)* the research question (Kitchenham and Charters [2007]; Kitchenham et al. [2009]) and *(iii)* meaningful synonyms and variant spellings. Whenever it was necessary, this search string was decomposed into several search terms (*e.g.* Recovery Block AND Service-Oriented Architectures) due to restrictions imposed by some of the search engines. The resulting search string is summarised in following:

Study Selection

The database searches resulted in a large number of candidate papers. We adopted study selection criteria to identify those studies that provide direct evidence about the research question.

Inclusion criteria:

- Approaches based on software diversity for FT-Compositions that specifically focused on web services. Additionally the solutions that were targeted supported one or more issues identified in the taxonomy (Figure 4),*i.e.*, selection of variant services, execution of variants and judgement on result acceptability.

Exclusion criteria:

- Solutions for reliable SOA-based applications employing solely replicas of identical services - although the adoption of identical replicas can improve system availability, they are not able to tolerate *software* faults (Gärtner [1999]; Lee and Anderson [1990]).
- Solutions for fault-tolerant SOAs based on data diverse software fault tolerance techniques.
- Solutions for fault-tolerant SOA relying solely on exception handling - variant services are not employed as part of the exception handling mechanism.
- Duplicate reports of the same solution - when several reports of the proposed solution exist in different papers the most complete version of the study was included in the review.
- Short papers, introductions to special issues, tutorials, and mini-tracks.
- Studies presented in languages other than English.
- Papers addressing empirical studies on fault tolerance based on design diversity applied to *SOAs* - not proposing any particular solution to employ FT-compositions.
- Grey literature, that is, informally published written material.

These criteria were applied as performed in (Kitchenham and Charters [2007]; Williams and Carver [2010]):

- Reading the title in order to eliminate any irrelevant papers.
- Reading the abstract and keywords to eliminate additional papers whose title may have fit, but abstract did not relate to the research question.
- Reading the introduction and, whenever it is necessary, the conclusion to eliminate additional papers whose abstract was not enough to decide whether the inclusion/exclusion criteria are applicable.
- Reading the remainder of the paper and including only those that addressed the research question.

Data Collection and Synthesis

We created a data extraction form to collect all the information needed to address the review question (Kitchenham and Charters [2007]). The contents of the designed data form are composed by (Kitchenham and Charters [2007]; Kitchenham et al. [2009]): the source (*e.g.* journal, conference) and full reference; date of extraction; summary of the proposed solution; supported design issues/solutions (Figure 4); and space for additional notes.

RESULTS AND DISCUSSION

Design Decision Guidelines to Realize Fault Tolerance in SOA

The proposed solution encompasses a set of guidelines to support the architect in key decisions relating to fault tolerance. The proposed guidelines address the design decisions of the taxonomy presented in Section 5 (Figure 4). Figure 5 presents the activities that are part of the proposed guidelines. First, we show guidelines which advise the architect to specify the failure modes of the system. Then, the guidelines lead the architect to specify the fault latency and the scenarios of fault tolerance. For example, Byzantine faults (intermittent faults) could be acceptable (Lee and Anderson [1990]; Randell [1975]) whereas other types of faults, such as permanent faults, may be unacceptable. This information may influence the choice of the adjudicator type (e.g., majority election, average value). Finally, the guidelines assist the architect in setting assumptions, in order to outline the scope of fault tolerance. After following the guidelines, the architect will have a classification of the features related to fault tolerance, following the classification of the taxonomy presented.

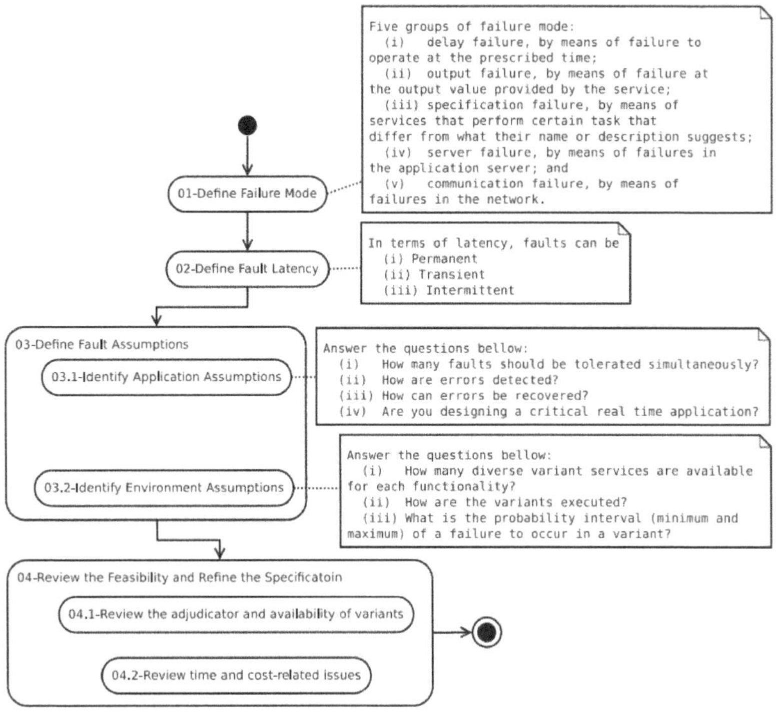

Figure 5 Activities of the proposed guideline.

At the end of the process, the architect can assess whether the projected solution is feasible with respect to the availability of resources: e.g., number of variants. Depending on the number of variants needed to meet the demands of the system, the architect can now assess if it is necessary to reduce the scope of fault tolerance. For example, intermittent faults, also known as Byzantine faults, are usually detected and tolerated utilizing design diversity and majority election techniques. In this case, the number of variants will be directly affected by the number of concurrent faults to be tolerated. Depending on the available variants, the number of concurrent tolerated faults should be decreased.

In the following sections (5 to 5) we suggest four steps for designing fault tolerance: (i) define failure mode; (ii) define fault latency; (iii) define fault assumptions; and (iv) review the feasibility and refine the designed solution. After reviewing the solution, the next step is to try to reuse existing solutions. To support the architect, Section 5 presents a systematic literature review that classifies existing approaches according to the same taxonomy presented in Section 5 that was also used by the guidelines presented here.

Define Failure Modes

Failure modes can be seen as ways in which a software, equipment, or machine failure can occur. The specification of the failure mode helps the identification of faults in applications, which are the underlying causes of failures or which ones initiate a process which leads to failure.

In terms of SOA-based applications, we consider five groups of failure modes: (i) delay failure, which is a failure to operate at the prescribed time; (ii) output failure, when the output value provided by the service is incorrect; (iii) specification failure, when a service performs a task that differs from what their name or description suggests; (iv) server failure, a failure in the application server; and (v) communication failure, a failure in the network.

The architect must indicate which failure modes need to be addressed within the application model. That is, if its behaviour detection and handling should be part of the application scope. The answer here should be either yes or no. Details about how to consider each group are defined in the next steps: fault latency and fault assumptions.

Define Fault Latency

Fault latency is defined as the interval between the moments of fault occurrence and error generation (Shin and Lee [1984]). This information is extremely important, since it directly affects how to handle the error caused by the fault. In terms of latency, faults can be permanent, transient or intermittent. Permanent faults are continuous and stable. In hardware, permanent faults reflect an irreversible physical change. Permanent faults are also known as "hard" faults. Transient faults result from temporary environmental conditions, and can be fixed by changing the respective conditions that cause the fault. Transient faults are also known as "soft" faults. Intermittent faults are only occasionally present due to unstable hardware or varying hardware or software states. Intermittent and transient faults are the major source of system errors. Even when it is not possible to repair the fault, the use of redundant resources allows the system to tolerate faults (Gärtner [1999]; Lee and Anderson [1990]). The manifestations of transient and intermittent faults and of incorrect hardware or software design are much more difficult to determine than permanent faults.

Fault latency is part of the fault model. The fault model is a design model that tries to predict what could go wrong, as well as the consequences of particular faults. In order to detail the fault model, the proposed guidelines state that, for each failure mode identified (Section 5), the architect has to specify how the error caused by the fault is expected to occur: permanently, transiently, or intermittently.

For example, a delay failure (failure mode) is characterised by performance problems, when a service says to execute in a certain period of time, but for some reason it is not able to do so. If the architect is considering this kind of failure in the failure mode, it is necessary to define how these failures can occur: permanently, in a transient way, or in an intermittent way. Considering it as a permanent fault, the error could be detected by time-out and a solution with two variant services would be sufficient to tolerate the error detect the problem by changing the faulty service to another one. If it is a transient fault caused by server overload, the handling could be, for example, to change the server. But assuming a fault model of intermittent faults, in some execution a certain service is faster than another, but in the following execution the scenario can be the opposite. So, redundant services could be executed in parallel and the adjudicator could consider the first reply it receives.

Define Fault Assumptions

The definition of *fault assumptions* contains information relating to the error detection and error recovery mechanisms. The proposed solution focuses on two types of assumption: (i) application assumptions; and (ii) environmental assumptions. Section 5 presents the guidelines for identifying assumptions related to the application, while Section 5 presents the guidelines for identifying assumptions related to the environment.

Identify Application Assumptions

In order to identify application assumptions, we outline four questions to be answered:

- *How many faults should be tolerated simultaneously?* The answer to this question should be a number. It will interfere with the number of variants required to tolerate the faults. This also depends on the adopted design solution.
- *How are errors detected?* The answer to this question can be either *by comparison* or *by checking a single result*. It aims to identify functionalities whose validity can be verified through acceptance tests, with no need of redundancy for error detection. The answer can also affect the number of variants required for fault tolerance.
- *How can errors be recovered?* The answer to this question can be either *forward* or *backward* error recovery, according to the error recovery strategy of the respective functionalities (see Section 5). The answer to this question should support the decision regarding how to execute variants. In some cases, when a forward error recovery strategy is more effective, a sequential execution is recommended. For example, when a billing system is executed in parallel, after processing redundant bills, some of them should be cancelled, since an undo operation is not applicable in such case.
- *Are you designing a critical real-time application?* The answer of this yes/no question also supports the decision of which execution strategy to use. In case of a critical real-time system, a parallel execution could be preferable, if redundancy is needed.

Identify Environment Assumptions

Environment assumptions are restrictions related to the services' availability, the diversity amongst the variant services available, as well as existing execution policies. For this, three questions should be answered:

- *How many diverse variant services are available for each functionality?* The answer to this question should be a number. It also supports the final decision regarding the appropriate design solution. For example, depending on the compatibility between the number of faults to be tolerated and the number of diverse variant services available, the feasibility of a fault-tolerant solution may not be possible.
- *How are the variants executed?* The answer to this question can be *for free*, *cheap*, or *expensive*. Such answer should support the decision of which execution strategy to use (sequential or in parallel). For example parallelism may have expensive running costs.
- *What is the probability interval (minimum and maximum) of a failure to occur in a variant?* The answer to this question can guide the architect in choosing and discarding variants based on monitoring data. Besides, this information may also interfere with the choice of the adjudicator, as discussed in Section 5.

Finally, for each failure mode and fault latency identified by the architect, a proper handling behaviour should be specified. Table 1 illustrates handling behaviour for errors related to faults, according to the failure mode and the assumed fault latency. The example considers scenarios involving the reliability quality attribute. It is important to know that the architect may assume more than one fault latency for the same failure mode. In these cases, the more general solution, which fits all the latencies, should be used.

Table 1 Example of fault tolerance specification using the guidelines

Failure mode	Fault latency	Fault assumption	How to tolerate
Delay	Permanent	Inefficient Algorithm	Change the faulty service to another one
		Hardware problem	Change the application server
	Transient	Server overload	Change the application server
	Intermittent	Environmental instability	Execution in parallel to get the fastest reply
Output	Permanent	Software bug	Use variant services to detect and majority election to tolerate

	Transient	Server overload	Use variant services to detect and majority election to tolerate
	Intermittent	Electromagnetic interference	Use variant services to detect and majority election to tolerate
Specification	Permanent	Malicious service	Use variant services to detect and majority
			election to tolerate
	Transient	DNS mistake due to environmental instability	Use variant services to detect and majority election to tolerate
	Intermittent	Unknown cause	Use variant services to detect and majority election to tolerate
Server	Permanent	Hardware failure	Change the application to a mirror server
	Transient	Memory overload	Change the application to a mirror server
	Intermittent	Environmental instability	Use redundant servers in parallel, and synchronisation algorithms for keeping the consistency among servers
Communication	Permanent	Breaking the optical fibber cable	Change the network link
	Transient	Network overload	Change the network link
	Intermittent	Electromagnetic interference	Use redundant communication channel in parallel

Review the Feasibility and Refine the Specification

After defining the initial specification related to fault tolerance, the last step is to review the feasibility of the designed solution and refine it based on concepts related to classical fault tolerance techniques. In order to make this task easier, in the following we provide a summary comparing classical fault tolerance techniques, which is important for choosing a design solution, giving a special attention to the type of adjudicator. It is important to stress that the design issues presented are compliant with the taxonomy presented in Figure 4. Instead of presenting a full discussion on such techniques, we summarise some of the findings on design diversity, in particular the findings related to non-functional characteristics of the described design solutions, represented by the taxonomy. The analysis of these characteristics provide a good support to define the system fault tolerance (*Section* 5). A summary of results and discussion for supporting the SOA architect on choosing fault tolerance techniques is presented in the following. A detailed discussion in the context of a literature review of existing solutions is presented in Section 5.

Review the Adjudicator and Availability of Variants

Firstly, it is essential to check the availability of variants that are sufficiently diverse in order to decrease the probability of occurrence of coincident failures (Eckhardt et al. [1991]; Hilford et al. [1997]; Knight and Leveson [1986]; Lyu et al. [1994]; Nascimento et al. [2012a]). Regarding the judgement on the result acceptability, the adjudicator would run its decision-making algorithm on the results and determine which one (if any) to output as the presumably correct result. Just as we can imagine different specific criteria for determining the 'best' item depending on what that item is, so we can use different criteria for selecting the 'correct' or 'most acceptable' result to output. The probabilities of activation of related faults between variants are likely to be greater for voters than for acceptance tests (ATs) (Arlat et al. [1988]; McAllister and Vouk [1996]). But in general, ATs are more difficult to construct in practice because they are strongly application-dependent and because it is not always possible to determine a criterion to judge variant results (Di Giandomenico and Strigini [1990]). As a consequence, voting is a more useful technique in a practical setting, because voting adjudicators are easier to develop (Wilfredo [2000]).

The exact majority voter is most appropriately used to examine integer or binary results, but it can be used on any type of input (Saglietti [1992]). The majority voter has a high probability of selecting the correct result value when the probability of a variant failure is less than 50% and the number of variants, n, is 'large' (Blough and Sullivan ([1990]) used n = 7 and n = 15 in the study). However, when the probability of a variant failure exceeds 50%, then the majority voter performs poorly (Blough and Sullivan [1990]). In fact, all voters have a high probability of selecting the correct result value when the probability of variant failures is less than 50% (Blough and Sullivan [1990]). A median voter can be defined for variant outputs consisting of a single value in an ordered space (*e.g.* real number). Median voter is a fast algorithm and is likely to select a correct result in the correct range (Blough and Sullivan [1990]). If it can be assumed that, for each input value, no incorrect result lies between two correct results, and that a majority of the replicas' outputs are correct, then the median voter produces a correct output (Pullum [2001]).

Consensus voting is more stable than majority voting and always offers reliability at least equivalent to majority voting (McAllister and Vouk [1996]; Vouk et al. [1993]). Nevertheless, in terms of implementation, the consensus voting algorithm is more complex than the majority one, since the consensus voting algorithm requires multiple comparisons (Lee and Anderson [1990]). Blough performed a study on the effectiveness of voting algorithms (Blough and Sullivan [1990]). He states that the median voter is expected to perform better than the mean voting strategy. He also shows the overall superiority of the median strategy over the majority voting scheme (Blough and Sullivan [1990]). Furthermore, under circumstances in which some or all variants might not produce their results (*e.g.* some or all variants not providing their results within the maximum expected time frame; catastrophic failure of some or all of the variants), dynamic voters are the best option since they can process zero to *n* inputs. Finally, acceptance tests, exact majority, consensus and dynamic voters can process any type of variant outputs, while the remaining adjudicators must receive inputs in an ordered space (Pullum [2001]).

We summarise some details of the described voters in Table 2, which is based on a summary table by Pullum ([2001]). We have added the type of variant results in which the voter is able to judge. This table states the corresponding recommended fault tolerance technique, given the type of variant results provided to the voter and the type of voter. To use this table, it is important to consider the primary concerns surrounding the application areas of the software system and details about the output space. For example, if safety is the primary concern, it is recommended to adopt the voter that would rather raise an exception and produce no selected output than present an incorrect output as a presumably correct one (*e.g.* the exact majority or dynamic majority voters) (Pullum [2001]). If the primary goal is to avoid cases in which the voter does not reach a decision, i.e., *an* answer is better than no answer, than it is sufficient to adopt the voter that reaches a 'No output' result least often (*e.g.* the median voter) (Pullum [2001]). Based on this criterion, exact majority voter, formal majority voter, and dynamic majority voter can be considered the safest voters, because they produce incorrect output 'only' in cases where most or all of the variants produce identical and wrong results.

Table 2 Voter results given details about variant output space ((Pullum[2001]) - page 310)

Variant results	**Voter**							
	Exact majority	**Me-dian**	**Mean**	**Weighted average**	**Con-sensus**	**Formal majority**	**Dynamic majority**	**Dynamic consensus**
All outputs identical and correct	C	C	C	PC	C	C	C	C
Majority Identical and correct	C	C	PC	PC	C	C	C	C
Plurality identical and correct	NO	PC	PC	PC	C	NO	NO	C
Distinct outputs, all correct	NO	C	PC	PC	NO	NO	NO	NO
Distinct outputs, all incor-rect	NO	I	PI	PI	NO	NO	NO	NO
Plurality identical and wrong	NO	PI	PI	PI	I	NO	NO	I
Majority identical and wrong	I	I	PI	PI	I	I	I	I
All outputs identical and wrong	I	I	I	I	I	I	I	I
Variant result type	Any type	Or-dered space	Ordered space	Ordered space	Any type	Floating-point arith-metic	Any type	Any type

The voter outputs are: ·C - Correct: The voter outputs a correct result; ·PC - Probably correct: The voter outputs a result that is probably correct, but may be incorrect; ·PI - Probably incorrect: The voter outputs a result that is probably incorrect, but may be correct; ·I - Incorrect: The voter outputs an incorrect result; ·NO - No output: The voter does not output a result; an exception is raised.

Review Time and Cost-Related Issues

With respect to the execution of variants, in the parallel scheme, there is an underlying assumption that sufficient hardware resources are available to enable the execution of variants concurrently. Even with sufficient parallelism, the execution time of this scheme will be constrained by the slowest version - there may be a substantial difference in the execution speeds of the fastest and slowest version because of the need to generate independent designs (Lee and Anderson [1990]). When variants are executed in parallel, there is also a synchronisation time overhead. The time required to execute variants in a sequential way will range from the execution time of the primary variant (if acceptance tests are employed and the primary result is acceptable) to the sum of execution time of all variants, *e.g.*if all variant results are subjected to ATs (Buys et al. [2011]). Nevertheless, this time will normally be constrained by the execution time of the primary variant (Lee and Anderson [1990]). Furthermore, under some circumstances, a specific execution scheme is not applied, *e.g.*, when there is a processing cost charged for the use of variant services, invoking them in parallel might incur in greater actual cost,*i.e.*, in sequential schemes, not all variants are necessarily executed (Zheng and Lyu [2010a]). Moreover, the error recovery strategy defined in the fault assumptions (backward or forward) might also interfere on the way variants should be executed.

In the following we present details about the systematic literature review involving solutions for composing fault-tolerant services. Such a review aims to support the architect in the task of reusing existing solution. The most relevant works are presented and classified in the target taxonomy (Figure 4).

Systematic Literature Review Results

In this section, we present the results obtained.

Search Results

The searches returned thousands of papers that were filtered down to 23, and then to 17 primary studies, three of which are journal articles (Mansour and Dillon [2011]; Yuhui and Romanovsky [2008]; Zheng and Lyu [2010a]), three book chapters (Dillen et al. [2012]; Gorbenko et al. [2005]; Kotonya and Hall [2010]), ten conference papers (Abdeldjelil et al. [2012]; Buys et al. [2011]; Gonçalves and Rubira [2010]; Gotze et al. [2008]; Looker et al. [2005]; Nascimento et al. [2011], [2012b]; Nourani [2011]; Santos et al. [2005]; Townend et al. [2005]), and one workshop paper (Laranjeiro and Vieira [2007]).

In the solutions by Dillen et al. ([2012]), Santos et al. ([2005]) and Mansour and Dillen ([2011]), despite each service being named a replica by the authors, these solutions were designed to tolerate different responses by means of adjudicator mechanisms. This suggests these solutions could be also implemented as a diversity-based solution. Therefore, these solutions were included as primary studies.

Regarding the papers excluded from the first filtered 23 publications, the articles (Zheng and Lyu [2008], [2010b]) are short versions of another article (Zheng and Lyu [2010a]), the article (Abdeldjelil et al. [2012]) is also an extended version of the article (Faci et al. [2011]). The study presented by Gorbenko et al. in (Gorbenko et al. [2009]) and by Nascimento et al. ([2012a]) are based, respectively, on the solutions proposed in (Gorbenko et al. [2005]) and in (Nascimento et al. [2012b]) - therefore, we consider the proposed solutions, i.e. (Gorbenko et al. [2005]; Nascimento et al. [2012b]), as primary studies. Xu ([2011]) examined challenges in the fields of dependability and security that need to be addressed carefully in order to provide sufficient support to enable service-oriented systems to offer non-trivial Quality of Service guarantees. Then, Xu presents several advanced techniques developed at the University of Leeds to achieve dependability and security in service-oriented systems and applications, including, the solution proposed by Townend et al. ([2005]). Therefore, only the work by Townend et al. ([2005]) is included as a primary study. Milanovic and Miroslaw ([2007]) also highlight the use of techniques to tolerate software faults in SOA, including techniques based on software diversity (e.g. N-Versions); however, no specific solution is proposed in this direction.

Classification of the Primary Studies

Y(yes), the design solution is supported by a primary study; **N(no)**, no information at all about the design solution is specified; **U(unknown)** according to the authors the design issue is supported, however, what design solutions are supported cannot be readily inferred.

It might be meaningless to rank the primary studies based solely on their 'quantity of *Yes*' since the studies present different purposes (e.g. some solutions are mainly focused on supporting the selection of variant services (Nascimento et al. [2012b]; Townend et al. [2005]), while other ones are focused on executing variant services (Gonçalves and Rubira [2010]; Yuhui and Romanovsky [2008])). Although it's difficult to compare these solutions, Section 5 presents non-functional characteristics related to the design solutions supported by the authors - thus supporting researchers' decision making when selecting design solutions more adjusted to different clients requirements.

In the next subsections, we discuss the answers to the two research questions presented in Section 5 and present the main proposed solutions regarding the design issues (Figure 4). Because of space limitations the summaries of solutions are representative rather than exhaustive.

Selection of Variant Services

The aims of selecting variants are twofold: *(i)* to increase the probability of selecting variants that are provided by different designs and implementations; *(ii)* to determine an appropriate degree and/or selection of variant services targeting an optimal trade-off between reliability measures as well as performance-related factors such as timeliness, cost and resource consumption. In general, variants have been chosen at different points during the software lifecycle. For instance, they can be chosen at design time by the engineer, configured manually once the software is deployed, or even be discovered and selected at runtime by the software itself.

The solutions by Townend et al. ([2005]) and by Nascimento et al. ([2012b]) address the issue of ensuring that variant services are diverse. Townend et al. ([2005]) aims to detect diverse designs during runtime. This is achieved by monitoring previous results and flow of data from a variant service using interaction provenance in order to reveal evidence that two variants share similar services or workflows. Such evidence may include matching common-mode failures that have propagated back from two variant services. Nascimento et al. ([2012b]) propose an experimental setup to investigate, from clients' viewpoint and by means of statistical tests, whether variant services present a difference in their outputs and their failure behaviours. Their solution also investigates if and by how much the use of FT-composition improves reliability when compared to a single non-fault-tolerant service (Nascimento et al. [2012b]).

Variant services may be chosen using different measurements at different points throughout the execution. Buys et al. ([2011]) and Dillen et al. ([2012]) propose a fault tolerance strategy that autonomously changes the amount of redundancy or the selection of variant services. The architecture proposed by Buys et al. ([2011]) bases this decision upon the current execution context and clients' requirements at the time of request. They propose a measure to infer combinations of variant services that are, in fact, effective. This measure quantifies the historical effectiveness of each variant service by penalising or rewarding it when it disagrees or complies with the majority decision respectively. Differently to this, Gotze et al. ([2008]) propose a solution where every atomic service provides information about its dependability attributes and every composite service has to provide additional information about their external services that are used to provide the desired functionality. The calculated dependability attributes and probability values of the resulting composite service are then used to manually optimize the composite service towards the user's expectations (Gotze et al. [2008]), differing from the solution by Buys ([2011]) and Dillen et al. ([2012]) in which variant services are automatically selected.

The solution by Nascimento et al. ([2011]), Abdeldjelil et al. ([2011],[2012]), Chen and Romanovsky ([2008]) and Zheng and Lyu ([2008],[2010b],[2010a]) allows the dynamic selection of variant services based on a priority schemes where the client defines requirements in terms of QoS. QoS values are updated by monitoring procedures in (Abdeldjelil et al. [2012]; Faci et al. [2011]; Nascimento et al. [2011]; Yuhui and Romanovsky [2008]) and by encouraging users to contribute their individually-obtained QoS information of the target Web services in (Zheng and Lyu [2008],[2010b],[2010a]). The solution by Kotonya and Stephen ([2010]) and by Mansour and Dillon ([2011]) support a QoS matching scheme that will prioritise services based on reliability and performance metrics. These metrics are not shared with the client, i.e., a client cannot express preference for specific QoS metrics. The solution by Gorbenko ([2005]) monitors dependability attributes and selects an appropriate service based on them. However, the motivation behind this solution was to manage service upgrades, i.e. switching from an old version to a new version online when the level of dependability of the new service is acceptable.

Execution of Variant Services

Both parallel and sequential execution schemes have been addressed within existing approaches. The solution by Nascimento et al. ([2012b]) does not aim to support multiple execution schemes. The solutions by Gotze et al. ([2008]), Townend et al. ([2005]) supports execution of variants; however, they do not specify how variants might be executed in parallel, sequentially or both. Most solutions support both execution schemes (Abdeldjelil et al. [2012]; Buys et al. [2011]; Dillen et al. [2012]; Gonçalves and Rubira [2010]; Gorbenko et al. [2005]; Laranjeiro and Vieira [2007]; Mansour and Dillon [2011]; Nascimento et al. [2011]; Nourani [2011]; Yuhui and Romanovsky [2008]; Zheng and Lyu [2008],[2010b],[2010a]) the solution by Looker et al. ([2005]), Santos et al. ([2005]) and by Kotonya and Stephen ([2010]) support the parallel execution of variants. An important characteristic of the execution scheme proposed by Laranjeiro and Vieira ([2007]) is that it can use functionally equivalent web services that have different interfaces, providing developers with more options to build their solutions (*i.e.* input/output adapters). However, their solution operates on a static connectivity mode, requiring static generation of local proxy classes for each variant service (Laranjeiro and Vieira [2007]). The solution by Abdeldjelil et al. ([2012]) allows for the execution of variant services that present diversity also in their interfaces and results by mapping operations and parameters in the domain ontology.

Judgement on Result Acceptability

A variety of decision mechanisms were found amongst the target papers. The main advantage of diversity-based solutions is that they allow for variant service responses to be compared using a large choice of voter and acceptance test techniques. For instance, majority, consensus, formal and dynamic voters are addressed by some of the existing approaches for FT-compositions. Acceptance tests (ATs) are also supported; however, as they are strongly application-dependent there are fewer approaches supporting ATs.

Majority voters

Majority voters are supported by Nourani et al. ([2009],[2011]), Looker et al. ([2005]), Nascimento et al. ([2011]) and Zheng and Lyu ([2008],[2010b],[2010a]). The solution by Nourani et al. ([2009],[2011]) supports the implementation of FT-compositions by means of the WS-BPEL. In this sense, the authors present details on the prototype implementation by identifying the BPEL structured activities adopted. The adjudication mechanism is also implemented as web service and invoked from a BPEL process. The authors mention the adoption of voters and adjudicators, including majority, dynamic, consensus, acceptance test and hybrid adjudicator. Nevertheless, no details on voting procedures are provided, except for the majority one. Differently from other solutions, they utilise diversity to allow two majority voting mechanisms to be applied to the same input set. In the BPEL process, if for any reason the voter faces faults or if there is an absence of consensus, the second version of voter is invoked using the same inputs. This avoids the voting process to becoming a single point of failure (Nourani [2009]; Nourani and Azgomi [2011]).

The Web Service-Fault Tolerance Mechanism (WS-FTM) proposed by Looker et al. ([2005]) supports the majority voter that allows generic result comparison. Nascimento et al. ([2011]) and Zheng and Lyu ([2008],[2010b],[2010a]) do not present additional information on voting procedures. We emphasize, however, that the solution by Zheng and Lyu ([2008],[2010b],[2010a]) supports different fault tolerance strategies and the authors describe in detail a dynamic fault tolerance strategy selection algorithm.

Consensus voters

A variety of solutions support consensus voters. Nourani et al. ([2009],[2011]) argues that their solution provides support consensus voters. In the solution by Santos et al. ([2005]), there is a component responsible for arbitrating the adjudicated output based on the output with the highest number of occurrences. Therefore, we inferred that their decision mechanism is based on the consensus voter. The benefits of diverse components is not only limited to the services, in the solution proposed by Laranjeiro and Vieira ([2007]) the voter protocol supports two voting mechanisms to be utilized at the same time: a unanimous voter and a consensus voter. Their solution also supports an evaluation mechanism that performs a continuous assessment of the quality of services. During the voting process, if an impasse occurs the QoS values of the variants are used to select one response. According to the authors, the impasse occurs whenever different variant results present the same number of occurrences (Laranjeiro and Vieira [2007]). However, in their solution, it is not clear how they judge variant result acceptability when variants are executed sequentially.

Formal voters

When dealing with greater variability in variant service interfaces, a straightforward consensus voting mechanism may not suffice. Some solutions accept a certain amount of variability and agree that a consensus is formed with multiple equivalent results. The solution by Dillen et al. ([2012]) supports formal consensus voting, called plurality voting in their paper. For each invocation of the scheme, the variant services will be partitioned based on the equivalence of their results. The result associated to the largest cluster will be accepted as the correct result (Dillen et al. [2012]). Abdeldjelil et al. ([2011],[2012]) describe a specific voting algorithm, called equivalence vote, that will decide if multiple concurrent service responses are equivalent or not. This is based on a pre-agreed amount of deviation for answers to be considered equivalent. Their algorithm requires the input to be an ordered set of equivalent results and also for the acceptable functional deviation to be specified.

Dynamic voters

Dynamic consensus and dynamic majority voters are supported by a number of solutions (Buys et al. [2011]; Gotze et al. [2008]; Nourani [2011]; Nourani and Azgomi [2009]; Townend et al. [2005]). This may be more suitable for applications where it is acceptable for some variant services to fail and an answer still be returned from the remaining variant services. Due to the intricacies of dynamic decision mechanisms defined in our taxonomy some classifications in our review have been changed from the classifications used in the target papers. The solution by Gotze et al. ([2008]) define three FT-protocols, namely, *one*, *any* and *majority*. Only the majority operator allows for the enhancement of reliability and availability. The remaining operators are mainly focused on achieving high levels of availability and are out of the scope of this work. They define the majority as an operation that schedules the same request to all defined services. Afterwards this operation uses the results of all services that did not fail and chooses the most common result. Based on this general definition, we inferred that their solution (according to our taxonomy) in fact supports the dynamic consensus voter instead of the majority one that has been specified by the authors (Gotze et al. [2008]).

According to Buys et al. ([2011]), their solution, called A-NVP composite, supports majority voting. However, for similar reasons to the Gotze et al. classification we decided their solution instead supports a dynamic majority voter. Moreover, the response latency of the A-NVP composite is guaranteed not to exceed a maximum response time defined by the client. If no absolute majority could be established before the maximum response time, an exception will be issued to signal that consensus could not be found (Buys et al. [2011]). In addition, according to Townend et al. ([2005]), their solution supports different types of voting algorithms to choose from. However, we inferred that the dynamic consensus voting is the only decision mechanism supported. The voter is dynamic as it can process 0 to *n*results, where *n* is the number of executed variant services. Specifically, the voting discards results of any variant service whose weighting falls below a user-defined value and subsequently performs consensus voting on the remaining results. The weighting is based on the confidence of that service returning a correct result.

Acceptance tests

Acceptance tests give the client the freedom to specify accepted values according to pre-defined requirements. Nascimento et al. ([2011]) propose a solution that supports a mechanism responsible for the error-processing technique, which in turn supports acceptance tests, voters and comparisons. The solution by Dillen et al. ([2012]) has been designed so that acceptance tests are not hardwired within the FT-composition. Instead, ATs can be configured at runtime through a parameterised assertion holding an *XPath* expression that will be used to assess if the variant result is acceptable The solution by Mansour and Dillon ([2011]) propose a scheme to combine variant web services into parallel and serial configurations with centralized coordination. In this case, the broker has an acceptance testing mechanism that examines the results returned from a particular web service. The acceptance test is conducted using the broker, which might be a single point of failure. To increase the reliability of the broker introduced in their systems and mask out errors at the broker level they suggest a modified general scheme based on triple modular redundancy and N-version programming, which also includes a voting algorithm. The ATs could be specified as examining a post-condition or inalterable association with the service. The solution by Zheng and Lyu ([2008],[2010b],[2010a]) and by Chen and Romanovsky ([2008]) supports recovery block strategy (RB), nevertheless, they do not mention any acceptance tests, the adjudicator employed in RB.

Other quality requirements

The solution by Gorbenko et al. ([2005]) supports an adjudicator, whose type is not explicitly specified, that is also responsible for reconfiguration, recovery of the failed releases and for logging the information which may be needed for further analysis (Gorbenko et al. [2005]). Extensibility is an important feature, and is important in SOA architecture when the context and available services are constantly changing. In the solution by Kotonya and Stephen ([2010]) different adjudicators might be plugged into their solutions. Also, new web services may be discovered and combined with the existing set of services. A particularly robust protocol detailed in this paper, Andros, provides a three-step consensus and authentication solution to tolerate Byzantine faults at a trade-off with system resources.

Chen and Romanovsky ([2008]) claim that although N-Version programming techniques require voting on results, in a real world application, it is not always possible to vote on results received from different services. In this sense, their solution for fault-tolerant SOAs supports well defined extension-points in which voting implementation might be included. The solution by Gonćalves and Rubira ([2010]) encapsulates the WS-Mediator proposed by Chen and Romanovsky ([2008]), therefore, it is possible to include voting implementations at extension-points of the WS-Mediator.

SOA Specific Requirements

The following discusses evidence that the target solution support specific SOA related quality requirements. The quality requirements selected include (i) interoperability capabilities, (ii) autonomic composition of services, (iii) QoS-aware service compositions and (iv) business-driven automated composition.

Since the studied solutions touch different phases of design, their implementation descriptions are not always available. For instance, some proposed solutions were based on abstract models or early stages of development and therefore it may not be appropriate to judge solutions against each other. Some solutions do not aim to present complete implementations as the contribution of the work is on a specific part of the system design.

Solutions supporting all SOA specific requirements

Seven solutions support all SOA specific requirements (Buys et al. [2011]; Dillen et al. [2012]; Gonçalves and Rubira [2010]; Kotonya and Hall [2010]; Nascimento et al. [2011]; Santos et al. [2005]; Townend et al. [2005]; Zheng and Lyu [2010a]).

The solution by Buys et al. ([2011]) is interoperable since it has been explicitly designed as a generic WSDM-enabled utility WS-Resource so as to support a diversity of applications without the need to generate application-specific proxy classes at design time. WSDM is a standard that defines how networked resources can be managed by exposing their capabilities and properties by means of a web service interface. This solution also supports an adaptive fault-tolerant strategy that autonomously tunes the amount of redundancy or dynamically alters the selection of variant services currently employed in the redundancy scheme. That is, their solution supports autonomic composition of services. Moreover, the proposed solution aims to achieve an optimal trade-off between dependability as well as performance-related objectives such as load balancing and timeliness.

Also, application-specific intricacies are taken into account, in that the redundancy dimensioning and variant selection models can be configured by means of a set of user-defined parameters. Therefore, the solutions supports both QoS-aware and business-driven automated compositions.

The FT-composition proposed by Townend et al. ([2005]) invokes variant services, and results are weighted based on a confidence metric for each service. The weighting algorithms, which are performed dynamically, take into account whether variant services are composed by common shared services and historic data of how often variant outputs agrees with the consensus. Services whose weighting is lower than a user-defined level are eliminated from the voting procedure for the remaining variants. Variant service endpoints are specified by the client. This means the solution is not able to dynamically bind new variants. Moreover, the functionalities of the proposed FT-compositions are exposed as web services operations. Therefore, we infer that this solution supports interoperable, QoS-aware, business-driven automated and autonomic compositions.

The solution proposed by Dillen *et al* ([2012]) dynamically manages the degree of redundancy of multi-version fault-tolerance mechanisms. The client specifies the parameters of the dependability requirements and its available budget at request level. The system will autonomously select an appropriate degree and selection of variants and integrate them within an appropriate fault-tolerant redundancy scheme. Their solution is also responsible for maintaining a pool of variants of a specific web service and is capable of autonomously deploying additional variants, or removing poorly performing variants.

Therefore, their solution supports all described SOA specific requirements.

Nascimento et al. ([2011]) proposes a feature model that captures the variabilities and commonalities among software fault tolerance strategies (for instance, recovery blocks, N-version programming and N-self-checking programming). The identified variability is mapped into design decisions represented as variation points into a Product Line Architecture. The authors propose an infrastructure that encompasses both the feature model and PLA and relies on key activities of the autonomic control loop (i.e. collect, analyze, plan and execute) to support dynamic management of software variability. Based on changes of *(i)* user requirements and *(ii)* QoS level, and high-level policies, which are represented as adaptation rules, the control loop decides an appropriate fault tolerance strategy to be executed. Consequently, this infrastructure is responsible for the dependable mediation logic between service clients and redundant services. Moreover, since functionally equivalent services may appear with completely different function names, input parameters and return types, hence complicating the dynamic discovery of redundant services. To alleviate this difficulty, their solution relies on the Semantic Web (SW) in order to support dynamic provision of redundant services by describing them in terms of semantics. Also the infrastructure itself may be deployed to be remotely accessible via web technology. Therefore, their solution supports all the described SOA specific requirements.

The FT-composition proposed by Santos *et al* ([2005]) relies on a set of components and services, some based on OMG's FT-CORBA standard's models and concepts. In order to create the groups of variant services, Santos *et al*([2005]) adopts the service domain concept. A service domain allows aggregation and sharing of multiple web service descriptions (WSDL). The binding information refers to the group, allowing several services to be virtualized as a single service. Their solution is able to dynamically add new variant services and the remove faulty variant services according to predefined rules. In particular, if a variant service presents a fault at the moment of its execution or does not respond within the time limit established in the service configuration, the faulty variant is removed from the service group. In this case, the faulty variant service stays out of the group until its state has been reestablished through the recovery mechanisms. In order to carry out the monitoring and recovery process, variant services must implement predefined interfaces. Therefore, their solution supports all the described SOA specific requirements.

Zheng and Lyu. ([2010a]) propose an adaptive fault tolerance strategy for automatic system reconfiguration at runtime based on the subjective user requirements and objective QoS information of the target Web services. Users are encouraged to contribute their individually-obtained QoS information of the target Web services by employing user-participation and collaboration. In this way, this solution is able to collect a large quantity of QoS data from the users located in different geographical locations under various network conditions. This data is used to objectively evaluate the target Web services. This solution supports various software fault tolerance techniques and adjusts the optimal fault tolerance strategy based on the overall QoS information and the individually recorded QoS information of the variant services.

The framework by Kotonya and Stephen ([2010]) supports interoperability capabilities, autonomic composition of services, QoS-aware service composition and and business-driven automated composition. Their framework implements fault tolerance protocols as process models and exposes them as discoverable services. At runtime, the framework provides a service differentiation mechanism based on quality of services. In this way, their solution is able to dynamically instantiate fault tolerance techniques tailored to the specific needs of different clients and contexts (e.g. requirements in terms of QoS).

Solutions supporting partial SOA specific requirements

The solution by Nourani et al. ([2009],[2011]) supports interoperability. Its variant execution scheme and adjudicators are offered as web services, and, in the prototype implementation, invoked in a fault-tolerant BPEL process that leverages variant web services.

The solution by Laranjeiro and Vieira ([2007]) support QoS-aware and business-driven automated service compositions as in their solution the web services execution sequence is defined based on the information available for each variant. The variant services are ranked based on evaluation metrics (for instance, response time, availability and correctness of variants) as selected by the programmer. The evaluation metrics might be collected offline (before deployment of variants) and online (during utilization of variants). However, the QoS values are not used to select variant services, since service endpoints are hard-coded. Their solution for fault-tolerant SOAs also supports interoperability capabilities by exposing their main functionalities by means of a proxy web service.

The solution by Chen and Romanovsky ([2008]), called WS-Mediator, supports Web service resilience-explicit dynamic reconfiguration in order to adapt fault-tolerance techniques and use the available service redundancy. Their solution monitors web services and generates resilience metadata representing dependability attributes, such as response time, failure rate, failure types and so on (Yuhui and Romanovsky[2008]). This metadata's structure can be designed for particular application scenarios and the resilience-explicit decision-making mechanism uses it to dynamically select the most dependable web service according to the client's preference. Nevertheless, the solution by Chen and Romanovsky ([2008]) cannot be directly accessible via web services technology because it is a Java stand-alone package. The solution by Gonćalves and Rubira ([2010]) extends WS-Mediator (Yuhui and Romanovsky[2008]) in order to make it interoperable. Therefore, the solution by Chen and Romanovsky ([2008]) supports autonomic composition of services, QoS-aware service composition and business-driven automated composition, while the solution by Gonćalves and Rubira ([2010]) supports these quality requirements and also interoperability capabilities.

The solution by Mansour and Dillon ([2011]) supports both autonomic composition of services and QoS-aware service composition. The solution develops a model used to improve the reliability of the composite service based on the prediction of the failure rates of individual services. For instance, it allows for execution schemes to be optimized by choosing effective rollback schemes. The focus of the solution is therefore to support self-optimizing autonomic composition of services. The approach subsequently allows for both the increased dependability of the composite service and increase trust from the end-user.

Discussion

Guidelines for designing fault-tolerant service applications

In order to evaluate the guidelines presented in Section 5 we gathered qualitative feedback using a questionnaire. Five graduate developers of service-based applications were given the questionnaire with questions about certain qualitative aspects of the guidelines. Two of the volunteers had experience on software fault tolerance techniques while three had no previous experience on designing fault-tolerant software. The questionnaire had a total of nine questions: (i) one to collect information about the previous experience of the volunteers when developing service-based applications; (ii) one to collect information about the previous experience of the volunteers when developing fault-tolerant software; and (iii) seven questions to collect information about qualitative aspects of the guidelines.

The seven qualitative questions were: (1) *What are the positive aspects of the guidelines?*; (2) *What are the negative aspects of the guidelines?* (3) *Would you use it to develop your next fault-tolerant web service?* (4) *Why?*(5) *Would you recommend the use of the presented guidelines to develop fault-tolerant web service?* (6) *Why?* (7)*Suggestions.* Except for Questions 3 and 5, which are yes/no questions, the other five qualitative questions had free answers.

All the volunteers agreed that the proposed guidelines make the design process more predictive and systematic. Moreover, according to the two volunteers that already had experience in designing fault-tolerant systems, the activities of the guidelines prevents important aspects of the software fault tolerance be neglected by the software designer. One of the volunteers suggested that the guidelines could be incorporated into a wizard tool to assist the designer in a more effective and easy to follow fashion.

Although the qualitative results are preliminary, they are important as a feedback and show a positive first impression that provides evidence that these guidelines are a potential help for less-experienced developers of fault-tolerant applications.

Systematic literature review

Related to the selection of variant services, we have considered two main issues, to select diverse variants and to determine an appropriate degree and/or selection of variant services. We should emphasize that these two different purposes are complementary. This is because the reliability of fault-tolerant compositions depends upon design diversity of their variant services to increase the probability that they fail on disjoint input spaces. For most of the proposed approaches for FT-compositions there is an underlying assumption that variant services can always be efficiently employed by means of diversity-based techniques (Gotze et al.[2008]; Kotonya and Hall[2010]; Zheng and Lyu[2008],[2010b],[2010a]). However, Nascimento et al. ([2012a]) presents an empirical study to investigate whether variant services are able to tolerate software faults. They concluded that the benefits of diversity-based solutions applied to SOAs are not straightforward. Even when variants seem to present design diversity, this diversity might not be sufficient to improve system reliability in case the chosen variants have coincident faults activated on important execution scenarios. That is, the chosen set of variants will impact on the success of the FT-strategy used.

Runtime decisions regarding which variant services are used require trade-offs according to which specific QoS attributes to use, and their feasibility of obtaining them. There are important considerations for delegating QoS responsibility to different components of the architecture. It may be less process intensive to require each atomic service to provide quality measurements of themselves; however, lack of trust or need to ensure data integrity may mean that QoS is monitored from the client. For instance, many approaches measure availability by monitoring the variant service 'heartbeat' - this is certainly feasible with most available services. However, a particular challenge for fault tolerance is to find a feasible way of measuring other QoS attributes, for example, the security of potential services, an issue tackled by Gotze et al. ([2008]) where various levels of service transparency are taken into account. Moreover, while many solutions provide means of optimizing service selection once the variant services have been chosen, we see there is a growing need to integrate test activities to ensure a specific service as being suitable as a candidate variant service. This is particularly needed with growing capabilities of fault-tolerant SOA in terms of autonomic searching, discovering and selection of variant services.

With respect to the execution scheme, both parallel and sequential execution schemes have been addressed. This is particularly important, as the type of execution scheme will affect important QoS attributes such as execution time and resource consumption (*Section* 5). Related to the decision mechanisms, it is important to notice that the expected behaviour of variant services is likely to affect the complexity of the chosen decision mechanism. For example, to choose among voting algorithms presented in the proposed taxonomy (Figure 4), we should consider the primary concerns surrounding the software's application and details about the output space (*Section* 5). As we can observe in the proposed classification there are still some adjudicators not addressed by current approaches for FT-compositions, e.g., median, mean voters and acceptance tests. One can claim that existing solutions might be easily extended.

On one hand, when looking beyond the implementation of solely the decision mechanism, we can also find interesting architectural solutions that provide additional functionality at the same point. For instance, by defining key extension points or ability for pluggable FT strategies enhances the flexibility and interoperability of fault-tolerant SOA design. Many publications that discuss this do not explicitly describe how to extend their solutions, therefore, the reader is unable to determine what interfaces must be implemented when inserting a custom adjudicator (Kotonya and Hall[2010]; Laranjeiro and Vieira[2007]; Nascimento et al.[2011]; Yuhui and Romanovsky[2008]). In fact adjudication procedures are marginally described. For example authors do not specify which type of variant outputs their solutions are able to process. Also, they don't specify how to navigate through elements and attributes in messages returned by the variant services in order to adjudicate the acceptability of specific fragments from these messages (Dillen et al.[2012]; Kotonya and Hall[2010]; Nascimento et al.[2011]; Santos et al.[2005]). In other words, most of the authors do not specify clear guidelines on the reuse and, in particular, customization of their decision mechanisms in practical settings.

In addition, related to the decision mechanism, many FT-protocols within diversity-based fault tolerance solutions frequently selected results based on properties other than the actual response values, such as response time or likelihood of failure. This perhaps reflects the reality that even when reliability of results is uncertain, the fastest response time remains one of the main sought-after service qualities. Alternatively, it highlights the need for future research to address these challenging issues. Finally, it is interesting to observe that although various design issues and respective design solutions related to software fault tolerance techniques have been supported, they are spread among existing approaches for FT-compositions. That is, there is no a single solution able to cope with conflicting client requirements by employing at the same time a wide variety of schemes to select and execute variant services and to determine the adjudicated result from the variant services. There is a lack of solutions able to bring out a set of closely related fault tolerance techniques based on design diversity in close accordance with customers' requirements and high-level policies (e.g. to adopt a fault tolerance technique based on parallel execution scheme for better response time).

From the 17 primary studies, 7 showed support for all SOA-specific requirements. In fact, design decisions chosen to support one SOA-specific requirement often addressed the others at the same time. For instance, mechanisms that gather QoS data can be utilised to select appropriate services. Consequently, the mechanisms to collect this information are often utilized to satisfy all requirements relating to the composition of services.

Many solutions provided QoS-aware service compositions. However, the way in which quality of service was measured may have been based on multiple properties such as response time, availability and correctness of variants or alternatively solely by monitoring the availability of a variant. As mentioned previously, these differences between solutions with respect to their underlying mechanisms for SOA-specific features impact on the capabilities of the SOA to satisfy the remaining design issues such as how to select, execute and judge variants.

Finally, we noticed that the field of defining fault-tolerant service compositions is relatively recent, since the analyzed solutions present illustrative examples to evaluate their feasibility. To the best of our knowledge there are no commercial or open source solutions for implementing fault-tolerant service composition based on design diversity.

THREATS TO VALIDITY

We identified some possible threats to validity (Wohlin et al.[2000]) and the measures we took to reduce the risks.

Internal Validity

In terms of internal validity, our study is based on 17 papers that matched our criteria (*Section* 5). This number is not high, nevertheless, it is representative of this area of research (Burrows et al.[2010]; Kitchenham et al.[2009]). To mitigate this risk, we adopted a search strategy that aims to detect as much of the relevant literature as possible (Kitchenham and Charters[2007]). Despite this, the size of the sample should be kept in mind when assessing the generality of our results.

Construct Validity

We identified two threats to construct validity: the study selection and data extraction are error-prone activities. Related to the study selection, this activity was performed by one of the researches at two different points in time, thus reducing the risk of having the inclusion/exclusion criteria applied inconsistently. Related to the data extraction, data might have been extracted in an inconsistent manner and to reduce this risk, as suggested by Kitchenham and Charters ([2007]), all primary studies were assigned to one of the researchers, responsible for extracting the data (Kitchenham and Charters[2007]). Another researcher was asked to perform data extraction on a subset of primary studies chosen at random (for instance, on 6 studies). Data from the researches were compared and disagreements were resolved by consensus among researchers.

Conclusion Validity

We identified one threat to conclusion validity, which is the reliability of the taxonomy itself used to classify the primary studies. To mitigate the risks of employing an inadequate taxonomy, before it was built, we had analysed the domain knowledge of software fault tolerance techniques based on design diversity in depth (e.g. (Elmendorf[1972]; Horning et al.[1974]; Kim[1984]; Laprie et al.[1990]; Lee and Anderson[1990]; Lyu[1996]; Pullum[2001]; Scott et al.[1987])).

RELATED WORK

We are not familiar with any work that surveys diverse fault-tolerant SOAs. As a consequence, we address, in turn, work related to literature review of fault tolerance techniques in general.

Garcia et al. ([2001]) present a comparative study of exception handling mechanisms for building dependable object-oriented software. The authors define a taxonomy to help address main basic technical aspects for a given exception handling proposal. By means of the proposed taxonomy, the authors survey various exception mechanisms implemented in different object-oriented languages, evaluates and compares different designs. Our classification of software fault tolerance solutions is also based on a general taxonomy of design issues. However, compared to their work, we do not provide a rating of the primary studies according to a quality assessment.

Carzaniga *et al* ([2008]) identify some key dimensions upon which they define a taxonomy of fault tolerance and self-healing techniques in order to survey and compare the different ways redundancy has been exploited in the software domain. These are the intention of redundancy (deliberate or opportunistic), the type of redundancy (code, data, environment), the nature of triggers and adjudicators that can activate redundant mechanisms and use their results (preventive - implicit adjudicator or reactive or- implicit/explicit adjudicator), and lastly the class of faults addressed by the redundancy mechanisms (Bohrbugs or Heisenbugs). The proposed taxonomy is used to classify well known techniques, for example, N-version programming, exception handling and data diversity. The concepts presented in their taxonomy and the ones presented in the taxonomy we employed are orthogonal. In fact, our classification is performed in lower level of abstraction.

Ammar et al. ([2000]) propose a survey of the different aspects of system fault tolerance and discuss some issues that arise in hardware fault tolerance and software fault tolerance. In this context, the authors distinguish information, spatial and temporal redundancy; present the three fundamental concepts of fault tolerance (i.e. failure, error, fault); describe the four steps of fault tolerance (i.e. error detection, damage assessment, error recovery, and fault removal) and relate these to the differences of redundant techniques for handling hardware as well as software faults. According to the authors, since redundancy may be used under a variety of forms to achieve fault tolerance, the design of a fault-tolerant system involves a set of trade-offs between redundancy requirements (imposed by the need for fault tolerance) and requirements of economy (economy of the process, and the product) (Ammar et al.[2000]). The authors also emphasize that program fault tolerance is no panacea, like almost everything in software engineering. We refer to their work for an interesting discussion on reasons to support this claim.

Florio and Blonda ([2008]) present a survey of linguistic structures for application-level fault tolerance (ALFT). The authors emphasize the importance of employing appropriate structuring techniques to support an adequate separation between the functional and fault tolerance concerns. They claim the design choice of which fault tolerance provisions to support can be conditioned by the adequacy of the syntactical structure at 'hosting' the various provisions, called *syntactical adequacy*. Moreover, offline and online (dynamic) management of fault tolerance provisions and their parameters may be an important requirement for managing the fault-tolerant code in an ALFT, called *adaptability*. These three properties, separation of concerns, adaptability and syntactical adequacy are referred as the *structural attributes* of ALFT. The structural attributes are adopted to classify and analyse a number of ALFTs, including, recovery blocks and n-version programming. This classification is also orthogonal to the classification we have provided.

CONCLUSION

Due to the low cost of reusing existing functionally equivalent services, called variant services, several approaches based on design diversity exist to support fault-tolerant Service-Oriented Architecture (SOA). These solutions operate in the communication between clients and variant services, which are structured in fault-tolerant compositions. Regarding fault tolerance based on software diversity, three major design issues need to be considered, namely, selection of variants; variant execution schemes; and judgement on results acceptability. These design issues may be realised by different design solutions. Different design decisions involve different measures of quality requirements (e.g. memory utilisation, execution time, reliability, financial costs and availability). With respect to service-oriented computing, it is well known that SOA systems *(i)* exhibit highly dynamic characteristics, and changes in the quality of services are likely to occur frequently and *(ii)* should support conflicting user requirements. Therefore, effective SOA solutions should address these design challenges.

In this paper we define a general taxonomy for these design challenges, their solutions, and functionalities required for the aggregation of multiple services into a single composite service. We also compare current design solutions and give an overview of their effectiveness. Based on this information and by means of systematic literature review method, we present a comprehensive survey of existing solutions for fault-tolerant service composition. The solutions were classified according to the elements of the proposed taxonomy and the checklist they support, thus facilitating the process of choosing from existing solutions by a SOA architect, according to specific needs of each SOA-application and execution environment. The classification guidelines support decisions related to four important aspects of fault-tolerant SOA-based applications: *(i)* failure mode, by defining the ways a failure can occur;*(ii)* fault latency, by defining details related to the failure behaviour, such as the interval between the moments of fault occurrences; *(iii)* fault assumptions, guiding the architect on the analysis of error detection and recovery mechanisms and the identification of restrictions related to the services available; and *(iv)* comparison amongst existing design solutions, by means of a systematic literature review which provides valuable information about the characteristics of classical software fault tolerance techniques.

DECLARATIONS

Acknowledgements

We would like to thank the anonymous referees, who helped to improve this paper. This research was partially supported by UOL (http://www.uol.com.br), through its UOL Bolsa Pesquisa program, process number 20120217172801. Cecília is supported by CNPq (305331/2009-4) and FAPESP (2010/00628-1). Fernando is supported by CNPq/Brazil (306619/2011-3), FACEPE/Brazil (APQ-0395-1.03/10 and APQ-1359-1.03/12), and by INES (CNPq 573964/2008-4 and FACEPE APQ-1037-1.03/08). Rachel is supported by EPSRC grant reference EP/K002465/1.

Authors' Contributions

ASN and RB planned the systematic review, carried it out and analyzed its results. ASN, RB and FC analyzed threats to the validity of the performed systematic review and the measures we took to reduce the risks. PHSB and ASN specified the design decision guidelines to realize fault tolerance in Service-Oriented Architecture (SOA). The format of the manuscript was decided by PHSB, ASN and RB. The manuscript was prepared by PHSB, corrections and reviews are made by RB, FC and CMFR. All authors read and approved the final manuscript.

REFERENCES

1. Abdeldjelil H, Faci N, Maamar Z, Benslimane D: A diversity-based approach for managing faults in web services. In *Proceedings of the IEEE 26th International Conference on Advanced Information Networking and Applications*. IEEE Computer Society, Los Alamitos, CA, USA; 2012:81–88.
2. Ammar HH, Cukic B, Mili A, Fuhrman C: A comparative analysis of hardware and software fault tolerance: impact on software reliability engineering. *Ann Software Eng* 2000, 10(1–4):103–150.
3. Anderson, T, Barrett PA, Halliwell DN, Moulding MR (1985) Software fault tolerance: An evaluation. IEEE Trans Software Eng SE-11(12): 1502–1510.
4. Arlat J, Kanoun K, Laprie JC: Dependability evaluation of software fault-tolerance. In *Digest of Papers of the 18th International Symposium on Fault-Tolerant Computing (FTCS'18)*. Society, Washington, DC, USA; 1988:142–177.
5. Avizienis A, Laprie JC, Randell B, Landwehr C: Basic concepts and taxonomy of dependable and secure computing.*IEEE Trans Dependable Secure Comput* 2004,1(1):11–33.
6. Blough DM, Sullivan GF: A comparison of voting strategies for fault-tolerant distributed systems. In *Proceedings of the 9th Symposium Reliable Distributed Systems (SRDS'09)*. IEEE Computer Society, Washington, DC, USA; 1990:136–145.
7. Broen RB: New voters for redundant systems. *J Dyn Syst Meas Contr* 1975,97(1):41–45.
8. Burrows R, Garcia A, Taiani F: Coupling metrics for aspect-oriented programming: A systematic review of maintainability studies. In *Evaluation of Novel Approaches to Software Engineering*. Edited by: Maciaszek L, Gonzalez-Perez C, Jablonski S. Springer, Berlin; 2010:277–290.
9. Buys J, De Florio V, Blondia C: Towards context-aware adaptive fault tolerance in soa applications. In *Proceedings of the 5th ACM International Conference on Distributed Event-Based System (DEBS'11)*. ACM, New York, NY, USA; 2011:63–74.
10. Cardozo ESF, Araújo Neto JBF, Barza A, França ACC, da Silva FQB: Scrum and productivity in software projects: a systematic literature review. In *Proceedings of the 14th International Conference on Evaluation and Assessment in Software Engineering (EASE'10)*. British Computer Society, Swinton, UK, UK; 2010:131–134.
11. Carzaniga A, Gorla A, Pezzè M: Handling software faults with redundancy. In *WADS, Lecture Notes in Computer Science, vol. 583*. Edited by: de Lemos R, Fabre JC,

Gacek C, Gadducci F, ter Beek MH. Springer, Berlin; 2008:148–171.

12. Daniels F, Kim K, Vouk MA: The reliable hybrid pattern: a generalized software fault tolerant design pattern. In*Proceedings of the 4th Conference of Patter Languages of Programming Conference (PloP'97)*. Washington University, St. Louis, MO, USA; 1997:1–9.

13. Di Giandomenico F, Strigini L: Adjudicators for diverse-redundant components. In *Proceedings of the 9th Symposium on Reliability in Distributed Software and Database Systems (SRDS'90)*. IEEE Computer Society, Washington, DC, USA; 1990:114–123.

14. Dillen R, Buys J, Florio V, Blondia C: Wsdm-enabled autonomic augmentation of classical multi-version software fault-tolerance mechanisms. In *Computer Safety, Reliability, and Security*. Edited by: Ortmeier F, Daniel P. Springer, Berlin; 2012:294–306.

15. Eckhardt, DE, Lee LD (1985) A theoretical basis for the analysis of multiversion software subject to coincident errors. IEEE Trans Software Eng SE-11(12): 1511–1517.

16. Eckhardt DE, Caglayan AK, Knight JC, Lee LD, McAllister DF, Vouk MA, Kelly JPJ: An experimental evaluation of software redundancy as a strategy for improving reliability. *IEEE Trans Software Eng* 1991,17(7):692–702.

17. Elmendorf, WR (1972) Fault-tolerant programming In: Proceedings of the 2nd IEEE International Symposium on Fault Tolerant Computing (FTCS'2), 79–83.

18. Faci N, Abdeldjelil H, Maamar Z, Benslimane D: Using diversity to design and deploy fault tolerant web services. In*Proceedings of the 20th IEEE International Workshop on Enabling Technologies: Infrastructure for Collaborative Enterprises (WETICE'11)*. IEEE Computer Society, Washington, DC, USA; 2011:73–78.

19. Florio VD, Blondia C: A survey of linguistic structures for application-level fault tolerance. *ACM Comput Surv*2008,40(2):6:1–6:37.

20. Garcia AF, Rubira CMF, Romanovsky AB, Xu J: A comparative study of exception handling mechanisms for building dependable object-oriented software. *J Syst Software* 2001,59(2):197–222.

21. Gärtner FC: Fundamentals of fault-tolerant distributed computing in asynchronous environments. *ACM Comput Surv* 1999,31(1):1–26.

22. Gonçalves EM, Rubira CMF: Archmeds: an infrastructure for dependable service-oriented architectures. In*Proceedings of the 17th IEEE International Conference and Workshops on the Engineering of Computer-Based Systems (ECBS'10)*. IEEE Computer Society, Washington, DC, USA; 2010:371–378.

23. Gorbenko A, Kharchenko V, Popov P, Romanovsky A: Dependable composite web services with components upgraded online. In *Architecting Dependable Systems III*. Edited by: Lemos R, Gacek C, Romanovsky A. Springer-Verlag, Berlin; 2005:92–121.

24. Gorbenko A, Kharchenko V, Romanovsky A: Using inherent service redundancy and diversity to ensure web services dependability. In *Methods, Models and Tools for Fault Tolerance*. Edited by: Butle M, Jones C, Romanovsky A, Troubitsyna E. Springer, Berlin; 2009:324–341.

25. Gorbenko A, Romanovsky A, Kharchenko V, Tarasyuk O: Dependability of service-oriented computing: time-probabilistic failure modelling. In *Software Engineering for Resilient Systems*. Edited by: Avgeriou P. Springer, Berlin; 2012:121–133.

26. Gotze J, Muller J, Muller P: Iterative service orchestration based on dependability attributes. In *Proceedings of the 34th Euromicro Conference on Software Engineering and Advanced Applications (SEAA'08)*. IEEE Computer Society, Washington, DC, USA; 2008:353–360.

27. Hilford V, Lyu MR, Cukic B, Jamoussi A, Bastani FB: Diversity in the software development process. In *Proceedings of the 3rd Workshop on Object-Oriented Real-Time Dependable Systems (WORDS,97)*. IEEE Computer Society, Washington, DC, USA; 1997:129–136.

28. Horning JJ, Lauer HC, Melliar-Smith PM, Randell B: A program structure for error detection and recovery. In*Proceedings of an International Symposium on Operating Systems: Theoretical and Practical Aspects*. Springer, London, UK; 1974:171–187.

29. Huhns MN, Singh MP: Service-oriented computing: key concepts and principles. *IEEE Internet Comput* 2005,9(1):75–81.

30. Jorgensen M, Shepperd M: A systematic review of software development cost estimation studies. *IEEE Trans Software Eng* 2007,33(1):33–53.

31. Kim KH: Distributed execution of recovery blocks: An approach to uniform treatment of hardware and software faults. In *Proceedings of 4th the International Conference on Distributed Computing Systems (ICDSC'84)*. IEEE Computer Society, Washington, DC, USA; 1984:526–532.

32. Kitchenham B, Charters S: *Guidelines for performing systematic literature reviews in software engineering. Tech. Rep. Technical Report EBSE 2007–001*. Department of Computer Science, University of Durham; 2007.

33. Kitchenham BA, Mendes E, Travassos GH: Cross versus within-company cost estimation studies: a systematic review. *IEEE Trans Software Eng* 2007,33(5):316–329.

34. Kitchenham BA, Pearl Brereton O, Budgen D, Turner M, Bailey J, Linkman S: Systematic literature reviews in software engineering - a systematic literature review. *Inform Software Tech* 2009,51(1):7–15.

35. Knight JC, Leveson NG: An experimental evaluation of the assumption of independence in multiversion programming. *IEEE Trans Software Eng* 1986,12(1):96–109.

36. Kotonya G, Hall S: A differentiation-aware fault-tolerant framework for web services. In *Service-Oriented Computing*. Edited by: Maglio PP, Weske M, Yang J, Fantinato M. Springer, Berlin; 2010:137–151.

37. Laprie JC, Béounes C, Kanoun K: Definition and analysis of hardware and software-fault-tolerant architectures. *Computer* 1990,23(7):39–51.

38. Laranjeiro N, Vieira M: Towards fault tolerance in web services compositions. In *Proceedings of the 2nd International Workshop on Engineering Fault Tolerant Systems (EFTS'07)*. ACM, New York, NY, USA; 2007.

39. Lee PA, Anderson T: *Fault tolerance: principles and practice*. Springer-Verlag New York, Inc., Secaucus; 1990.

40. Looker N, Munro M, Xu J: Increasing web service dependability through consensus voting. In *Proceedings of the 29th annual International Conference on Computer Software and Applications (COMPSAC-W'05)*. IEEE Computer Society, Washington, DC, USA; 2005:66–69.

41. Lyu MR: *Handbook of Software Reliability Engineering*. Inc., Hightstown; 1996.

42. Lyu MR, Chen JH, Avizienis A: Experience in metrics and measurements of n-version programming. *Int J Reliab Qual Saf Eng* 1994,1(1):41–62.

43. Mansour H, Dillon T: Dependability and rollback recovery for composite web services. *IEEE Trans Serv Comput*2011,4(4):328–339.

44. McAllister, DF, Vouk MA (1996) Handbook of software reliability engineering, 567–614.. McGraw-Hill, Inc., Hightstown. chap Fault-tolerant Software Reliability Engineering, ., [http://dl.acm.org/citation.cfm?id=.239425239466]

45. Milanovic N, Malek M: Service-oriented operating system: A key element in improving service availability. In*Proceedings of the 4th International Symposium on Service Availability (ISAS '07)*. Springer, Berlin; 2007:31–42.

46. Nascimento, AS, Rubira CMF, Lee J (2011) An spl approach for adaptive fault tolerance in soa In: Proceedings of the 15th International Software Product Line Conference (SPLC'11), 1–8.

47. Nascimento, AS, Castor F, Rubira CMF, Burrows R (2012a) An empirical study on design diversity of functionally equivalent web services In: Proceedings of the 7th International Conference on Availability, Reliability and Security (ARES'12), 236–241.. ACM, New York, NY, USA.

48. Nascimento, AS, Castor F, Rubira CMF, Burrows R (2012b) An experimental setup to assess design diversity of functionally equivalent services In: Proceedings of the 16th International Conference on Evaluation and Assessment in Software Engineering (EASE'12), 177–186.. IET, Herts, UK.

49. Nascimento AS, Rubira CMF, Burrows R, Castor F: A model-driven infrastructure for developing product line architectures using cvl. In *Proceedings of the 7th International Conferences on Self-Adaptative and Self-Organizing Systems (SBCARS'13)*. IEEE Computer Society, Washington, DC, USA; 2013.

50. Nourani E: A new architecture for dependable web services using n-version programming. In *Proceedings of 3rd International Conference on Computer Research and Development (ICCRD'11)*. IEEE Computer Society, Washington, DC, USA; 2011:333–336.

51. Nourani, E, Azgomi MA (2009) A design pattern for dependable web services using design diversity techniques and ws-bpel In: Proceedings of the 6th International Conference on Innovations in Information Technology (IIT'09), 290–294.

52. Papazoglou MP, Heuvel WJ: Service oriented architectures: approaches, technologies and research issues. *Int J Very Large Data Bases* 2007,16(3):389–415.

53. Papazoglou MP, Traverso P, Dustdar S, Leymann F: Service-oriented computing research roadmap. In *Dagstuhl Seminar Proceedings 05462*. Universidad de Talca, Talca; 2006:1–29.

54. Papazoglou MP, Traverso P, Dustdar S, Leymann F: Service-oriented computing: state of the art and research challenges. *Computer* 2007,40(11):38–45.

55. Pullum LL: *Software fault tolerance techniques and implementation*. Artech House, Inc., Norwood; 2001. MATH

56. Randell, B (1975) System structure for software fault tolerance In: Proceedings of the 1st International Conference on Reliable Software, 437–449.

57. Saglietti F: The impact of voter granularity in fault-tolerant software on system reliability and availability. In*Software Fault Tolerance*. Edited by: Kersken M, Saglietti F. Springer-Verlag, Berlin; 1992:199–212.

58. Santos GT, Lung LC, Montez C: Ftweb: a fault tolerant infrastructure for web services. In *Proceedings of the 9th IEEE International EDOC Enterprise Computing Conference (EDOC '05)*. IEEE Computer Society, Washington, DC, USA; 2005:95–105.

59. Scott RK, Gault JW, Mcallister DF: Fault-tolerant software reliability modeling. *IEEE Trans Software Eng SE*1987,13(5):582–592.

60. Shin K, Lee YH: Error detection process: model, design, and its impact on computer performance. *IEEE Trans Comput* 1984,33(6):529–540.

61. Townend P, Groth P, Xu J: A provenance-aware weighted fault tolerance scheme for service-based applications. In*Proceedings of the 8th IEEE International Symposium on Object-Oriented Real-Time Distributed Computing (ISORC'05)*. IEEE Computer Society, Washington, DC, USA; 2005:258–266.

62. Trivedi KS, Grottke M, Andrade E: Software fault mitigation and availability assurance techniques. *Int J Syst Assur Eng Manage* 2010,1(4):340–350.

63. Vouk MA, Mcallister DF, Eckhardt DE, Kim K: An empirical evaluation of consensus voting and consensus recovery block reliability in the presence of failure correlation. *J Comput Software Eng* 1993,1(10):364–388.

64. Wilfredo, T (2000) Software fault tolerance: a tutorial. Tech. Rep. Technical Report NASA/TM-2000–210616, National Aeronautics and Space Administration (NASA).

65. Williams BJ, Carver JC: Characterizing software architecture changes: A systematic review. *Inform Software Tech*2010,52(1):31–51.

66. Wohlin C, Runeson P, Höst M, Ohlsson MC, Regnell B, Wesslén A: *Experimentation in Software Engineering:*

An Introduction. Kluwer Academic Publishers, Norwell; 2000.

67. Xu J: Achieving dependability in service-oriented systems. In *Dependable and Historic Computing*. Edited by: Jones CB, Lloyd JL. Springer, Berlin; 2011:504–522.
68. Yuhui C, Romanovsky A: Improving the dependability of web services integration. *IT Professional* 2008,10(3):29–35.
69. Zheng Z, Lyu MR: Ws-dream: a distributed reliability assessment mechanism for web services. In *Proceedings of the International Conference on Dependable Systems and Networks*. IEEE Computer Society, Washington, DC, USA; 2008:392–397.
70. Zheng, Z, Lyu MR (2010a) An adaptive qos-aware fault tolerance strategy for web services. Empir Software Eng 15(4): 323–345.
71. Zheng, Z, Lyu MR (2010b) Collaborative reliability prediction of service-oriented systems In: Proceedings of the 32nd ACM/IEEE International Conference on Software Engineering (ICSE'10), 35–44.

CHAPTER 7

DESIGNING CONCEPTUAL FRAMEWORK FOR ALIGNING SERVICE ORIENTED ARCHITECTURE WITH BUSINESS PROCESS

Zulqarnain Abdul Jabbar, Manoj Kumar, Asia Samreen

Keywords: SOA, Process Maturity, Conceptual Framework, YAWL

INTRODUCTION

A business process is a collection of activities that takes one or more kinds of input and creates an output that is of value to the customer [1] . Business Process Reengineering (BPR) is a process-centered change management tool that is used to control the dynamic behavior of business processes and that allows us to examine business processes and redesign them, and thus can improve the service effectiveness and cost efficiency.

Section 1 gives the introduction of Service Oriented Architecture with basic and enhanced framework of SOA. In Section 2, we will discuss various issues related to business process reengineering, service oriented architecture and enterprise service bus. Section 2 will summarize the research done in the domain of BPR, SOA's approaches/structure, failure/success indicators for SOA, SOA impacts and its implementation in different industries. In Section 3, we will discuss the methodology used in our research. Section 4 will simulate the implementation of Service Oriented Architecture. Conclusion and future work will be presented in the next section.

Service Oriented Architecture

Service Oriented Architecture (SOA) is a services based software integration solution for most of the systems. It is a loosely-coupled architecture designed to meet the business needs of the organization.

Citation: Jabbar, Z. , Kumar, M. and Samreen, A. (2015) Designing Conceptual Framework for Aligning Service Oriented Architecture with Business Process. Journal of Computer and Communications, 3, 11-22. doi: 10.4236/jcc.2015.34002.

Key features of Service oriented architecture are:

- Divides our code in reusable modules and encapsulates design decisions in modules.
- Modules should be combined with each other following loose coupling for different purposes.
- Easily respond to changes and make maintainability easier.
- Improves productivity, agility, and speed for both business and IT.
- Aligns IT services to business and delivers faster services.

Reusability, flexibility and maintainability are the main powers of service oriented architecture.

SOA can provide following benefits to business.

- Efficiency: Transform business processes from replicated processes into highly leveraged shared services that cost less to maintain.
- Responsiveness: Rapid adaptation and delivery of key business services are to meet market demands for increased service levels to customers, employees, and partners.
- Adaptability: More effectively rollout changes throughput the business with minimal complexity and effort, saving time and money.

Basic interactions of web services in SOA are given in Figure 1.

Basic Framework of SOA

Service providers publish their services in a service directory called Universal Description, Discovery and Integration UDDI. Services' description and their usage are defined using Web Service Description Language in XML format. Service requester search for the desired service in service directory and send a request to the service provider to bind or use the service. Message passing between service provider and service requester is managed by the SOAP protocol in XML format.

Enhanced Framework of SOA

There could be multiple requesters for a service at a time and it is difficult for the provider to serve all requestors without any delay. In this situation, ESB Enterprise Service Bus serves as a middleware between service provider and requesters and is responsible to manage connection and interaction between service provider and service requesters. It is like a Hub in networking.

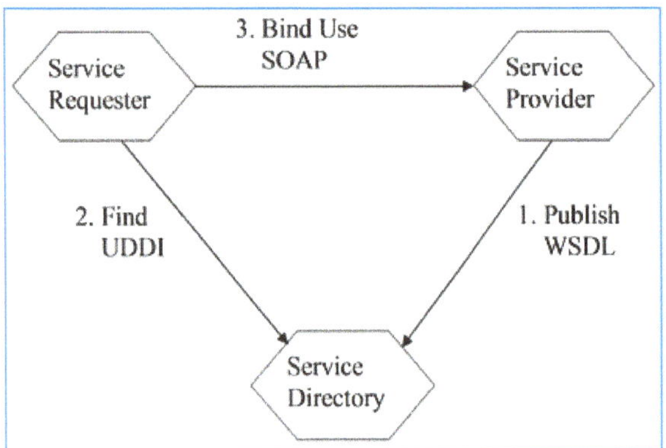

Figure 1. Framework of SOA.

Some web services standards discussed in different research are; WSDL, SOAP, UDDI, ESB, and BPEL.

WSDL: Web service description language is an XML file used to define what service is and how to interact with it [2] ?

UDDI: Universal Description, Discovery and Integration. It is used to register web services.

ESB: ESB serves as a middleware in SOA. Service provider publishes services on ESB and service users can invoke the services on the ESB according to their business requirements [3] . ESB provides a set of infrastructure capabilities, implemented by middleware technology, that enable the integration of services in an SOA.

SOAP: Simple Object Access Protocol provides a framework that manages the interaction between requester and responder through message passing. An example of SOAP format is in Figure 2.

BPEL: Business Process Execution Language is an XML based standard for defining business processes. It supports processes which exchange information by using web service interfaces [4] .

REVIEW OF VARIOUS ISSUES

We studied various issues regarding SOA. These issues are very important because to design a framework based on web-services it requires to tackle critical complications carefully.

Business Process Reengineering

Business process is the most abstract entity of process technology. Two important aspects of dynamic behavior of a business process are, 1) variability (e.g. customer arrival or customer service time), 2) Interdependence (number of decision points that affect the overall performance of the system) [5] .

In order to control this dynamic behavior of business process, a methodology of Business Process Reengineering BPR was introduced to accommodate changes to business processes and to align the business processes with the strategic aims of the organizations. Improvements in efficiency, effectiveness, productivity, speed of services, and cost savings are the primary objective of Business Process Reengineering [1] . Business Process Reengineering implementation has been done in many organizations especially in the western world in order to improve the organizational performance [6] .

Enterprise Service Bus

Service Oriented Architecture SOA is a software integration solution for most of the systems. It is a loosely- coupled architecture designed to meet the business needs of the organization. SOA is defined as an approach used to fulfill the requirements of loosely coupled, standard-based distributed computing which is protocol- independent as well. Enterprise Service Bus (ESB) serves as an integration and communication backbone in SOA approach. ESB utilizes web services standards to support communication patterns over multiple transport protocols and is responsible for the control, flow, and translations of all messages between services using different messaging protocols. SOA is a flexible architecture in terms that larger applications are modularized into services to unify business processes [7] .

Construction Principles for SOA

Architecture is basically a workflow framework including standards, processes and procedures for implementation and SOA is one of the widely used architecture in enterprises that can effectively handle the rapid changes in architecture. Load testing, performance testing, and security testing are mostly done for SOA based systems.

```
http://mygateway.com/services/createOrder
<order>
    <id>1234</id>
    <customer_id>AB35</customer_id>
    <line>
        <item>
            <part_no>127.871</part_no>
            <quantity>2</quantity>
```

Figure 2. Example of SOAP.

Service level agreement SLA is an agreement between consumer and service provider that is used to verify the QoS of services [2] . SOA allows business transactions among loosely connected service in heterogeneous environment. Flexibility and agility are the strengths of the architectural model provided by SOA to implement business process. Design principles of SOA are service contract, loose coupling, abstraction, reusability, autonomy, statelessness, discoverability and composition [8] .

Factors to Be Considered to Implement SOA

Some researchers discuss the impacts of the SOA implementation in organizations and the factors causing the success or failure of SOA implementation. Many factors are considered as essential success factors for SOA implementation. Some of the factors suggested by different authors are; reusability, complexity, governance, lack of skills in developers, lack of expertise and possible business models, organizational strategy/structure/culture, granularity of services, integration of applications, network governance, agile development, stakeholder's participation, business leadership, security, web services standards, system potential and strategy for migration, risk assessment and complexity increment. Architects and SOA implementers must have to consider the essential factors for SOA implementation as per business domain [9] .

Information Security

Information security challenges should be considered during SOA implementation. Some challenges such as loosely coupled services, service contract, abstraction, reusability, autonomy, statelessness, discoverability, and composition have been discussed in literature. Some of the controls for providing solutions for these challenge are; SOA information security governance, SOA information security management, SOA information security model, and Policy information security framework [8] .

Limited Recourses of Small Devices

Mobile (a low band-width and low computational device) data streaming applications can face problems in SOA environment due to the difference of attributes of service provider and consumer. For example, service provider provides video stream at 150 MB/sec but the consumer speed is just 5 MB/sec. A generic framework prototype is presented for managing and disseminating streaming data within an SOA environment [10] .

Rapid Change in Consumer Demands

As the enterprises approaches towards business globalization, the rapidly increasing consumer demands become a big challenge. Solution for this problem is the agility of business and IT. Integration of traditional and new IT systems is a major issuer so the integration of logistic information system is a crucial issue for modern business. Logistic information system has several subsystems like purchasing, warehouse etc. and needs to contact with third parties like suppliers, customers etc. A general design based on SOA and ESB can be described for the integration of distributed logistic information systems [11] .

Areas of SOA Application

Problems associated with the development of e-government in Southern African Development Community are analyzed and an SOA framework is proposed as a solution that can integrate back-end legacy systems and deploy services [12] . E-banking can provide many benefits to customers, banks, enterprise and also offers green banking. SOA adoption can provide many benefits to e-banking like efficiency, agility, flexibility etc. [13] . Non-integrated nature of healthcare systems causes loss of tens of thousands of patients per year due to the medical errors. So there was a need to increase the success rate of SOA adaptation in healthcare systems. SOA implementation can extend the body of knowledge in healthcare organizations [14] . An architectural baseline is proposed by Kim et al. to design and implement the SOA based Operation Support System model for telecommunication providers'. The model can be extended to other domains like diverse service provisioning [15] .

METHODOLOGY/MODELING

In this research, we are going to suggest a workflow to an organization to help them out to integrate multiple software systems based on Service Oriented Architecture and will present the simulation of the suggested workflow.

Background Knowledge of Organization

A well-known and well managed organization is working in education sector and providing free education to needy children all over the country. The organization is non-profitable and running its setup based on the donations collecting from donors.

Basic School Information

Classification of the educational units in this organization is described in Table 1 below.

IT Landscape

School Management System (SMS) is the center point of their IT landscape, enabling them to input relevant school information and disseminate information to all stakeholders from decision makers at the HO/RO level to those who make and implement decisions at the AO and Principal level. Current system is represented by Figure 3(a) while required system should be interactive that is shown inFigure 3(b).

As till Dec 2014, the organization has already grown to 900 units with 160,000 students. Their growth pattern is displayed in Figure 4.

Scope of the Suggested Workflow

We shall cover the data synchronization task between two systems SMS and HRMIS for this organization in our suggested workflow.

Focus Areas of SMS

The main areas of the SMS and related sections are illustrated in Figure 5.

Workflow

Purpose

Integration between HRMIS and SMS will be a two way process passing selected fields from SMS to HRMIS and vice versa at predefined intervals.

How Will It Be Done?

Web services will be designed for pushing information to HRMIS and for pulling information from HRMIS.

Table 1. Classification of the educational units.

Classification	Definition	Naming convention
Region	Region is a geographical entity organized roughly along provincial boundaries	South, South West, North, North West
Area	An Area is an administrative unit created (and occasionally revised) to reflect an optimal composition of school units and campuses	Based on main City in the Area, as determined by the respective Regional Manager
Cluster	Cluster is logical grouping of Campuses in close proximity (typically less than 5 km) and is meant for administrative and expansion planning	Based on main Town in the cluster.
Campus	Campus is a concrete structure designed to house a single or multiple school units.	Usually named after the Build Donor
E-Compound	E-compound refers to a group of campuses located in close proximity to another within the same boundary wall, although they operate as independent units	S/4/05 which means that this E-Compound was the fourth E-Compound made in the year 2005 in South
School	School is a function of campus (that houses the school), shift (morning, afternoon) and type (primary, secondary)	<Campus Name><Type><Shift> e.g. Khaliq Noorani Primary Morning
Unit	Unit is the most basic form of classification based on Capacity of the school	1P, 2P, 1S, 2S etc.

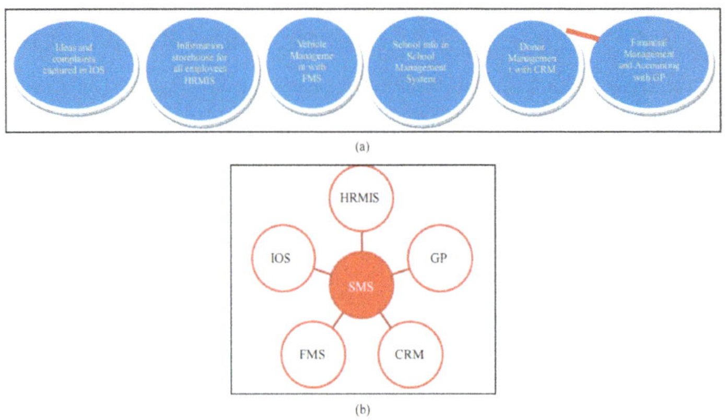

Figure 3. (a) AS-IS-IT landscape; (b) To-Be-IT landscape.

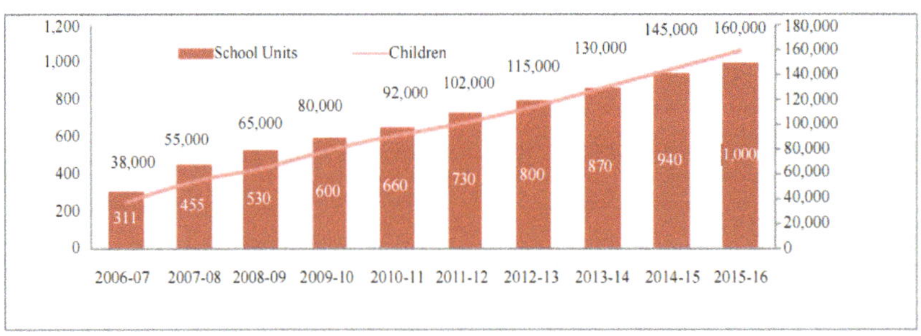

Figure 4. Growth pattern.

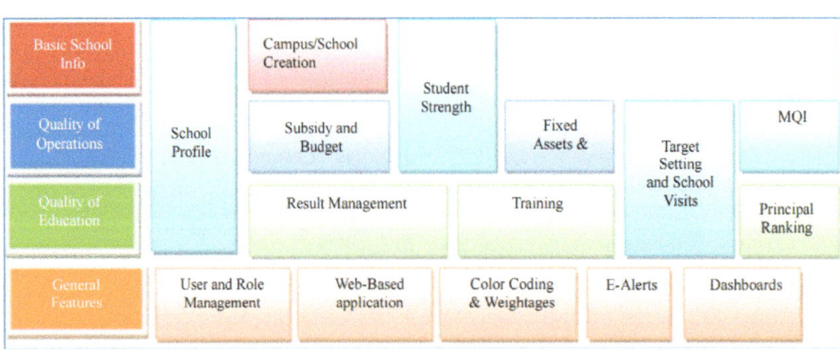

Figure 5. Main areas of SMS.

This is the most secure manner of integration as no application will need to interact with the database directly. Web service can also utilize the methods and functions already built in the system. This will also be a more flexible approach when more systems (such as CRM, GP) will require two way communications with SMS going forward. Both web services, will be registered on UDDI so that the web service can operate at all times after required authentication.

Some important features of the web service are as follows:

- Web Service will send and receive only those fields as defined by business users of SMS and HRMIS. Ideally, as the needs of business users evolve, an appointed system administrator should have the option to add more fields so that more information can be passed/ retrieved vis-à-vis the web service.
- For SMS specifically, the web service will always update existing school information for example staff strength and staff credentials and not create new school. The web service will be able to update selected fields, not delete any data point.
- The web service will not be event based, rather it would be linked to predefined intervals. At specified time, web services will be called to read and write data. Hence all changes done to school data within the SMS over the period will get updated in HRMIS in bulk.

It is recommended that this practice should be done thrice a year i.e. end of April (when new schools are created), end of August (when school information like signage are likely to be finalized), end of November (when midterm results are finalized along with some minor changes in school information).

SMS will also need HR data to be updated at defined intervals. Most likely, this information should get updated twice a year one in end of May (when teachers, faculty have been assigned to schools) and once in November (in case there is any change in faculty information).

Required Fields Mapping (Table 2)

Table 2. Required fields mapping.

Fields for HRMIS from SMS	Fields for SMS from HRMIS
School_Name	Principal's Contact No.
School_Full_Name	Area Manager's Contact No.
Start_Date	Regional Manager Contact No.
End_Date	Principal Name
School_Address	No. of Principal
City_ID	No. of Admin Assistant
Number_Of_Students	No. of Driver
Telephone_No	No. of Chowkidar
Emp_ID(principle)	Total No. of Staff
Country_ID	Break up of Admin staff and teaching staff
State_Province_ID	No. of Teachers
campusID	Break down of teacher by subject
CostCenterCode	Teachers' Quality: by Qualification and experience
noOfClasses (No. of Units)	Teachers' Availability: Shortages
establishmentYear	Principal Qualification
Shift	-
typeOfSchool	-
Email	-
phoneCode	-
RegionName	-
Branch_Code	-
Region_ID	-
Branch_Name	-
Area ID	-
Cluster	-
APR (Annual Percentage Result)	-
E-compound	-
District	-
Tehsil/Town	-
Location	-

Proposed Solution for Integration

Now we describe our solution to the problem to integrate interactively all the web-service in use for any organization. Figure 6 shows how the web services will interact with their respective application database and over all interaction with other web services.

Here is how this will work:

- Each application (SMS, HRMIS, CRM etc.) have its own Web Service which is responsible to handle all requests related to that application. So, SMS Web Service does not know how the HRMIS web service will update or fetch data from HRMIS database.
- We have a "Scheduled Integration Service" which is serving a center point for communications for all the applications. Important points for this application are:
  - This will be a windows service or scheduled task which we will setup on a server or machine. We will need to discuss how to define the scheduling logic for this application.
  - This application will use the web services to retrieve and update data for one application to another application.
  - Application will maintain a log of all the operations/errors.

SIMULATION

Here we'll present a simulated workflow for the SOA implementation for that organization. Simulation is performed using the software YAWL (Yet Another Workflow Language).

Introduction to YAWL

Based on a rigorous analysis of existing workflow management systems and workflow languages, a new work- flow language called YAWL (Yet Another Workflow Language) was developed by Wil van der Aalst (Eindhoven University of Technology, the Netherlands) and Arthur ter Hofstede (Queensland University of Technology, Australia) in 2002. This language was based on the one hand on Petri nets, a well-established concurrency theory with a graphical representation, and on the other hand on the well-known Workflow Patterns. The work- flow Patterns form a generally accepted benchmark for the suitability of a process specification language. Petri nets can capture quite a few of the identified control-flow patterns, but they lack support for the multiple instance patterns, the cancellation patterns and the generalized OR-join. YAWL therefore extends Petri nets with dedicated constructs to deal with these patterns [16] .

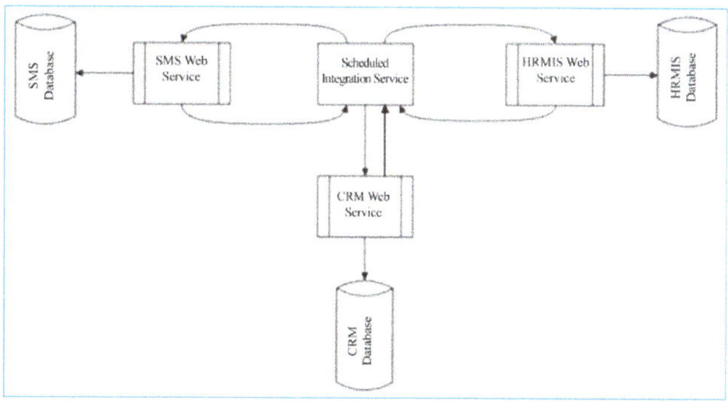

Figure 6. How web services interact.

Workflow for the Data Synchronization Using Web Services

In this section, we will describe the main workflow of our suggested framework.

Workflow in YAWL

This workflow presents the entire data sync process between SMS and HRMIS system. Similar work flow can be created for the data sync process between SMS and GP, SMS and FMS, SMS and CRM (Figure 7).

Data Sync Process for HRMIS System

Schedule Integration Service that is running on the SMS system will invoke and send a request to Request To SMS to Pull Data task with the output variable RequestType = SMS. Request to SMS to Pull Data task takes the input of RequestType = SMS and calls the Authentication 1 task with 2 output variables which are Userid = smsuser and Password = sms123. This task will authenticate the requester and invokes the SMS Web Service with output variable authentic = true. SMS Web Service gives a flag of servicestart = true to Service Pulls the Data from SMS DB task. This task will getdata in string or json string format from sms database and senddata in string or json format to the Send Data to Requester 1 task. This task will pass the senddata string to Push Received Data in HRMIS task that will finally push data in HRMIS database.

Simulation Result

This simulation doesn't only gives the workflow model but also gives a XML based specification. This specification clearly defines the input/output parameters and invoke condition for all services participated in the workflow. This specification will help in the final implementation of the services based model. A code snippet of the XML based specification for the service Invoke_HRMIS_Web_Service is given below:

<specification uri="SOA_Simulation">

< metaData >

< creator>Zul_qarnain</creator >

< description>No description provided</description >

<version>0.1</version>

<persistent>false</persistent>

<identifier>UID_63f35c80-ec0f-4773-af4e-6f2d3b84d5f7</ identifier>

</metaData>

<xs:schemaxmlns:xs="http://www.w3.org/2001/ XMLSchema"/>

<decomposition id=Decomposition1 isRootNet="true" xsi:type="NetFactsType">

<localVariable>

<index>0</index>

<name>RequestType</name>

<type>string</type>

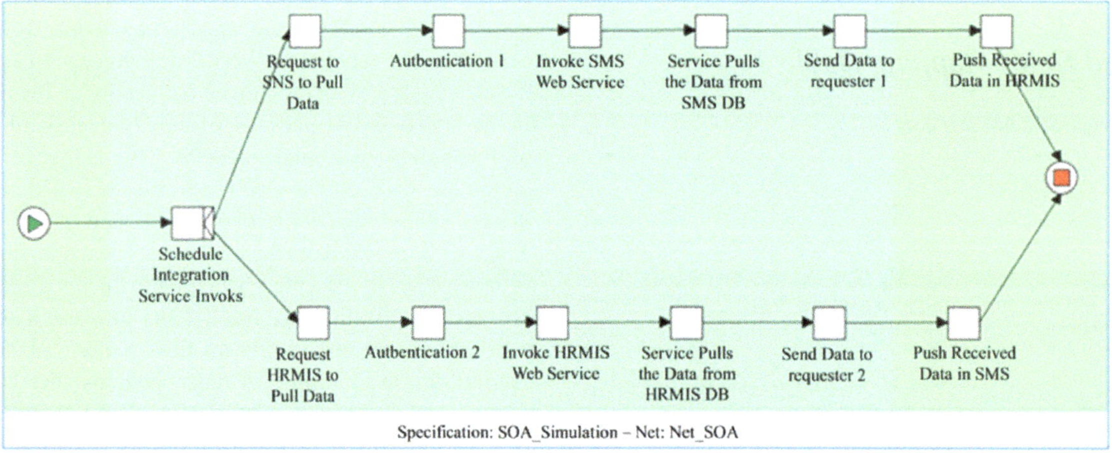

Figure 7. Example of workflow in YAWL.

<namespace>http://www.w3.org/2001/XMLSchema </ namespace >

<initialValue/>

</localVariable>

<localVariable>

<index>1</index><name>Userid</name>

<type>string</type>

<namespace>http://www.w3.org/2001/XMLSchema </ namespace>

<initialValue/>

</localVariable>

<localVariable>

<index>2</index><name>Password

<type>string</type >

<namespace>http://www.w3.org/2001/XMLSchema </ namespace>

<initialValue/>

</localVariable>

<processControlElements>

<inputCondition id=InputCondition1>

<flowsInto>

<nextElementRef id=""Schedule_Integration_Service_ Invoks""/>

</flowsInto>

</inputCondition>

<task id=Task1>

```
<name>Invoke HRMIS Web Service</name>
<flowsInto>
<nextElementRef id="“Service_Pulls_the_Data_from_HRMIS_DB””/>
</flowsInto>
<join code=“xor”/>
<split code=“and”/>
<startingMappings>
<mapping>
<expression query=“<authentic>{/Net_SOA/authentic/text()}</authentic>”/>
<mapsTo>authentic</mapsTo>
</mapping>
</startingMappings>
<completedMappings>
<mapping>
<expression query=“<servicestart>{/Invoke_HRMIS_Web_Service/servicestart/text()}</servicestart>”/>
<mapsTo>servicestart</mapsTo>
</mapping>
</completedMappings>
<resourcing>
<offer initiator=“user”/>
<allocate initiator=“user”/>
<start initiator=“user”/>
</resourcing>
<decomposesTo id=DecomposesTo1/>
</task>
<outputCondition id="“OutputCondition””/>
</processControlElements>
</decomposition>
</specification>
<layout>
<locale language=“en” country=“US”/>
<specification id=Specification1>
<size w=“58” h=“28”/>
<net id=Net1 bgColor=“-3342388”>
<container id=Container1>
<vertex>
<attributes>
<bounds x=“552” y=“376” w=“32” h=“32”/>
</attributes>
</vertex>
<label>
<attributes>
<bounds x=“520” y=“408” w=“96” h=“40”/>
</attributes>
</label>
</container>
<flow source=“Authentication” target=“Invoke_HRMIS_Web_Service”>
<ports in=“13” out=“12”/>
<attributes>
<lineStyle>11</lineStyle>
</attributes>
</flow>
<flow source=“Invoke_HRMIS_Web_Service” target=“Service_Pulls_the_Data_from_HRMIS_DB”>
<ports in=“13” out=“12”/>
<attributes>
<lineStyle>11
</attributes>
</flow>
</net>
</specification>
</layout></specificationSet>
```


CONCLUSIONS/FUTURE WORK

The dynamic behavior of the business processes can be well controlled by aligning the business processes with the web services using the service oriented architecture. SOA doesn’t only allow business process reengineering in an efficient manner, but its loosely coupled nature also helps organizations to evaluate their process and to accommodate changes in process without affecting the entire architecture. Most of the organizations are getting benefit of the SOA by mapping their business processes to web services and by using a middle ware in the form of Enterprise Service Bus to control traffic (requests) to web services to serve the required purpose. In this research, we are focusing on an organization of education sector and suggesting a workflow to them for the mapping of their business processes to web services. In this workflow, we suggested a web services-based solution to them. We performed the simulation of the suggested workflow using YAWL (Yet Another Workflow Language). We gave the complete specification of the suggested workflow in XML format as well. This XML based workflow describes the data flow in this workflow. No one presents this type of workflow for the requirement of the information synchronization in multiple systems. We are the first, proposing this solution and this is an easiest and cheapest solution for the automated information synchronization among multiple systems.

In next phase, we will present a workflow for the dynamic service replacement in SOA.

ACKNOWLEDGEMENTS

We would like to pay special thanks to Allah (SWT) who gave us the opportunity to complete this thesis.

We would like to pay thanks to our seniors and teachers, who guided us in the light of their previous professional experiences and knowledge.

Zulqarnain Abdul Jabbar, Manoj Kumar, Asia Samreen In the last, we are also thankful to our family, friends, fellows, and colleagues who supported us in their best.

REFERENCES

1. Hammer, M. and Champy, J. (1993) Reengineering the Corporation: A Manifesto for Business Revolution. Harper Collins Books, NY. [Paper reference:2]
2. Parveen, T. and Tilley, S. (2008) A Research Agenda for Testing SOA-Based Systems. Proceedings of System Conference 2008—IEEE international Systems Conference, Montreal, 7-10 April 2008, 1-6. http://dx.doi.org/10.1109/SYSTEMS.2008.4519032 [Paper reference:2]
3. Zhu, C.S., Chai, M.M., Lu, Y.F. and Guo, Y.D. (2013) Service Oriented Architecture Design of Energy Consumption Information System about Petroleum Enterprise. IEEE International Conference on Computational and Information Sciences, Shiyang, 21-23 June 2013, 1174-1177. http://dx.doi.org/10.1109/ICCIS.2013.311 [Paper reference:1]
4. Arslan, F. (2012) Towards Service Oriented Architecture (SOA) for Massive Multiplayer Online Games (MMOG). IEEE 14th International Conference on Modelling and Simulation, Cambridge, 28-30 March 2012, 538-543. http://dx.doi.org/10.1109/UKSim.2012.82 [Paper reference:1]
5. Greasley, A. (2003) Using Business Process Simulation within a Business Process Reengineering Approach. Business Process Management Journal, 9, 408-420. http://dx.doi.org/10.1108/14637150310484481 [Paper reference:1]
6. Weerakkody, V. and Currie, W. (2003) Integrating Business Process Reengineering with Information Systems Development: Issues and Implications. BPM 2003, 302-320. [Paper reference:1]
7. Papazoglou, M.P. and ven den Heuvel, W.-J. (2007) Service Oriented Architecture: Approaches, Technologies and Re- search Issues. The VLDB Journal, 16, 389-415. http://dx.doi.org/10.1007/s00778-007-0044-3 [Paper reference:1]
8. Chetty, J. and Coetzee, M. (2010) Towards an Information Security Framework for Service Oriented Architecture. Information Security for South Africa, Sandton, 2-4 August 2010, 1-8. http://dx.doi.org/10.1109/ISSA.2010.5588272 [Paper reference:2]
9. Waris, M., Khan, S.A. and Fakhar, M.Z. (2013) Factors Effecting Service Oriented Architecture Implementation. Sci- ence and Information Conference, 1-7. [Paper reference:1]
10. Ahmed, N., Linderman, M. and Bryant, J. (2010) Towards Mobile Data Streaming in Service Oriented Architecture. 29th IEEE International Symposium on Reliable Distributed Systems, New Delhi, 31 October-3 November 2010, 323- 327.http://dx.doi.org/10.1109/SRDS.2010.45 [Paper reference:1]
11. Zhang, L.Y., Li, J.Q. and Yu, M. (2006) An Integration Research on Service Oriented Architecture (SOA) for Logistic Information System. IEEE International Conference on Service Operations and Logistics, and Informatics, Shanghai, 21-23 June 2006, 1059-1063. http://dx.doi.org/10.1109/SOLI.2006.328898 [Paper reference:1]
12. Ramtohul, A. and Soyjaudah, K.M.S. (2013) Service-Orientation Method to Realise Government e-Services in SADC. VINE: The Journal of Information and Knowledge Management Systems, 43, 237-258. http://dx.doi.org/10.1108/03055721311329972 [Paper reference:1]
13. Basias, N., Themistocleous, M. and Morabito, V. (2013) SOA Adoption in e-Banking. Journal of Enterprise Information Management, 26, 719-739.http://dx.doi.org/10.1108/JEIM-07-2013-0042 [Paper reference:1]
14. Koumadities, K. and Themistocleous, M. (2013) SOA Implementation Critical Success Factors in Healthcare. Journal of Enterprise Information Management, 26, 343-362.http://dx.doi.org/10.1108/JEIM-06-2012-0036 [Paper reference:1]
15. Kim, J.W. and Lim, K.J. (2007) An Approach to Service-Oriented Architecture Using Web Services and BPM in the Telecom-OSS Domain. Internet Research, 17, 99-107.http://dx.doi.org/10.1108/10662240710730524 [Paper reference:1]
16. The YAWL Foundation (2004-2014) YAWL-User Manual. [Paper reference:1]

CHAPTER 8

SOAP-BASED SECURITY INTERACTION OF WEB SERVICE IN HETEROGENEOUS PLATFORMS

Tao Xu, Chunxiao Yi

Keywords: SOAP, Heterogeneous, Web Service, SIMSA, Security Interaction

INTRODUCTION

With the growth of the Service-oriented Architecture (SOA) application scale, there are hundreds of services in a large company. Different services may be deployed to platforms from different vendors, and different services installed in different locations have different access rights and security policy (encryption, signature, prevention of attacks, etc.). How to guarantee the security of services has become hot spot in foreign research institutions and scholars. IBM Tokyo Research Institute (Fumiko Satoh et al.) puts forward the best practice models and support tools for the specific service safety profile construction for the IBM Websphere Server according to security policy using mapping rules [1]. Microsoft Research in University of Cambridge (Karthikeyan Bhargavan et al.) [2] publishes a security policy configuration guidance to help developers construct the security policies of Web service according to security requirements. IBM Research Division in New York (Sam Weber et al.) [3] points out that there are a large number of heterogeneous platforms and different platforms have many Web Service standards and complex technologies. Even if there is a variety of "best security practices mode", it is still very difficult to ensure how to achieve the proper security.

Although SOA has solved the Web services called in heterogeneous platforms, and there are relevant security standards (WS-Security) of security information exchange between different platforms, WS-Security only gives an abstract framework to achieve security goals, including XML signatures, encryption, authentication and authorization. As for how to use them to achieve the goal of SOA security, it presents a challenge both in theoretical and technical practices [4,5].

Authentication policies and SOAP message-based security interactive study of Web services in heterogeneous platforms have been proposed in this paper. First the security feature of heterogeneous platforms is analyzed, and then the details of the security interaction model of heterogeneous platform named SIMSA is given. Combined with concrete application examples, user authenticcation during a Web service call as well as the safe handling of SOAP messages in heterogeneous platforms is achieved. The security model provides theoretical support for the security interacts of Web services in heterogeneous platforms and is verified by experiments. This model ensures the security interactions of Web service effectively.

SECURITY FEATURES OF HETEROGENEOUS PLATFORM

SOA needs a wide range of interoperability between services. In the development of Web service's logic functionality, if the security features are designed, Web services will become extremely complex and service performance and scalability will be greatly reduced. In terms of the analysis on the security needs and consideration of a variety of security measures, it cannot be sure whether the security components are appropriately organized and whether the system is more secure [6,7]. Security issues of Web services in SOA should be out of service functions, and the security requirements of Web services can be achieved through appropriate security configuration and mechanism. In this way, it can not only ensure the simplicity of design and call of Web services, but also can achieve the security of SOAP messaging [8,9].

An application system is usually based on a platform such as Microsoft. NET or Apache Axis. The service platform has its own security solution such as Microsoft's WSE (Web Service Enhancement) and Axis's of Rampart, etc. For the same security policy such as using certificates to sign the message, it can be achieved in the same platform for service requester to sign the

Citation: Tao Xu, Chunxiao Yi, SOAP-Based Security Interaction of Web Service in Heterogeneous Platforms, doi:10.4236/jis.2011.21001

message and service provider to do signature verification. If the service requester and provider are in different platforms, the security interoperability can not be guaranteed.

Each application platform has its own security mechanisms and security API. When using SOA to integrate enterprise application, services of different applications may be deployed in different application platforms and security requirements may be achieved by different security policy and platform technology. Then it needs an agent mechanism dealing with service security to package the specific realization of platform security from the logic, so that the security SOAP information of heterogeneous platform can be consistently understood and treatment.

Security processing mechanisms of Web services in heterogeneous platform provide security policy configuration and security implementation method of SOAP message [4]. Security service agents use WS-Security and other specifications to achieve the following three aspects of security requirements of SOAP message [10, 11]:

- Message integrity

WS-Security takes XML signature to do digital signature for SOAP message to ensure that SOAP message passes through intermediate nodes without being tampered.

- Message confidentiality

WS-Security uses XML Encryption to encrypt the SOAP message, so that the message sender can ensure that the contents of SOAP message can be achieved by the intended recipient uniquely. In this way, even if SOAP messages are listened, listeners cannot extract confidential information from the messages.

- Message authenticity

WS-Security introduces the concept of security tokens, which can represent the identity of the message sender. Combined with digital signatures, the message recipient can confirm the legitimacy and authenticity of the SOAP message sender.

SECURITY MODEL FOR HETEROGENEOUS WEB SERVICES SIMSA

Security framework and configuration strategies for heterogeneous platforms are quite different. Therefore, in order to achieve the security interaction of Web service in heterogeneous platforms, a third-party certification agency must be added. It can complete the relevant certification according to the request of the client. After the verification, client could send a request to call the Web service. To ensure the safety of service call process, both the client and Web server set the security service agent module to conduct safe handling to SOAP messages in the service interaction, including the signature and encryption of the SOAP message. The authentication module of client user is added to Web server, and only after the verification can client call the Web service. In this way, the security interactions of Web services in heterogeneous platforms can be achieved.

Combined with WS-Security specification, a security model of Web services in heterogeneous platform named SIMSA is constructed in this paper (shown in Figure 1). SIMSA model is mainly based on the extension of SOAP header including signature, encryption and authentication. The various components and functions of the security model are described as follows.

SIMSA Model Composition

- UDDI Server

Its main function is to store service descriptions by category. It can be a private registry, such as Capeconnect's UDDI Registry server, or it can also be a public registry, such as IBM Corporation and Microsoft's UDDI registry.

- Third-Party Certification Agency

It is used to verify the client's identity information, and only the users who pass through the authentication can send service requests to the Web server.

- WSDL Builder

It is used to describe how to use SOAP to invoke the Web service, and its function is to generate the corresponding WSDL document.

- Security Service Agent

It is the core module of the model. It is responsible for the security of Web service during transmission and achieves the security requirements of the model includeing signature and encryption of the SOAP message.

- User Authentication Policy

It is also the core module of the model. It is responseble for the request verification of client's identity, and only authenticated users can call the appropriate Web service.

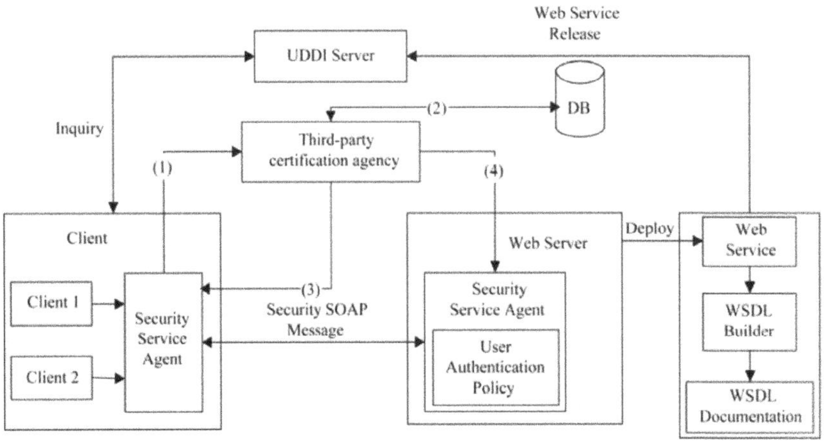

Figure 1. SIMSA Model.

Third-Party Certification Agency of SIMSA Model

In order to provide reliable authentication information for the Web server, SIMSA adds a third-party certification agency. Certification agency will compare the requestor's information such as usernames, passwords and permissions and other information with that stored in the certification database (DB in Figure 1). It can provide users with the information needed to verify to invoke Web services. This information is encapsulated in an encrypted message, and this message will be sent to the Web server with the user's SOAP message, waiting for the server's validation. In order to formally describe the process of third-party certification agency, Table 1 defines the parameters and function description.

The formal description of certification process in thirdparty certification agency is shown as follows (the following numbers correspond to that in SIMSA):

- Client's security service agent sends user information to the third-party certification agency:

$$CSP \rightarrow AC : SOAP(IDc, PWDc, IDs) \quad (1)$$

- Third-party certification agency gets the user information (including user name, password, etc.) and compares them with that in the database:

$$AC : COMPARE(IDc, PWDc) \quad (2)$$

- After the comparison, if properly the third-party certification agency will return a message encrypted with the Key, and otherwise it will reject the user's authenticcation request.

$$AC \rightarrow CSP : SOAP(Message) \quad (3)$$

- The third-party certification agency sends the Key used to encrypt the Message to the Web server:

$$AC \rightarrow SSP : SOAP(Key) \quad (4)$$

Web Server's User Authentication of SIMSA Model

When the client's security service agent receives the encrypted Message that the third-party certification agency returns, the client can use the Message to invoke the Web service in the server. The SOAP message that client's security service agent sends to the Web server's security service agent includes the client ID and Message, and its formal description is:

$$CSP \rightarrow SSP : SOAP(Head(IDc, Message), Body) \quad (5)$$

When the SOAP message including the client ID and the Message reaches the Web server's security service agent, the security service agent must verify the SOAP message whether the client has the permission to call the Web service. In the process it will verify whether the ID included in the Message is the same as the client claims, if they are the same client could invoke the Web service. A user authentication policy is designed in the server's security service agent for the authentication of the client ID. The user authentication policy is shown in Figure 2.

The process of Web server's user authentication is:

- Extract the Key used to encrypt Message from the SOAP message that third-party certification agency sends.
- Extract the client ID and Message from the SOAP message that client sends.
- Use the Key to decrypt the Message and extract the client ID that the Message contains.
- Verify whether the ID that client claims is the same as that in the Message, if they are the same, the client will be allowed to call the Web service, otherwise authentication will fail.

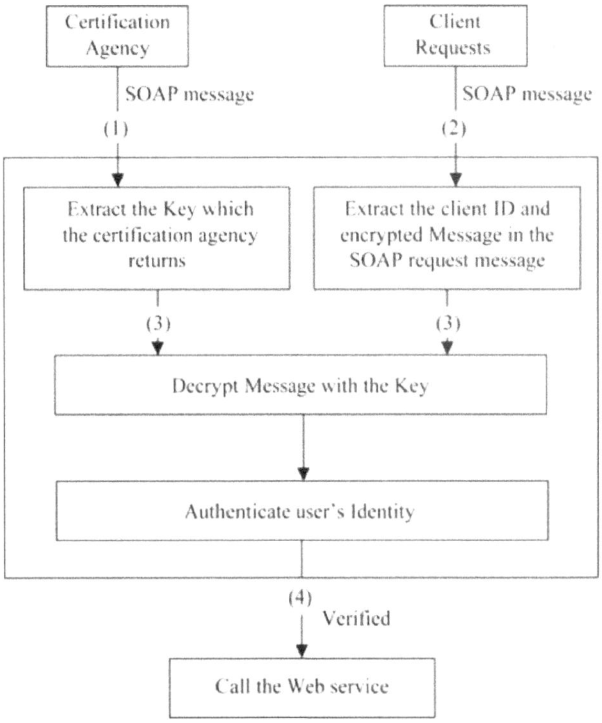

Figure 2. User Authentication Policy.

Security Service Agent of SIMSA Model

After the user's request passes through the identity validation in the Web server, a connection is established between the Web server and client, and customers can call the Web service. In order to ensure the security of Web services exchanged between heterogeneous platforms, the SOAP messages transmitted between the server and client must be handled safely. The security service agent module of SIMSA implements these security requirements, and it achieves security interaction of end to end in message-level mainly through the security extension of SOAP message. This module is to realize the signature and encryption of SOAP message. Figure 3 shows the security service agent module of SIMSA.

To formally descript the security interaction process of SOAP messages between heterogeneous platforms, Table 2 defines the relevant parameters and their functions.

Table 2. Parameter description of security interaction in heterogeneous platform.

Abbreviation	Content
S,C	Web server and client built on different platforms
Cc	Client certificate
Cs	Server certificate
Pu(cert)	Public key of cert
Pr(cert)	Private key of cert
Mes	SOAP Message
S(Pr(cert), Mes)	Use the private key of cert to sign the Mes
Dm	The digital signature of Mes
VS(Mes, Pu(cert), Dm)	Use the public key of cert to validate the digital signature of Mes
E(Pu(cert), Mes)	Use the public key of cert to encrypt the Mes
DE(Pr(cert), Mes)	Use the private key of cert to decrypt the Mes

The simplest form of security interaction of SOAP message is that a signed and encrypted Web service request M1 is sent to the server security service agent from the client security service agent and corresponding to that the server security service agent will return a response message M2 which has been handled safely to the client security service agent. The security interaction process of SOAP message can be formally described as:

- Client request: encrypt and sign the request message.

$$C \to S: E(Pu(Cs), M_1), S(\Pr(Cc), M_1) \quad (6)$$

- Server: verify the signature and decrypt the request message

$$S: VS(M_1, Pu(Cc), Dm_1), DE(\Pr(Cs), M_1) \quad (7)$$

- Server response: encrypt and sign the response message.

$$S \to C: E(Pu(Cc), M_2), S(\Pr(Cs), M_2) \quad (8)$$

- Client: verify the signature and decrypt the response message

$$C: VS(M_2, Pu(Cs), Dm_2), DE(\Pr(Cc), M_2) \quad (9)$$

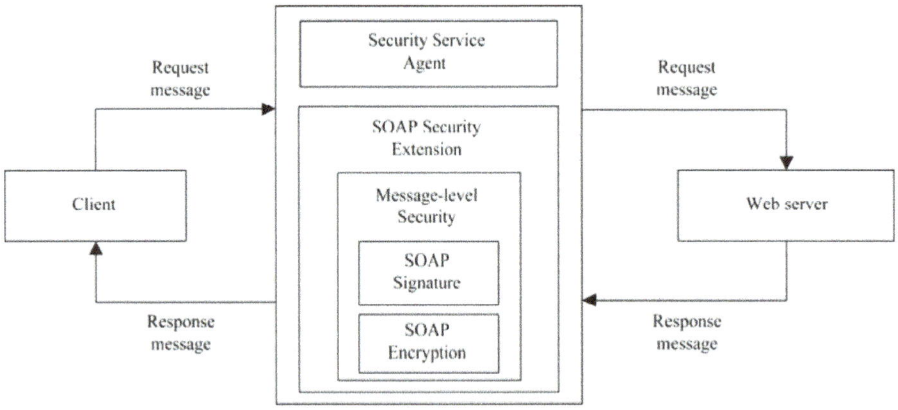

Figure 3. Security Service Agent Module.

SECURITY INTERACTIVE EXAMPLE

The user authentication module and security service agent module of the SIMSA are realized in this paper. They implement the user authentication in heterogeneous platforms and security extension of SOAP message during the process of Web service interaction.

User Authentication Implementation

The client sends the request SOAP message to the thirdparty certification agency. The message's format is shown in Figure 4, in which shows the information required certification agency to verify; specifies the client ID; specifies client password and specifies server ID.

The third-party certification agency queries the database to verify the client request SOAP message and after that it returns an encrypted SOAP message including the client ID and the encrypted Message to the client. The message's format is shown in Figure 5, in which contains the encrypted information.

The third-party certification agency sends the encrypttion key which is used to encrypt the Message to the Web server. The encryption key can be used to decrypt the Message in the user authentication security strategy when the client calls the Web service. The SOAP message's format is shown in Figure 6.

```
<soapenv:Header xmlns:wsa="http://www.w3.org/2005/
    08addressing">
      <authentication>
          <clientID>admin</clientID>
          <password>admin123</password>
          <serverID>server</serverID>
      </ authentication>
   </soapenv:Header>
```

Figure 4. Client Request SOAP Message.

```
<soapenv:Header xmlns:wsa="http://www.w3.org/2005/
    08addressing">
    <ToClient>
        <clientID>admin</clientID>
        <Message>encrypted message…</Message>
    </ ToClient>
</soapenv:Header>
```

Figure 5. SOAP message that certification agency returned to the client.

```
<soapenv:Header xmlns:wsa="http://www.w3.org/2005/
    08addressing">
    <ToServer>
        <key>Key</key>
    </ ToServer>
</soapenv:Header>
```

Figure 6. SOAP message that certification agency returned to the server.

```
<?xml version='1.0' encoding='utf-8'?>
<soapenv:Envelopexmlns:soapenv="http://www.w3.org/2003/
 05/soap-envelope">
<soaenv:Header xmlns:wsa="http://www.w3.org/2005/
 08/addressing">
  <wsse:Security xmlns:wsse="http://docs.oasis-open.org
   /wss/2004/01/oasis-200401-wss-wssecurity-secext-1.0.xsd
   " soapenv:mustUnderstand="true">
   <ds:Signature>
     <ds:SignedInfo>
       <ds:CanonicalizationMethod Algorithm="http://
           www.w3.org/2001/10/xml-exc-c14n#" />
       <ds:SignatureMethod Algorithm="http://www.w3.org
           /2000/09/xmldsig#rsa-sha1" />
       <ds:Reference URI="#id-8303462">
         <ds:Transforms>
           <ds:Transform Algorithm="http://www.w3.org
            /2001/10/xml-exc-c14n#" />
           </ds:Transforms>
         <ds:DigestMethod Algorithm="http://www.w3.org
           /2000/09/xmldsig#sha1" />
         <ds:DigestValue>q0ut1qK9WER7MXSuX
         4vV4wYS3oQ=</ds:DigestValue>
       </ds:Reference>
     </ds:SignedInfo>
     <ds:SignatureValue>
       SKPKP5ICsX/lcZzCdYxk0cAsQV6Gbyau0bBJvpq
       NKL/kSyh9KvUMJIJ7i96gT46tCdexHne+LzE2CO
       1xUkBLDv8+zX049Klk++BdqiuZLF6PB/X79dqyd
       RIWYOMYuN2nMvP5Qdo3MzYOvvi2K7w3gcbiy
       euDwmWglkeR8iCqHvk=
     </ds:SignatureValue>
     <ds:KeyInfo Id="KeyId-11463270">
       <wsse:SecurityTokenReference xmlns:wsu="http://
        docs.oasis-open.org/wss/2004/01/oasis-200401-wss-
        wssecurity-utility-1.0.xsd" wsu:Id="STRId-367156">
       <ds:X509Data>
         <ds:X509IssuerSerial>
          <ds:X509IssuerName>CN=Sample Client,OU=
             Rampart,O=Apache,L=Colombo,ST=Western,
            C=LK</ds:X509IssuerName>
          <ds:X509SerialNumber>1187603652
          </ds:X509SerialNumber>
         </ds:X509IssuerSerial>
       </ds:X509Data>
      </wsse:SecurityTokenReference>
   </ds:KeyInfo>
   </ds:Signature>
 </wsse:Security>
 <wsa:To>http://10.6.233.177:8080/axis2/services/Signiture.
   signitureHttpSoap12Endpoint/</wsa:To>
   <wsa:MessageID>urn:uuid:22EC2A05BDC41A98491289
   284864538</wsa:MessageID>
 <wsa:Action>urn:echo</wsa:Action>
</soapenv:Header>
<soapenv:Body>
 <xenc:EncryptedData>
 ……
 </xenc:EncryptedData>
</soapenv:Body>
</soapenv:Envelope>
```

Figure 7. Security SOAP Message.

SOAP Message Signed and Encrypted by Security Service Agent

The SOAP message output from the server security service agent is signed and encrypted. The signed part of the message is shown in Figure 7. mainly consists of three parts: , and . also contains three parts including , and . indicates the algorithm that signature used; indicates the algorithm need to be used to generate the abstract data; specifies the abstract data. points out the signature value. shows the information of the certificate which signature uses, including the data of the X.509 certificate and the information of the certificate publisher. contains only one element named which indicates the encrypted information. As the encrypted information is too large, the part of the information is omitted.

From Figure 7 it can be seen that the SOAP message has been successfully signed and encrypted which ensures the security of SOAP messages transmitted between different platforms.

CONCLUSIONS

SOA promotes the application and integration of information technology, but the security of application and integration is much more complex. In connection with SOA application and integration practice, the security issues of Web service in the SOA architecture have been proposed. In order to solve these issues, a security interactive model of heterogeneous platform named SIMSA is designed. This model realizes security requirements during the process of calling Web services in heterogeneous platform. By making client authentication, signing and encrypting SOAP message in the process of Web service interaction in heterogeneous platform, it achieves the security interaction of Web service in heterogeneous platform, which greatly enhances Web service's security features.

REFERENCES

1. F. Satoh, et al., "Adding Authentication to Model Driven Security," IEEE International Conference on Web Services (ICWS), Chicago, 2006, pp. 585-594. doi:10.1109/ ICWS.2006.25
2. K. Bhargavan, C. Fournet, et al., "An Advisor for Web Services Security Policies," Proceedings of the 2005 workshop on Secure web services, New York, 2005, pp. 1-9. doi:10.1145/1103022.1103024
3. S. Weber, P. Austel and M. McIntosh, "A Framework for Multi-Platform SOA Security Analyses," IEEE International Conference on Web Service, Salt Lake City, 2007, pp. 102-109.
4. J. Viega, "Why Applying Standards to Web Services is not Enough," IEEE Security and Privacy, Vol. 4, No. 4, 2006, pp. 25-31. doi:10.1109/MSP.2006.110
5. Z. P. Liu, D. D. Zhou, L. Y. Xue, X. M. Chang and X. J. Song, "A Security Model of Web Service Based on SOAP," Journal of Wuhan University in Chinese, Vol. 52, No. 5, 2006, pp. 570-573.
6. L. Y. Tang and S. H. Qing, "Administration of Multiple Roles in the Hybrid RBAC-DTE Policy," Chinese Journal of Computers, in Chinese, Vol. 29, No. 8, 2006, pp. 1419-1425.
7. X. M. Wang and Z. T Zhao, "Role-Based Access Control Model of Temporal Object," Acta Electronica Sinica, in Chinese, Vol. 33, No. 9, 2005, pp. 1634-1638.
8. W. F. Zheng, T. Xu and Q. F Gu, "Design and Implementation of Core Service in Civil Aviation Integrated Information Platform," Computer Engineering, In Chinese, Vol. 34, No. 21, 2008, pp. 267-269.
9. R. Bunge, S. Chung, B. Endicott-Popovsky and D. McLane, "An Operational Framework for Service Oriented Architecture Network Security," Proceedings of the 41st Hawaii International Conference on System Sciences, Waikoloa, 2008, pp. 312-320.
10. N. Bieberstein, S. Bose, M. Fiammante, K. Jones, R. Shah and Z. Ning, "Service-Oriented Architecture Guide," in Chinese, Posts & Telecom Press, Beijing, 2008, pp. 160-166.
11. Z. P. Liu, X. M. Chang, D. D. Zhou and X. J. Song, "A Safe ID Authentication Policy in Web Service," Journal of Computer Research and Development, in Chinese, Vol. 43, 2006, pp. 551-555.

CHAPTER 9

ENHANCED PROGRAM COMPREHENSION FOR SERVICE ORIENTED ARCHITECTURE (SOA) SYSTEMS

Eman El-Sheikh, Thomas Reichherzer, Laura White, Norman Wilde, John Coffey, Sikha Bagui, George Goehring, Arthur Baskin

Keywords: Service Oriented Architecture; Software Maintenance; Program Comprehension; Intelligent Search; Abstraction; Visualization; Web Services

INTRODUCTION

The emergence of Service Oriented Architecture (SOA) has created a new generation of information technology systems that support mission critical tasks in government and industry. Unfortunately, like each previous generation of software, SOA is also likely to create some new challenges for software maintainers.

Definitions of SOA vary [1], but generally they describe large systems-of-systems [2] in which composite applications are created by orchestrating loosely-coupled service components that run on different nodes and that communicate via message passing. An infrastructure layer, sometimes called an Enterprise Service Bus (ESB), mediates the communication, providing features such as routing, security, and data transformation.

The fundamental technique is the concept of service interface contracts, which play a critical role in allowing communication among the various components. The services are heterogeneous in both implementation language and operating environment, distributed geographically, and, possibly most important, commonly distributed in ownership. A main attraction of SOA is that it enables collaborations that cross company and organizational boundaries.

These characteristics of SOA aggravate the issue of program comprehension, which has been at the heart of the software maintenance problem for all previous generations of software. It is very important for a maintainer to understand software at a deep level before making changes; modifications made based on imperfect understanding are highly likely to fail, possibly with disastrous consequences. Such deep knowledge is, in practice, best obtained from skilled software engineers who have participated in the system's creation. Software maintenance typically becomes difficult and expensive precisely at the time when such individuals disperse, and take their expertise with them.

Most SOA composite applications are still young, so the challenges of SOA maintenance are still emerging. SOA implementations vary greatly so it is not clear that a typical SOA maintenance environment may look like. However, we hypothesize that SOA maintainers may face a situation similar to that is shown in **Figure 1**.

As illustrated in **Figure 1**, the maintainer works for one particular organization and typically has access to the services operated by that organization, which may be a mixture of components large and small, legacy and new, and implemented in different languages and styles. Further, these services interoperate with components owned and controlled by other organizations, and here the maintainer's information may be more fragmentary. The maintainer is unlikely to have, or desire, access to source code. Documentation may be partial and not always upto-date. The one guaranteed-correct item will likely be the service interface description. If, as is often recommended, web services standards are being followed, then this description will take the form of a Web Services Description Language (WSDL) service interface and an Extensible Markup Language (XML) Schema Definition (XSD) for service datatypes. These documents must be current for the components to interoperate correctly at runtime.

In addition to source code, WSDLs and XSDs, there may be a plethora of other documents that shed light on how SOA

Citation: E. El-Sheikh, T. Reichherzer, L. White, N. Wilde, J. Coffey, S. Bagui, G. Goehring and A. Baskin, " Enhanced Program Comprehension for Service Oriented Architecture (SOA) Systems," doi: 10.4236/jsea.2013.69054.

composite applications actually work. These may include configuration files for the ESB and application servers in which the code is deployed, Business Process Execution Language (BPEL) orchestration instructions that tie component services together, project files describing the build process, and unstructured documentation in various formats; all of which may help provide insight into system operation.

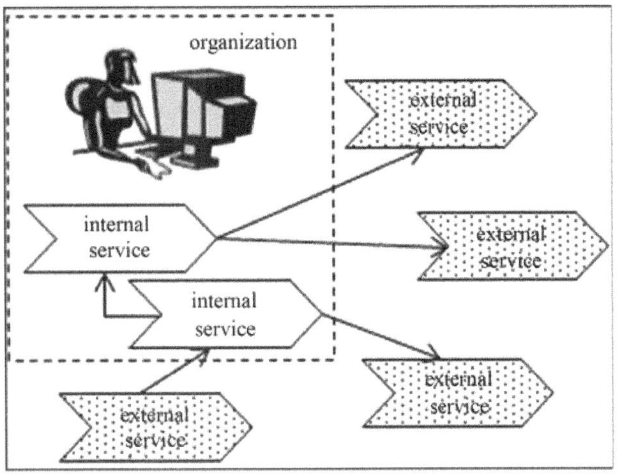

Figure 1. Typical SOA maintenance environment for a composite application.

In this environment, how will a SOA maintainer go about performing enhancements, adaptations or bug fixes? We hypothesize that the maintainer will follow advice that is as old as the software engineering profession: start by gathering all available information that is relevant to the problem [3]. That gathering process must include searches in the collection of documents described in the previous paragraph.

Our research group has been studying how intelligent search techniques could help ease the challenges of SOA maintenance. We have constructed a SOA search tool called SOAMiner—not as a finished product for immediate use—but rather as a research tool to explore the information needs of those maintaining SOA systems [4]. The research reported here builds upon and expands a two-part case study reported in Reichherzer [5] and White [6], which focused on observing software engineers as they use the search tool to help identify what SOA maintainers will want to know. This paper reports on additional analysis of the case study results and the development of methods and tools to enhance program comprehension for SOA systems.

From previous research results and related literature, it has become clear that naive search can be helpful, but for the combination of structured and unstructured SOA documents, it would be much more useful to combine simple text-based search with additional visualizations and abstractions of the information in the documents. More advanced search and visualization techniques will, for example, simplify the task of locating domain concepts within the system and perform impact analysis for proposed code enhancements.

In the remainder of this paper, we present our most recent research on enhancing program comprehension for SOA systems. Section 2 summarizes related research in the area of comprehension and maintenance of SOA systems. We then describe challenges in SOA comprehendsion and how intelligent search techniques and our search tool, SOA Miner, can contribute to improved understanding of those systems. Section 4 describes a case study that explores search within the context of maintenance for two different SOA applications, followed by the results, which highlight the need for specific abstractions that distill pertinent from irrelevant information. Section 5 presents additional analysis of the case study results as well as several visualization methods to enhance comprehension. Novel research reported in Sections 5 and 6 focuses on enhancing program comprehension for SOA systems through the development of various types of visualizations of the identified abstractions, including trees and Entity Relationship visualizations and a visualization tool, SOA Intel. The paper ends with a discussion of conclusions and plans for future work.

RELATED WORK

A review of recent related work identifies the aspects of SOA that may make comprehension and maintenance even more difficult than it was with earlier systems [7- 10]. Some of the main factors discussed are:

- The heterogeneity of SOA applications: expertise in many different languages and environments may be needed.
- The distributed ownership of services: source code or key documents may not be made available to the maintainers for business reasons.
- Poorly coordinated changes: multiple fielded versions of services arise as different service owners are driven by different business needs.

Researchers have also considered the organizational structures needed to support SOA maintenance. KajkoMattson, Lewis, and Smith [11] discuss how organizations adding SOA applications to their maintenance workload influence traditional IT roles. Several new roles emerge—which need to be filled—and new problems arise such as the prioritization of changes requested by different partners.

Recently, Papazoglou, Andrikopoulos, and Benbernou [12] described the problems of managing versions as a SOA system evolves. They distinguish between shallow service changes, which are localized in their impact, and deep changes, which may cascade to other services. For deep changes they suggest that a gap-analysis model should be constructed to identify the differences between an as-is currently deployed system and a to-be system with desired changes implemented. This suggestion highlights the importance of program comprehension since the creation of such a gap-analysis model would require a deep understanding of the services making up the as-is SOA system.

Our literature review identified only one paper that reports on experiences with program comprehension related to a specific interoperable system. Gold and Bennett [13] describe a research prototype web services system for integrating health care data from multiple providers. The project used the UK's National Health Service as an example. Their work suggests that there are many consequences which result from widespread distributed ownership of services. Maintainers will generally have to rely on WSDLs as descriptions of external services; however, WSDLs have many limitations with respect to comprehension since they are designed primarily to allow runtime calling of services. The maintainer will not be able to drill down into the code to get richer information since the code for an external service will most likely not be available to the maintainer. Gold and Bennett [13] argue further that since there are many service owners, the maintainer of a SOA composite application may need to deal with frequent unanticipated changes in external services with which he is interoperating. The maintainer will need to re-read updated WSDL interfaces and analyze the changes to identify necessary modifications to his own code. Time may be very short when there is a need to comprehend a modified service and make adjustments.

Little research has been conducted specifically on maintenance tools for Service Oriented Architecture systems. However, some researchers have proposed the use of dynamic analysis to aid in SOA understanding. Dynamic analysis involves collecting execution data, such as a trace from a running system in either a test environment or in a live deployed environment. The Web Services Navigator tool, described by a group at IBM, collects trace data from a SOA application and provides five different views of the executing system [14]. Coffey, White, Wilde and Simmons [15] use dynamic analysis to address the problem of locating the message interchanges associated with a particular user feature in a SOA system. A rather different form of dynamic analysis involves hypothesizing an interface contract for an unfamiliar service and sending it a series of messages to confirm the correctness of the hypothesis [16]. Analysis of execution data can be a powerful way to gain understanding of software. However, dynamic analysis is not always practical because of the difficulty of collecting the necessary data when dealing with large systems running across many nodes.

SOA SEARCH SUPPORT

SOA Artifacts

An alternative approach to analyzing systems dynamically is to analyze the artifacts that build them. In the case of SOA composite applications, SOA artifacts include a variety of different files that provide insight into the architecture of a SOA system and the messages exchanged between its services. The artifacts are automatically produced by SOA development and deployment tools and formatted according to standardized SOA Web languages, such as WSDLs, Simple Object Access Protocol (SOAP), XSD, and more. Since machines produce them from annotations in source code and user-specified deployment and integration information, the artifacts tend to be diverse and complex sometimes involving hundreds of lines of XML encoded descriptions that makes them difficult to inspect (the PAVER™ system described below has 10 WSDL files and 63 XSD files with a total of 49,000 lines and 14,000 lines of XML code respectively). Moreover, the SOA Web languages provide flexibility in the encodings of service and data descriptions, resulting in syntactic differences in SOA artifacts that further complicate their analysis. Yet, information that the artifacts contain is important to understand how a SOA composite application works. For example, the implementation of a service is described by a WSDL interface description, a type of contract that allows services to be loosely coupled. Among other things, the description includes operations of services, messages that may be exchanged between services along with data type information. Such information is valuable to software maintainers that will ultimately need to understand how services communicate and what data they exchange to make any changes to them consistent with the longterm maintenance goals of SOA composite applications.

Challenges in SOA Comprehension

Maintaining SOA composite applications requires a deeper understanding of the applications' services, their operations, and exchanged messages. To illustrate the maintenance challenges that engineers face, consider a few excerpts from the Web Auto Parts example discussed in more detail later. The artifacts include a BPEL file (Order Processing.bpel) that orchestrates multiple services to search inventories in the store for auto parts, computes taxes and shipping costs, among others, a WSDL file (Inventory Repository Artifacts.wsdl) that fronts the company's inventory database and a data type definition file (Inventory Query.xsd) that describes message data to and from the inventory repository. A maintainer that needs to know the data being passed when inventory is checked needs to step through a number of artifact files to answer this question, searching the files for text labels that match the names of services, operations, and data involved in the inventory check. A strategy to find the hidden information within the SOA artifacts may involve the following sequence of steps:

- Examine the BPEL file to search for a partner service that involves inventory checks in the processing of an order.
- Identify the partner link type associated with the partner service.
- Look for the WSDL service interface file that implements the partner link type. This specific information is not available in the BPEL code. It must be discovered manually by matching tag names across the different WSDL files.
- Find the operations associated with the service in the service interface file.
- Identify the operation involved in the inventory check using the name of the operation and keywords for filtering.
- Search for the correct input message specified by the operation. The input message contains the data type for the data passed to the service.
- Find the data type within the same WSDL file or imported XSD files.
- If the data type is a complex type, identify the parts of the type. This may involve additional searches for more data types.

In conclusion, multiple searches are needed through various SOA artifacts to answer a maintenance question. In the specific case of Web Auto Parts, service names, operations, and messages include keywords in their labels that made it possible to identify the correct data type. The discovery of such information requires an in-depth understanding of the languages encoding the SOA artifacts as well as their relationships.

SOA Miner: A Search Tool

Scenarios such as the one described above lead us to believe that future SOA maintainers will need the ability to search quickly across multiple document types and to integrate multiple kinds of information as they build their conceptual picture of a composite SOA application. However, there is not yet any published experience about what actual types of searches SOA maintainers will want to perform.

To explore this question, we have developed a prototype SOA search tool called SOA Miner, as a research prototype to explore information needs. SOA Miner currently focuses on searches of documents having XML structure since WSDLs, XSDs, BPELs and many ESB configuration files take this form. SOA Miner is built on the Apache Solr search tool [17], with an interface derived from AJAX-Solr [18]. To use SOA Miner, the software engineer indexes the collection of files that have an XML structure and then queries the collection using the interface shown in **Figure 2**. In this interface, the current query is shown on the upper left and the current set of result tags are displayed on the right.

TWO-PART CASE STUDY OF SOA SEARCH

General Structure

We performed a two-part case study of SOA systems to gain insight into what SOA maintainers would want to know as they try to understand a SOA composite application and perform a maintenance task. The objectives and methods of the two parts were the same, but since SOA systems are very diverse, we found two different composite applications representing different implementtation approaches to services-based computing. The case study thus involves two different "units of analysis" within a single context as described by Runeson and Host [19].

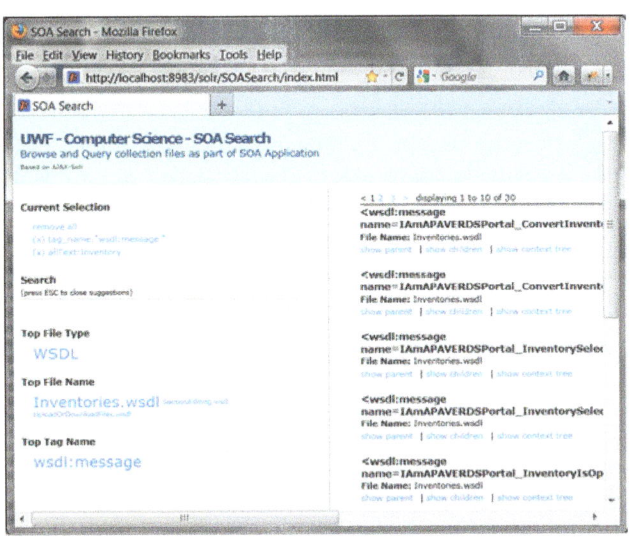

Figure 2. SOA Miner screenshot.

The main research question for the case study was: What abstractions would SOA maintainers find useful to help them understand a composite application?

The method for each part of the study followed the same steps. We started from a non-trivial services-based system and indexed artifacts from it such as WSDLs and XSDs. We also developed a list of questions to answer about the specific SOA application. The questions were loosely based on the search questions that Sim, Clarke, and Holt [20] found that software engineers asked when maintaining traditional software systems. The questions included both concept location queries that look for domain concepts (e.g., "What services/operations/messages deal with parts inventory?") and impact analysis queries (e.g., "If I change this data type, what code is affected?").

Case study participants were first provided some training in using the tool. Then they used it individually to respond to the questions while "thinking out loud" to verbalize their thought processes. An observer noted the searches they made and the areas where they seemed to encounter difficulties. Finally, for each part of the study, there was a group debrief session with all participants to discuss the results and contribute suggestions for improved search and visualization support.

The Web Auto Parts System

The first unit of analysis involved a hypothetical online automobile parts dealer called Web Auto Parts [5]. Web Auto Parts models an Internet start-up company that is using SOA for rapid development. Its software uses BPEL for orchestration of commercially available external services from well-known vendors. As shown in **Figure 3**, the Order Processing workflow for Web Auto Parts has two stubbed in-house BPEL services (Order Processing and Inventory Repository) and four comercially available external services:

- Amazon Web Services-Simple DB (data base) and Simple Queue Service (message queuing).
- StrikeIron.com-Tax Data Basic (sales tax rates).
- Ecocoma-USPS (shipping costs).

Web Auto Parts is, of course, much smaller than most real SOA applications as shown in **Table 1**. However, it is useful for a case study since it consists of syntactically correct BPEL code and contains XSD and WSDL documents typical of current industrial practice.

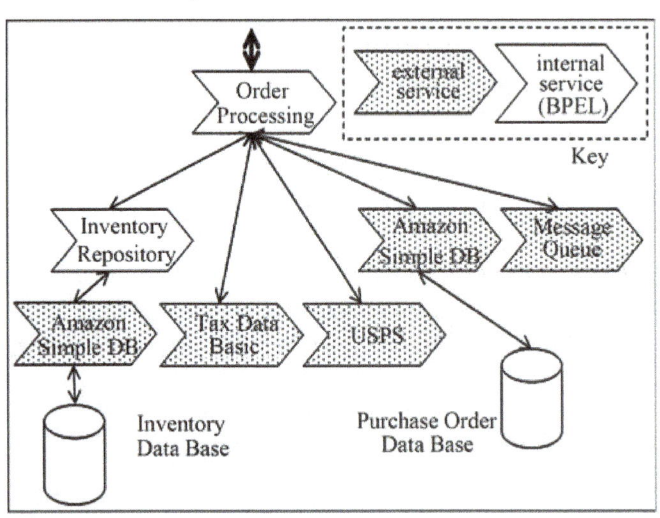

Figure 3. Web Auto Parts-services in the order processing workflow.

Table 1. SOA artifacts of web Auto Parts

Filename	Lines of Code
wsdl.AmazonSimpleDB	611
xml.deploy	51
xsd.InventoryQuery	28
wsdl.InventoryRepositoryArtifacts	69
bpel.OrderProcessing	118
bpelex.OrderProcessing	55
xsd.PurchaseOrder	36
dlws.QueueService	1043
wsd.51TaxDataBasic	436
wsdl.usps	197
Total	2644

Study participants were three computer science faculty members who were familiar with the basic concepts of SOA. However, only one of them had any SOA programming experience or experience with WSDLs, XSDs and BPEL. They were given only very general information about Web Auto Parts and about the Order Processing workflow, typical of what a maintainer might have in dealing with an unfamiliar application.

The PAVER™ System

The second unit of analysis involved a full-scale industrial SOA application called PAVER™ [6]. It included a graduate student and professional software engineers experienced in services computing. PAVER™ is a pavement management system for condition-based maintenance management of airport pavements and roadways. The version used in this study had 10 services, which totaled approximately 400,000 lines of Visual Basic code. PAVER™ can be used by pavement engineers in several ways: 1) to develop an inventory of the pavements to be managed; 2) to collect distress data about inventory items using an international standard for such field observations; 3) to model pavement condition over time, and 4) to plan budgets for repair work in order to make the best use of limited resources.

The PAVER™ system is not a typical SOA application because it uses SOA principles to manage the separation of what appears to the user as a unified system into a family of components that are mostly independent yet closely cooperate. The system uses Microsoft's Windows Communication Foundation (WCF) to implement a family of cooperating services that span the major modules within PAVER™. The WSDL and XSD files are generated automatically from interface definitions using specialized WCF tags, and can be used to describe the services in a standard way.

The case study followed the same structure described in Section 4.1, with pre-indexing of the WSDLs and XSDs, a training exercise for the participants, a main study using a questionnaire, and a debrief session. However, the main study was structured somewhat differently since the study dealt with a real application and some participants were professional software engineers having experience with that application. The main study took place in three phases as follows:

- First, a graduate student with some SOA background but no PAVER™ experience went through the questions in a university setting.
- Second, a software engineer at the company that develops PAVER™ worked on the questions and related SOA Miner's responses to his insight from developing the PAVER™ code.
- Third, two software engineers from the PAVER™ development company used SOA Miner searches and compared the results with information obtainable from Microsoft's Visual Studio™ programming environment used in their daily work. They also experimented with allowing Visual Studio to generate a stub client for one of the services to see what information was recoverable in that way.

Case Study Results: Identified Abstractions

Almost all search tools present a low-level worm's eye view of the subject matter. Just as a source code search tool may identify many isolated lines that match search criteria, SOAMiner finds many isolated XML tags. To make changes successfully, a maintainer needs to create for himself a higher-level conceptual view of the software, and this may require many searches. We would like to supplement search results with higher-level abstractions to speed up the maintainers work. For example, a click on a search result could provide a pop-up showing how that isolated result fits into a larger picture as shown in **Figure 4**.

The case study identified a variety of such abstractions. They could be classified roughly as service linkage abstractions that pull together distant information across service boundaries, and summarizing abstractions that eliminate verbose syntax that may hinder understanding. A third category, datatype abstractions, has characteristics of both categories and, because of its importance, is discussed separately in Section 5.

The service linkage abstractions summarize logical chains in XML, which are found by tracing names from one XML element to another. Case study participants identified several relationships between service definitions and service invocations that they felt would help answer questions such as: How do services call each other?

High level-service invokes service. This abstraction would summarize chains similar to:

(BPEL file)

(BPEL file)

(WSDL file)

(WSDL file)

This abstraction essentially ties a BPEL process to the services that it may use since a partner link of the correct type has been declared. It does not establish if or where such usage actually takes place. However the abstraction can provide a high-level view of the potential relationships in a composite application and supports further exploration of input and output data.

Low level-process invokes operation. Summarizes chains similar to:

(BPEL file)

(BPEL file)

(WSDL file)

(WSDL file)

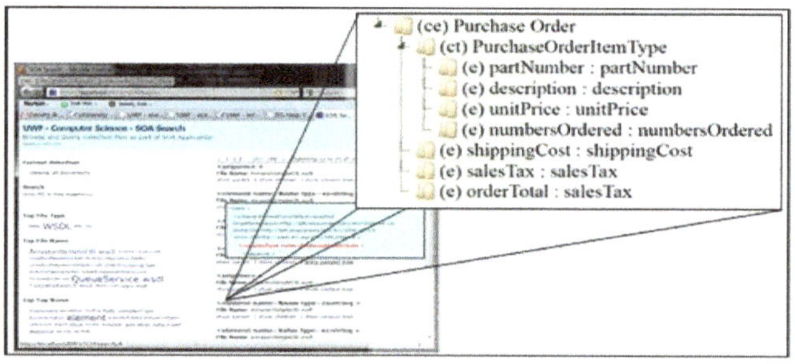

Figure 4. Displaying an abstraction in a search result.

(WSDL file)

(BPEL file of invoked service)

This abstraction ties a BPEL invocation of an operation on a service to the high-level WSDL description and through that to a BPEL implementation of the called operation. This particular chain enables the maintainer to examine the actual code that may be implementing a called service.

Low level—"called by". Summarizes chains similar to:

(BPEL file of invoked service)

(BPEL file of invoked service)

(BPEL file of calling service)

(BPEL file of calling service)

This abstraction allows a maintainer to understand how other BPEL processes may invoke a particular operation implemented in BPEL.

Summarizing abstractions are needed because XML is so verbose and because WSDL and XSD files are often machine generated, making them still more verbose. All the study participants noted that the WSDL/XSD description of a service was too dispersed and hard to navigate. In debrief sessions they all agreed that one solution would be a simple expandable tree abstraction of a service as shown in **Figure 5**. This eliminates many XML tags and provides a more compact description that should be adequate for many purposes.

The best example of machine generated verbosity identified in these studies comes from WCF generated XSD files. **Figure 6** shows how WCF has generated five tags encapsulating an empty , simply to convey the information that the response to a Report Delete operation is empty. The single word "void" could replace the whole structure.

DATATYPE ABSTRACTION AND VISUALIZATION

This research analyzes and expands upon the results of the case study described above to facilitate enhanced program comprehension for SOA systems.

```
+ service
  + operation
    + input message
      + datatype
    + output message
      + datatype
```

Figure 5. Expandable tree abstraction of a service.

```
<xs:element
name="ReportDeleteResponse">
  <xs:complexType>
    <xs:sequence/>
  </xs:complexType>
</xs:element>
```

Figure 6. Datatype description of a void return type.

The case study results showed that naive search can be helpful, but for the combination of structured and unstructured SOA documents, it would be much more useful to combine simple text-based search with additional visualizations and abstractions of the information in the documents. As a result, more advanced search and visualization techniques were developed to simplify the task of locating domain concepts within the system and of performing impact analysis for proposed code enhancements. More specifically, the case study results demonstrated the need for specific abstractions that distill pertinent from irrelevant information and for visualizations to display the pertinent information to software maintainers. This section presents methods that we have developed to enhance SOA program comprehension, including an enhanced search and visualization tool, and tree and Entity Relationship (ER) visualizations of the identified abstractions.

Analysis of the Case Study Results

The results of the case study highlighted the challenge in understanding SOA datatypes and their significance in SOA program comprehension. Experienced study participants emphasized the importance of understanding the data model underlying a SOA application before making any changes to it. The results indicated that while searches for services and for operations went fairly smoothly, searches related to datatypes were substantially more difficult. Data definition information is spread across multiple tags, such as and tags in WSDLs, and , and tags in XSDs. Since a search result shows individual matching tags, the user often has to make multiple searches to identify the entire structure. It is not even easy for SOA maintainers to know in which files to search for datatype information since service authors may choose to reference separate XSD files or to incorporate such information directly into the section of the WSDL itself.

Additionally, the results suggested that it was easy to make time-consuming mistakes in trying to locate datatype information. For example in trying to find the data passed in an inventory query, participants searched for a tag matching the string "inventtoryQuery". However, in an XSD, the datatype can be named in either an tag as depicted in **Figure 7**, or in a tag. Much time may be lost if the maintainer searches on the wrong alternative.

Due to the variety of difficulties identified with datatypes, a high priority for enhanced SOA program comprehension is to provide a compact way of abstracting and visualizing them. An abstraction would be constructed by walking the XML structure and collecting references to each datatype and the elements and types it contains. For visualizing the resulting abstraction, we employ two strategies, a tree view and an ER view, each with its advantages and disadvantages.

```
<element name="inventoryQuery">
  <complexType>
    <sequence>
...
```

Figure 7. Datatype named in the tag.

Tree Visualization of Datatypes

A tree visualization would use an expandable tree view of datatypes. For example, consider a simple XSD element from the section of the Amazon Simple DB WSDL file. Select Response is the payload of the Select Response Msg, which is the result of the Select operation in Amazon Simple DB. The XSD definition of Select Response is:

Here we see that the element Select Response has two child elements that reference Select Result and ResponseMetadata so we would next have to locate these elements. If we continue this location process in total we would need to identify five separate elements scattered throughout Amazon Simple DB WSDL.

As a first visualization alternative, we could display a compact expandable tree view for Select Response:

CES-Select Response

+E-element-Select Result

+E-element-Response Metadata This view uses abbreviations to summarize commonly occurring structures. "CES" denotes a "complex element sequence" and "E" an "element". The view has "+" symbols next to the child elements indicating that they can be expanded. In a user interface, a click on the "+" would expand the tree to show additional information. This allows dependencies for an element to be aggregated and displayed without requiring additional queries by the user. The fully expanded tree view for Select Response is as follows:

CES-Select Response

-E-element-Select Result CES-Select Result

-E-element-Item CTS-Item E-element-Name

-E-element-Attribute CTS-Attribute E-element-Name E-element-Value E-element-Next Token

-E-element-Response Metadata CES-Response Metadata E-element-RequestId E-element-Box Usage However, for a complete visualization of a datatype it would be useful to show how it is used; a right-click or other gesture could show a list of the elements that depend upon it, as shown below. For example, ResponseMetadata is utilized by additional XSD elements besides Select Response. In fact, in this particular WSDL, Response Metadata is a common element of all "response" elements. The enumeration of these dependencies, listed below, provides additional invaluable information about the layout of SOA artifacts.

Response Metadata References:

-Select Result

-Batch Delete Attributes Response

-Delete Attributes Response

-Get Attributes Response

-Batch Put Attributes Response

-Put Attributes Response

-Delete Domain Response

-Domain Metadata Response

-List Domains Response

-Create Domain Response

Entity Relationship Visualization of Datatypes

An alternative to the tree view involves generating an Entity Relationship (ER) view of SOA datatypes. ER diagrams present an abstraction of a data model composed of entities, relationships and attributes. ER diagrams show how entities, which contain attributes, are related, but are not limited to a hierarchical structure. Since not all relationships between data elements are hierarchical in nature or necessarily have a tree structure, the ER model is an effective way of showing all relationships between entities, and has become an established method of presenting relationships between data elements or entities [21].

Entities or complex types (in XML), are depicted by rectangles in ER visualization and are units used to hold data or concepts of data. Characteristics of complex types are referred to as attributes in ER visualization and are depicted in ER diagrams as ovals attached to the entities. Relationships between the entities, denoted by element refs (in XML), are depicted by diamonds in ER diagrams. ER diagrams also show how many of one element is related to another element. For example, as shown in Figure 8, we can see that one Select Result element can be related to many Items, or one Item can be related to many Attributes. And we can also see immediately that Response Meta Data is related to several other entities, not shown in the figure for the sake of brevity.

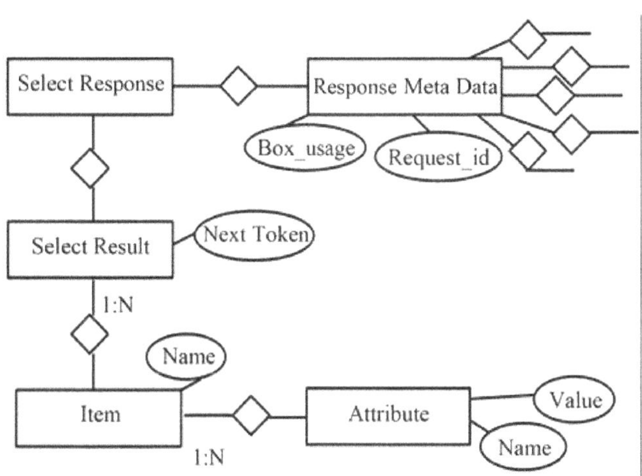

Figure 8. ER visualization of the select response element.

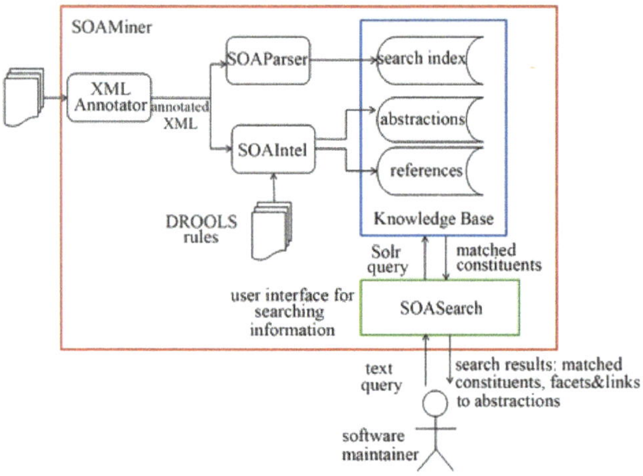

Figure 9. SOA Miner and SOA Intel architecture.

The expandable tree visualization has the advantage of being more compact than an ER diagram and it has a textual representation that could be easier to display in a web browser or similar interactive interface. On the other hand the ER visualization makes use of a well-known modeling method that will be familiar to many software engineers and perhaps conveys more information without the need for mouse clicks or other navigational gestures.

ENHANCING SOA SEARCH WITH SOA INTEL

Modern search technology can help users quickly identify pieces of information whether on the Web or in documents including SOA artifacts. Search can support program comprehension of complex, heterogeneous SOA systems by discovering patterns and links across the various types of documents that compromise SOA composite applications. Research involving SOA Miner has demonstrated the usefulness of exposing information in SOA artifacts to software engineers that can help with maintenance activities. However, search tools can only discover and present patterns as they exist in the documents themselves encoded in the language of the indexed documents. As the case study results have shown, what maintainers need to know most is conceptual information about the composite application, not syntactic information included in the SOA artifacts. They need to know what services are involved in a composite application and what data is being exchanged among services. Thus, while search is useful, we need to be able to transform the search results into meaningful entities. The identified abstractions discussed earlier represent those meaningful units.

Compiling abstractions from the diverse artifacts of SOA composite applications requires interpretation and knowledge of the language that encodes the artifacts. A difficulty is that in the SOA open environment, the relevant abstractions will vary from system to system and over time as standards, practices and tools change.

Thus, we need a flexible approach to complement SOA search and automate the discovery of abstractions within the SOA artifacts. An ideal tool would index the collection of artifacts from a composite application and provide maintainers with two types of information:

1) Abstractions where it can discover them, or
2) Text snippets taken from the artifacts where it cannot.

The tool would also allow for the definition of additional abstractions so that more and more search results can be of the first category. Such a tool would have to be flexible to adapt to a wide range of SOA artifacts from different environments and allow for the inclusion of new abstractions as they are identified by software engineers.

In an effort to extend SOA Miner with the kinds of search capabilities identified from an analysis of the case study results outlined above, we developed SOA Intel, a tool to discover abstractions within SOA artifacts. Figure 9 shows the relationship between SOA Miner, SOA Intel, the SOA artifacts and software maintainers. As shown in the figure, a software maintainer submits a text query using the SOA Search interface. SOA Intel then uses knowledge-based systems methods and applies a rule-based approach to build abstractions from the artifacts. Next, SOA Miner indexes these abstractions to provide them to users upon request. A reasoning engine automates the process of the expert's analysis of SOA artifacts by executing chains of rules on the artifacts once they are committed to the engine's working memory. Matching rules build and store the abstractions in working memory, which can then lead to the discovery of additional abstractions and relationships between them. Finally, after all rules have fired, working memory may be queried to collect the abstractions and store them for future retrieval by SOA Miner in response to user-entered search queries. Each abstraction is formatted as an XML snippet that includes constituents and relations from the SOA artifacts to model the abstraction. More details on the rules can be found in [22].

Rule engines have traditionally been used to capture expert problem solving as a set of rules and apply them to reason about a solution for a new problem. Through experiments and case studies involving domain experts, we can create a set of rules that identify abstractions within the SOA artifacts, and extract and transform them into human-readable representations. In essence, the rules are designed to capture an expert's experience with identifying useful excerpts of information relevant to maintenance problems.

DISCUSSION AND CONCLUSIONS

SOA offers the prospect for greater interoperability among software systems by enabling developers to configure software as services and to interconnect services with other services independent of differences in operating platform and programming and communicating languages. Resulting systems can bridge heterogeneous environments of platforms and languages across institutional boundaries. However, the new languages, infrastructures and flexibility that accompany SOA also introduce new complexities.

From the perspective of software maintenance, SOA systems require:

1) An in-depth understanding of the mechanics involved in the deployment of composite applications and their interaction;
2) Expertise in many different languages and environments that make up a SOA composite application, and
3) Insight into the distribution and ownership of services.

These new challenges make it difficult for maintainers to determine how an existing SOA system actually works.

We believe that searching techniques can help maintainers locate needed information in the large body of artifacts that describe a SOA application. However, search will need to be accompanied by a process of abstraction and visualization to enhance the comprehension of search results. Additional analysis of the case study results identified some of the abstractions and visualizations needed to enhance SOA program comprehension. These were classified as service linking abstractions to identify relationships between services, summarizing abstractions to remove unneeded verbose syntax, and data type visualizations to help understand the data that services share. These abstractions and visualizations distill useful information by compiling dependencies among services and references of messages to data types into single, coherent units free from syntactic overhead of XML encoded machine descriptions. Several visualizations were developed, including trees, Entity Relationships and the framework for an intelligent search-based visualization tool.

Several directions for future work can be explored to provide further support for program comprehension of SOA systems. We are exploring methods for semantic analysis of SOA composite applications, including concept maps [23] and ontologies. Future tools to support SOA maintainers could build on ontologies describing the web services standards, the most common extensions to these standards, and domain concepts from different problem domains such as health care, travel, etc. Information from the ontologies could be used in several ways. It could provide searchable help that a SOA maintainer could use in interpreting the WSDL, XSD, and other documents encountered in his work. It could also provide input for search tools such as SOA Miner for synonym analysis of queries and help prioritize query results.

Research into program comprehension for SOA systems is still at a very early stage and doubtless, many novel tools and techniques remain to be developed. However, as an initial step, we think that search enhanced by abstraction and visualization can make an important contribution in addressing the emerging challenges of SOA maintenance.

ACKNOWLEDGEMENTS

Work described in this paper was partially supported by the University of West Florida Foundation under the Nystul Eminent Scholar Endowment. We would like to thank UWF graduate students Douglas Leal, Joshua Dault and Juan Gil Restrepo who implemented and tested different versions of SOA Miner, and Ben Hartmann and Mircea Manea, Software Engineers at Intelligent Information Technologies, for their participation in the PAVER™ case study.

REFERENCES

1. N. Josuttis, "SOA in Practice: The Art of Distributed Software Design," O'Reilly Media, Sebastopol, 2007.
2. G. Lewis, E. Morris, S. Simanta and D. Smith, "Service Orientation and Systems of Systems," IEEE Software, Vol. 28, No. 1, 2011, pp. 58-63. doi:10.1109/MS.2011.15
3. S. D. Fay and D. G. Holmes, "Help! I Have to Update an Undocumented Program," Proceedings of the IEEE Conference on Software Maintenance-1985, Washington DC, 11-13 November 1985, pp. 192-204.
4. L. White, T. Reichherzer, J. Coffey, N. Wilde and S. Simmons, "Maintenance of Service Oriented Architecture Composite Applications: Static and Dynamic Support," Journal of Software Maintenance and Evolution: Research and Practice, Vol. 25, No. 1, 2011, pp. 97-109. doi:10.1002/smr.568
5. T. Reichherzer, E. El-Sheikh, N. Wilde, L. White, J. Coffey and S. Simmons, "Towards Intelligent Search Support for Web Services Evolution: Identifying the Right Abstractions," Proceedings of 2011 13th IEEE International Symposium on Web Systems Evolution (WSE), Williamsburg, 30 September 2011, pp. 53-58. doi:10.1109/WSE.2011.6081819
6. L. White, N. Wilde, T. Reichherzer, E. El-Sheikh, G. Goehring, A. Baskin, B. Hartmann and M. Manea, "Understanding Interoperable Systems: Challenges for the Maintenance of SOA Applications," Proceedings of the 45th Hawaii International Conference on System Sciences (HICSS), Maui, 4-7 January 2012, pp. 2199-2206.
7. G. Canfora and M. Di Penta, "New Frontiers of Reverse Engineering," Proceedings of the 29th International Conference on Software Engineering, Minneapolis, 20-26 May 2007, pp. 326-341. doi:10.1109/FOSE.2007.15
8. N. Gold, C. Knight, A. Mohan and M. Munro, "Understanding Service-Oriented Software," IEEE Software, Vol. 21, No. 2, 2004, pp. 71-77. doi:10.1109/MS.2004.1270766
9. K. Kontogiannis, "Challenges and Opportunities Related to the Design, Deployment and Operation of Web Services," Proceedings of the 24th Conference on Software Maintenance, Beijing, 28 September-4 October 2008, pp. 11-20. doi:10.1109/FOSM.2008.4659244
10. G. A. Lewis and D. B. Smith, "Service-Oriented Architecture and Its Implications for Software Maintenance and Evolution," Proceedings of the 24th Conference on Software Maintenance, Bejing, 28 September-4 October 2008, pp. 1-10.doi:10.1109/FOSM.2008.4659243
11. M. Kajko-Mattsson, G. A. Lewis and D. B. Smith, "Evolution and Maintenance of SOA-Based Systems at SAS," Proceedings of the 41st Annual Hawaii International Conference on System Sciences (HICSS), Waikoloa, 7-10 January 2008, p. 119.doi:10.1109/HICSS.2008.154
12. M. P. Papazoglou, V. Andrikopoulos and S. Benbernou, "Managing Evolving Services," IEEE Software, Vol. 28, No. 3, 2011, pp. 49-55. doi:10.1109/MS.2011.26
13. N. Gold and K. Bennett, "Program Comprehension for Web Services," Proceedings of the 12th IEEE International Workshop on Program Comprehension, Bari, 24- 26 June 2004, p. 151.
14. W. De Pauw, M. Lei, E. Pring, L. Villard, M. Arnold and J. F. Morar, "Web Services Navigator: Visualizing the Execution of Web Services," IBM Systems Journal, Vol. 44, No. 4, 2005, pp. 821-845. doi:10.1147/sj.444.0821
15. J. Coffey, L. White, N. Wilde and S. Simmons, "Locating Software Features in a SOA Composite Application," Proceedings of the 8th IEEE European Conference on

Web Services (ECOWS'10), Ayia Napa, 1-3 December 2010, pp. 99-106.doi:10.1109/ECOWS.2010.28

16. S. Halle, T. Bultan, G. Hughes, M. Alkhalaf and R. Villemaire, "Runtime Verification of Web Service Interface Contracts," Computer, Vol. 43, No. 3, 2010, pp. 59-66.doi:10.1109/MC.2010.76

17. Apache Software Foundation, "Apache Solr," 2011. http://lucene.apache.org/solr/

18. GitHub Inc., "Evolvingweb/AJAX-Solr," 2012. http://github.com/evolvingweb/ajax-solr

19. P. Runeson and M. Host, "Guidelines for Conducting and Reporting Case Study Research in Software Engineering," Empirical Software Engineering, Vol. 14, No. 2, 2009, pp. 131-164. doi:10.1007/s10664-008-9102-8

20. S. E. Sim, C. L. A. Clarke and R. C. Holt, "Archetypal Source Code Searches: A Survey of Software Developers and Maintainers," Proceedings of the 6th International Workshop on Program Comprehension (IWPC'98), Ischia, 26 June 1998, pp. 180-187.doi:10.1109/WPC.1998.693351

21. S. Bagui and R. Earp, "Database Design Using EntityRelationship Diagrams," 2nd Edition, Auerbach Publications, Boca Raton, 2012.

22. G. Goehring, T. Reichherzer, E. El-Sheikh, D. Snider, N. Wilde, S. Bagui, J. Coffey and L. White, "A KnowledgeBased System Approach for Extracting Abstractions from Service Oriented Architecture Artifacts," International Journal of Advanced Research in Artificial Intelligence, Vol. 2, No. 3, 2013, pp. 44-52.

23. J. Novak and D. Gowin, "Learning How to Learn," Cambridge University Press, New York, 1984. doi:10.1017/CBO9781139173469

Section III - Different SOA Use-Case Scenarios

CHAPTER 10 SERVICE-ORIENTED DATA MINING

Derya Birant

INTRODUCTION

A service is a software building block capable of fulfilling a given task or a distinct business function through a well-defined interface, loosely-coupled interface. Services are like "black boxes", since they operate independently within the system, external components are not aware of how they perform their function, they only care that they return the expected result.

The Service Oriented Architecture (SOA) is a flexible set of design principles used for building flexible, modular, and interoperable software applications. SOA represents a standard model for resource sharing in distributed systems and offers a generic framework towards the integration of diverse systems. Thus, information technology strategy is turning to SOA in order to make better use of current resources, adapt to more rapidly changes and larger development. Another principle of SOA is the reusable software components within different applications and processes.

A Web Service (WS) is a collection of functions that are packaged as a single entity and published to the network for use by other applications through a standard protocol. It offers the possibility of transparent integration between heterogeneous platforms and applications. The popularity of web services is mainly due to the availability of web service standards and the adoption of universally accepted technologies, including XML, SOAP, WSDL and UDDI.

The most important implementation of SOA is represented by web services. Web servicebased SOAs are now widely accepted for on-demand computing as well as for developing more interoperable systems. They provide integration of computational services that can communicate and coordinate with each other to perform goal-directed activities. Among intelligent systems, Data Mining (DM) has been the center of much attention, because it focuses on extracting useful information from large volumes of data. However, building scalable, extensible, interoperable, modular and easy-to-use data mining systems has proved to be difficult. In response, we propose SOMiner (Service Oriented Miner), a service-oriented architecture for data mining that relies on web services to achieve extensibility and interoperability, offers simple abstractions for users, provides scalability by cutting down overhead on the number of web services ported to the platform and supports computationally intensive processing on large amounts of data.

This chapter proposes SOMiner, a flexible service-oriented data mining architecture that incorporates the main phases of knowledge discovery process: data preprocessing, data mining (model construction), result filtering, model validation and model visualization. This architecture is composed of generic and specific web services that provide a large collection of machine learning algorithms written for knowledge discovery tasks such as classification, clustering, and association rules, which can be invoked through a common GUI. We developed a platform-independent interface that users are able to browse the available data mining methods provided, and generate models using the chosen method via this interface. SOMiner is designed to handle large volumes of data, high computational demands, and to be able to serve a very high user population.

The main purpose of this chapter is to resolve the problems that appear widely in the current data mining applications, such as low level of resource sharing, difficult to use data mining algorithms one after another and so on. It explores the advantages of serviceoriented data mining and proposes a novel system named SOMiner. SOMiner offers the necessary support for the implementation of knowledge discovery workflows and has a workflow engine to enable users to compose KDD services for the solution of a particular problem. One important characteristic separates the SOMiner

Citation: Derya Birant (2011). Service-Oriented Data Mining, New Fundamental Technologies in Data Mining, Prof. Kimito Funatsu (Ed.), InTech, DOI: 10.5772/14066.

from its predecessors: it also proposes Semantic Web Services for building a comprehensive high-level framework for distributed knowledge discovery in SOA models.

In this chapter, proposed system has also been illustrated with a case study that data mining algorithms have been used in a service-based architecture by utilizing web services and a knowledge workflow has been constructed to represent potentially repeatable sequences of data mining steps. On the basis of the experimental results, we can conclude that a serviceoriented data mining architecture can be effectively used to develop KDD applications.

The remainder of the chapter is organized as follows. Section 2 reviews the literature, discusses the results in the context of related work, presents a background about SOA+Data Mining approach and describes how related work supports the integrated process. Section 3 presents a detailed description of our system, its features and components, then, describes how a client interface interacts with the designed services and specifies the advantages of the new system. Section 4 demonstrates how the proposed model can be used to analyze a real world data, illustrates all levels of system design in details based on a case study and presents the results obtained from experimental studies. Furthermore, it also describes an evaluation of the system based on the case study and discusses preliminary considerations regarding system implementation and performance. Finally, Section 5 provides a short summary, some concluding remarks and possible future works.

BACKGROUND

Related work

The Web is not the only area that has been mentioned by the SOA paradigm. Also the Grid can provide a framework whereby a great number of services can be dynamically located, managed and securely executed according to the principles of on-demand computing. Since Grids proved effective as platforms for data-intensive computing, some grid-based data mining systems have been proposed such as DataMiningGrid (Stankovski et al., 2008), KnowledgeGrid (K-Grid) (Congiusta et al., 2007), Data Mining Grid Architecture (DMGA) (Perez et al., 2007), GridMiner (Brezany et al., 2005), and Federated Analysis Environment for Heterogeneous Intelligent Mining (FAEHIM) (Ali et al., 2005). A significant difference of these systems from our system (SOMiner) is that they use grid-based solutions and focus on grid-related topics and grid-based aspects such as resource brokering, resource discovery, resource selection, job scheduling and grid security.

Another grid-based and service-based data mining approaches are ChinaGrid (Wu et al., 2009) and Weka4WS (Talia and Trunfio, 2007). A grid middleware ChinaGrid consists of services (data management service, storage resource management service, replication management service, etc.) to offers the fundamental support for data mining applications. Another framework Weka4WS extends the Weka toolkit for supporting distributed data mining on grid environments and for supporting mobile data mining services. Weka4WS adopts the emerging Web Services Resource Framework (WSRF) for accessing remote data mining algorithms and managing distributed computations. In comparison, SOMiner tackles scalability and extensibility problems with availability of web services, without using a grid platform.

Some systems distribute the execution within grid computing environments based on the resource allocation and management provided by a resource broker. For example, Congiusta et al. (2008) introduced a general approach for exploiting grid computing to support distributed data mining by using grids as decentralized high performance platforms where to execute data mining tasks and knowledge discovery algorithms and applications. Talia 2009 discussed a strategy based on the use of services for the design of open distributed knowledge discovery tasks and applications on grids and distributed systems. On the contrary, SOMiner exposes all its functionalities as Web Services, which enable important benefits, such as dynamic service discovery and composition, standard support for authorization and cryptography, and so on.

A few research frameworks currently exist for deploying specific data mining applications on application-specific data. For example, Swain et al. (2010) proposed a distributed system (P-found) that allows scientists to share large volume of protein data i.e. consisting of terabytes and to perform distributed data mining on this dataset. Another example, Jackson et al. (2007) described the development of a Virtual Organisation (VO) to support distributed diagnostics and to address the complex data mining challenges in the condition health monitoring applications. Similarly, Yamany et al. (2010) proposed services (for providing intelligent security), which use three different data mining techniques: the association rules, which helps to predict security attacks, the OnLine Analytical Processing (OLAP) cube, for authorization, and clustering algorithms, which facilitate access control rights representation and automation. However, differently from SOMiner, these works include application-specific services i.e. related to protein folding simulations or condition health monitoring or security attacks.

Research projects such as the Anteater (Guedes et al., 2006) and the DisDaMin (Distributed Data Mining) (Olejnik et al., 2009) have built distributed data mining environments, mainly focusing on parallelism. Anteater uses parallel algorithms for data mining such as parallel implementations of Apriori (for frequent item set mining), ID3 (for building classifiers) and K-Means (for clustering). DisDaMin project was addressed distributed discovery and knowledge discovery through parallelization of data mining tasks. However it is difficult to implement the parallel versions of some data mining algorithms. Thus, SOMiner provides parallelism through the execution of traditional data mining algorithms in parallel with different web services on different nodes.

Several studies mainly related to the implementation details of data mining services on different software development platforms. For example, Du et al. (2008) presented a way to set up a framework for designing the data mining system based on SOA by the use of WCF (Windows Communication Foundation). Similarly, Chen et al. (2006) presented architecture for data mining metadata web services based on Java Data Ming (JDM) in a grid environment.

Several previous works proposed a service-oriented computing model for data mining by providing a markup language. For example, Discovery Net (Sairafi et al., 2003) provided a Discovery Process Markup Language (DPML) which is an XML-based representation of the workflows. Tsai & Tsai (2005) introduced a Dynamic Data Mining Process (DDMP) system in which web services are dynamically linked using Business Process Execution Language for Web Service (BPEL4WS) to construct a desired data mining process. Their model was described by Predictive Model Markup Language (PMML) for data analysis.

A few works have been done in developing service-based data mining systems for general purposes. On the other side, Ari et al., 2008 integrated data mining models with business services using a SOA to provide real-time Business Intelligence (BI), instead of traditional BI. They accessed and used data mining model predictions via web services from their platform. Their purposes were managing data mining models and making business-critical decisions. While some existing systems such as (Chen et al., 2003) only provide the specialized data mining functionality, SOMiner includes functionality for designing complete knowledge discovery processes such as data preprocessing, pattern evaluation, result filtering and visualization.

Our approach is not similar in many aspects to other studies that provided a service-based middleware for data mining. First, SOMiner has no any restriction with regard to data mining domains, applications, techniques or technology. It supports a simple interface and a service composition mechanism to realize customized data mining processes and to execute a multi-step data mining application, while some systems seem to lack a proper workflow editing and management facility. SOMiner tackles scalability and extensibility problems with availability of web services, without using a grid platform. Besides data mining services, SOMiner provides services implementing the main steps of a KDD process such as data preprocessing, pattern evaluation, result filtering and visualization. Most existing systems don't adequately address all these concerns together.

To the best of our knowledge, none of the existing systems makes use of Semantic Web Services as a technology. Therefore, SOMiner is the first system leveraging Semantic Web Services for building a comprehensive high-level framework for distributed knowledge discovery in SOA models, supporting also the integration of data mining algorithms exposed through an interface that abstracts the technical details of data mining algorithms.

SOA + Data Mining

Simple client-server data mining solutions have scalability limitations that are obvious when we consider both multiple large databases and large numbers of users. Furthermore, these solutions require significant computational resources, which might not be widely available. For these reasons, in this study, we propose service-oriented data mining solutions to be able to expand the computing capacity simply and transparently, by just advertising new services through an interface.

On the other side, while traditional Grid systems are rather monolithic, characterized by a rigid structure; the SOA offers a generic approach towards the integration of diverse systems. Additional features of SOA, such as interoperability, self-containment of services, and stateless services, bring more value than a grid-based solution. In SOA+Data Mining model, SOA enables the assembly of web services through parts of the data mining applications, regardless of their implementation details, deployment location, and initial objective of their development. In other words, SOA can be viewed as architecture that provides the ability to build data mining applications that can be composed at runtime using already existing web services which can be invoked over a network.

MINING IN A SERVICE-ORIENTED ARCHITECTURE

SOMiner Architecture

This chapter proposes a new system SOMiner (Service Oriented Miner) that offers to users high-level abstractions and a set of web services by which it is possible to integrate resources in a SOA model to support all phases of the knowledge discovery process such as data management, data mining, and knowledge representation. SOMiner is easily extensible due to its use of web services and the natural structure of SOA - just adding new resources (data sets, servers, interfaces and algorithms) by simply advertising them to the application servers.

The SOMiner architecture is based on the standard life cycle of knowledge discovery process. In short, users of the system can be able to understand what data is in which database as well as their meaning, select the data on which they want to work, choose and apply data mining algorithms to the data, have the patterns represented in an intuitive way, receive the evaluation results of patterns mined, and possibly return to any of the previous steps for new tries.

SOMiner is composed of six layers: data layer, application layer, user layer, data mining service layer, semantic layer and complementary service layer. A high speed enterprise service bus integrates all these layers, including data warehouses, web services, users, and business applications.

The SOMiner architecture is depicted in the diagram of Fig. 1. It is an execution environment that is designed and implemented according to a multi-layer structure. All interaction during the processing of a user request happens over the Web, based on a user interface that controls access to the individual services. An example knowledge discovery workflow is as follows: when the business application gets a request from a user, it firstly calls data preparation web service to make dataset ready for data mining task(s), and then related data mining service(s) is activated for analyzing data. After that, evaluation service is invoked as a complementary service to validate data mining results. Finally, presentation service is called to represent knowledge in a manner (i.e. drawing conclusions) as to facilitate inference from data mining results.

Data Layer: The Data Layer (DL) is responsible for the publication and searching of data to be mined (data sources), as well as handling metadata describing data sources. In other words, they are responsible for the access interface to data sets and all associated metadata. The metadata are in XML and describes each attribute's type, whether they represent continuous or categorized entities, and other things.

DL includes services: Data Access Service (DAS), Data Replication Service (DRS), and Data Discovery Service (DDS). Additional specific services can also be defined for the data management without changes in the rest of the framework.

The DAS can retrieve descriptions of the data, transfer bases from one node to another, and execute SQL-based queries on the data. Data can be fed into the DAS from existing data warehouses or from other sources (flat files, data marts, web documents etc.) when it has already been preprocessed, cleaned, and organized. The DRS deals with data replication task which is one important aspect related to SOA model. DDS improves the discovery phase in SOA for mining applications.

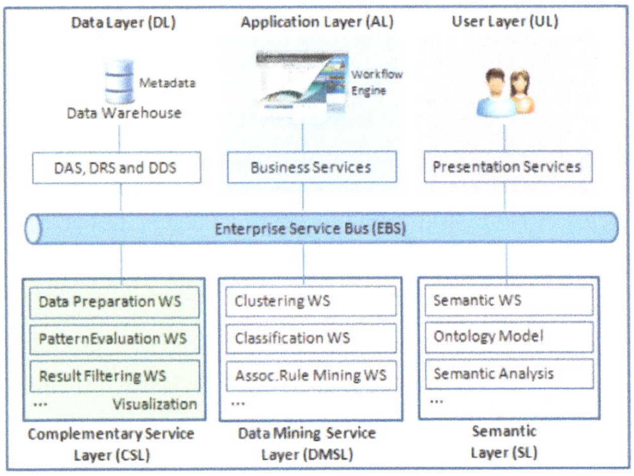

Figure 1. SOMiner: a service-oriented architecture (SOA) for data mining

Application Layer: Application Layer (AL) is responsible for business services related to the application. Users don't interact directly with all services or servers - that's also the responsibility of the AL. It controls user interaction and returns the results to any user action. When a user starts building a data mining application, the AL looks for available data warehouses, queries them about their data and presents that information back to the user along with metadata. The user then selects a dataset, perhaps even further defines data preprocessing operations according to certain criteria. The AL then identifies which data mining services are available, along with their algorithms. When the user chooses the data mining algorithm and defines the arguments of it, the task is then ready to be processed. For the latter task, the AL informs the result filtering, pattern evaluation and visualization services. Complementary service layer builds these operations and sends the results back to the AL for presentation. SOMiner saves all these tasks to the user's list from which it can be scheduled for execution, edited for updates, or selected for visualization again.

User Layer: User Layer (UL) provides the user interaction with the system. The Results Presentation Services (RPS) offer facilities for presenting and visualizing the extracted knowledge models (e.g., association rules, classification rules, and clustering models). As mentioned before, a user can publish and search resources and services, design and submit data mining applications, and visualize results. Such users may want to make specific choices in terms of defining and configuring a data mining process such as algorithm selection, parameter setting, and preference specification for web services used to execute a particular data mining application. However, with the transparency advantage, end users have limited knowledge of the underlying data mining and web service technologies.

Data Mining Service Layer: Data Mining Service Layer (DMSL) is the fundamental layer in the SOMiner system. This layer is composed of generic and specific web services that provide a large collection of machine learning algorithms written for knowledge discovery tasks. In DMSL, each web service provides a different data mining task such as classification, clustering and association rule mining (ARM). They can be published, searched and invoked separately or consecutively through a common GUI. Enabling these web services for running on large-scale SOA systems facilitates the development of flexible, scalable and distributed data mining applications.

This layer processes datasets and produces data mining results as output. To handle very huge datasets and the associated computational costs, the DMSL can be distributed over more than one node. The drawback related to this layer, however, is that it is now necessary to implement a web service for each data mining algorithm. This is a time consuming process, and requires the scientist to have some understanding of web services.

Complementary Service Layer: Complementary Service Layer (CSL) provides knowledge discovery processes such as data preparation, pattern evaluation, result filtering, visualization, except data mining process. Data Preparation Service provides data preprocessing operations such as data collection, data integration, data cleaning, data transformation, and data reduction. Pattern Evaluation Service performs the validation of data mining results to ensure the correctness of the output and the accuracy of the model. This service provides validation methods such as Simple Validation, Cross Validation, nFold Cross Validation, Sum of Square Errors (SSE), Mean Square Error (MSE), Entropy and Purity. If validation results are not satisfactory, data mining services can be re-executed with different parameters more than one times until finding an accurate model and result set.

Result Filtering Service allows users to consider only some part of results set in visualization or to highlight particular subsets of patterns mined. Users may use this service to find the most interesting rules in the set or to indicate rules that have a given item in the rule consequent. Similarly, in ARM, users may want to observe only association rules with kitemsets, where k is number of items provided by user. Visualization is often seen as a key component within many data mining applications. An important aspect of SOMiner is its visualization capability, which helps users from other areas of expertise easily understand the output of data mining algorithms. For example, a graph can be plotted using an appropriate visualize for displaying clustering results or a tree can be plotted to visualize classification (decision tree) results. Visualization capability can be provided by using different drawing libraries.

Semantic Layer: On the basis of those previous experiences we argue that it is necessary to design and implement semantic web services that will be provided by the Semantic Layer (SL), i.e. ontology model, to offer the semantic description of the functionalities. Enterprise Service Bus: The Enterprise Service Bus (ESB) is a middleware technology providing the necessary characteristics in order to support SOA. ESB can be sometimes considered as being the seventh layer of the architecture. The ESB layer offers the necessary support for transport interconnections. Translation specifications are provided to the ESB in a standard format and the ESB provides translation facilities. In other words, the ESB is used as a means to integrate and deploy a dynamic workbench for the web service collaboration. With the help of the ESB, services are exposed in a uniform manner, such that any user, who is able to consume web services over a generic or specific transport, is able to access them. The ESB keeps a registry of all connected parts, and routes messages between these parts. Since the ESB is solving all integration issues, each layer only focuses on its own functionalities.

SOMiner is easily extensible, as such; administrators easily add new servers or web services or databases as long as they have an interface; they can increase computing power by adding services or databases to independent mining servers or nodes. Similarly, end users can use any server or service for their task, as long as the application server allows it.

Application Modeling and Representation

SOMiner has the capability of composition of services, that is, the ability to create workflows, which allows several services to be scheduled in a flexible manner to build a solution for a problem. As shown in Fig. 2, a service composition can be made in three ways: horizontal, vertical and hybrid. Horizontal composition refers to a chain-like combination of different functional services; typically the output of one service corresponds to the input of another service, and so on. One common example of horizontal composition is the combination of pre-processing, data mining and post-processing functions for completing KDD process. In vertical composition, several services, which carry out the same or different functionalities, can be executed at the same time on different datasets or on different data portions. By using vertical composition, it is possible to improve the performance in a parallel way. Hybrid composition combines horizontal and vertical compositions, and provides one-to-many cardinality, typically the output of one service corresponds to the input of more than one services or vice versa.

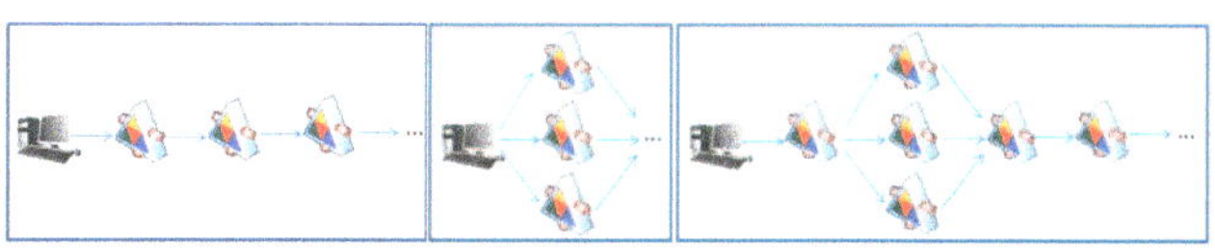

Figure 2. Workflow types: horizontal composition, vertical composition, and hybrid

A workflow in SOMiner consists of a set of KDD services exposed via an interface and a toolbox which contains set of tools to interact with web services. The interface provides the users a simple way to design and execute complex data mining applications by exploiting the advantages coming from a SOA environment. In particular, it offers a set of facilities to design data mining applications starting from a view of available data, web services, and data mining algorithms to different steps for displaying results. A user needs only a browser to access SOMiner resources. The toolbox lets users choose from different visual components to perform KDD tasks, reducing the need for training users in data mining specifics, since many details of the application, such as the data mining algorithms, are hidden behind this visual notation.

Designing and executing a data mining application over the SOMiner is a multi-step task that involves interactions and information flows between services at the different levels of the architecture. We designed toolbox as a set of components that offer services through well defined interfaces, so that users can employ them as needed to meet the application needs. SOMiners's components are based on major points of the KDD problem that the architecture should address, such as accessing to a database, executing a mining task(s), and visualizing the results.

Fig. 3 shows a screenshot from the interface which allows the construction of knowledge discovery flows in SOMiner. While, on the left hand side, the user is provided with a collection of tools (toolbox) to perform KDD tasks, on the right hand side, the user is provided with workspace for composing services to build an application. Tasks are visual components that can be graphically connected to create a particular knowledge workflow. The connection between tasks is made by dragging an arrow from the output node of the sending task to the input node of the receiving task. Sample workflow in Fig. 3 was composed of seven services: data preparation, clustering, evaluation of clustering results,

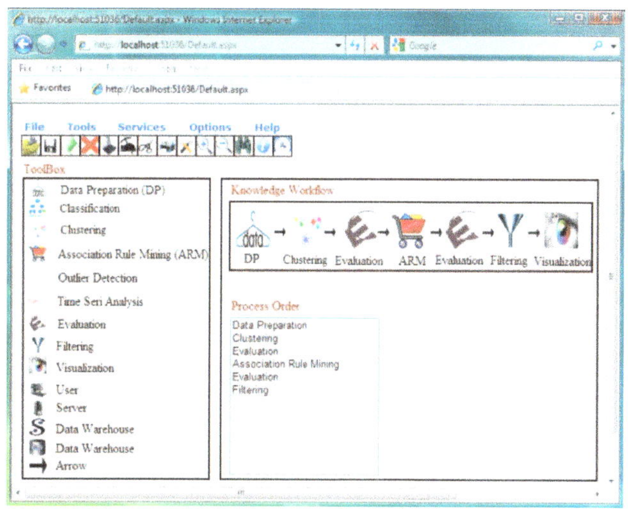

Figure 3. Screenshot from the interface used for the construction of knowledge workflows

ARM, evaluation of association rules, filtering results according to user requests, and visualization. Interaction between the workflow engine and each web service instance is supported through pre-defined SOAP messages. If a user chooses a particular web service from the place on the composition area, a URL specifying the location of the WSDL document can be seen, along with the data types that are necessary to invoke the particular web service.

Advantages of Service-Oriented Data Mining

Adopting SOA for data mining has at least three advantages: (i) implementing data mining services without having to deal with interfacing details such as the messaging protocol, (ii) extending and modifying data mining applications by simply creating or discovering new services, and (iii) focusing on business or science problems without having to worry about data mining implementations. (Cheung et al., 2006) Some key advantages of service-oriented data mining system (SOMiner) include the following:

1. Transparency: End-users can be able to carry out the data mining tasks without needing to understand

detailed aspects of the underlying data mining algorithms. Furthermore, end-users can be able to concentrate on the knowledge discovery application they must develop, without worrying about the SOA infrastructure and its low-level details.

2. Application development support: Developers of data mining solutions can be able to enable existing data mining applications, techniques and resources with little or no intervention in existing application code.
3 .Interoperability: The system will be based on widely used web service technology. As a key feature, web services are the elementary facilitators of interoperability in the case of SOAs.
4. Extensibility: System provides extensibility by allowing existing systems to integrate with new tasks, just adding new resources (data sets, servers, interfaces and algorithms) by simply advertising them to the system.
5. Parallelism: System supports processing on large amounts of data through parallelism.
6. Different parts of the computation are executed in parallel on different nodes, taking advantage at the same time of data distribution and web service distribution.
7. Workflow capabilities: The system facilitates the construction of knowledge discovery workflows. Thus, users can reuse some parts of the previously composed service flows to further strengthen the data mining application development's agility.
8. Maintainability: System provides maintainability by allowing existing systems to change only a partial task(s) and thus to adapt more rapidly to changing in data mining applications.
9. Visual abilities: An important aspect of the system is its visual components, since many details of the application are hidden behind this visual notation.
10. Fault tolerance: The application can continue to operation without interruption in the presence of partial network failures, or failures of the some software components, taking advantage of data distribution and web service distribution.

Collaborative: A number of science and engineering projects can be performed in collaborative mode with physically distributed participants.

A significant advantage of SOMiner over previous systems is that SOMiner is intended for using semantic web services to the semantic level, i.e. ontology model and offer the semantic description of the functionalities. For example, it allows integration of data mining tasks with ontology information available from the web.

Overall, we believe the collection of advantages and features of SOMiner make it a unique and competitive contender for developing new data mining applications on service-oriented computing environments.

CASE STUDY

SOMiner at work

In this section, we describe a case study and experimental results obtained by the construction of a knowledge workflow in which data in a data warehouse was analyzed by using clustering and ARM algorithms, with the goal of evaluating the performance of the system. In the case study, interface within the SOMiner framework has been used to implement a data mining application related to dried fruit industry, and obtained significant results in terms of performance. The analyzed data provided by a dried fruits company in Turkey consists of about three years of sales data collected within the period January 2005 and April 2008. The complete data that consists of five tables (customers, products, sales, sales details, and branches) included about 56,000 customers, 325 products, 721,000 sales and 3,420,000 sales details. Fig. 4 shows the star schema of the data warehouse that consists of a fact table with many dimensions.

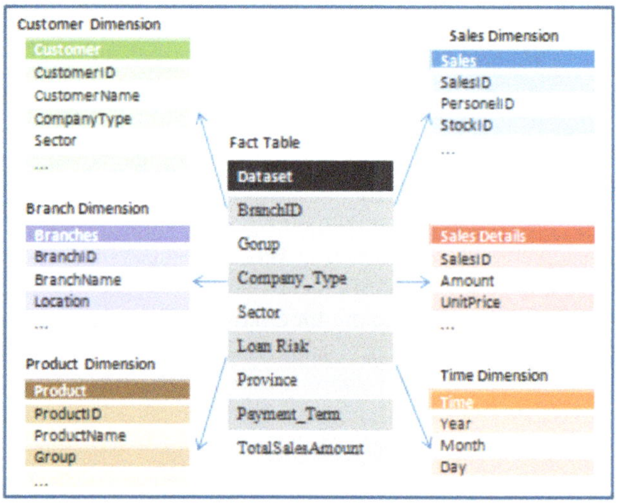

Figure 4. Star schema of the data warehouse used in the case study

In the case study, once clustering task was used to find customer segments with similar profiles, and then association rule mining was carried out to the each customer segment for product recommendation. The main advantage of this application is to be able to adopt different product recommendations for different customer segments. Based on our servicebased data mining architecture, Fig. 5 shows the knowledge discovery workflow constructed in this case study, which represents pre-processing steps, potentially repeatable sequences of data mining tasks and post-preprocessing steps. So, we defined a data mining application as an executable software program that performs two data mining tasks and some complementary tasks.

In the scenario, first, (1) the client sends a business request and then (2) this request is sent to application server for invoking data preparation service. After data-preprocessing, (3) data warehouse is generated, (4) clustering service is invoked to segment customers, and then (5) clustering results are evaluated to ensure the quality of clusters. After this step, (6) more than one ARM web services are executed in parallel for discovering association rules for different customer segments. (7) After the evaluation of ARM results by using Lift and Loevinger thresholds, (8) the results are filtered according to user-defined parameters to highlight particular subsets of patterns mined. For example, users may want to observe only association rules with k-itemsets, where k is number of items provided by user. Finally, (9) visualization service is invoked to plot a graph for displaying results.

Figure 5. An example knowledge discovery workflow

Given the design and implementation benefits discussed in section 3.3, another key aspect in evaluating the system is related to its performance in supporting data mining services execution. In order to evaluate the performance of the system, we performed some experiments to measure execution times of the different steps. The data mining application described above has been tested on deployments composed from 4 association rule mining (ARM) web services; in other words, customers are firstly divided into 4 groups (customer segments), and then 4 ARM web services are executed in parallel for different customer segments (clusters). Each node was a 2.4 GHz Centrino with 4 GB main memory and network connection speed was 100.0 Mbps. We performed all experiments with a minimum support value of 0.2 percent. In the experiments, we used different datasets with sizes ranging from 5Mbytes to 20Mbytes.

While in the clustering experiments we used the customer and their transactions (sales) data available at the data warehouse, in the ARM, we used products and transaction details (sales details) data. Expectation-Maximization (EM) algorithm for clustering task and Apriori algorithm for ARM were implemented as two separate web services. The execution times have been shown in Table 1. It reports the times needed to complete the different phases: file transfer, data preparation, task submission (invoking the services), data mining (clustering and ARM), and results notification (result evaluation and visualization).

Values reported in the Table 1 refer to the execution times obtained for different dataset sizes. The table shows that the data mining phase takes averagely 81.1% of the total execution time, while the file transfer phase fluctuate around 12.8%. The overhead due to the other operations – data preparation, task submission, result evaluation and visualization – is very low with respect to the overall execution time, decreasing from 6.5% to 5.4% with the growth of the dataset size. The results also show that we achieved efficiencies greater than 73 percent, when we execute 4 web services in parallel, instead of one web service.

Table 1. Execution times (in milliseconds) needed to complete the different phases

Dataset Size	File Transfer	Data Prepar.	Task Submission	Data Mining			Results Notification
				EM	Apriori	Total	
5 MB	3,640	1,820	212	7,110	29,156	36,266	691
10 MB	5,437	1,995	253	13,251	24,031	37,282	720
15 MB	8,287	2,064	248	18,343	23,477	41,820	862
20 MB	11,071	2,218	264	34,528	23,233	57,761	1,485

The file transfer and data mining execution times changed because of the different dataset sizes and algorithm complexity. In particular, the file transfer execution time ranged from 3,640 ms for the dataset of 5MB to 11,071 ms for the dataset of 20MB, while the data mining execution time ranged from 36,266 ms for the dataset 5 MB to 57,761 ms for 20MB. In general, it can be observed that the overhead introduced by the SOA model is not critical with respect to the duration of the service-specific operations. This is particularly true in typical KDD applications, in which data mining algorithms working on large datasets are expected to take a long processing time. On the basis of our experimental results, we conclude that SOA model can be effectively used to develop services for KDD applications.

DISCUSSION AND EVALUATION

The case study has been useful for evaluating the overall system under different aspects, including its performance. Given these basic results, we can conclude that SOMiner is suitable to be exploited for developing services and knowledge discovery applications in SOA.

In order to improve the performance moreover, the following proposals should be considered:

- To avoid delays due to data transfers during computation, every mining server should have an associated local data server, in which data is kept before the mining task executes.
- To reduce computational costs, data mining algorithms should be implemented in more than one web services which are located over different nodes. This allows the execution of the data mining components in the knowledge flow on different web services.
- To reduce computational costs, the same web services should be located over more than one node. In this way, the overall execution time can be significantly reduced because different parts of the computation are executed in parallel on different nodes, taking advantage at the same time of data distribution.
- To get results faster, if the server is busy with another task, it should send the user an identifier to use in any further communication regarding that task. A number of idle workstations should be used to execute data mining

web services, the availability of scalable algorithms is key to effectively using the resources.

Overall we believe the collection of features of SOMiner make it a unique and competitive contender for developing new data mining applications on service-oriented computing environments.

CONCLUSION

Data mining services in SOA are key elements for practitioners who need to develop knowledge discovery applications that use large and remotely dispersed datasets and/or computers to get results in reasonable times and improve their competitiveness. In this chapter, we address the definition and composition of services for implementing knowledge discovery applications on SOA model. We propose a new system, SOMiner that supports knowledge discovery on SOA model by providing mechanisms and higher level services for composing existing data mining services as structured, compound services and interface to allow users to design, store, share, and re-execute their applications, as well as manage their output results.

SOMiner allows miners to create and manage complex knowledge discovery applications composed as workflows that integrate data sets and mining tools provided as services in SOA. Critical features of the system include flexibility, extensibility, scalability, conceptual simplicity and ease of use. One of the goals with SOMiner was to create a data mining system that doesn't require users to know details about the algorithms and their related concepts. To achieve that, we designed an interface and toolkit, handling most of the technical details transparently, so that results would be shown in a simple way. Furthermore, this is the first time that a service-oriented data mining architecture proposes a solution with semantic web services. In experimental studies, the system has been evaluated on the basis of a case study related to marketing. According to the experimental results, we conclude that SOA model can be effectively used to develop services for knowledge discovery applications.

Some further works can be added to make the system perform better. First, security problems (authorization, authentication, etc.) related to the adoption of web services can be solved. Second, a tool can be developed to automatically transfer the current traditional data mining applications to the service-oriented data mining framework.

REFERENCES

1. Ali, A.S.; Rana, O. & Taylor, I. (2005). Web services composition for distributed data mining, Proceedings of the 2005 IEEE International Conference on Parallel Processing Workshops, ICPPW'05, pp. 11-18, ISBN: 0-7695-2381-1, Oslo, Norway, June 2005, IEEE Computer Society, Washington, DC, USA.
2. Ari, I.; Li, J.; Kozlov, A. & Dekhil, M. (2008). Data mining model management to support real-time business intelligence in service-oriented architectures, HP Software University Association Workshop, White papers, Morocco, June 2008, HewlettPackard.
3. Brezany, P.; Janciak, I. & Tjoa, A.M. (2005). GridMiner: A fundamental infrastructure for building intelligent grid systems, Proceedings of the 2005 IEEE/WIC/ACM International Conference on Web Intelligence (WI'05), pp. 150-156, ISBN: 0-7695-2415-x, Compiegne, France, September 2005, IEEE Computer Society.
4. Chen, N.; Marques, N.C. & Bolloju, N. (2003). A Web Service-based approach for data mining in distributed environments, Proceedings of the 1st Workshop on Web Services: Modeling, Architecture and Infrastructure (WSMAI-2003), pp. 74-81, ISBN 972-98816-4-2, Angers, France, April 2003, ICEIS Press 2003.
5. Chen, P.; Wang, B.; Xu, L.; Wu, B. & Zhou, G. (2006). The design of data mining metadata web service architecture based on JDM in grid environment, Proceedings of First International Symposium on Pervasive Computing and Applications, pp. 684-689, ISBN: 1-4244-0326-x, Urumqi, China, August 2006, IEEE.
6. Cheung, W.K.; Zhang, X-F.; Wong, H-F.; Liu, J.; Luo, Z-W. & Tong, F.C.H., (2006). Serviceoriented distributed data mining, IEEE Internet Computing, Vol. 10, No. 4, (July/August 2006) pp. 44-54, ISSN:1089-7801.
7. Congiusta, A.; Talia, D. & Trunfio, P. (2007). Distributed data mining services leveraging WSRF, Future Generation Computer Systems, Vol. 23, No. 1, (January 2007) 34–41, ISSN: 0167-739X.
8. Congiusta, A.; Talia, D. & Trunfio, P. (2008). Service-oriented middleware for distributed data mining on the grid, Journal of Parallel and Distributed Computing, Vol. 68, No. 1, (January 2008) 3-15, ISSN: 0743-7315.
9. Du, H.; Zhang, B. & Chen, D. (2008). Design and actualization of SOA-based data mining system, Proceedings of 9th International Conference on Computer-Aided Industrial Design and Conceptual Design (CAID/CD), pp. 338–342, ISBN: 978-1-4244-3290-5, Kunming, November 2008.
10. Guedes, D.; Meira, W.J. & Ferreira, R. (2006). Anteater: A service-oriented architecture for high-performance data mining, IEEE Internet Computing, Vol. 10, No. 4, (July/August 2006) 36–43, ISSN: 1089-7801.
11. Jackson, T.; Jessop, M.; Fletcher, M. & Austin, J. (2007). A virtual organisation deployed on a service orientated architecture for distributed data mining applications, Grid-Based Problem Solving Environments, Vol. 239, Gaffney, P.W.; Pool, J.C.T. (Eds.), pp. 155- 170, Springer Boston, ISSN: 1571-5736.
12. Olejnik, R.; Fortiş, T.-F. & Toursel, B. (2009) Web services oriented data mining in knowledge architecture, Future Generation Computer Systems, Vol. 25, No. 4, (April 2009) 436-443, ISSN: 0167-739X.
13. Perez, M.; Sanchez, A.; Robles, V.; Herrero, P. & Pena, J.M. (2007). Design and implementation of a data mining grid-aware architecture, Future Generation Computer Systems, Vol. 23, No. 1, (January 2007) 42–47, ISSN: 0167-739X.
14. Sairafi, S.A.; Emmanouil, F.S.; Ghanem, M.; Giannadakis, N.; Guo, Y.; Kalaitzopolous, D.; Osmond, M.; Rowe, A.; Syed, J. & Wendel, P. (2003). The design of discovery net: Towards open grid services for knowledge discovery, International Journal of High Performance Computing Applications, Vol. 17, No. 3, (August 2003) 297–315, ISSN: 1094-3420.

15. Stankovski, V.; Swain, M.; Kravtsov, V.; Niessen, T.; Wegener, D.; Kindermann, J. & Dubitzky, W. (2008). Grid-enabling data mining applications with DataMiningGrid: An architectural perspective, Future Generation Computer Systems, Vol. 24, No. 4, (April 2008) 259–279, ISSN: 0167-739X.

16. Swain, M.; Silva, C.G.; Loureiro-Ferreira, N.; Ostropytskyy, V.; Brito, J.; Riche, O.; Stahl, F.; Dubitzky, W. & Brito, R.M.M. (2009). P-found: Grid-enabling distributed repositories of protein folding and unfolding simulations for data mining, Future Generation Computer Systems, Vol. 26, No. 3, (March 2010) 424-433, ISSN: 0167-739X.

17. Talia, D. (2009). Distributed data mining tasks and patterns as services, Euro-Par 2008 Workshops - Parallel Processing, Lecture Notes in Computer Science, pp. 415-422, Springer Berlin / Heidelberg, ISSN: 0302-9743.

18. Talia D. & Trunfio, P. (2007). How distributed data mining tasks can thrive as services on grids, National Science Foundation Symposium on Next Generation of Data Mining and Cyber-Enabled Discovery for Innovation (NGDM'07), Baltimore, USA, October 2007.

19. Tsai, C.-Y. & Tsai, M.-H. (2005). A dynamic web service based data mining process system, Proceedings of the 2005 The Fifth International Conference on Computer and Information Technology (CIT'05), pp. 1033-1039, IEEE Computer Society, Washington, DC, USA.

20. Wu, S.; Wang, W.; Xiong, M. & Jin, H. (2009). Data management services in ChinaGrid for data mining applications, Emerging Technologies in Knowledge Discovery and Data Mining, pp. 421-432, Springer Berlin / Heidelberg, ISSN: 0302-9743.

21. Yamany, H.F.; Capretz, M. & Alliso, D.S. (2010). Intelligent security and access control framework for service-oriented architecture, Information and Software Technology, Vol. 52, No. 2, (February 2010) 220-236, ISSN: 0950-5849.

CHAPTER 11 SOA-BASED AERONAUTICAL SERVICE INTEGRATION

Yifang Liu, Yongqiang Cheng, Yim Fun Hu, Prashant Pillai and Vincenzo Esposito

INTRODUCTION

Over the past two decades, the air transport industry has experienced continuous growth. The demand for passenger air traffic is forecast to double the current level by about 2025 (European Organisation for the Safety of Air Navigation [EUROCONTROL], 2006). Smallto-medium sized low cost airlines in Europe such as EasyJet and Ryanair have observed a considerable percentage of passenger increase between 2008 and 2009 due to the growth in the number of regional airports and more choices offered on international destinations (EasyJet & Ryanair, 2009). To accommodate such growth and changes in new flight patterns and strategies, it is of paramount importance to ensure air transport communication systems around the globe be integrated to enable efficient air-to-ground and ground-to-ground communications for global air traffic management and coordination.

Traditional approaches for aeronautical system integration in the past impose a high level of system dependencies; a fixed connection is required to be set up every time a new application is added. Therefore, aviation companies are facing continuous investment increase every time a new connection is established. This situation discourages enterprises from fulfilling grater business values by adding interior constraints; it restricts the number of applications and services that can be integrated into the existing IT infrastructure. In safety-critical systems in the aeronautical context, overloaded complex system structure will increase the chances of operational failures and jeopardise passenger safety. Therefore, it is important to devise a suitable architecture which minimises system dependencies and allows new applications to be integrated easily with the lowest IT maintenance budget. A layer-extensible blueprint in a Service-Oriented Architecture (SOA) is considered as a solution in this case for the integration of future aeronautical communication systems. The proposed framework should allow consistent data capturing and sharing among all end users who are involved in the global aircraft operations in the 2020 timeframe and beyond. In recent years, the SESAR SWIM (Single European Sky Air Traffic Management Research System Wide Information Management) concept has reflected the emerging needs and willingness of Air Traffic Management (ATM) organisations in transforming proprietary ATM systems into a standardised and interoperable information pool in the pan-European aeronautical network. As the challenge still exists where the ATM stakeholders today do not want to deal with the complexity of the lower communication layers, SOA is considered as one of the most effective emerging technologies to provide a scalable, flexible and interoperable system framework, according the adoption of the SOA paradigm in the global SWIM studies (Houdebert & Ayral, 2010; Luckenbaugh et al., 2007). However, SWIM focuses on ground-to-ground aeronautical services. In extending the SWIM ideology to an airborne context, the EU FP7 project SANDRA (Seamless Aeronautical Networking through integration of Data-Links, Radios and Antennas) continues with the SOA notion in air-to-ground information exchange, service composition and integration to provide a complete and coherent set of communication services for Next Generation global Air Traffic Management.

Building on the investigation and analysis of the existing industrial programmes targeting aeronautical service integration, this chapter provides an introduction of the SOA-based

Citation: Yifang Liu, Yongqiang Cheng, Yim Fun Hu, Prashant Pillai and Vincenzo Esposito (2011). SOA-Based Aeronautical Service Integration, Future Aeronautical Communications, Dr. Simon Plass (Ed.), InTech, DOI: 10.5772/29307.

future avionic systems. Section two outlines the middleware concept, the service-oriented architecture, its implementation technologies and the use of SOA design solutions forming an integrated ATM framework. Section three summarises the SOA-based future aeronautical communication referring to the SESAR and FAA (Federal Aviation Administration) SWIM approaches for information fusion and dissemination for ground-toground service integration. The SWIM ATM added-value services, data access services and technical services defined in Section three are used as a baseline for the definition of the SANDRA Airborne Middleware (SAM) through the utilisation of a set of airborne/ground data domain objects, as described in Section four. Finally, analysis of the service improvement methods and the technology options for future ATM system realisation is addressed at the end of this chapter.

SOA IN AERONAUTICAL COMMUNICATION

SOA is an emerging middleware approach for linking various legacy systems into a standard platform to achieve a highly interoperable and collaborative communication infrastructure. It permits the separation of legacy system service interfaces from the underlying implementation, thus to reduce technology-dependent attributes of the system. SOA promotes service reusability and interoperability through a set of standardised data schemas used in the discovery and self-description of each course-grained, composed and loosely-coupled service.

The SOA capabilities are seen as an enabler for the realisation of the EUROCONTROL SESAR concept (EUROCONTROL, 2008), which explicitly states the focus on the global ATM interoperability with regard to the semantics of the data exchanged, the protocols and the overall quality of dialogue in terms of Communication, Navigation and Surveillance (CNS). According to the ICAO 2010 operational opportunity report (International Civil Aviation Organisation [ICAO], 2010), the European ATM Master Plan defines the "path" towards achieving performance goals by adopting the service-oriented architecture as agreed at the European Union ministerial level. The main targets are to:

- Enable a 10% reduction in CO_2 emissions per flight
- Reduce ATM costs by 50%
- Enable a 3 times increase in capacity
- Improve safety by a factor of 10

Supported by state-of-the-art and innovative technologies designed to eliminate fragmentation in the future European ATM system, SOA-based middleware reflects the operational, technological and regulatory requirements of the future ATM infrastructure while serving for the improvement of system efficiency and interoperability.

Middleware and Service-Oriented Architecture

Definition of Middleware

The term middleware was first introduced in 1968 and had only gained its popularity until it was formally used as an integration platform to connect different systems and applications since the 1980s. The role of middleware varies in different domains. In the scope of enterprise applications integration, middleware is called plumbing because it connects two applications and passes data in between (Simon, 2003). For purpose such as data integration of heterogeneous networks across different geographical locations, especially in the Air Traffic Management context, middleware is a distributed software layer that sits above the operating system and below the application layer and abstract the heterogeneity of the underlying environment. Middleware provides an integrated distributed environment whose objective is to simplify the task of programming and managing distributed applications (Campbell et al., 1999).

The common types of middleware are Message-Oriented Middleware (MOM), adaptive and reflective middleware and transaction middleware. Middleware can be grouped according to different technologies, such as grid middleware, peer-to-peer middleware and real-time middleware concerning the Quality of Service, security, performance, Model-Driven Architecture, Service-Oriented Architecture and more (Mahmoud, 2004). In aviation, the shift from proprietary air traffic control systems into a standardised and interoperable platform embracing the middleware approach facilitates the communication and integration of a wide range of ground-based and air-to-ground system applications operating across the networks. The middleware acts as an intermediary enabling direct communication with the legacy technology interfaces, to minimise system dependency.

Definition of Service-Oriented Architecture

As an embodiment of the middleware concept, SOA is a paradigm for the integration of various applications running on heterogeneous platforms using common standards. It is designed to consolidate the system capabilities for the organisation and utilisation of data distribution managed by different ownership domains. The term "service" can be defined as a single or multiple operational functions offered by a software system for the fulfilment of business objectives, for example, flight plan filing, aircraft tracking, controller-pilot communication and passenger logistics management. The specification of services may be modified as the business objectives and operations change.

There are eight design principles that affect the design of services and SOA-based system integration (Erl, 2009):

- *Standard Service Contract* – Services within the same service inventory should have the same contract design standards.
- *Service Loose Coupling* – Service contracts ensure the service consumers are decoupled from their surrounding environment.
- *Service Abstraction* – Information contained in the service contracts are limited to what is published.
- *Service Reusability* – Services contain and express agnostic logic and can be reused as enterprise resources.
- *Service Autonomy* – Services exercise a high level of control over their underlying runtime execution environment.
- *Service Statelessness* – Minimised resource consumption by deferring the management of state information when necessary.
- *Service Discoverability* – Services described with metadata can be effectively discovered and interpreted.

- *Service Composability* – Services are effective composition participants.

The SOA concept as a recommendation for system integration is an emerging approach in the ATM development programmes in Europe and North America. It offers a uniform platform, which supports the registration, discovery and administration of individual business process with use capabilities to produce desired effects consistent with measurable preconditions and expectations in a short timeframe.

Rooted in the Business Process Management (BPM) notion, SOA is a holistic mechanism for the alignment and harmonisation of an enterprise and its IT development as:

- SOA encompasses the tools and methodologies for capturing business design, and uses that design information to help improve the business.
- SOA covers the programming model, tools, and techniques for implementing the business design in information systems.
- SOA contains the middleware infrastructure for hosting that implementation.
- SOA encompasses the management of that implementation to ensure availability to the business and efficient use of resources in the execution of that implementation.
- SOA encompasses the establishment of who has authority and the processes that are used to control changes in the business design and its implementation.

The SOA principles and standards highlight the significance of loosely coupled and reusable services in the software architecture perspective. Services are independent and are accessed via standardised interfaces as a frontend of the massive network resources. The advantage lies at the transparent communication SOA offers to end-systems (technology-agnostic), and hence, to effectively demonstrate the application of data-centric information sharing. The SWIM infrastructure provides the basis for information exchange between systems based on the principles of SOA.

SOA Implementation Technologies

The definition of SOA emphasises that the concept of service-orientation is a paradigm solely. SOA is remarkable for its flexibility allowing many types of system interactions to be performed based on a series of pre-defined architectural patterns. From the functional point of view, classification of business process and service interaction modelling are two dominant motives at system planning and design stage. Afterwards, the realisation of software services supporting these interactions requires the state-of-the-art technologies to be defined. Technology-independence is one of the most important criterions in terms of technology evaluation.

The paragraphs below provide a general overview on common technologies for the implementation of a service-oriented architecture of which are used in aeronautical communication.

BPM, BPMN and BPEL

In the past 30 years, the growing concept of Business Process Management (BPM) has shifted from the use of static business process flowcharts in unchanging organisations to dynamic corporate processes which can be accessed by collaborating partners in a more flexible and efficient way. A business process can be summarised as a collection of structured activity to produce a specific business service or product. BPM introduces sophisticated software and best practices targeting the modelling, simulation, automation and management of cooperative operations with dynamic business priorities.

Business Process Modelling Notation (BPMN) is a visual language with graphical notations for the modelling of business processes. It presents the business activities, tasks and their relations in a business process diagram (Juric et al, 2008). BPMN can be used in collaborative processes and internal business processes. The BPMN models in future aeronautical communication should appear as a mixture of both intra-business and interbusiness flows reflecting the concept of Collaborative Decision Making (CDM).

To implement the modelled business interactions, Business Process Execution Language (BPEL) enables the service orchestration for composed service and business processes reinforcing service reusability and loose coupling. BPEL conducts the orchestration of services. It is mapped from the BPMN diagram for service execution, and thus allowing integrated monitoring functions to be applied. The predominant standard for BPEL is the Business Process Execution Language for Web Services (BPEL4WS v1.1) in 2003 (Andrews et al, 2003), defined in the human-readable Extensive Mark-up Language.

Based on the BPM-related concepts, the SESAR SWIM Program has addressed the need to derive a common view on the ATM business processes for accessing SWIM ATM Data and ATM functionalities. The development of a formal business process model has been recommended and it is essential to follow standard IT industry practices through the use of enterprise architecture modelling techniques.

Web Services

The Web Service infrastructure is one of the most common approaches for the realisation of SOA. It is recognised as a predominant technology framework in the avionic industry for the realisation of the SWIM infrastructure. The World Wide Web Consortium (W3C) defines Web services as a standard software system for interoperating different software applications running on a variety of platforms and/or frameworks (W3C, 2004). A Web service supports interoperable machine-to-machine interaction over a network based on the Web service stack illustrated in Fig. 1.

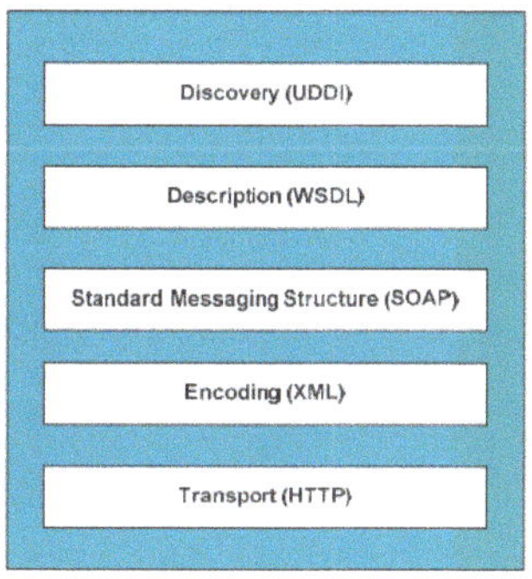

Figure 1. Web service stack.

- HTTP – Hypertext Transfer Protocol (HTTP) located in the lowest level of the Web service stack supports the distribution of information across networks. Web applications usually use HTTP on port 80 and HTTPS on port 443 for security purposes. Web service uses SOAP as a messaging protocol over HTTP.
- XML –Extensible Mark-up Language (XML) data formatted with XML tags. Data exchanged between services could be described in XML Schema Definition (XSD) conforming to the SOAP as a messaging standard.
- SOAP and transport protocols – Simple Object Access Protocol (SOAP) as a standard messaging protocol, and other transport protocols such as HTTP, FTP, SMTP and JMS are common protocols for web service communication.
- WSDL – Web Service Description Language (WSDL) is an XML formatted file used to abstractly describe the network services corresponding to the endpoints. WSDL defines the service details (contracts) between service consumers and providers. Messages, port types for specific operations, bindings, services containing SOAP addresses are key elements of a WSDL file.

Web service stands out for its standardised languages and specifications. Nevertheless, the verbose structure and the long processing time of XML schema are two major constraints. Therefore, it is essential to define suitable mechanisms to improve the efficiency of XML applied in aeronautical communication where the performance level should be optimised in order to ensure the Quality of Service. As addressed in Section 4, the matching of Abstract Syntax Notation One (ASN.1) and XML and compression mechanisms can be considered as potential solutions.

Message-Oriented Middleware

Message-Oriented Middleware (MOM) is a software term that connects multiple systems in a network for data distribution, typically in a service-oriented architecture. It is inspired from the conventional client/server architecture nevertheless, with advanced features allowing both synchronous and asynchronous communication. Such feature is beneficial in providing a messaging platform accessed by global ATM systems.

The introduction of MOM enhances the level of quality attributes such as performance, scalability, flexibility and interoperability. MOM provides Java Message Service (JMS) as the standard Application Programming Interface (API) to perform the message broker function and to support client application.

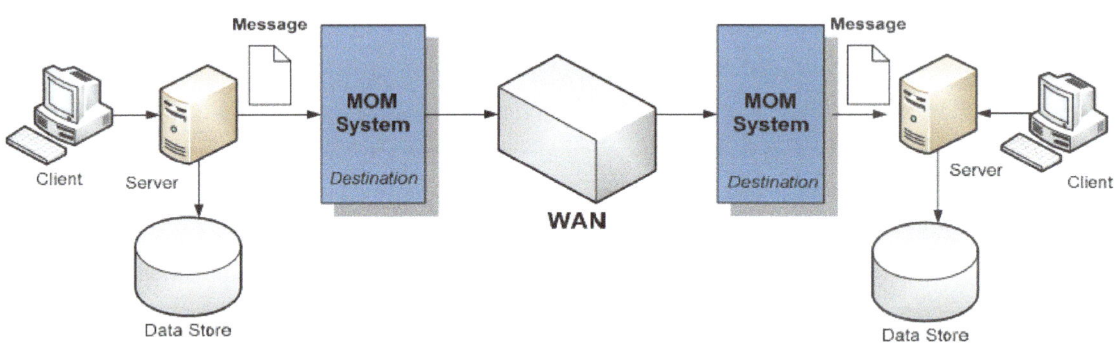

Figure 2. MOM system architecture.

As indicated in Fig. 2, a MOM system can deliver message across networks via a centralised message server or it can distribute routing and delivery functions to each client machine. The client can continue requesting information from the data store or performing other operations while delivering messages to the JMS API.

Enterprise Service Bus

An Enterprise Service Bus (ESB) is a common implementation solution that allows services to be used in a productive system. An ESB provides coarse-grained interfaces with the purpose of sharing data asynchronously between applications. Such integration architecture pulls together applications and discrete integration components to create assemblies of services to form composite business processes, which in turn automate business functions in a real-time enterprise. The rise of multiple ESBs is a result of iterative SOA implementation approaches.

An ESB provides (but not limited to) the following functions:

- Messaging functions, such as transformation, delivery and routing
- Service registry and metadata management for the storage and discovery of services
- Adapter functions supporting various communication protocols
- Support to allow service composition/orchestration in business processes through WSBPEL.
- Security management in order to provide authorization, authentication, and the creation of the policies
- Management monitoring and configuration of the management, components life cycle, logging and auditing

Data Distribution Service

Data Distribution Service (DDS) is a newly adopted middleware specification for distributed real-time applications introduced by Real-Time Innovations (RTI) in 2003. It is a standard implementation of Object Management Group (OMG) and is used in many time-critical and data-critical applications such as industrial automation, robotics, air traffic control and monitoring and transaction processing.

DDS is aimed at a diverse community of users requiring data-centric publish/subscribe with high flexibility, performance, portability and configurable data distribution management using the topic channels. Such publish/subscribe based communication model is used for sending and receiving data, events, and commands among the service nodes managed by different publishers (containing any number of DataWriters) and subscribers (containing any number of DataReaders) connected to the Global Data Space for resources sharing.

The development trend of DDS, e.g. the amalgamation with Web Services standards is driving DDS to a maturing SOA solution for future aeronautical service integration.

Common Object Request Broker Architecture

Common Object Request Broker Architecture, namely CORBA, is a specification defined by the OMG for system integration of aeronautical legacies. However, as the Web Service based solutions are gradually gaining recognition, CORBA is shifting to a legacy category.

SOA and air Traffic Management

The investigation and analysis of SESAR SWIM-SUIT (System-Wide Information Management SUpported by Innovative Technologies) and the FAA SWIM prototypes reveal substantive findings on service integration of ground-to-ground communication in a service-oriented architecture (EUROCONTROL, 2008; FAA, 2010). Implementation of the functional framework is carried out using Web Services, JMS, DDS and ESB to support one-to-one, one-to-many and event-based communication via request/reply and publish/subscribe message exchange patterns. It is envisaged that the SWIM-based SANDRA Airborne Middleware and future air traffic management infrastructure will also consider SOA as a baseline for seamless aeronautical communication in the next decades.

THE SWIM SOA APPROACH

SWIM overview

System Wide Information Management, namely SWIM, is an information sharing concept leading to the development of a number of technology programmes conducted by both the FAA, as the Next Generation Air Transportation System (NextGen), and EUROCONTROL to facilitate the information sharing and global situation awareness in the future aeronautical context. In the past, the state-of-the-art to connect different ATM systems required a fixed connection and application-level data interfaces to be set up individually between each system. SWIM is essentially introduced to reduce the high degree of system dependence by providing a Network Centric environment to enhance the flexibility of aeronautical system integration.

ICAO Global ATM Operational Concept definition of SWIM (SWIM-SUIT, 2008):

"System Wide Information management aims at integrating the ATM network in the information sense, not just in the systems sense. The fundamental change of paradigm forms the basis for the migration from the one-to-one message excha is geographically dispersed sources collaboratively updating the same piece of infornge concept of the past to the many-to-many information distribution model of the future, thatmation, with many geographically dispersed destinations needing to maintain situational awareness with regard to changes in that piece of information. Successfully managing the quality, integrity and accessibility of this complex, growing web of distributed, fast changing, shared ATM information, called the virtual information pool, can be considered as the main operational enabler for the operational concept."

FAA description of SWIM (SWIM-SUIT, 2008):

"To streamline the evolution and modernization process, SWIM concept is to support loosely coupled, many-to-many data exchange interfaces. When implemented, SWIM will allow information producers and consumers to exchange data in a secure, robust, standards-based, loosely coupled environment." [...] "Exploitation of advancing technology that moves from an application centric to a data-centric paradigm – that is, providing users the ability to access applications and service through web services – an information environment comprised of interoperable computing and communications components."

The EUROCONTROL SESAR definition of SWIM (SWIM-SUIT, 2008):

"SWIM represents added value also in terms of facilitating general accessibility. Focus shifts from the producer of information to information itself and generalised access to information (as opposed of prepackaged sets as is the case today) enables users to create their own applications which best suit their mission needs. In the ATM network, almost every participant is a producer as well as a consumer of information. It is not desirable to decide in advance who will need what information, from whom and when. The key issue is to decouple producer of information from the possible consumer in such a way that the number and nature of the consumers can evolve through time. On the contrary for what concerns the producers of information it is of the utmost importance to agree on the level of interoperability required with other ATM stakeholders that may have to contribute to the elaboration of the consistent and consolidated view of the reference data. For that purpose, the SWIM participants have to share:

- A reference Data and Services model,
- A set of agreed cooperation patterns (Rules, Roles and Responsibilities),
- A set of technical services necessary to support system interactions,
- An access to the SWIM physical network.

In short, SWIM provides the mechanisms which support the partners in managing the Rules, Roles and Responsibilities (the 3Rs) of information sharing. This determines which kind of information is shared by whom, with whom, where, when, why, how, how much, how often, at which quality level, in what form, for which purpose, at which cost, under which liability, under which circumstances, security level of air traffic management. The 3Rs must also be properly addressed both in terms of institutional and Information Communication Technology (ICT) aspects.

SWIM in Europe

Since 1997, EUROCONTROL's Experimental Centre has been participating in the SWIMSUIT Project, an initiative laying some of the foundations of SWIM. In 2008, the EUROCONTROL launched SWIM-SUIT as an underlying work package of SESAR with the aim to facilitate aeronautical information sharing with regarding to flight data, airport operational status, weather information and special use of airspace and restrictions. The information sharing targets a number of operators working with the ATM systems in aspects such as airline operation control, administration, air traffic services and passenger and logistics management.

Building on top of the SWIM concept, the SWIM-SUIT Project was designed to allow expedite and secure access and conveyance of vital information supported by the process of collaborative decision making with the adoption of the state-of-the art technologies, for achieving efficient and effective cross-domain operations.

Scope and Timeline

The SESAR Concept of operations for the long-term time frame calls for an overall European ATM system (EATMS) that is fully interconnected via a SWIM network. As illustrated in Fig. 3, the connected systems include:

- Pan-European systems for managing Europe/network-wide information services;
- Civilian and Military ATC systems;
- Airspace users systems (Military, Scheduled and on-demand civilian operators);
- Airports;
- Aircraft.

Such a system (or rather a "system of systems") requires a move from point-to-point message exchange to the sharing of information within a common virtual information pool. The SWIM architecture will permit actors to focus upon the information itself, rather than the systems that produce / manage the information.

The SESAR SWIM environment, given its wide reaching scope, will require a progressive, iterative and constant implementation programme. The following diagram outlines the current SESAR view on the various developments streams (hence, the deployment begins progressively following the end of a development stream).

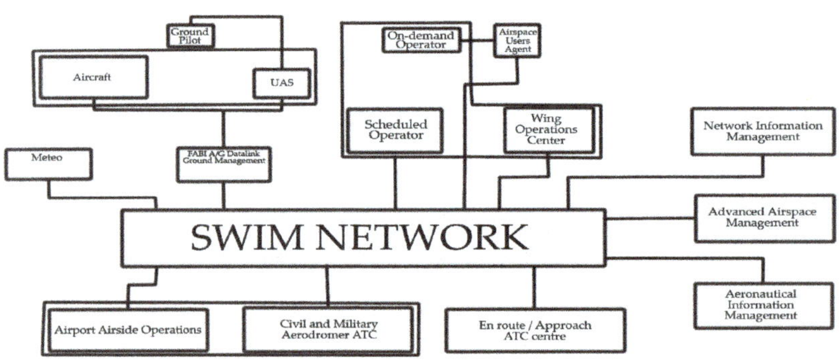

Figure 3. SESAR SWIM architecture.

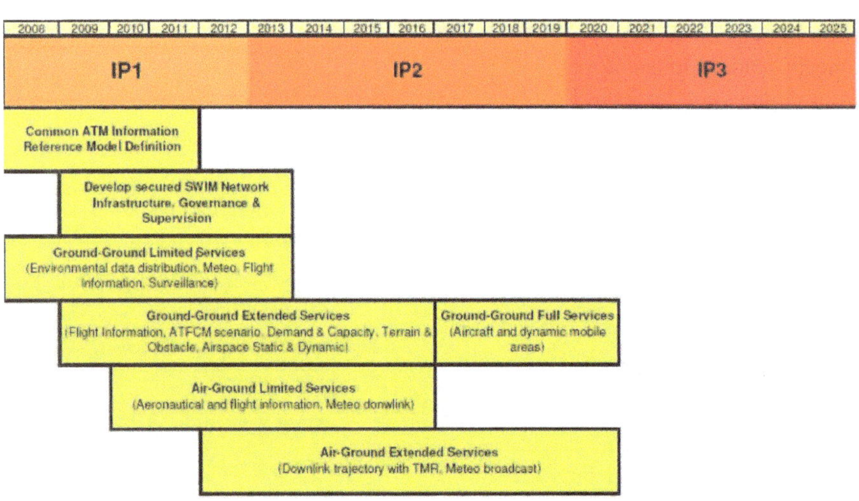

Figure 4. SESAR SWIM implementation timeline.

Data sharing and Services

The SESAR SWIM environment expects at least the following data to be shared across the SESAR-defined time frames, known as the short-term/medium planning, long-term planning, and the execution and post-execution phase:

- Flight Data - Flight Structure, Flight Script, Taxi Plan, Trajectory, What-If Flight and Context, and departure and arrival related data represented in the Flight Object Model (The European Organisation for Civil Aviation Equipment [EUROCAE], 2006)
- Surveillance Data - System Track, Sensor Descriptions, Aircraft Track, Traffic Advisory and ASAS Alert
- Aeronautical Data - Aerodrome Data, Heliport Data, Airspace Data, Navigation aids Data, Terrain and Obstacles Data and Aircraft Data with details described in (Aeronautical Information Exchange Model [AIXM], 2011)
- Meteo Data - Aerodrome Weather, Area Weather and Met Hazard with details described in (Weather Information Exchange Model [WXXM], 2011.)
- Capacity and Demand Data - Configuration Plan, Traffic and Airspace Demand, Traffic
- Load and Demand Capacity Balancing Measures
- ATFCM Scenario Data - Demand Capacity Balancing (DCB) Scenario, Flow Measures and DCB Scenario Catalogue

System Architecture

Fig. 5 illustrates a layered conceptual view of the SWIM architecture:

- SWIM network – the physical pan-European network along with the essential technical IP building blocks (e.g. transport protocols, firewalls).
- SWIM Technical Services – the core technical services that SWIM will provide to all connected systems. These services are built, as far as possible, upon standard IT middleware technologies.
- SWIM ATM Data Access Services – this layer embodies the "SWIM virtual information pool". It provides access via defined services to the standardised SWIM ATM Data model. The data access services are typically be categorised into different domains (e.g. FlightDataAccess, MeteoDataAccess).
- SWIM ATM Added-value services – this layer contains services that provide access (perhaps distantly) to added-value ATM functionality beyond that of the "virtual information pool". Typically, this layer could contain CDM type applications/services.

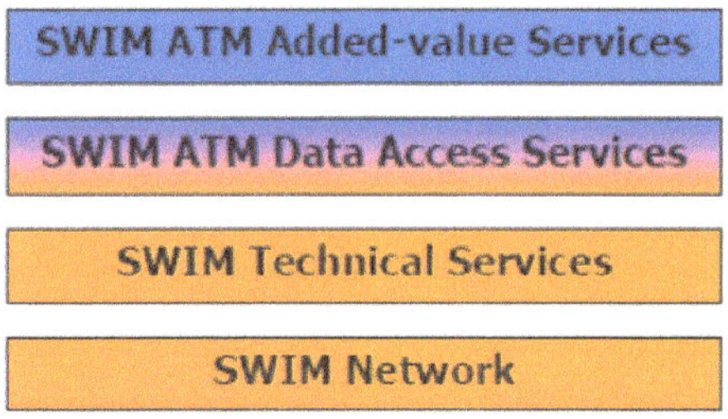

Figure 5. SWIM layered architecture.

From a domain viewpoint, the layers can be divided into two main groups:

- SWIM Infrastructure – SWIM Network, SWIM Technical Services, and SWIM ATM Data Access Services (partial), which represent a common SWIM IT infrastructure, consisting of both turn-key solutions and toolkit/frameworks, upon which is built the SWIM ATM functionality.
- SWIM ATM functionality – SWIM ATM Added-value Services, SWIM ATM Data Access Services (partial), representing the domain specific functionality.
- The SWIM infrastructure is spread out amongst the (legacy) ATM systems that form a part of the overall European ATM system (the "system of systems"). Each ATM system, typically composed of a number of major subsystems, implementing domain specific functionality will now include a "SWIM / IOP Management subsystem" which:
- Contains the (or parts of) SWIM Infrastructure functionality shown above;
- Connects the legacy system functionality to the SWIM environment;
- Translates standard SWIM ATM data structures into the appropriate legacy system data formats.

Services in SWIM are defined in a domain-specific manner providing a wide range of standard functional interfaces to support the communication and collaboration between participants connected to the SWIM network. Data collected from both the SWIM-enabled applications and ATM legacy systems, via the SWIM external adapter, is transmitted through the SWIM Ground/Ground gateways, namely the SWIM-BOXes, for the facilitation of data sharing.

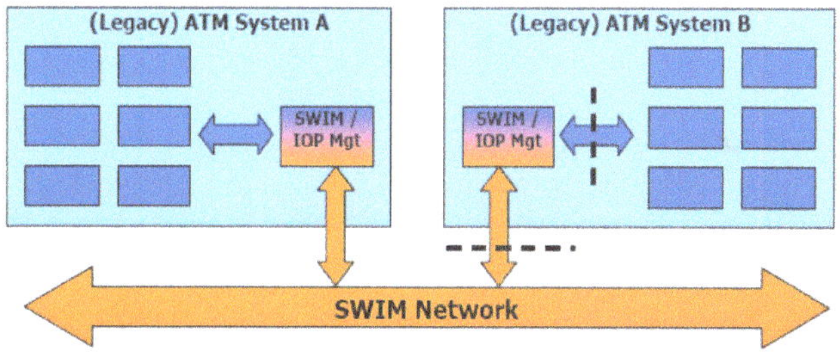

Figure 6. SWIM/ATM system viewpoint.

SWIM in the U.S.

The SWIM Program in the United States was originated in 1997 as the EUROCONTROL initially presented the SWIM concept to FAA. The concept was under development ever since until the ICAO Global ATM Operational Concept adopted the SWIM concept in 2005. SWIM is now a part of development project in the United States NextGen framework for the development and integration of the National Air Space (NAS) systems for greater sharing of ATM system information on airport operational status, weather information, flight data, status of special use airspace, and NAS restrictions.

Scope and Timeline

The FAA has established a notion called "Core Services" as a consistent capability existing at each node to provide a uniform mechanism for communicating among nodes. Fig. 7 illustrates the FAA view of how Core Services fit into the overall SWIM architecture.

The following system cores are included:

- En Route Automation Modernization(ERAM)
- Weather Message Switching Centre Replacement (WMSCR)
- Traffic Flow Management System (TFMS)
- FAA Telecommunications Infrastructure (FTI)
- Special Use Airspace Management System (SAMS)
- Central Processor (CP)
- National Airspace System (NAS)
- Electronic Flight Strip Terminal System (EFSTS)
- Airport Surface Detection Equipment –Model X (ASDE-X)
- Flight Data Input Output (FDIO)
- Terminal Data Link System (TDLS)
- Runway Visual Range (RVR)
- Air Route Traffic Control Centre (ARTCC)
- William J Hughes Technical Centre (WJHTC)

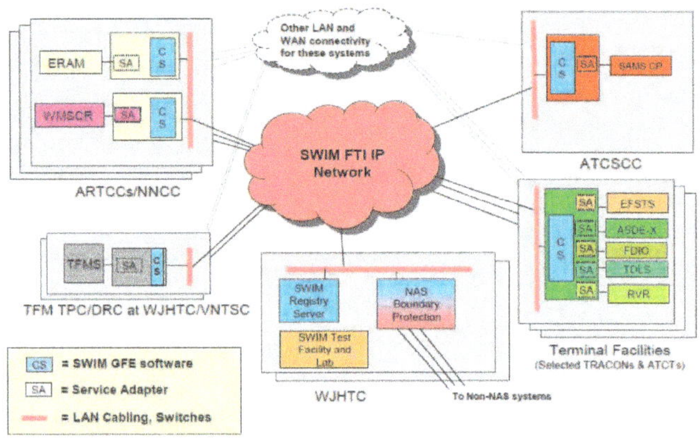

Figure 7. FAA SWIM architecture with core services.

Fig. 7 raises the question of what specific capabilities are comprised in these Core Services. The FAA has proposed the core capabilities in Fig. 8 below.

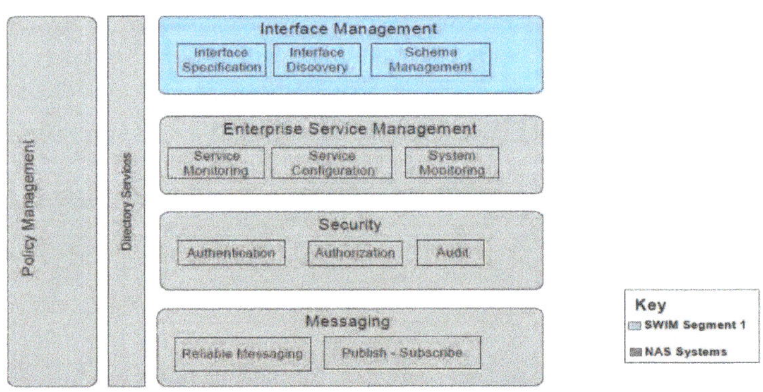

Figure 8. SWIM Segment 1 Core Capabilities.

The FAA organizes SWIM's initial Core Services into four groups (SESAR shares the same

Core Services grouping as FAA):

- Interface Management
- Messaging
- Security
- Enterprise Service Management

FAA SWIM will be deployed in segments (stages), with the first segment planned for the

2008-2012 timeframe though the NextGen has a long planning horizon (20+ years).

Data Sharing and Services

The Segment 1 business services are defined in the SWIM Final Program Requirements. It identifies and describes the services in the following categories for example:

Flight and Flow Management

- Flight Data Publication
- Terminal Data Publication
- Flow Data Publication
- Runway Visual Range (RVR) Data Publication

Aeronautical Information Management

- Special Use Area (SUA) Data Publication
- Corridor Integrated Weather System (CIWS) Data Publication
- Integrated Terminal Weather Service (ITWS) Data Publication

System Architecture

In response to the FAA SWIM program using SOA, Government Electronics & Information Technology Association (GEIA) which is a trade association that includes many industry partners who support the FAA, provides the industry solution, shown in following figure, both adheres to the overall SOA and to the FAA SWIM vision

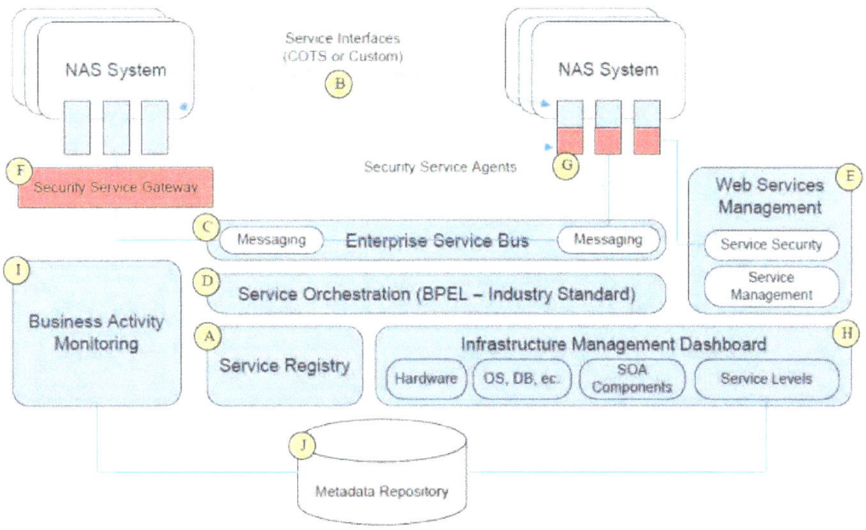

Figure 9. GEIA SOA Architecture for SWIM (GEIA, 2008).

The GEIA architecture above supports the FAA Service groupings via the following subsystems, according to the "SOA Best Practices –Industry Input" (GEIA, 2008).

- Interface Management (A, B)
- Messaging (C, D)
- Security (E, F, G)
- Enterprise Service Management (H, I, J)

SANDRA – EXTENDING SWIM ONBOARD

SANDRA overview

Building on the SESAR SWIM concept for information fusion and dissemination for groundto-ground service integration, the EU FP7 project SANDRA (Seamless Aeronautical Networking through integration of Data-Links, Radios and Antennas) extends the ideology of SWIM to cover air-to-ground information exchange, service composition and integration to provide a complete and coherent set of communication services for future global Air Traffic Management in the 2020 timeframe. To ensure the integration of different service domains onboard legacy applications with very diverse requirements, the SANDRA communication system will represent a key enabler for the global provision of distributed services for Collaborative Decision Making based on the SWIM concept, and for meeting the high market demand for broadband passenger and enhanced cabin communication services.

As a case study, the paragraphs below concentrate on the SANDRA Airborne Middleware design and how such architecture can be realised using the various SOA technologies. Focusing on communications related aspects, the following high-level requirements are identified to allow future systems to be compatible with the expected air-traffic growth:

- Pilots situation awareness shall be improved
- Capacity at airports, as today's main limiting structural factors, shall be increased
- ATS shall be primarily based on highly reliable data communication
- AOC data traffic shall strongly increase for efficient airline operations
- Passengers and cabin communications systems shall be further developed
- Safety critical applications shall need diverse means to reach ground for global availability and higher reliability
- A simplification of on-board network architecture shall need convergence of protocols and interfaces

In order to satisfy the objectives (middleware aspect only), a possible airborne middleware architecture in SANDRA is defined aiming at the interoperation with the ground systems utilizing SOA. To define the airborne middleware architecture, analysis of air/ground (A/G) information exchange is carried out focusing on the definition of the A/G data domain services and functional interfaces based on the SWIM information infrastructure. A combination of mechanisms to improve the A/G data exchange is proposed in dealing with the limited bandwidth available for over the SANDRA Data Link. The A/G integration architecture is defined containing a set of core infrastructural subsystems.

Analysis of air/ground Information Exchange

The SESAR SWIM environment expects at least the following data to be shared:

- Flight Data
- Surveillance Data
- Aeronautical Data
- Meteo Data
- Capacity and Demand Data
- ATFCM Scenario Data

SWIM ATM Information Model

The ATM information to be exchanged via SWIM Network needs to be modelled explicitly, to allow a precise and concrete definition to be agreed. Previous work has already defined data models and required services within specific domains (e.g. Aeronautical Information and Flight Information), but this is not the case for all types of information. The services in support to SWIM are organized around a number of central themes called profiles.

An overall ATM Information Reference Model is required to define the semantics of all the ATM information to be exchanged. This model will form the master definition, subsets of which would be used in lower level models, supporting interoperability for each of the datasharing domains.

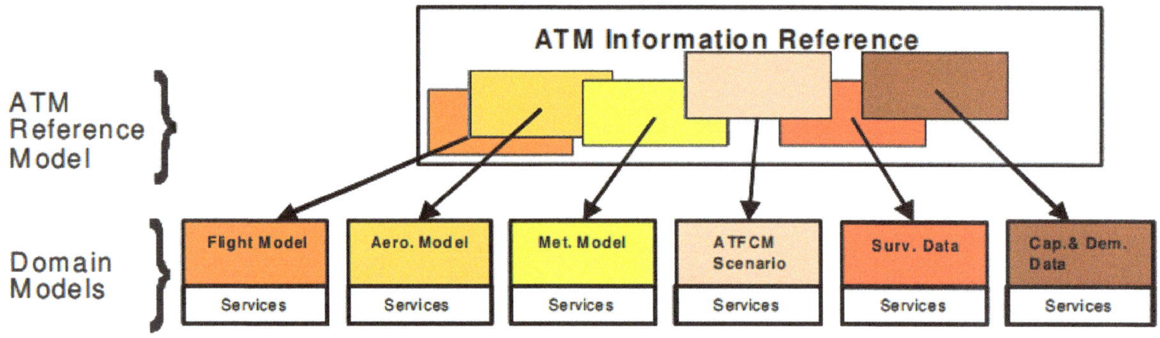

Figure 10. SESAR ATM Reference Information Model.

The ATM Information reference would be a key asset in the ATM System design and would sit above a set of domain-specific, platform independent models which may overlap with each other, without being incompatible. The overall reference model and existing models such as OATA, FOIPS, OMEGA, AIXM etc., will need to be reconciled.

From these models, the specific SWIM exchange formats (i.e. on the wire exchange formats) can then be defined. SWIM assumes that the data handed over to SWIM Node services is already in the canonical ATM information model. There will be no mappings from/to the canonical data model in the data domain components. If such mappings are required, they have to be implemented in the SWIM Applications adapters. The data domain components perform data conversions for encryption/decryption and data filtering on the canonical data.

SWIM ATM information services

The ATM information services are all services that can be called on the northbound external interface of a SWIM Node. These are application services and data access services. Fig. 11 shows a typical scenario: A simple request/reply service invocation results in a data change (on ATM System B) that is followed by a publish/subscribe exchange to distribute the changed data. In this case the ATM information service call is initially triggered by the SWIM Application Adapter on System A. System B is identified as the master of the data and the service call is forwarded to System B where the operation is performed. If the operation results in a data change, this is distributed to all relevant subscribers.

Only the initial service call originates outside of SWIM, all the other information flows are triggered by the SWIM infrastructure. This requires some sort of service orchestration inside of SWIM.

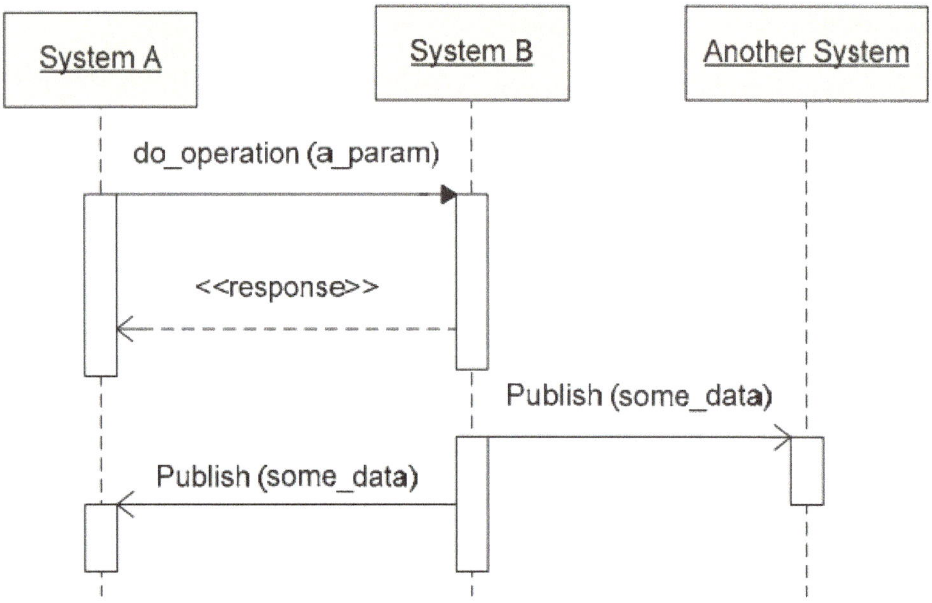

Figure 11. Interaction Scenario.

SANDRA Data Domain Concept

In order to respect the SWIM Data Domain Concept, described in SESAR as "Profiles", the SANDRA Airborne Middleware (SAM) provides a more generic approach to allow different kind of data sharing/services over SANDRA data links without any kind of restrictions, but just working on XML Optimised Representations of Shared Data. Fig. 12 below clarifies the Data Domain Object (DDO) concept: as the Flight Object on SWIM Ground Side is described as composed by different Flight Object Clusters with an XML Representation, SANDRA DDO provides a more generic view of the same thing, in particular it is composed by different Data Object Clusters and, with this assertion, we can describe any kind of Data Domain (Meteo, Aeronautical, Flight, etc) using this kind of representation for specific entities.

For example, SANDRA supports the EUROCAE ED133 Flight Object services (EUROCAE, 2009) through the DataDomainObject.

Improving the Air/Ground Data Exchange Services

SANDRA will provide a generic representation for the shared data over SAM, in particular, analysing the last image it is possible to discover two kinds of representations for the same information:

- DataDomainObject (DDOject): it contains "n" DDObjectClusters of each with an Object Identifier and multiple Object Release Identifiers described in XML
- DataObjectSummary: it contains just one data object cluster the Distribution List cluster that contains information about the participants over the DDObject shared information. A release identifier, contained also in the DDObject, gives information about the actual releases of the single clusters contained into the DDObject.

These two representations are important in order to reduce the traffic between the involved stakeholders: the first one is the full data representation that each involved stakeholder has to save locally; the usually shared information that informs which is the last "present" information is given by the DDObjectSummary.

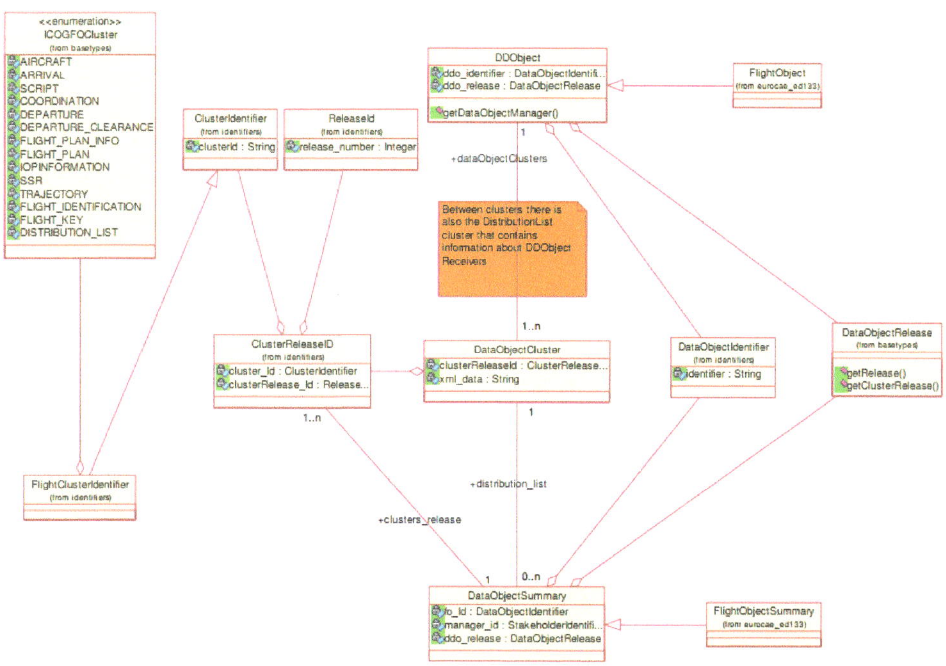

Figure 12. SAM Data Domain Object.

Once the new AIRBORNE requests a subscription, it receives all the summaries of DDObject of interests (based on particular AIRBORNE StakeholderIdentifier). The SWIM Ground infrastructure may need to be extended in order to identify the objects exchanged to support SWIM A/G communication. For example, it may be useful to link the specific DDObjects (Meteo information, Flights over the trajectory, etc) to a Trajectory for distribution of the DDObjectSummaries of interest to subscribed aircrafts only.

SANDRA targets to reduce the traffic on the Air/Ground data link by designing a more schematic yet lightweight communication protocol. However, a publish operation for distributing the whole clusters information in XML format incurs a large overhead and high bandwidth usage. In order to reduce the amount of shared information, two important operations are applied to the XML format:

- Compression: A number of compression techniques can be used to reduce "drastically" the XML shared information size.
- Data Manipulation: the XML format is extremely schematic and there are techniques that can allow simple updates over an original data.
- In considering the above, the requirements for data exchange optimisations are identified as follows:

- A common data representation to optimise the shared data is required
- An XML-based shared data content is required
- A complete knowledge of Shared Information by the ground system is required in order to share essential information starting from an airborne stored one.

To respect these few but extremely important requirements, the DDObject with its inner XML clusters are introduced. Concerning the Ground side DDObjects knowledge, a "DataRepository" component to store all the DDObject Cluster Releases of each DDObject is defined. The "Delta" concept for the differentiation and integration of XML data is applied using the information stored in the "DataRepository".

Based on the SESAR SWIM study, the "publish" and the "read" operations are the two most critical operations to integrate compression and data manipulation concepts into SAM:

- Applying "Delta" Concept: Once the DDObject Manager requires an update on an already shared DDObject, it requests a publish operation of the DDObjectSummary that contains the DDObject Identifier, DDObject Release and Distribution Cluster for such information to be received by airborne applications that have already been subscribed to and registered on the DDObject Domain, also given that the DDObject is created and updated. Under this premise, the airborne application knows the "stored" DDObject Release and the new Release Identifier that was just published. Knowing this information the application can request a "read" operation signalling the "stored" release to enable the ground side to compare the release values of the newly published DDObject and the one that is stored by the airborne application. Once the SWIM Ground locates the clusters identifier to update using a DDObject repository that contains all the DDObject Releases clusters, it can be possible to identify the differences between the XML file stored in the airborne application and that in the newly shared clusters. The difference in the XML contents, XML Diff, can then be sent as a reply message to the read operation signalled by the airborne application.
- Applying Compression Concept: Compression can be defined at different layers, in particular at the "message" layer and at the "parameter" layer. In order to design the SANDRA Middleware, Web Service technology and, in particular, the shared messages – SOAPMessages to realise the request/reply pattern are applied. Previous studies show that it is possible to compress SOAP messages before sending out the requests and to decompress them once received at the destination. In addition, with the "Delta" Concept, the SOAP message body will contain only a "read reply" message with just the differences between the "Airborne Stored DDObject Clusters" and "Ground Updated Clusters" as parameters. As a result, the SOAP Body contains only the XML Diff content. Applying XML Compression over XML Diff will further reduce the shared packet size.

The same compression can be however applied to the publish operation since all the DDObjects has the same data structure XML Based. Hence, it is possible to compress the publish topics clusters - the whole clusters for DDObjects and just the Distribution Cluster for the DDObjectSummaries before publishing.

The SANDRA Airborne Middleware Architecture

The SANDRA Airborne Middleware architecture as shown in Fig. 13 has the scope to provide services to airborne applications and to the ground-based Air Ground Data Link Ground Management System (AGDLGMS) gateway over the SANDRA A/G Network. In order to establish such a connection, a set of external interfaces are defined for use in the ground side to communicate with SWIM Ground Gateway and airborne side to realise the communication with SWIM airborne applications.

A detailed SAM system architecture, as illustrated in Fig. 14, includes the AGDLGMS entity residing on the ground is communicating with the other SWIM G/G Gateways via the SWIM Ground Network; and also the SANDRA Airborne Middleware, via the SANDRA A/G Data Link. The SAM provides two kinds of external interfaces:

- SAMUtilityService Interface: this interface has to provide the utility services requests such as Subscription, Un-subscription and the set of connected Airborne status
- SAMBusinessService Interface: this interface has to provide the business services requests, in particular creation, update, handover, read, and so on.

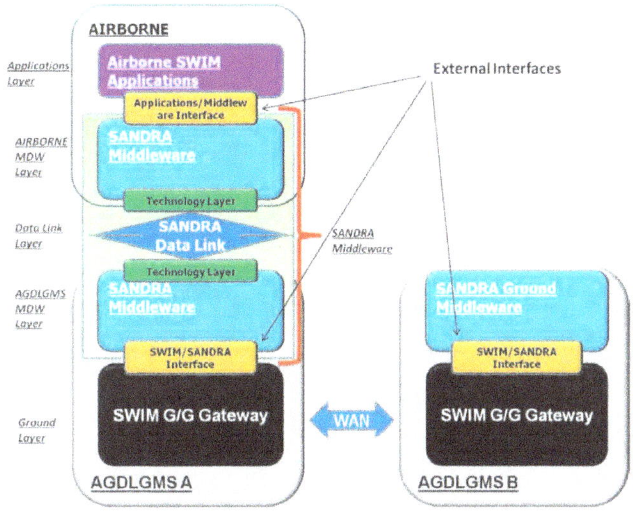

Figure 13. SAM Architecture Overview.

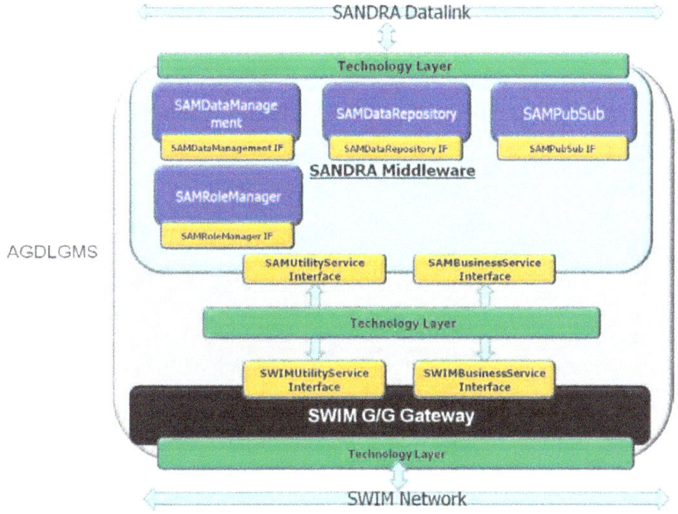

Figure 14. SAM Architecture Details.

As described in the following paragraphs, both the airborne and ground SANDRA middleware segments should provide the core infrastructural functions to support the aeronautical operations via the defined SAM interfaces. Core services are defined in alignment with the EUROCONTROL and FAA SWIM approach to construct a coherent SWIM infrastructure around the globe.

Interface Management

The interface management provides capabilities that enable service providers to publish information about services and service consumers to discover service information. In addition to the generic service registration/publication and discovery, user registration and subscription for notification are also associated supporting functionalities.

The interface management of the SANDRA system should support the manipulation of information from the service registry, shown as follows:

- Service Registration: the ability for a user to register a service to the system.
- Service Lookup: the ability for a user to look for (discover) a registered service.
- Service Invocation: the ability to invoke an identified and possibly distant service.

A service provider registers the service endpoints on a local registry. For routing purposes, the lookup service will be invoked if the service consumer does not know the endpoint of a specific service. However, this also depends on the message exchange pattern being applied. Both Flight Object key selection and content-based search support the service discovery.

Messaging Services

The messaging services provided SAM the messaging mechanisms to enable the communication between service providers (publishers) and consumers (subscribers) in a loosely-coupled manner. However, these roles may vary in different scenarios. The decoupling feature of participants not only reduces chances of synchronisation, but also ensures the transparency and autonomy of services. Several mechanisms are introduced here to support a variety of services invocation styles and data exchange protocols:

- Publish/Subscribe with notification: allow publishers to check the subscribed users for the actual notification type and send them the subscribed notification.

- Request/Response: allows service client to request information from the server through for example, RPC-style client/server communication.

The adoption of Web Services and JMS allows both synchronous and asynchronous messaging for the realisation of various aeronautical operations across all data domains.

Security Services

The security services offered by SAM focus on aspects such as user role management, access control, the encryption and decryption of messages as well as service security monitoring. The Lightweight Directory Access Protocol (LDAP) user registry is considered in the design phase to provide security functions.

A common approach is introduced to allow service consumers to gain restricted access only on specific tasks by building a standalone authentication and user management application that can be accessed as a service in a SOA framework. Operational services/ processes that require proof of identity will access this shared user account; thereby the shared function can be repurposed across all tasks. In this scenario, the shared user account service will be reusable for different business processes. This includes the following aspects:

- Authentication: this function provides password features for user login.
- Authorisation: this function provides user access control.
- Logging: this function stores the user actions in a security log and alerts unauthorized operations according to the security requirements (SANDRA, 2010).

Enterprise Service Management

Enterprise Service Management (ESM) includes the governance and monitoring of services.

It provides passive and active management of services at run time while performing overall management operations of systems and applications. SAM should also provide core functions to collect the Service Level Agreement (SLA) and policy-related metrics to ensure QoS. An SLA refers to a set of performance figures that are indicated in the service contract shared by a service provider and the consumer(s) of that service. Guaranteed operation time, i.e. system uptime, downtime and response time, as well as capacity of the system are the most common figures. The topics covered are:

- Fault monitoring and reporting: with this function the administrator can monitor and manage the service faults.
- Performance monitoring and reporting: with this function the administrator can monitor the performance level of the services.
- Enterprise configuration: with this function the administrator can perform system configuration (e.g. service setup and software configuration) through GUI.
- SANDRA service management: with this function the administrator can monitor the quality level of services, according to the QoS requirements (SANDRA, 2010).

Technology Choices

A number of technologies are proposed for the realisation of the SANDRA Airborne Middleware in a service-oriented architecture. Evaluation of the suitable technologies is performed based on the three following steps:

- The propose of candidate technologies
- A list of evaluation criteria taking into account the system requirements and communication patterns of SWIM, SWIM-SUIT and SANDRA Airborne Middleware (SAM)
- Technology selection based on the rating of each technology against the quality attributes to define a technology selection matrix

In summary, it is envisaged that Web Service is the one of the most appropriate technologies in future aeronautical communication considering its standardisation, interoperability and compatibility with the ground SWIM infrastructure. It is also suitable in the airborne context for its maturity and integration features. Web services provide the support for the realisation of a SOAP-based SOA infrastructure incorporating the MOM JMS API for providing pragmatic request/reply and publish/subscribe messaging mechanisms. The Enterprise Service Bus is considered as an alternative approach for system implementation in addition to Web Service and MOM/ JMS. DDS outstands for its excellent network performance. Therefore, it is envisioned as an emerging candidate technology for highefficient and technology-independent data distribution along the refinement of its specification. The SWIM-SUIT project has also concluded with the same prospect and adopted DDS for the SWIM-BOX implementation on ground.

The evaluation of the implementation software indicates that Apache and JBoss frameworks are respectively the most and second-most appropriate technologies. The scores are obtained based on the aggregation of a Web service infrastructure, a messaging backbone (MOM) and an ESB for service composition and system integration. Here, the following sets of technology options are proposed:

- Apache CXF, Apache ActiveMQ, Apache Camel, and Apache ServiceMix or Apache Synapse - Apache CXF and ActiveMQ compose a lightweight system framework for onboard systems. Apache Camel can be used for advanced routing and mediation functions if required. Apache Synapse can be used as a replacement of ServiceMix to achieve a more lightweight system. System bridging is required for achieving full interoperability with SWIM-SUIT.
- JBoss Application Server/JBoss ESB, and HornetQ - direct integration with SWIM-SUIT, thus to achieve full interoperability. HornetQ is claimed to have better performance among all message brokers available.
- XOperator or XMLUnit - used for comparing, summarising and synchronising XML documents for the realisation of the "Delta" data sharing in the SWIM context, i.e. to support operations such as "getDataDiff", "makeDataDiff" and "integrateDataDiff" in the "SAMDataRepository" and "SAMDataManagement".
- FastInfoset and Fast Web Service - used for converting test-based XML into binarybased ASN.1 FastInfoset provided by the JAX-WS interface within Java

framework while remaining the capability to allow message transmission using SOAP. No additional tool is required for this approach. Although the support for Fast Web Service has yet become sufficient, the approach is envisioned for SAM development.

CONCLUSION

With an appreciation of envisioning the future aeronautical communication system in a service-oriented architecture, this chapter summarises the ongoing development of avionic service integration and the utilisation prospects of the middleware and SOA concepts in the 2020 timeframe and beyond. SWIM, as an architectural blueprint, is envisaged as a baseline solution in dealing with the growth of airline passenger and the increasing complexity of aeronautical operations. The state-of-the-art SWIM system architectures proposed by worldleading aviation organisations, e.g. EUROCONTROL and FAA allow Air Traffic Management stakeholders around the globe to obtain coherent and persistent knowledge of relevant system data regarding the flights in operation.

To continue with the ground-based SWIM programmes, this chapter proposes a possible SANDRA Airborne Middleware approach for the integration of airborne/ground Air Traffic Management systems for SOA-based future aeronautical service integration. Analysis of airborne/ground information exchange targeting on the domain-based operations and interactions are defined according to the added-value services, data access services and technical services in the SWIM context. An architectural overview of the SANDRA Airborne Middleware is illustrated featuring the connections between the onboard middleware and the SWIM Ground Gateways with its underlying system infrastructure. The "Delta" concept and compression mechanisms are proposed to optimise system performance and message exchange based on the selected technologies.

ACKNOWLEDGMENT

The research leading to these results has been partially funded by the European Community's Seventh Framework Programme (FP7/2007-2013) under Grant Agreement n°233679. The SANDRA project is a Large Scale Integrating Project for the FP7 Topic AAT.2008.4.4.2 (Integrated approach to network centric aircraft communications for global aircraft operations). The project has 31 partners and started on 1st October 2009. In addition, as an acknowledgement from the authors, the chapter represents only the opinion of the authors but not the whole SANDRA Consortium.

REFERENCES

1. AIXM. (2011) AIXM Aeronautical Information Exchange Model, 12.12.2010, Available from http://www.aixm.aero/public/subsite_homepage/homepage.html
2. Andrews, T.; Curbera, F.; Dholakia, H.; Goland, Y.; Klein, J.; Leymann, F.; Liu, K.; Roller, D.; Smith, D.; Thatte, S.; Trickovic,I. & Weerawarana, S. (5th May 2003). Business Process Execution Language for Web Services Version 1.1, 24.11.2010, Available from http://xml.coverpages.org/BPELv11-May052003Final.pdf
3. Campbell, A.T.; Coulson, G. & Kounavis, M.E. (1999). Managing Complexity: Middleware Explained, IEEE Computer Society IT Professional, vol. 1, September | October 1999, pp. 22-28.
4. EasyJet & Ryanair. (2009). Ryanair and EasyJet continue strong growth, British Airways' struggles continue in Oct-2009.
5. Erl, T. (2009). SOA design patterns (Ed. 1), Prentice Hall PTR, ISBN: 9780136135166, New Jersey, USA.
6. EUROCAE. (2006). D7 Flight Object Interoperability Proposed Standard (FOIPS) Study. Issue 1.4.
7. EUROCAE. (2009) ED-133 Flight Object Interoperability Specification.
8. EUROCONTROL. (2006). Long-Term Forecast Flight Movements (2006 - 2025) v1.0, EUROCONTROL.
9. EUROCONTROL. (2008). What is SESAR WP 14 SWIM technical architecture, 21.10.2010, Available from http://www.swim-suit.aero/swimsuit/project.php
10. EUROCONTROL. (2011). Weather Information Exchange Model, 12.12.2010, Available from http://www.eurocontrol.int/aim/public/standard_page/met_wie.html
11. FAA. (28th April 2010). SWIM Documents, 11.11.2010, Available from http://www.faa.gov/about/office_org/headquarters_offices/ato/service_units/techops/atc_comms_services/swim/documentation/GEIA. (March 2008) FAA SWIM Program SOA Best Practices - Industry Input
12. Houdebert, R. & Ayral, B. (2010). Making SWIM Interoperable between US and Europe, Integrated Communications Navigation and Surveillance (ICNS) Conference Proceedings of IEEE, Herndon, Virginia, USA, May 11-13, 2010.
13. ICAO. (2010). Operational Opportunity. ICAO Environmental Report 2010, Chapter 3, pp.96-125
14. Luckenbaugh, G.; Landriau. S.; Dehn, J. & Rudolph, S. (2007). Service Oriented Architecture for the Next Generation Air Transportation System, Integrated Communications Navigation and Surveillance (ICNS) Conference Proceedings of IEEE, Herndon, Virginia, USA, May 1-3, 2007.
15. Mahmoud, Q. H. (2004) Middleware for Communications (Ed. 1), John Wiley & Sons, Inc., ISBN: 0470862068, New York, USA.
16. SANDRA. (June 2010) Deliverable D3.1.1 SANDRA Detailed Network Requirements v1.0.
17. Simon, R. (2003) Middleware, In: The Internet Encyclopedia, Bidgoli, H., vol. 1, 603-613, John Wiley & Sons, Inc. ISBN: 978-0-471-22202-6, New Jersey, USA.
18. SWIM-SUIT. (June 2008) Deliverable D1.5.1 Overall SWIM Users Requirements v01.
19. W3C. (2004) Web Services Architecture, 11.02.2004, Available from http://www.w3.org/TR/ws-arch/

CHAPTER 12 BUSINESS INTELLIGENCE IN TELECOMS INDUSTRY

Tanko Ishaya and Musiliudeen Folarin

INTRODUCTION

Mobile market is becoming saturated and competitive in telecoms industry. As a result, these organizations are becoming more and more conscious about the advantages of data and information kept in their organization, the need to integrate these large volumes of data and to utilize these information to support the quality of their decision-making, in order to stay at a competitive advantage and to increase profit (Wu et al, 2007; Pareek, 2006). The profitability of these industry is clearly linked to its subscriber base which again depends on number of active customers, duration of calls made by customers, quality of service, price as compare to others, and ability to satisfy customers (Pareek, 2006). To properly utilize the relationships between all the profitability attributes, there is a clear demand for quality Business Intelligence (BI) (Wu et al, 2007; Pareek, 2006). BI is the combination of business processes with the use of IT Systems such as DWs, Data Marts, Metadata Data Mining, ETL, Query and Reporting Software, OLAP, and Visualization (Kudyba and Hoptroff, 2001; Pareek,2006) to support decision-making in an organization.

However, studies have shown that many researchers view BI from different perspectives. For example, Power (2003) considers BI as a data driven decision support system while others such as Rus and Toader (2008), and Kulkarni et al (2010) considered BI as strategic information system capable of providing actionable information through a centralized data repository, sourced from numerous sources, transformed into meaningful information via BI analytical tools, to facilitate business insights leading to informed decisions. Ishaya et al. (2007) shared similar view with Rus and Toader (2008) and further classified Information System in an organization into two broad categories: Operational Support Systems (OSS) which are systems that supports day-to-day business operational data and Decision Support Systems (DSS) which are systems that support decision-making. Ranjan (2009) defined BI as a way and method of improving business performance by making actionable information available for decision makers in an organization. BI is also defined as "the communication facility serving the conduct of a business, the notion of intelligence is the ability to apprehend the interrelationship of presented facts in such a way as to guide action towards a desired goal" (Rus and Toader, 2008). Hence, BI can be define as a process and methods of improving decision-making through a combination of business processes and effective utilization of IT to integrate data and information from various OSS into DWs , using data mining to analyze the data, and generating high-level report in a timely and user friendly manner for the decision makers in an organization.

BI assists corporate managers and decision makers to make relevant, accurate, timely and smart decision in an organization and thus lead to increase in productivity and profitability of an organization (Gordon et al, 2006; Ranjan, 2009). BI is a field of building "information that is conclusive, fact-based, and actionable"(Pareek, 2006). Therefore, BI expose the importance of data and information kept by various organizations, which can be used to help in accurate and efficient decision-making based on the facts rather than human reasons (Ishaya et al, 2007). The competitive forces common in the world of business today require a business organization to operate efficiently and productively in order to maintain and support market share, profitability and shareholder values (Atre, 2003; Madnick et al,

Citation: Tanko Ishaya and Musiliudeen Folarin (2012). Business Intelligence in Telecoms Industry, Dr. Daniel Catalan-Matamoros (Ed.), InTech, DOI: 10.5772/33065.

2009). BI use traditional Extracts, Transform and Load (ETL) for data integration from Operational Support System (OSS) such as CRM, Decision Support System (DSS), Supply Chain Management (SCM), Enterprise Resource Planning (ERP), and E-business application (Pareek, 2006), which involve complex rule and long-running business processes during business downtime and which may span days as emphased in Gordon et al(2006). Current implementation of BI in telecoms organization is still based on traditional approach to data integration, which is static in nature. This approach may not meet up with constantly changing analysis required to support decision-making due to its static nature and direct end-to-end BI tools (Wu et al, 2007). Million of Call Details Record (CDR) are being generated daily and as services providers add new services to ensures customer satisfaction, customer's data will continue to grow exponentially, which can be difficult to analyze at a reasonable time and cost (Gordon et al, 2006; Ranjan, 2009). Therefore, there is need for a Service Oriented (SO) approach to BI in order to provide real-time data analysis. The SO approach will also provide an open, interoperable and potentially collaborative means of proving BI (Berthold et al, 2010).

This chapter presents an investigation into the integration and analysis of data from CRM and CDR of Telecoms operators using SO approach to assist the organization in making real-time and accurate decision about the customer tariff plan to ensure customer satisfaction which in return can lead to increase in profit.

The research has investigated the use of SO approach to BI in Telecoms organizations towards providing real-time and accurate decision support about customer tariff plan in order to ensure customer satisfaction. The chapter presents:

- A thorough review of current approaches/technologies to BI with telecoms industry and data sources –such as CDR, Billing system and CRM
- The development of Service Oriented Business Intelligence (SOBI) architecture based on an analysis of existing architectures/models and customer requirements that were captured through questionnaires. The architecture integrates integrate data from heterogeneous data sources of these organizations.
- Development of a SOBI prototype system that simulates the basic operation of a typical telecoms organization.
- An evaluation of the architecture and potential effectiveness using the implemented prototype

A BACKGROUND TO BI WITHIN TELECOMS

Advancement in the use of information technology (IT) over the past 50 years to collect, keep, extract, analyze and communicate data and information (Kudyba and Hoptroff, 2001) has lead business organizations through an era of OSS (Pareek, 2006). With these OSS, business organizations are able to keep lots of data about customers and daily operation and they now want to turn these data into actionable information. Since there are different perspectives to BI, there are also differing challenges of BI applications between organisations. The table below presents an analysis of some of the challenges that different industries face in implementing BI applications.

Table 1. BI Challenges in various Industries

Industry	Application	Challenge
Telecommunication	CRM, DSS	Legal Issues (Griffin, 2003; Kudyba and Hoptroff 2001). Ethical Issues (Griffin, 2003). Collaboration Business Platforms (Griffin, 2003; Atre, 2003; Johnstone and Wong, 2008). Improper Implementation (Ishaya and Rigneau, 2007; Levine, 2002). Minimization of time (Griffin, 2003).
Construction	DSS	Data Quality (Madnick et al, 2009; Ishaya and Julian 2007; Ishaya and Rigneau, 2007)
Retail Sale	CRM, DSS	Collaboration Business Platforms (Griffin, 2003; Atre, 2003).
E-Commerce	CRM	Data Quality (Madnick et al, 2009; Ishaya and Julian 2007; Ishaya and Rigneau, 2007). Improper Implementation (Ishaya and Rigneau, 2007; Levine, 2002)
Insurance	DSS	Ethical Issues (Witten and Frank, 2005) Legal Issues (Witten and Frank, 2005)

As can be seen from Table 1 above, collaborative business platforms is a fundamental challenge as also identified in Bethold et al(2010) that require investigating within telecoms industry. This section presents a review of BI, implementation of BI within Telecoms industry, and data sources use for data warehouses (DWs) and BI in Telecoms industry and an analysis of the data sources within the industry.

A Review of Current Approaches to BI in Telecoms Industry

Application of BI in Telecoms Industry has been focused mainly on customer management, fraud management, knowledge discovery and key performance indicators (Christine normile 2006). Each application has its own process and the processes are often automated in the Telecoms industry. BI combines business processes with IT systems to support decision-making in an organization. The IT systems used in BI such as DWs, OLAP, and Reporting have their own processes and combination of these processes made up the processes of BI. Business processes in BI are business rules defined by each Telecoms organization base on the business requirement and objectives. If for instance, the objective of Telecoms Company is to manage customers, then customer satisfaction becomes the business requirement and as a result, a set of rules are developed to define the processes required to achieve the requirement.

The process of CRM in Telecoms industry involves three steps, which are customer identification, understanding, and interaction as shown in Figure 1 below.

Figure 1. Process of CRM in telecoms (Normile, 2006)

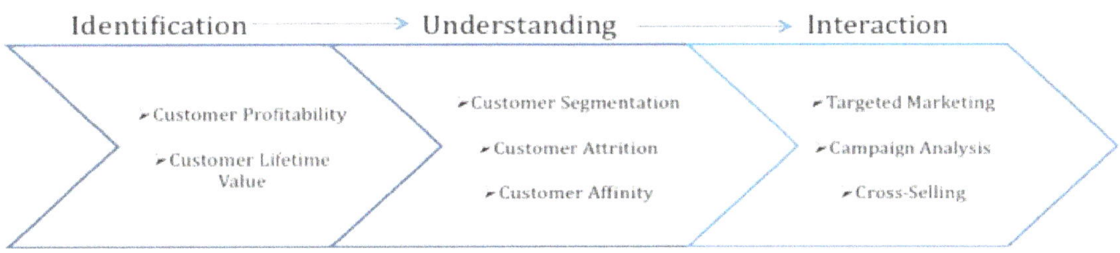

The following section provides a brief description of the main components:

Identification

Customer identification is very important to Telecom operators and it starts from counting the number of subscriber base via a unique identification MSISDN and to identify the most profitable and potential profitable customers in the future. In the past, Telecom operators were more concerned about the number of subscribers with a simple view that the more the subscribers the more their turn over until recently when the telecoms operators started applying BI before they discover many unknowns such as the differences in the contribution of each subscriber (Normile, 2006). Hence, they need to define business rule to identify customers who are the most profitable among their customer base and who are the less profitable. These set of business rules help the company to keep the profitable customer to ensure stable income while the less profitable one can also give an insight about the reasons why they are not profitable, which may be due to wrong offerings, low income or bad network in their location and so on. To determine the overall customer profitability, the operators need to calculate the costs of serving customers over a period of time and revenue realized over the same period of time (Normile, 2006).

The second attribute in the identification component is the Customer Lifetime Value (CLV), which is the value in terms of money that a telecoms operator can realize from the customer over long-term (Cunningham et al, 2004). Analysis of CLV could tell if a customer is likely to be more profitable in the future or not and a customer may also serve as reference to a profitable customer (Normile, 2006). CLV is also used to justify the cost of customer acquisition. For example, if it will cost £20 to acquire a customer and CLV is about £50, then the cost may be considered justifiable.

Understanding

In order for services or products offering to be successful, there is need for proper understanding of the needs and wants of customers. Due to large number of customers, it is always good to divide them into groups for close observation before drilling down to individual customer. Segmentation is used to segment customers with common relationships. These segments now become a unique entities and the future relationship with the segments can be tailored accordingly. Through segmentation we can identify market potential relationship between products and each customer in the segments and decisions can be made about which product is likely to be interested to the segments (Lee and Park, 2005).

Customer affinity is also referred to as market-basket analysis and this analysis tells what segments of customer are likely to buy from a group of products. Affinity analysis is usually done using association techniques to predict the right combination of products and services for a customer or segment of customer (Normile, 2006). The last in the process of CRM is customer interaction, after identifying the type of customers and understand their usage pattern; the next step is to start interacting with the customers. Targeted Marketing, Campaign Analysis, and Cross-selling are ways of interacting with the customer (Normile, 2006).

Interaction

In targeted marketing, particular group of customer segmentation are the target and once the customer segments are identified, BI tools can be used to develop a predictive model to determine buying propensity of the segment towards both new and existing products (Normile, 2006). Campaign analysis is the analysis of impact of a promotion or marketing advertisement on a particular service or product. Market affinity and market target and knowledge of past success or failure are the prerequisites of campaign analysis (Normile, 2006). Cross-selling is way of using existing data via BI tools to gain quick insight into what could be the new products that may be requested or required by the customers so that the right offer can be made to the customers when interacting or making contact with them. Cross-selling also make used of association technique to achieve it aim (Normile, 2006). However, for this to be more effective, it is important to ensure that the data captured about customers is of quality in nature. The importance of data quality for data mining has been well discussed in Ishaya and Rigneau (2007), and Griffin (2003).

Implementation of BI in Telecoms Industry

The processes of BI in Telecoms Industry are usually implemented using traditional BI approaches as shown in figure 2 below.

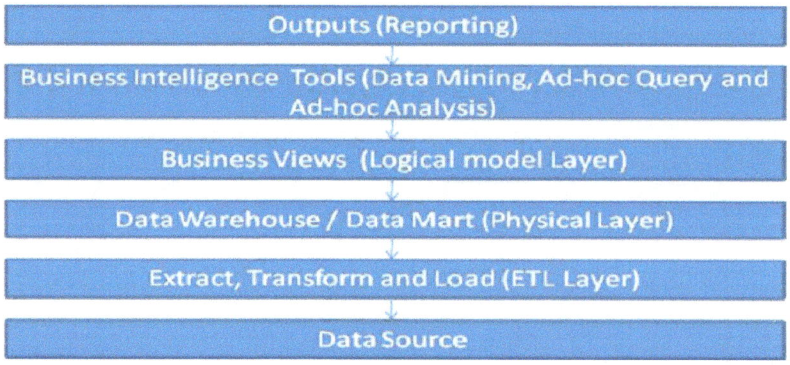

Figure 2. Traditional Approach to BI (Wu et al, 2007)

As shown in figure 2 above, BI integrates data and information from various sdata source using the ETL process to extract transactional data, transform and upload data into DWs. After loading the data into DWs, Data mining tools such as OLAP and ad-hoc query operate on the vast amount of information stored in the DWs or Datamarts to produce business related report in a timely (near real-time) and friendly format. However, traditional approach to BI takes much longer time to process and as competition increases among business organizations, this approach to data integration may not meet up with constantly changing analysis needed to support decision-making due to the static and time dependent nature of DWs and direct end to end BI tools. Millions of CDRs data are being generated daily and as service providers add new services to ensure customer satisfaction, customer's data will continue to grow exponentially and it can be difficult to analyze these vast amounts of data at a reasonable time and cost (Cunningham el al, 2004). Therefore, there is the need for SO and dynamic approach to BI that would allow for flexibility, collaboration and both real-time and historic data processing and analysis of the vast amount of data and information keep in Telecoms Industry.

An analysis of Telecoms Data Sources

Data sources for BI can be from OOS, external source, archived data, and information from other DWs (Ranjan, 2009). Weiss (2004) described three major data keep by telecoms organizations as CDR, Network Data, and CRM. Also Johnstone et al (2008) recognized Network Switches, Billing System and Service Records as part of data sources in telecoms organizations. The data sources for BI in Telecoms industry can be grouped into internal and external data sources as discussed in section 2.3.1 and 2.3.2 respectively. Data sources can also be classified into structure and unstructured data. The structure data referred to as data from structured databases such as relational and xml while unstructured data are data from text file, PDF, Web pages, and so on.

Internal Data Sources

The Internal data sources are data generate from OSS and examples include CDR, CRM, Billing Systems, and Service Records. CDR is generated directly from the telco's network switch. Billing System extract part of CDR, CRM and Service Records for billing purpose and merge the bill to customer via the mobile number after calculating the bill.

CDR is a computer record containing details of calls such as the number making the call, number receiving the call, date and time of call, call duration, call route, call type, the number charged for the call, telephone switch identity, record identity, and fault condition encountered during the call usually generated by charging system of the telephone switch. The sending telephone switches keep the CDR progressively until the end of the call, after which the Telecoms billing support system can retrieve and process the CDR for billing. Mobile CDR may contain information on more than one call type or traffic such as voice calls, Short Message Service (SMS), and other data services traffic (Johnstone and Wong, 2008). Due to valuable information contain in the CDR, Telecom operators can utilize CDR information as a data source for DWs and BI. The mediation module prepares CDR data for billing by cleaning and transforming CDRs into format that is accessible by the billing system (Johnstone and Wong, 2008). Figure 3 below shows a simple billing process and explanation on how the billing system work is provided.

All mobile calls passes through Mobile Switch Centre (MSC) for the purpose of routing and to generate, collect, and store CDR records. If the call is a local call, the call traffic is connected through MSC to a public-switched telephone network (PSTN) for a fixed-line network or directly to MSC of another mobile operator network. But in the case of International Direct Dialling (IDD) call, the traffic is routed from MSC to an international toll gateway (ITG) or other IDD services providers (Johnstone and Wong, 2008). The SMS CDR is being generated and recorded by Short Message Service Centre (SMSC). SMSC provides a store and forward function delivering SMS messages to the users' destination when they are available while destination mobile operator has a SMSC designated to the respective SMS message partners or SMS clearinghouse for further delivery (Johnstone and Wong, 2008). Global System for Mobile Communication (GSM), 2G General Packet Radio Service (GPRS), 2.5G GPRS and 3G GPRS offers data services and the usage of data services are recorded by GPRS Support Note (SGSN) and Gateway GPRS (GGSN). Data collected from the SGSN and the GGSN is first sent to a dedicated charging gateway (CG) before being forwarded to the mediation module. The major function of a CG is to collect CDRs from both the SSGN and GGSN, buffering and transferring CDRs to the mediation module of the billing system (Johnstone and Wong, 2008). The mediation module also contains a filtering rule algorithm. The filtering rules are a programming conditions base on the business requirements. It is very important to ensure that appropriate and complete information is delivered to the billing system for rating and necessary calculation, and the service type must be mapped accurately against the corresponding rate for accurate billing (Johnstone and Wong, 2008).

The main reasons for developing CRM is to manage customer by identifying who the customer is, understanding what customer needs and value of each customer, and interacting with them base on the information at hand. CRM also combine data from CDR, Billing System, and Customer profile and Service Record (Weiss, 2004) to give more information about the customer in order to make more accurate and stronger decision to be able to make right offer to the right customer at the right time.

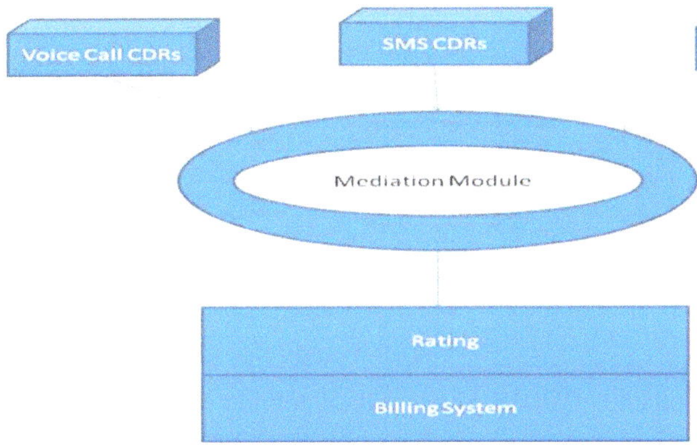

Figure 3. Simple billing process (Johnstone and Wong, 2008)

External Data Sources

The external data sources are data retrieved from external network domain such as Telecoms regulatory body and specialist vendor in the public or social network domain. Among the information retrieved from external source are customer profile information such as income, age, habits and gender and competitor's products, prices, and sales. External data sources are very expenses due to unstructured format, which need to undergo extra and complex transformation before loading into the DWs.

This section has presented a review of BI in Telecoms industry by a way of justifying a need for SOBI approach to BI in order to ensure flexible, collaborative and both real-time and historic data analysis of vast amount of data and information available within the industry. In the next section, a proposed SOBI architecture is presented and discussed.

A PROPOSED SERVICE ORIENTED BUSINESS INTELLIGENCE (SOBI) ARCHITECTURE

Based on the review presented in the previous section, it is clear that telecoms industries need BI that is capable of performing real-time analysis on vast amount of CDR data generated and able to analyze historical data of CDR to identify customer value and make strategic decision to retain, attract new customer, and to ensure their satisfaction towards increasing profitability. A service-oriented-architecture (SOA) is an architecture upon which different standalone services can be loosely coupled over distributed systems (Hu et al, 2011). They are business-centric IT architectural approach that supports the integration of business as connected and repeatable business services. A fundamental advantage of these services is that they can communicate with each other even though each service has different underlying implementation platforms. It is therefore clear that a Service Oriented (SO) approach will provide a common, open, and interoperable solution to the problem encountered in traditional BI. While, SO approach is being used within many industries, its advantages are yet to be fully harnessed within the telecoms industry. SO can be adopted for agile and flexible applications, application-application integration, high-frequency events, real-time data analysis, reusable of services components, proper data formats and structures, and encapsulates and abstracts functionality (Gordon et al, 2006). This section presents the development of Service Oriented Business Intelligence (SOBI) architecture based on an analysis of existing architectures/models and customer requirements that were captured through questionnaires. The architecture integrates data from heterogeneous data sources of the organization.

The SOBI architectural framework intends to leverages the strengths of BI and SO while defining guiding principle to ensure that the fundamental tenets of each of the component architectures are not broken. SO allows distributed application development through interfaces capable of exchange messages through. In SOBI paradigms, BI is seen as a collection of Services such as Data Services, Transformation Services and so on, while SO is seen as a collection of data sources and event source. A service can promptly be opened "as a data source with the introduction of a simple facade layer that provides a mapping between the BI interface and interface exposed by the service" (Gordon et al, 2006). The facade layer also transforms the results set of the call from data schema used on the service bus to data format expected by the BI platform and returns the result to the caller. The section is organised as follows: Section 3.1 describes the general approach used in the development of the proposed architecture. Section 3.2 presents an analysis and discussion of the customer satisfaction surveys and interviews undertaken to help capture a set of user requirements for SOBI. Section 3.3 presents a review of current BI architectures, which was also used in analysing the SOBI requirements presented in Section 3.4. Section 3.5 finally presents the proposed architecture.

Methodology

A mixed methods approach was used in developing the SOBI Architecture. First we conducted a customer satisfaction survey via a questionnaire to capture customer requirements, and business requirement by interviewing a few Telecoms operators. Second, the requirements were used in the context of existing models. A phone simulator was developed to generate and store CDR data in OSS database since we couldn't not lay our hands on the CRM and CDR dataset from the telecoms operator that promised to provide us with such data. Samples of other data such as customer profile, tariff plan, route, rate, algorithm, route, location, and services are provided in the OOS database. A DW was developed and data and information was extracted from OSS databases to populate the DW. The customer questionnaire survey data was collected to capture requirements required for the development of the SOBI architecture. The interview was conducted with Telecoms operator to understand business rules and requirements, which form the business processes towards development of SOBI architecture.

Customer Satisfaction Surveys and Interviews

An interview was conducted with two Telecoms analysts who are making use of BI report for decision-making and BI application developer analyst. One of the Telecoms analysts works with Vodafone as Online Services Senior Executive and the second works with Etisalat Nigeria as Product Specialist-Post-paid/Corporate Solutions. The first interview with Vodafone BI analyst was carried out face to face while the subsequent interview was conducted via email. Interview with Etisalat Nigeria Analyst was through email and interview with BI application developer was through online blog. During the interview, we were able to understand the type of data kept in Telecoms industry and the necessary reports needed to support decision-making process. Also, we were able to capture business rule and processes to ensure customer satisfaction, which eventually form the Telecoms operator requirement to develop SOBI architecture.

The interview conducted with Telecoms analyst also assisted in understanding the processes, which helped in the design of the questionnaire that was administered to customers. The interview with BI application developer gave us more details on how Telecoms operator system works. A questionnaire was developed and administered online by sending a link of the survey to a list of postgraduate students of the University of Hull and other individuals across UK that have volunteered to participate in the study. The questionnaire was made anonymous by making sure that personal information - such as name, telephone number, and addresses were not been included. This is in order to ensure that we conform to privacy law. The questionnaire was divided into sections. Section one captured some of the generic participant's personal details such as gender, age group, region and country of residence, education level, industry sector, and current position.

Section two covers customer mobile information such as how long a customer has been using their provider's SIMcard, the name of the provider, the reasons and name of second provider for those using multiple SIMcards. Section three covers the customer usage information such as services and tariff plan used by the customer, reasons for choosing particular tariff plan and the level of their satisfaction with services, tariff plan and quality of network.

A total number of 42 customers participated in the survey with results presented in Table 2 below. A number of responses for each question in the questionnaire vary due to the option given to customers to skip or even opt out of the survey at any time, which was one of the stated conditions in the letter of consent. The analysis of the result showed that 47.6% and 52.4% are male and female who participated in the survey respectively. 66% are within the age of 18 and 30 and 90.5% are currently residing in UK and 9.5% residing in other countries. 17 out of 38 responses equivalent to 44.7% have been using their provider SIMcards for less than one year, 39.5% have been using provider SIMcard for one to five years and 15.8% have maintained their SIMcard providers for more than five years. O2 happened to be the preferred provide for most of the participants followed by Vodafone and Orange. 20.0% used two SIMcards due to lack of variation of services, and 70.0% leave the previous provide for the current one because the current provider offer competitive tariff. 23 out of 27 responses equivalent to 85.2% of customer used their current SIMcard. 66.7% make local call every day, 25.0% make international calls every day, 46.9% make long duration call of 5 min and above every day, 78.1% send text messages every day, 25.0% used the internet every day, and 37.5% send or check email every day while none of them send video messages, download music and video at all on a daily basis.

Services	Daily	Weekly	Monthly	Yearly	Never	No of Response
Local call	66.7%	15.2%	15.2%	-	3.0%	33
International call	25.0%	25.0%	12.5%	15.6%	21.9%	32
Make 5 min call and above	46.9%	25.0%	18.8%	-	9.4%	32
Text messages	78.1%	15.6%	3.1%	3.1%	-	32
Video messages	-	6.5%	9.7%	3.2%	80.6%	31
Internet browsing	25.0%	12.5%	12.5%	-	50.0%	32
Check and send email	37.5%	3.1%	12.5%	-	46.9%	32
Download music	-	3.1%	25.0%	3.1%	68.8%	32
Download video	-	3.1%	25.0%	-	71.9%	32

Table 2. Customer usage habit over time on various services

Customer tariff plan was also captured during the survey, with results presented in Table 3 below. 18 out of 32 responses equivalent to 56.3% of the customers are using Pas As You Go tariff plan also known as pre-paid package, 43.8% are using Contract Package also known as post-paid package while none of them were using a roaming tariff plan. The reason for choosing a particular tariff plan varies among the customers. 21 out of 28 responses equivalent to 75% choose tariff plan because they were more cheaper them, 14.3% choose a particular tariff plan because they were not aware of others, 10.7% choose tariff plan because of the availability of free international call, 3.67% choose a particular tariff plan because of more number of free international text, 14.3% choose tariff plan because of more number of free local call, and 10.7% choose tariff plan because of more number of free local text. The survey also captured the level of customer satisfaction on some charges and promotional offers.

Table 3. Customer satisfaction surveys

	Strongly Satisfied	Satisfied	Neutral	Dissatisfied	Strongly Dissatisfied	No of Response
Charges on Pay As You Go	16.7%	33.3%	26.7%	3.3%	20.0%	30
Promo offer on Pay As You Go	10.3%	24.1%	51.7%	10.3%	3.4%	29
Charges on Contract Package	-	39.3%	35.7%	10.7%	14.3%	28
Free call on Contract Package	11.1%	40.7%	40.7%	-	7.4%	27
Free text on Contract Package	18.5%	37.0%	37.0%	-	7.4%	27

From the table above, customers are satisfied except on promotional offer where customers are neutral. These levels of satisfaction indicate where Telecom operators' analysis needs to concentrate in order to know if a customer is satisfied or not. Hence tariff plan and associated benefit need to meet the preference of the customer especially on Pay AS You Go tariff plan.

The survey further captured what will be customer next step if Telecoms operator want to use business rule of £20 usage in a month to identify loyal customer by getting the monthly usage and call of 5 min and above before and after asking customers how likely they are likely to make more call and used £20 in a month. 17 out of 33 responses equivalent to 51.5% of customers used £20 and above while 24.2% used less than £20 in a month. 18.8% of customers make 5 min call and above in a month as shown in table 1000 above. But after asking the question, the customers responses show that 14 out of 32 equivalents to 43.8% of customers are very likely to make more call, 18.8% are likely to make more call, 6.3% are not likely to make more call, and 9.4% are very unlikely to make more call if Telecoms operator is ready to reduce price on long duration call. Also, 6 out of 31 equivalents to 19.4% of customer are very likely to used £20, 25.8% are likely to used £20, 32.3% say nothing, 12.9% are unlikely to used £20, and 9.7% are very unlikely to used £20 in a month. This show that customer are willing to make more call but £20 average set by the Telecoms operator is too much for them and hence majority of customer may not be satisfied with promotional offer targeting customer with £20 usage in a month and can also be the reason why customer are not satisfied with promo offer on Pay As You Go as the case of this survey.

Analysis of Current BI Architecture

As discussed, traditional BI has been designed with focus on historical data usually provided by DWs and used for strategic decision which may span days but as business activities continue to evolve there is need for multi-tier data analytics application and leverage analytics of data, event, and content (Atre, 2008; Berthold, 2010). Current approach to BI has changed beyond traditional approach (as previously discussed) in other industries such as E-commerce and a good example is Amazon.com, but Telecom Operators are just on the way to follow this trend. Telecoms Operators are now structuring OSS towards SO which in return will aid SOBI. Figure 4 below shows the component of SOBI architecture proposed by Wu et al. (2007).

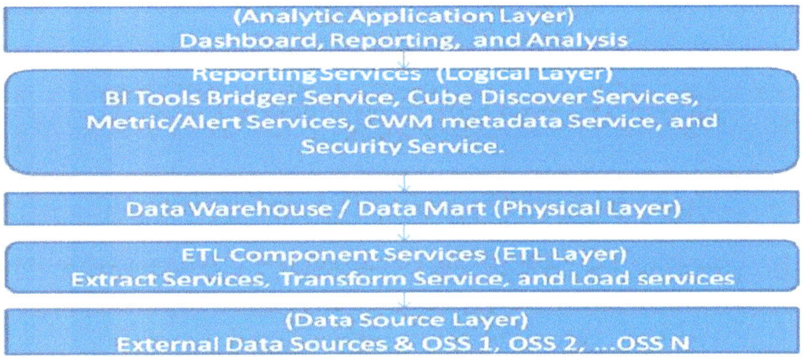

Figure 4. Current BI Architecture (Wu et al, 2007)

Wu et al. (2007), described SO architecture as an improvement on the traditional BI architecture by implementing ETL Layer and Logical Layer as web component services and thus leverage SO and BI architecture.

Requirements analysis for SOBI architecture Based on survey analysis, interviews and a review of related models, the following requirements were identified as fundamental in the development of SOBI architecture.

- Telecoms operators need to analyze both real-time and historical data. Real-time analysis such as registering an event on CDR record to identifying customer making long duration call and automatically billing them base on predefined tariff plan to such transactions and inform the customer about it. This can speed up decision-making process and communication. Analysis of historical data can provide adequate review of what tariff plan need to be set up, and other required services by which category or individual customer.
- Telecoms operator managers need to have a quick summary of customer satisfaction. While it is important to go through in-depth customer satisfaction analysis by the managers or the analyst, it also important to have a quick overview customer satisfaction levels.
- Telecoms operators need to analyze customer usage pattern in various dimensions. This is important in order to understand why customers have behaved in a particular way at a particular time. For example, customers may have different calling habits depending on tariff plan, available service, time of the day, and so on. These analyses also enable the discovery of hidden behaviour, which has not been noticed in the past.
- Telecoms operators need to be able to drill down and drill up while analysing the customer usage pattern. This is also supporting requirement No. 3 mentioned above.
- Telecoms operators need BI architecture that is flexible to change in the business activities, which usually lead to changes in business requirement. Change is inevitable in business activities, therefore the more flexible to adapt to change, the more Telecoms operator will be able to survive the competitive environment.
- Telecoms operators need to ensure security of data stored in the OSS and DWs and during analysis. Security of operational data and customer information is very important to prevent loss, stolen, damage and authorise person from accessing the information while in storage or during analysis.
- Telecoms operators need to combine call details with customer profile and demographic for more accurate decision making about customer satisfaction. For example customer that is 60 years of age and above may make less calls but there may be an issue of customer dissatisfaction when customer within the age of 20-40 is making less call.

From the customer's point of view, the following requirements were identified:

- Customers need reasonable tariffs and would wish that the tariffs were dynamically adjustable to suite individual demands, which clearly suggest a need for a personalised plan where possible.
- The customers need to be aware of current promotion and contract packages.
- Customers need quality of service

There are also a number of technical and non-technical requirements

The Proposed SOBI Architecture

The SOBI architecture was developed based on the general requirements presented in Section 3.4. The architecture is an extension of the one developed in Wu et al. (2007). Main extension is the clear emphasis on the analysis of events that should be performed on CDR data. Figure 5 below shows the developed SOBI architecture.

The SOBI architecture consists of five layers, which are Data Source Layer, ETL Layer, Physical Layer, Logical Layer, and Application Layer. Each of these layers defines a set of business processes to ensure a successful BI project. Each of the layers has been briefly described below, with a more technical insight provided in the implementation of the SOBI prototype simulator.

- Data Source Layer is the OSS database where day-to-day business transaction data are stored. Data Source Layer can also be an external source such as data from a survey company. SOBI architecture had been designed to allow analytics of events on the CDR data source in order to provide more real time analysis. The Data Source Layer stored day-to-day business activities of Telecoms operators in OOS database. In order to design OSS database, we need data modelling using ERM or Normalization approach to ensure that the entities in OSS database are normalized to the third normal form. This is very essential to prevent data inconsistency, data redundancy, and anomalies, which reduce the quality of data and thus make ETL process very complex and can even result into poor quality BI.

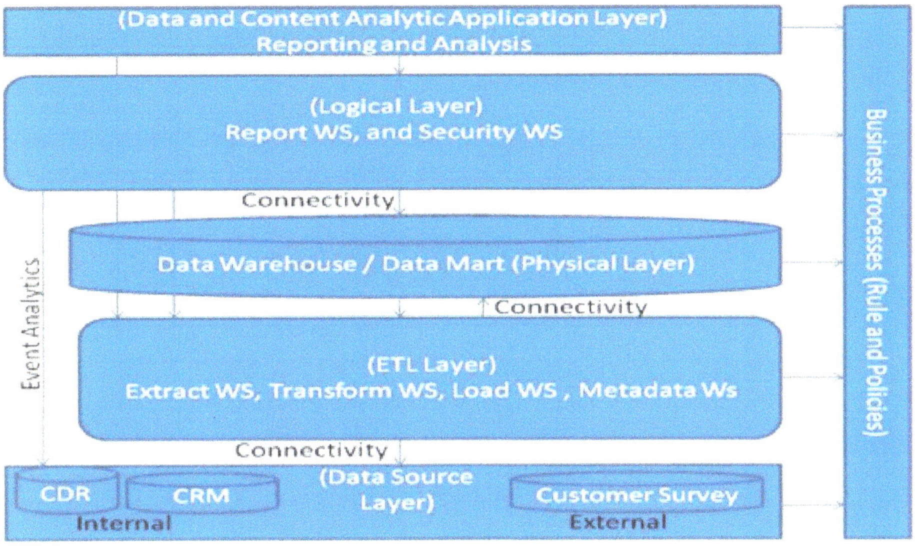

Figure 5. SOBI architecture

- ETL Layer consists of Extract, Transform, and Loading Services. The extract service extract all the required data from the OSS databases, transform service transform the data into a format required by the DWs while the function of loading service is to load the data and information into the DWs. The design of ETL Layer starts with the identification of the exact data that need to be extracted, the quality of the data and additional information necessary to provide complete and meaningful information. Business processes must be followed during ETL Layer design. Business processes determine when operational data is available for ETL, reformatting of OSS into a unified format, reconciling the data redundancy, and cleansing the dirty data found in the source system.
- The Physical Layer is the data repository centre of SOBI architecture and this is the layer where DWs are required to be developed. DWs have processes and architecture have been discussed in section 2. Before designing DWs, it is important to have DWs specific technical and functional requirements from the general requirements performed in section 3.
- The Logical Layer of SOBI architecture focuses on the development of business logic. This includes appropriate activities that are required to be monitored, those that trigger other events/services, design of variable billing algorithms, tariffs, etc. This layer represents the logical view of the entire Telecoms operator data Business logic and rules regarding security, privacy, etc also falls within this layer.
- The Application Layer is the presentation layer where data are display in form of reporting tools using tables, charts, etc to aid visualization. This layer is where reporting and complex analysis are performed and rendered to the BI end user. OLAP and data mining technique will be adopted for reporting and forecasting respectively. OLAP provide summary data and information, which can also be drill down, roll up, slice and dice. Appropriate data mining techniques such as segmentation and exponential smoothing can be applied for specific objectives, such as the ability to predict customer satisfaction level and forecast the average usage of customer respectively.

The developed SOBI architecture will be evaluated by the prototype application, which will be discussed in the next section

DEVELOPMENT OF A SOBI PROTOTYPE SIMULATOR

According to Atre and Moss (2003), BI applications require a dynamic system development approach. Since it was not possible to have access to some telecoms data, it became necessary to design a simulator to demonstrate and further reflect on the developed SOBI architecture presented in Section 3. The design of the simulator was done according to the five layers of the architecture - Data Source Layer, ETL Layer, Physical Layer, Logical Layer and Application Layer. The focus of the prototype was on the generation of CDR and CRM data, extraction, transformation and loading of the data into developed DWs. The prototype also covered report generation to demonstrate how such reports could assist Telecoms operator to analyze the customer call details over time and able to identify the relationship between tariff plan and customer usage. The prototype is limited to only call service categorise by local and international call.

Prototype Requirement Analysis

After reviewing service oriented development technologies, the prototype was design and implemented using PHP WS technology at the server side, JavaScript at the client side, and Ajax to provide dynamic interaction between the client and the server. The data source and DWs was designed and implemented using MySQL RDBMS running on Apache server with PHP installed on the server. WS was configured with SOAP extensions in the PHP library. The prototype also required sample data of CDR and CRM from Telecoms operator but a call simulator will be developed since samples data are not available.

- The prototype is expected to allow user to simulate a call and generate the CDR data set.
- Extract data from OSS, transform data and load into DWs.
- Analyze customer call details to know the customer satisfaction level.
- Identify relationship between customer usage and tariff plan.
- Provide details information about customer in segment of the tariff plan.

The overall design of the simulator is shown in Figure 6 below.

The simulator also required the design of the data source layer in order to provide the OSS data required for the development of other layers. The entities necessary for Telecoms operator to store customer call details included Mediation, TariffPlan, TariffAlgorithm, Rate, Billing, Route, Location, Service, ServiceType, Customer, CDR, etc. At the physical layer, a DW has been design to provide the required data repository for the SOBI prototype simulator. Before designing the DW, it was important to have the DW specific technical and functional requirements. A star schema of the DW containing a customer fact table and the associated dimensions were designed as shown in Figure 7.

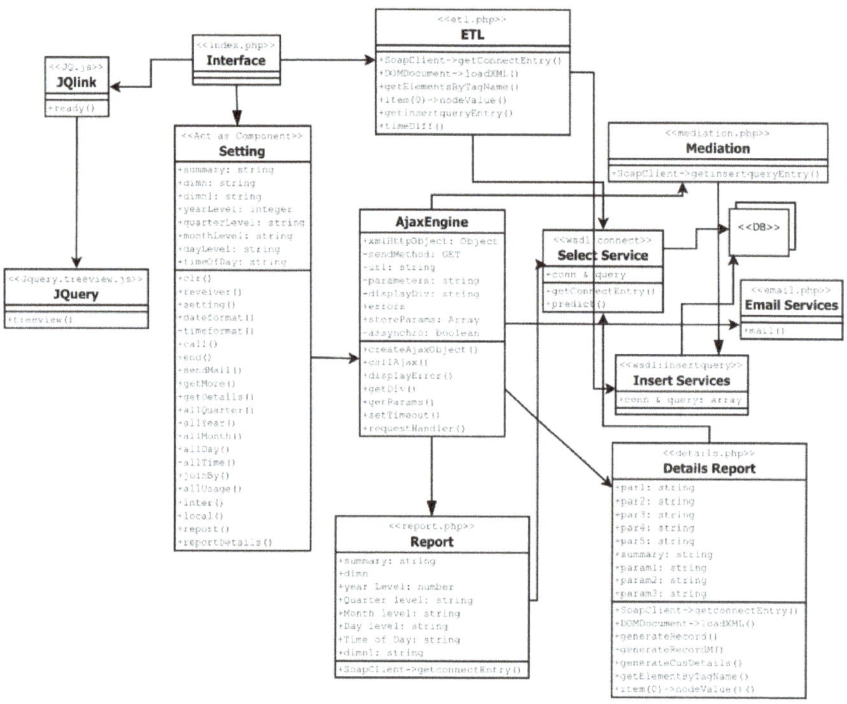

Figure 6. Class diagram of the SOBI prototype simulator

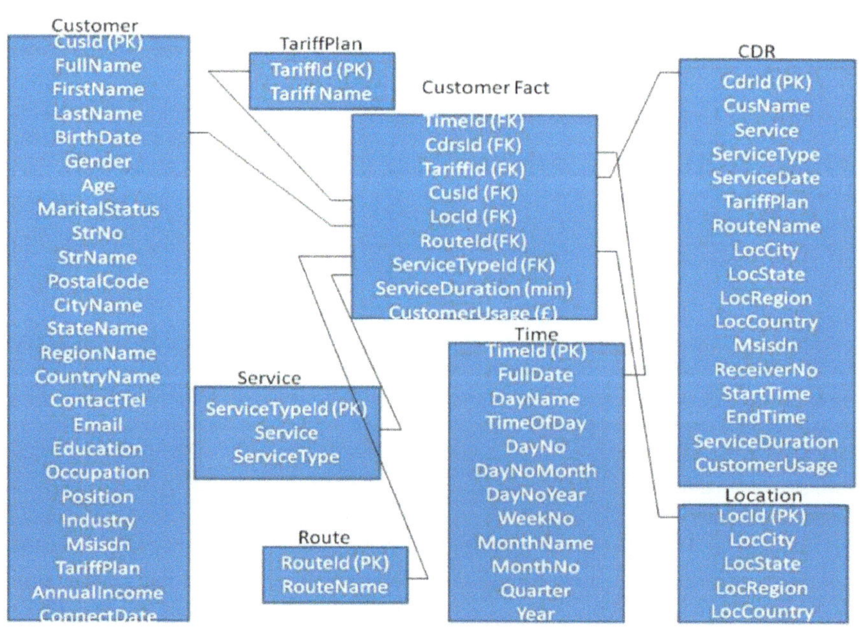

Figure 7. Star schema of customer fact.

As shown from Figure 7 above, the Customer Fact is in the centre surrounded by the dimension table. The time dimension will make it easy to view ServiceDuration and CustomerUsage on daily, weekly, monthly, quarterly and yearly basis. Other physical layer designs included data marts, metadata, backup and recovery, data aggregation, etc.

Prototype Implementation

The implementation of SOBI prototype is divided into Data Source, DWs, analytical and presentation tools. The simulator prototype was implemented using service-oriented technologies. As shown in Figure 6, the prototype has a single interface using JavaScript at the client side to capture the request of the user and pass it to the Ajax Engine which then send the request to the server where the WS class component are located. The ETL processes are being handled by etl.php. The index.php is the interface to invoke the ETL process and the interface will refresh to reflect the newly loaded data. The interface has a tree view menu list elements that is dynamically handled using the JQuery class. Setting.js acts as a listener to every change that occurs and passes the necessary parameter to the Ajax.class.js, which sends the request to the server and handles the response, which is display on the client side. Other components of the class diagram are discussed below.

The Insert Service has a WSDL, which specified the input and output parameter operations. The array of input parameter contains the host, username, password, database, table, and query. This service is used to insert CDR data generated by the call simulator into the OSS database on MySQL server and is also used to load the transformed data into DW in another MySQL database on the same server. This class has also been developed to connect with Postgre SQL. This is the usefulness of SOBI, the interoperability and the reusability and flexibility that WS brings.

The select service also has WSDL and WS server class that perform the requested operation. The select service has input parameter as an array, which contains the same content as insert service and another additional parameter, which specified what type of string to be returned by the service. The service can return XML or HTML string depending on the expected result output. The HTML string has been specially developed to generate html table of any column and row without knowing the structure of the table. What is requires is the correct query. Similarly, XML file is generated using DOMDocument object class. The select service also has a function that calculates single exponential smoothing technique. This function takes the row of average usage query result accordingly and applies the formula to forecast the next average usage.

The report has been implemented using the select service to select from the database and send the return HTML string from the select service to Ajax Engine which passes it to JavaScript which is using DOM Objects to display the table in a specified div (cont) in the index.php corresponding to the specified of the interface report area. The report service contain series of next if statement which determines what query to be executed before invoking the select service. The details report could have been part of Report Service discussed above but it has been move to another PHP file for simplicity, readability and to avoid confusion as a result of the complexity of the if statement involved in both reports. Parameters sent by the Ajax is also examined to determine which query is required and responses returned from Select Service is handle using DOMDocument to load the XML string and generate html table which is sent back to the Ajax Engine.

Mediation Service get all the call simulator parameter sent by setting.js through Ajax Engine and invoke Select Service to get other information such as customer id of the caller and tariff plan. It has functions that calculate the duration and bill the customer before invoking Insert Service to insert the CDR data into the OOS database.

The extract, transform, and load services, which have been design separately during the SOBI system design, are now implemented together as a single service. The Select Service was invoked to select the current data from the source system and transformation process was carried out before invoking the Insert Service to load into the DW.

During data transformation, the content of DW table was compare with sources in order to select the current information. PK and FK relationships are used to get the actual data from the sources system. The dimension and fact table was loaded during the ETL. The Email Service gets the necessary parameter such as message, receiver email and name from client side through JavaScript and Ajax Engine. Email Service used PHP mail function to sent mail and returns nothing back to the Ajax Engine.

The prototype was evaluated by developing a set of tasks that will enable telecoms analysts to perform customer call usage analysis through simulated calls and whether or not they could make informed decisions about specific customer. The evaluation was carried out by the telecom analysts were interviewed during the requirements gathering stage. Evaluation results clearly indicates a great potential of using SOBI in telecoms industry.

CONCLUSION

This chapter presents an investigation into the integration and analysis of data from CRM and CDR of Telecoms operators using SO approach to assist the organization in making real-time and accurate decision about the customer tariff plan to ensure customer satisfaction which in return can lead to increase in profit. The prototype was evaluated against the potential outcome of the research study. The SOBI architecture and design was able to achieve all but the prototype has not been able to achieve everything.

Analytic events on CDR, ability to offer the right product to the right customer, and security of WS have not been achieved. This is due to limitation of the prototype scope and it is expected that the prototype will have to go through next iteration of the software engineering process. Telecoms operator cannot do without SOBI in the competitive market and ability to analyze make decision, and act on the decision in time could be an advantage to exploit market opportunity. SOBI architecture have been developed and designed to achieve this but the prototype have not been able to evaluate everything about SOBI. Therefore, we need to implement other aspect and re-evaluate the SOBI architecture and design.

REFERENCES

1. Atre, S. (2008), Successful Business Intelligence: Secrets to Making BI a Killer App, the McGraw-Hill Companies, ISBN: 978-0-07-149851-7, Available at http://books.google.co.uk/ accessed [19 July 2010].
2. Atre, S. (2003), The Top 10 Critical Challenges for Business Intelligence Success, White Paper Article, Available at http://www.computerworld.com/computerworld/records/images/pdf/BusIntel lWPonline.pdf accessed [19 July 2010].
3. Berthold, H., Rosch P., Zoller S., Wortmann F., Carenini A., Campbell S., Bisson P., and Strohmaier F. (2010) , An Architecture for Ad-Hoc and Collaborative Business Intelligence, ACM Conference Proceeding Series Vol. 426, Proceeding of the 2010 EDBT/ICDT Workshops, Lausanne, Switzerland, ISBN:978-1-60558-990-9, Article No. 13, Available at http://portal.acm.org/citation.cfm accessed [28 June 2010].
4. Christensen, E., Curbera, F., Meredith, G., and Weerawarana, S. (2001), Web Services Description Language (WSDL) 1.1, W3C, Available at http://www.w3.org/TR/wsdl, accessed [5th August 2010].
5. Chung, W. and Chen, H. (2009), Handbooks in Information Systems Series: Business Computing, Volume 3, Edited by Gediminas, A. and Alok, G.,Emerald Group Publishing Limited, ISBN:978-1-84855-264-7, Available at http://books.google.co.uk/books accessed [14 June 2010] , pp. 373-396.
6. Cunningham, C., Song, L., and Chen, P.P. (2004), Data Warehouse Design to support Customer Relationship Management Analyses, Data Warehousing and OLAP, Proceedings of the 7th ACM international workshop on Data warehousing and OLAP, Washington DC, USA, ISBN: 1-58113-977-2, pp. 14-22, Available at http://portal.acm.org accessed [8th July 2010].
7. Gordon, S., Grigg, R., Horne, M., and Thurman, S. (2006), Service-Oriented Business Intelligence, Microsoft, Available at http://msdn.microsoft.com/enus/library/bb245659.aspx accessed[18 June 2010].
8. Griffin, J. (2003), A Challenge for the Telecom Industry: Converging Enterprise Portals and Business Intelligence to Produce a Collaborative Business Platform, Information Management Magazine, August 2003, Available at http://www.informationmanagement.com/issues/20030801/7154-1.html accessed [6th July 2010].
9. Hadden, J., Tiwari, A., Roy, R., and Ruta, D. (2007), Computer assisted customer churn management: State-of-the-art and Future Trends, Computers and Operations Research vol.34, No.10, pp2902-2917
10. Han, J., and Kamber, M. (2006), Data Mining : Concepts and Techniques, Morgan Kaufmann, Second Edition, ISBN:1-55860-901-6.
11. Hu, J., Khalil, I., Han, S., and Mahmood, A (2011). Seamless integration of dependability and security concepts in SOA: A feedback control system based framework and taxonomy. Journal of Network and Computer Applications Vol 34(4), July 2011, pp1150-1159
12. Hung, S.Y, Yen, D.C, and Wang, H.Y. (2006), Applying Data Mining to Telecom Churn Management, Expert Systems with Application Vol.31, Issue 3, pp. 515-524, available at linkinghub.elsevier.com/retrieve/pii/S0957417405002654, accessed [2nd July 2010].
13. Hwang, H., Jung, T., and Suh, E.(2004), An LTV model and customer segmentation based on customer value: a case study on the wireless telecommunication industry, Expert Systems with Application Vol.26, Issue 2, pp.181-188, Available at http://www.sciencedirect.com/science accessed[8th July 2010].
14. Ishaya, T., Chadband, J., and Grierson, L. (2007), Integrating Enterprise Data for Decision Support in Construction Organisations, Proceedings of the 9th International Conference Organisations Systems , Funchal, Madeira, Portugal, ICEIS(1) : 534-539.
15. Ishaya, T., and Rigneau, J. (2007), Data Quality for Effective E-Commerce Customer Relationship Management, Proceedings of the 9th International Conference on Enterprise Information Systems, Funchal, Madeira, Portugal, ICEIS (4): 92-100.
16. Johnstone, D., and Wong, C.Y. (2008), Billing Audit on a Mobile Operator-Call Detail Record, Information Systems Control Journal, Vol. 3.
17. Kudyba, S. and Hoptroff, R. (2001), Business Intelligence A Guide to Productivity, Idea Group Publishing, ISBN: 1-930708-03-3, Available at http://www.igi-global.com accessed [14 June 2010].
18. Kleinbaum, D.G, Kupper, L.L, Nizam, and Muller, K.E. (2008), applied regression analysis and other multivariable methods, Fourth Edition, ISBN: 13:978-0-495-38496-0. Available at http://books.google.co.uk/ accessed [12 July 2010].
19. Kulkarni, U., Power, D. J. and Sharda, R. (2007), Decision Support for Global Enterprises: Annals of Information Systems, Vol. 1, Springer, Available at http://www.springerlink.com/content/g02v70027227648u/fulltext.pdf accessed [15 June 2010].
20. Lee, J.H., and Park, S.C.(2005), Intelligent profitable customers segmentation system based on business on business intelligence tools, Expert Systems with Application Vol.29, pp.145-152, Available at http://www.sci.brooklyn.cuny.edu/~kopec/cis718/fall_2005/sdarticle2.pdf accessed[5th July 2010].
21. Levin, S. (2002), Lessons in CRM: when it comes to caring for customers, telecom firms need to wise up. Here's a primer of best practices, complied from a roster of CRM experts - Telecom Corporate, Telecom Asia, Available at http://findarticles.com/p/articles/mi_m0FGI/is_10_13/ai_94010195/, accessed [8th July 2010].
22. Madnick, S.E, Lee, Y.W, and Zhu H. (2009), Overview and Framework for data and Information quality research, ACM Journal, Data Information Quality 1(1)
23. MetaGroup, (2004), Data Mining Tools: METAspectrunSM Evaluation, Available at http://www.oracle.com/technology/products/bi/odm/pdf/odm_metaspectrum _1004.pdf accessed [30 July 2010].

24. Moss, L.T., and Atre, S. (2003), Business Intelligence Roadmap: The Complete Project Lifecycle for Decision-Support Applications, Addison-Wesley, ISBN: 0-201-78420-3.

25. Pareek, D. (2006), Business Intelligence for telecommunications, Auerbach Publications, ISBN: 0-8493-8792-2.

26. Patrick, P. (2005), Impact of SOA on Enterprise Information Architectures, International Conference on Management of Data archive, Proceedings of the 2005 ACM SIGMOD International Conference on Management of Data, pp. 844-848.

27. Power, D., J. (2003), A Brief History of Decision Support Systems, version 2.8, DSSResources.COM, Available at http://dssresources.com/history/dsshistoryv28.html accessed [15 June 2010].

28. Ranjan, J. (2009), Business Intelligence: Concepts, Components, Technique and Benefits, Journal of Theoretical and Applied Information Technology, Vol.9, No.1, Available at http://www.jatit.org/volumes/research-papers/Vol9No1/9Vol9No1.pdf accessed on [26 July 2010].

29. Rus, V.R., and Toader, V. (2008), Business Intelligence for hotels' Management Performance, International Journal of Business Research, FindArticles.com, Available at http://findarticles.com/p/articles/mi_6773/is_4_8/ai_n31136506/ accessed [14 June 2010].

30. Schnjakin, M., Menzel M., and Meinel C. (2009) , A pattern-driven security for serviceoriented architectures, Conference on Computer and Communications Security, Proceeding of the 2009 ACM workshop on Secure web services, Chicago, Illinios, USA, ISBN:978-60558-789-9, pp. 13-20, Available at http://portal.acm.org/citation.cfm accessed [28 June 2010].

31. Watson, H.J. (2005), Real Time: The Next Generation of Decision Support Data Management, Business Intelligence Journal, Vol. 10, No.3, pp. 4-6.

32. Weiss, G.M. (2004), Data Mining in Telecommunications, kluwer, 2004.

33. Witten, I.H, and Frank, E. (2005), Data Mining: Practical Machine Learning Tools and Techniques, Second Edition, ISBN: 0-12-088407-0, Available at http://books.google.co.uk/ accessed [12 July 2010].

34. Wu, L., Barash, G. And Bartolini, C. (2007), A Service Oriented Architecture for Business Intelligence, IEEE International Conference on Service-Oriented Computing and Application (SOCA'07), Newport, Beach.

CHAPTER 13

A SERVICE ORIENTED ANALYTICS FRAMEWORK FOR MULTI-LEVEL MARKETING BUSINESS

Rich C. Lee

Keywords: Software Engineering, SOA, Business Analytics, Big Data, GNU-R

INTRODUCTION

The Big Data is a short hand term for advancing technology trends that open the door to a new approach to disclose the meaning behind the business activities and then based on the findings to make decisions with quality. Enterprise performance relies on the responsiveness and the quality of decision-making. Decision-making is based on rationale of the knowledge which enterprise has possessed. Enterprise knowledge is accumulated and compiled by the information, and the information is generated from the raw data by business activities. The decision makers have to develop a feasible approach to acquire sufficient knowledge and on the situation where makes a confident enough decision to support business needs [1]. Today's good decisions are driven by reliable data. Business managers and professionals are increaseingly required to justify decisions based on data. They need statistical model-based decision support systems [2]. Enterprise strives on process improvement and variation reduction; it requires a disciplined, data-driven approach to reach business goals. Statistics helps enterprise describing in quantitative way about how well the processes are performing, transform raw data to valuable information, and later become useful knowledge.

Analyzing data, deriving information, and accumulateing knowledge is not handy in most enterprise's information environment currently. First analysts must know where the desired data is, and ask IT professionals to retrieve that data, save it into files, store them under a shared folder over network, and then develop statistical models. If data is considerably large and fast-updated, it will make the statistical process more inconveniently. If other analysts concern just a portion of the data or the data is not fully covered, IT professionals must repeat these resource-exhausting tasks again for each of them respectively. Another drawback is the poor reusability if the statistical procedures are not shared. In fact, enterprise knowledge does not just cover the information but also the processes of how information was derived. These processes ensure the reproducibility of knowledge that is a part of the enterprise intelligent properties. To reach this objective, a software application—the Business intelligence (BI)-is used to analyze enterprise data; it requires expertise to design and manage those analytical models, it is usually rather expensive and complicated requiring IT professionals and software vendor's intensive assistance. Not like commercial BI software, GNUR is a flexible and extendable language and environment for statistical computing and graphics; it has been widely used in many applications for years. The analysts who are planning to use GNU-R can find abundant resources over the Internet to ease their learning curves. Thus, GNU-R is more cost-effective as a statistical engine automating analytical processes than commercial BI software. It is worthy to develop a statistical service engine solution using R to improve enterprise knowledge generating and reusability.

However, developing such statistical service engine solution to meet time-to-market objective within budget, it is important to know why most software projects failed: 1) unrealistic or unarticulated project goals; 2) inaccurate estimates of needed resources; 3) badly defined system requirements; 4) poor reporting of the project's status; 5) unmanaged risks; 6) poor communication among customers, developers; and users 7) use of immature technology; 8) inability to handle the project's complexity; 9) sloppy development practices;

Citation: R. Lee, "A Service Oriented Analytics Framework for Multi-Level Marketing Business," doi: 10.4236/jsea.2012.58061.

10) poor project management; 11) stakeholder politics; 12) commercial pressures [3]. The third factor attracts the most concerns; mainly because during the software development it has not considered the non-functional requirements during the development. These non-functional requirements are to ensure the software capability does meet business goal with less Total Cost of Ownership (TCO).

The Statistical Service Engine solution helps analysts offer their business's performance perspectives to enterprise, and enhance their daily decision making by reusing these statistical inferences, in a more effective way. Although GNU-R has the ability to access the databases directly from analysts' desktops, but such an approach might cause security breach if database schemas are disclosed, and potentially jeopardize the performance of databases to serve the designated business activities if databases were inappropriately accessed. On the other hand, the analysts expect the solution will eventually execute the submitted GNU-R scripts on behalf of them at most appropriate timing. There for the solution must be under a unified flexible reliable robust mechanism integrating the backend processes—running GNU-R scripts on distributed servers.

To adopt such a unified flexible reliable robust mechanism, the Enterprise Service Bus (ESB) is a proven approach to meet the requirements; it is an infrastructure which underpins a fully integrated and flexible end-toend Service-Oriented Architecture (SOA). The ESB enables SOA by providing the connectivity layer between services [4]. The ESB combines event-driven and service oriented approaches to simplify the integration of business units, bridging heterogeneous platforms and environments. The ESB acts as an intermediary layer to enable communication between different application processes. A service deployed onto an ESB can be triggered by a consumer or an event. It supports synchronous and a synchronous, facilitating interactions between one or many applications (One-to-One or Many-to-Many communications) [5], this is a vital scheme to the statistical service engine solution.

To maximize the reusability and the influence of statistical inferences to enterprise, the user-friendliness of the solution is very crucial to the acquisition and disemination of business knowledge. The user-friendliness increases user's perceived ease-of-use against a system. Accumulating knowledge is a complex and dynamic process; it needs continuously reshaping the appearance of the knowledge by enhancing the solution's usability. Usability, a synonym of user-friendliness, is a core term in human-computer interaction. The platform portability is another important consideration of technology selection for the solution. Java is well-known for better portability, and its portlet technology—a proven approach of better usability—can enable users to dynamically construct and reconstruct Web applications of information convergence in run time to resolving urgent and unplanned business requirements [6].

QUALITY ATTRIBUTES OF STATISTICAL SERVICE ENGINE SOLUTION

It is obvious and important that the Statistical Job Engine software requires high quality because business decisions depend on it. Software quality needs attributes to measure and evaluate to meet business requirements. In Software Engineering perspective, the requirements cover 1) functional; 2) non-functional. These Quality Attributes are for those non-functional requirements covering: 1) functionality; 2) usability; 3) reliability; 4) performance; 5) supportability [7]. The solution especially focuses on the reliability and supportability attributes. Reliability is "a set of attributes that bear on the capability of software to maintain its level of performance under stated conditions for a stated period of time", it consists of three sub-factors: 1) Maturity is the frequency of software faults; 2) Fault Tolerance is the ability of software to deal with of software faults or infringement of its specified interface; 3) Recoverability is the capability to recover data affected in case of a failure and measured by the time and effort needed for it [8]. Supportability includes 1) Testability; 2) Extensibility; 3) Adaptability; 4) Maintainability; 5) Compatibility; 6) Configurability; 7) Serviceability; 8) Installability; 9) Localizability; 10) Portability [7]. Table 1 exhibit the most concerned attributes as follows.

STATISTICAL SERVICE ENGINE

GNU-R provides a powerful programming language and a statistical environment; it is very extensible, with over hundreds of add-on packages obtainable from CRAN (the "Comprehensive R Archive Network"), providing high quality of graphical output [9]. The r-base-core is a universe/math package described as a GNU R core of statistical computation and graphics system. GNU R script can access databases by r-cran-rodbc package through Open Data Base Connectivity (ODBC). The package should be platform independent and provide access to any database for which a driver exists [10]. Table 2 shows how R script access database through ODBC. In many occasions, the source data for statistical analysis is sophisticated and requires complex process to generate it. Using Java servlet technology is a common practice. Using servlet to populate complex data from various sources and transform them into desired format. The HTTP output format should be text/plain with tab delimiter for data columns. Table 3shows how R script gets data from web. Graphics help user to comprehend the trend and the meaning behind statistical figures intuitively. Normally statist uses tool to visualize the statisticcal graphics; the Statistical Job Engine runs GNU-R scripts on behalf of the statist, it must save the graphics to image file so that the statist can visualize the image file later. Table 4 shows how R script saves graphics into image file. Java program has two approaches of executing GNU-R script 1) using Runtime.getRuntime().exec(); 2) using JRI as the interface to GNU-R. It allows Java program to take control over R. Table 5 shows how Java program interacts with R.

Table 1. Quality attributes requirements

Quality Attribute		*Requirement*
Reliability	Maturity	Using Proven Technologies.
	Fault Tolerance	Job Execution at All Times.
	Recoverability	Job Automatically Resumed When Failed.
Supportability	Testability	Feature Self-Tests at Any Time.
	Extensibility	Adding More Computing Resources at Any Time.
	Adaptability	Standard Protocols of Service Integration.
	Maintainability	Providing a Management Console.
	Compatibility	None
	Configurability	Providing a Management Console.
	Serviceability	7 × 24 Operations.

THE ARCHITECTURE OF STATISTICAL SERVICE ENGINE SOLUTION

Based on the above-mentioned required Quality Attributes, Statistical analysis takes time and consumes computing resources; it means the response time varies from the complexity of the task. Asynchronous messaging tactics is the solution for time-consuming requests. In asynchronous messaging, the process response does not return immediately but some time later in a different communication session. The user does not wait for the process result at the request time but retrieve the result later after the called process finished or failed from another request [11]. Asynchronous messaging relies on message-oriented middleware (MOM). The MOM creates a "software bus" for integrating heterogeneous applications [12]. Messages are distributed across applications running on different servers; its reliability and robustness is crucial to MOM. An Enterprise Service Bus is an open standards, message based, distributed integration infrastructure that provides routing, invocation and mediation services to facilitate the interactions of disparate distributed applications and services in a secure and reliable manner [13]. Figure 1 illustrates the system architecture of the Statistical Service Engine.

The Statistical Job Portal server provides a number of predefined statistical procedures and ad-hoc analysis to users. The Enterprise Service Bus server receives messages, the statistical job requests, from the Statistical Job Portal server and dispatches them accordingly. GNU-R Engine is a set of Blade servers executing GNU-R scripts designated by the messages. The script may retrieve data from the Database servers or the File Repository server. The application servers are user process engines populating source data on the Database servers or the File Repository server. The File Repository server also stores the statistical results expecting users to retrieve later. The statistical job request is in XML format covering the following fields shown in the Table 6.

Figure 2 illustrates the Activity Diagram of the solution. There are two routes: 1) Predefined; 2) Ad-hoc Statistical Job. When user select a predefined job from the Statistical Job Portal, the responded portal event sends the Statistical Job Request message to Message Queue. One of the GNU-R Engine server gets the routed message from Enterprise Message Bus and does the following tasks:

1) Predefined Statistical Job:
   a) Loads predefined GNU-R script.
   b) Replaces the paramters (i.e. ResultDestinamtion, ServerID, and DateRange, etc.).

Table 2. GNU-R uses ODBC example.

1	`myChannel <- odbcConnect("ResellerTransaction")`
2	`sqlSave(myChannel, PerfInfo, rownames="EventDate", verbose=TRUE)`
3	`sqlQuery(myChannel, paste("SELECT EventDate, CPU from PerfInfo", "WHERE EventDate > '2012/04/27' ORDER BY EventDate"))`
4	`close(myChannel)`

Table 3. GNU-R reads data from HTTP.

1	`mySourceData <- readtable("http://172.16.5.23/getResellerData")`

Table 4. GNU-R saves graphics to image file.

1	setwd('/data/images')
2	reset <- par(no.readonly=TRUE)
3	par(mfrow=c(1,3))
4	plot(x[,1],x[,2],xlim=c(min(x[,1],x[,2]),max(x[,1],x[,2])), ylim=c(min(x[,1],x[,2]),max(x[,1],x[,2])))
5	plot(x[,1],x[,3],xlim=c(min(x[,1],x[,3]),max(x[,1],x[,3])), ylim=c(min(x[,1],x[,3]),max(x[,1],x[,3])))
6	plot(x[,2],x[,3],xlim=c(min(x[,2],x[,3]),max(x[,2],x[,3])), ylim=c(min(x[,2],x[,3]),max(x[,2],x[,3])))
7	savePlot('myPlot',type="jpg")
8	par(reset)

Table 5. JRI interacts with GNU-R example

1	Rengine re=new Rengine (args, false, new TextConsole());
2	REXP x;
3	re.eval("print(1:10/3)");
4	System.out.println(x=re.eval("iris"));
5	RVector v = x.asVector();
6	if (v.getNames()!=null) { System.out.println("has names:"); for (Enumeration e=v.getNames().elements(); e.hasMoreElements();) { System.out.println(e.nextElement()); } }
7	if (true) { System.out.println("Console:"); re.startMainLoop(); } else { re.end(); System.out.println("end"); }

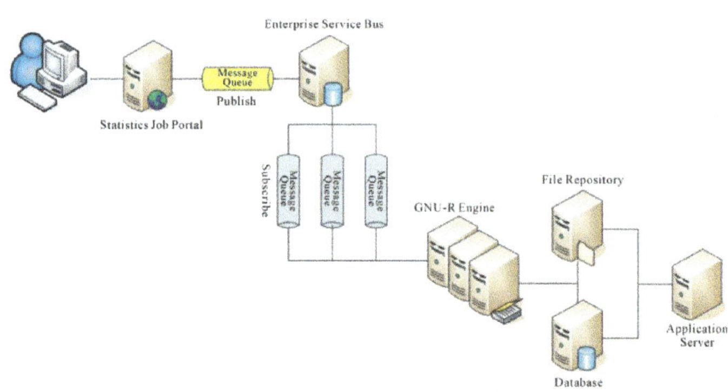

Figure 1. Statistical service engine solution.

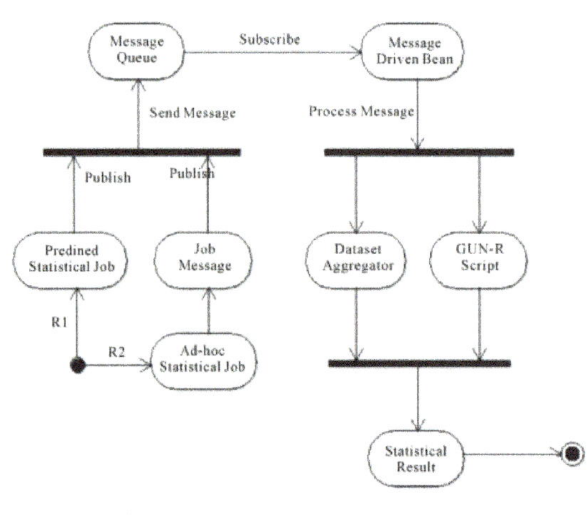

Figure 2. Activity diagram of statistical service engine solution.

c) Spawns GNU-R interpreter ro run the prepared script.

d) Retrieves data from File Repository and Database.

e) Populates the statistical result on File Repository.

f) If Result Destination > 0 emails the statistical result to the requested user.

2) Ad-Hoc Statistical Job:

a) Loads the GNU-R script from the message received.

b) Spawns GNU-R interpreter to run the prepared script.

c) Retrieves the designated data from File Repository and Database.

d) Populates the statistical result on File Repository.

e) If Result Destination > 0 emails the statistical result to the requested user.

The user can view the statistical result from the Statistical Job Portal under [My Job Results] web page if Result Destination! = 1. The web page [My Job Results] lists down the statistical results of previous submitted jobs with hyperlinks.

Table 6. Statistical job request

Field	*Description*	*Example*
User ID	User Identification	richlee@tw.ibm.com
Submit Date Time	Job Submitted Date/Time	20120427-164530
Job ID	Statistical Job Identification	Statistics Summary: 00: Ad-hoc 01: Reseller 02: Level 03: Sales Regression 11: Sales~Level Moving Average: 21: Total Sales 22: Sales by Level
Ad-Hoc Script	GNU-R Script	If Job ID==00
Source Data	Statistics Source Data	If Job ID==00, /DB1205/20120531.RData
Result Destination	Statistics Result Destination	0: Web 1: Email 2: Both
Server ID	Server Identification	DB1205
Date Range	Date Range of Performance Counters	20050901 ~ 20120531

EMPIRICAL CASE

More people are accepting the self-care concept in natural health regimens as the complementary and alternative medicine has become a key driver for wellness foods industry business. Many wellness food companies rely on multi-level marketing—directly selling products through individuals' social networks—for their business development. However, promoting wellness foods via multilevel selling model has been a challenge for years to business owners including both companies and the associated resellers. The research subject is a very successful biological company selling a series of products containing Reishi and uses the multi-level marketing as their primary tool of business development. This company faced high competition from the wellness foods market, and the products sales did not grow as expected. So, the company wished to disclose which link had gone wrong; based on the research findings, to develop associated business policies to secure its market position. This company encourages the resellers to pursue higher level position for better product discount rates. In the beginning, the resellers who were also consumers too, they move up to higher levels—bronze, silver, gold, platinum, and titan—in turn by the increasing the sales amount and developing deeper levels in distributing channels. Regardless in which level, some resellers became hibernate for not having any transaction for at any giving period. Once a hibernated reseller resumes the sales, the reseller is back to the original level and gets the discounts accordingly. Few resellers were able to move up to next level position successfully, while most resellers remain staying in the current level. The research objective was to identify whether the current distributed channels have any pattern; if there was any, what would be the pattern.

Since this company was looking for a possible pattern among these discrete states—the resellers role change, the paper mapped the business questions onto the Discrete-Time Markov Chain (DTMC) problem domain. The DTMC is a random process that moves among various states in a "memory-less" fashion. The analysis of DTMC problem depends on a Transition Diagram and maps the diagram onto a corresponding Transition Matrix, so that the researcher can solve the problem by manipulating the matrix calculation. The DTMC concerns about whether the state will become stable and how many terms that each state needs to shift to others respectively in the run-run. Let P_{ij} denote the probability of moving from state i to state j during a time step. The Transition Matrix P is in m × n dimension, $1 \le i \le m$, $1 \le j \le n$. If there exists an n elements steady-state row vector $\mu = [\mu_1 \quad \mu_2 \quad \cdots \quad \mu_i]$, such that:

$$\mu \cdot P = \mu \tag{1}$$

$$\sum_{i}^{n} \mu_i = 1 \tag{2}$$

If there is a solution for the linear Equations (1) and (2), then the steady-state vector exists. On the other hand, three column vectors of the same m elements M, M_0, and I; while M contains the terms required for state S_i changes to other states S_j respectively; M_0 is derived from M that excludes the term for recurrence of state S_i; and all the elements of I are ones, such that:

$$M = \begin{bmatrix} m_{i1} \\ m_{i2} \\ m_{ii} \\ \vdots \\ m_{ij} \end{bmatrix} \quad M_0 = \begin{bmatrix} m_{i1} \\ m_{i2} \\ 0 \\ \vdots \\ m_{ij} \end{bmatrix} \quad I = \begin{bmatrix} 1 \\ 1 \\ \cdots \\ 1 \end{bmatrix}$$

$$M = I + P \cdot M_0 \qquad (3)$$

By solving the linear equations derived from (3), the terms required for state S_i shifting to other states S_j will be disclosed respectively. If S_i is an absorbing state, it means that there is a probability of P_{ii} for continuously staying in the state S_i.

This company has several datasets with vast amount of records about the resellers and the associated transactions. This paper exported these records for past decade into separate annual aggregated dataset files; the files were named after the year of the exported records respectively. There were two additional marks as the file name suffix; using P was for new product introduced, B was for bonus plan changed, and PB if both cases happened. Each annual aggregated dataset consists of the following information: 1) Reseller ID; 2) Reseller Level; 3) Date of Level Promoted; and 4) Sales Amount. By issuing the following SQL statement against each year's dataset file to get the number of resellers and the sales amount for each level:

"SELECT RESELLER_LEVEL, COUNT (RESELLER_ID) AS NUM_ALL_RESELLER, SUM (SALES_AMOUNT) ASLEVEL_AMOUNT FROM RESELLER_TRANS GROUP BY RESELLER_ID"

This paper conducted a series of statistical processes of ANOVA (Analysis of Variance) to see if there was any difference between ordinary datasets and those files with additional marks. The result showed that it did make differece when new products was introduced to the market or the bonus plan was changed by company's policy. By issuing a series of SQL statements as follows against each year's dataset file to get the proportions of each level:

"SELECT RESELLER_LEVEL, COUNT (RESELLER_ID) AS NUM_HIBERNATE_RESELLER FROM RESELLER_TRANS WHERE SALES_AMOUNT = 0 GROUP BY RESELLER_ID"

"SELECT RESELLER_LEVEL, COUNT (RESELLER_ID) AS NUM_PROMOTED_RESELLER FROM RESELLER_TRANS WHERE YEAR (PROMOTED_DATE) -@DATA_YEAR GROUP BY RESELLER_ID"

Therefore, the number of resellers remained in their current levels—NUM_RESELLER—was calculated by the following formula:

$$\begin{aligned} &NUM\_RESELLER \\ &= NUM\_ALL\_RESELLER \\ &\quad -(NUM\_HIBERNATE\_RESELLER \\ &\quad + NUM\_PROMOTED\_RESELLER) \end{aligned}$$

By using these three numbers—NUM_RESELLER, NUM_PROMOTED_RESELLER, and NUM_HIBER NATE_RESELLER—this paper got the probabilities of each state respectively. Figure 3 illustrated the Markov Chain Transition Diagram and Figure 4 illustrated the associated Transition Matrix for the business problem. According to Formula (2), the probability of Hibernate for a state can be derived by one minus the sum of other states's probability. To solve this business problem, this paper applied the GNU-R's capabilities of Matrix Calculation and Linear Equations Solution. Table 7illustrated how GNU-R manipulate the matrix and find the soluton of linear equations. Another example showed a GNU-R script to calculate the visiting times of each state and the average travel times before shifting into an absorbing state, and the probabilities of non-absorbing states shifting to those absorbing states. The absorbing state in DTMC is a state that never shifts out once entering it. To do the calculation, the analysist needs to transform the transition matrix—m denotes the number of transsition states and n is number of absorbing states—intoan absorbing form consisting of four quadrual parts: 1) Q is a square matrix of m; 2) R is non-zero matrix of m × n; 3) I is an identity matrix of n; and 4) 0 is a zero-matrix of n × m. The example does the rest of the calculation automatically. Table 8 illustrated the GNU-R script for the calculation.

This paper disclosed the business problem which had been a long-time mistery to their operation of the company. By taking advantage of the automation of the whole analytical process, the company is able to adjust its policy to better business result.

Table 7. Linear equation solution sample

Solv	$a_{11}x + a_{12}y = a_{13} \quad a_{21}x + a_{22}.y = a_{23}$	
1	myEq <- array(0, c(2, 2))	
2	myEq[1, 1] = 1 myEq[1, 2] = 1 myEq[2, 1] = 1 myEq[2, 2] = −3	#a_{11} #a_{12} #a_{21} #a_{21}
3	myEqVal <- array(0, c(2, 1))	#a_{13}
4	myEqVal[1, 1] = 1 myEqVal[2, 1] = 0	#a_{23}
5	myAnswer <- solve(myEq, myEqVal) print(myAnswer)	

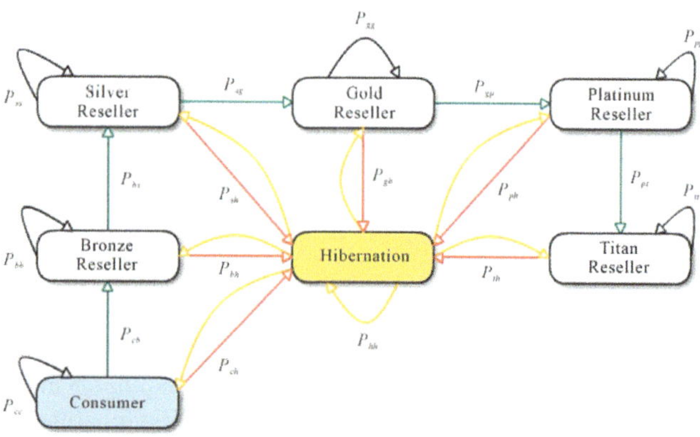

Figure 3. State transition diagram.

$$
P = \begin{array}{c} \\ \end{array}
\begin{array}{c|ccccccc|}
 & Consumer & Bronze & Silver & Gold & Platinum & Titan & Hibernate \\
\hline
Consumer & P_{cc} & P_{cb} & 0 & 0 & 0 & 0 & P_{ch} = 1-(P_{cc}+P_{cb}) \\
Bronze & 0 & P_{bb} & P_{bs} & 0 & 0 & 0 & P_{bh} = 1-(P_{bb}+P_{bs}) \\
Silver & 0 & 0 & P_{ss} & P_{sg} & 0 & 0 & P_{sh} = 1-(P_{ss}+P_{sg}) \\
Gold & 0 & 0 & 0 & P_{gg} & P_{gp} & 0 & P_{gh} = 1-(P_{gg}+P_{gp}) \\
Platinum & 0 & 0 & 0 & 0 & P_{pp} & P_{pt} & P_{ph} = 1-(P_{pp}+P_{pt}) \\
Titan & 0 & 0 & 0 & 0 & 0 & P_{tt} & P_{th} = 1-(P_{tt}) \\
Hibernate & P_{hc} & P_{hb} & P_{hs} & P_{hg} & P_{hp} & P_{ht} & P_{hh} = 1-(\sum P_{hi})
\end{array}
$$

Figure 4. Transition matrix.

Table 8. Example of calculating an absorbing matrix

1	I <- array (0, c(n, n))
	# Assign Values to I
	Q <- array (0, c(m, m))
	# Assign Values to Q	

2	N = solve (I − Q)	$N=(I-Q)^{-1}$
3	T = N %*% I	$T = N \cdot I$

4	R <- array(0, c(m, n))
	# Assign Values to R
	B = N %*% R
		$B = N \cdot R$

5	Print (N) Print (T) Print (B)	

These business findings inspired the company to dedicate more resources to develop and explore the undisclosed business intelligence. The proposed Statistical Service Engine Solution makes this automation more seamless and handy for the anlysts and the executives to make business decision swiftly with quality.

CONCLUSIONS AND FUTURE WORK

To increase business competitiveness requires continuous innovation and operation excellence. Re-examining the data business activities and finding patterns and trends in various statistical perspectives help enterprise making rational decisions swiftly. Knowledge Management offers a collaborative platform to acquire, compile, diseminating, and reuse the knowledge to elicit creative and improve operation efficiency. A more intense use of knowledge management platform has both a direct and indirect (innovation-mediated) positive effects on enterprise performance [14]. To make knowledge management platform success, the users' perceived usefulness and user satisfaction is the key [15]. Based on useful statistical results, it disclosed the implications of business competitiveness improvement will stimulate and inspire employees' further finding by reusing these statistical procedures and the data. This reinforced process makes employees use knowledge management platform more intensively and help them making business decision more rational and swiftly. To realize this goal, a more convenient solution is called to help analysts retrieve data, reuse statistical procedures, and disseminate the findings easier. This paper answered such need and presented a reliable robust architecture on top of Enterprise Service Bus; it also showed how GNU-R scripts access vivid data from databases, generate statistical graphics and save them to image files. In software engineering perspective, this paper demonstrated how to define and measure the quality attributes of the solution to ensure the solution will meet business requirements during the development cycle.

The proposed solution is still very primitive but workable. More useful statistical models should be developed and categorized. The solution has more room in the reuse and dissemination of statistical work products. To integrate with existing proven knowledge management platform product seems to be a practical approach via Web Services. First is to configure appropriate taxonomy and document hierarchical folders for statistical results. Second is to apply Ajax technology to embed the statistical job submission form from the proposed solution. Third is to design an interface to check in the statistical results from the file repository to the knowledge management platform by Web Service calls. Fourth since the computing resources (i.e. CPU, MEM, and I/O) consumption is determined by the complexity of statistical model and the volume of data, the GNU-R Engine must re-dispatch the job to another available message queue if resource-shortage failure occurs. To resolve that, designating a First-in-First-out (FIFO) sequential processing queue on a dedicated blade server to handle those earlier failed requests should be a feasible approach. Lastly, this paper urges employees to take advantage of existing data and transform them into useful knowledge to enhance the quality of decision making in their enterprises and let statistics become the core of strategy reasoning.

REFERENCES

1. B. P. Kumar, J. Selvam, V. Meenakshi, K. Kanthi, A. Suseela and V. L. Kumar, "Business Decision Making, Management and Information Technology," Ubiquity, Vol. 2007, 2007, p. 4. doi:10.1145/1226690.1232401
2. H. Arsham, "Statistical Thinking for Managerial Decisions," 9th Edition, 2011. http://home.ubalt.edu/ntsbarsh/Business-stat/opre504.htm
3. R. N. Charette, "Why Software Fails," IEEE Spectrum, Vol. 42, No. 9, 2005, p. 36.doi:10.1109/MSPEC.2005.1502528

4. M. T. Schmidt, B. Hutchison, P. Lambros and R. Phippen, "The Enterprise Service Bus: Making Service-Oriented Architecture Real," IBM Systems Journal, Vol. 44, No. 4, 2005, pp. 781-797. doi:10.1147/sj.444.0781

5. J. L. Maréchaux, "Combining Service-Oriented Architecture and Event-Driven Architecture Using an Enterprise Service Bus," IBM Developer Works, 2006.

6. Y. Wei, Z. Sun, X. Chen and F. Zhang, "A Service-Portlet Based Visual Paradigm for Personalized Convergence of Information Resources," 2nd IEEE International Conference on Computer Science and Information Technology, Beijing, 8-11 August 2009.

7. L. Chung and J. do Prado Leite, "On Non-Functional Requirements in Software Engineering," Conceptual Modeling: Foundations and Applications, Vol. 5600, 2009, pp. 363-379. [Paper reference:2]

8. B. Behkamal, M. Kahani and M. K. Akbari, "Customizing ISO 9126 Quality Model for Evaluation of B2B Applications," Information and Software Technology, Vol. 51, No. 3, 2009, pp. 599-609. doi:10.1016/j.infsof.2008.08.001

9. A. T. Yalta and R. Lucchetti, "The GNU/Linux Platform and Freedom Respecting Software for Economists," Journal of Applied Econometrics, Vol. 23, No. 2, 2008, pp. 279-286.doi:10.1002/jae.990

10. M. Lapsley and B. Ripley, "ODBC Database Access," 2011. http://cran.r-project.org/web/packages/RODBC/RODBC.pdf

11. A. Friis-Christensen, N. Ostländer, M. Lutz and L. Bernard, "Designing Service Architectures for Distributed Geoprocessing: Challenges and Future Directions," Transactions in GIS, Vol. 11, No. 6, 2007, pp. 799-818. doi:10.1111/j.1467-9671.2007.01075.x

12. C. F. Liao, Y. W. Jong and L. C. Fu, "Toward a Message-Oriented Application Model and Its Middleware Support in Ubiquitous Environments," Proceedings of the 2008 International Conference on Multimedia and Ubiquitous Engineering, IEEE Computer Society, Washington, 2008, pp. 298-303. doi:10.1109/MUE.2008.24

13. F. Menge, "Enterprise Service Bus," 2007.

14. A. Vaccaro, R. Parente and F. M. Veloso, "Knowledge Management Tools, Inter-Organizational Relationships, Innovation and Firm Performance," Technological Forecasting and Social Change, Vol. 77, No. 7, 2010, pp. 1076-1089.doi:10.1016/j.techfore.2010.02.006

15. U. R. Kulkarni, S. Ravindran and R. Freeze, "A Knowledge Management Success Model: Theoretical Development and Empirical Validation," Journal of Management Information Systems, Vol. 23, No. 3, 2007, pp. 309-347. doi:10.2753/MIS0742-1222230311

CHAPTER 14

UNDERSTANDING SOA PERSPECTIVE OF E-GOVERNANCE

Harekrishna Misra

INTRODUCTION

Role of information and communication technologies (ICT) in managing business processes has been phenomenal. Today, ICT is aggressively used for development process and results are showing positively in this direction. E-governance projects are no exception. In today's context, e-governance projects have become a part of national policies across the world. Globally, e-governance projects have remained restricted to delivering government interfaces digitally with the focus to optimize transaction latency, improving transparency and extending on-line services. However, e-governance projects have fallen short of citizen expectations in developing countries (Mehdi, 2005). Most of the developing countries around the world have adopted e-governance systems strategically to provide better, transparent and value added services to its citizens with the help of ICT. Millennium development goals (MDG) have also included ICT as means of development (WSIS, (2004)). In India there is rapid progress in implementing e-governance strategy keeping pace with the global scenario. With the national e-governance plan (NeGP), the pace of progress in setting up information technology (IT) infrastructure has been accelerated (Ramarao et al. (2004)). NeGP has identified various projects on "Mission Mode" for scale up nationally and have allocated funds for "Common Service Centres" (CSC) for deployment of ICT enabled services including e-governance services at the door steps of citizens (Chandrashekhar, (2006); NeGP, (2005)). Besides, there are many mission mode projects like Gramin Gyan Abhiyan (GGA) as per agenda set through Mission 2007, National Rural Employment Guaranty Act (NREGA) and Ministry of Company Affairs (MCA-21) have been taken up. However, alike the experiences worldwide (Heeks, (2006)), the scale up exercise for egovernance has not been yielding results as expected in India (Janssen, (2005); Mishra, (2007)). Various reasons including inadequate local level planning with least participation of citizens and challenging situations to spread effective infrastructure contribute to this poor adoption of e-governance services. Despite improved ICT infrastructure, penetration of telephony and internet, Indian e-governance applications and services are below expected levels of delivery standards.

In this paper, it is posited that e-governance projects in India need to follow SOA principles in order to make them successful in terms of sustainability, providing appropriate services to citizens. It is argued that Indian e-governance initiatives to be termed successful should pay special attention to rural areas. Rural areas in India are largely challenged by digital divides (social, educational, health etc.) and rural development largely influences overall development of Indian economy which is related to citizen services, especially value added rural services (Riley, (2003)). It is considered important that e-governance services should be available to rural citizens on demand and through proper orchestration of inputs received from various service provisioning agencies involved in the initiative. Essentially, SOA principles provide such ambience and in this paper its contributions are discussed to extend desired support to e-governance initiatives in India.

The organization of the paper is as follows. In section two, e-governance scenario in global context is discussed with specific reference to development perspectives in India. It aims at providing an appreciation of what is happening in India vis-à-vis global efforts in this direction. In section three

Citation: Harekrishna Misra (2010). Understanding SOA Perspective of e-Governance, User Interfaces, Rita Matrai (Ed.), InTech, DOI: 10.5772/9495.

architectural issues are discussed with specific reference to egovernance systems. A framework is presented in this section to understand the feasibility of Indian e-governance systems with development perspective. Rationale for deployment of SOA principles and their relevance in e-governance systems in Indian context are discussed in this section. In section four, SOA based architectural framework is presented. It includes a scenario built through SOA architecture to showcase the possible effect of SOA principles in order to appreciate citizen centric services taking scale-up issues into consideration. Unified Modelling Language (UML) is used for presenting the architecture and its possible use. Through this language, the scenario is presented to explain the path to reflect the underpinnings of orchestration of services on demand and service provisioning through egovernance initiatives for effective implementation SOA principles. In section five, two popular e-governance models implemented in India are taken for discussion based the SOA principles and an evaluation is done to understand the scope for further value addition in rendering citizen centric services. While concluding in section six, future direction of the work is described.

INDIAN E-GOVERNANCE SYSTEMS: DEVELOPMENT PERSPECTIVE

Conceptualization and implementation of E-governance projects have gradually gained momentum in recent years and many pilot projects have been taken up by governments worldwide. Most of the governments have transformed their pilot activities to real projects with scale up strategies (ADB,(2008)). European Union has strategies to collaborate and unify e-governance services across all its member states (Benamou, N. (2006)). Interoperability has been a critical evaluation criterion for enabling interstate transactions, managing information flow seamlessly and overseeing the backend process for effective delivery of citizen services. According to the European Commission (European Commission, 2004,2006) survey an average of 84% of all public services was available online in the EU member states much have been done for effective citizen transactions (Capgemini, (2007)). Despite such good efforts, EU countries largely acknowledge that though supply of e-governance services is rather not a problem, meeting the demands is actually a challenge before the strategic implementers. Globally, contemporary egovernance strategies therefore, profess for e-inclusion, e-participation and citizen centric services. E-Governance applications expect integrated efforts to improve citizen interfaces and citizen centric services while scaling up to make the government's withdrawal strategy feasible. These withdrawal strategies include involvement of private-public partnership, citizen inclusiveness and a proper revenue model among other critical parameters.

In India, e-governance system is still evolving and is not free from challenges as experienced in global terms. Mixed results of e-governance projects are experienced due to poor participation of important stakeholders - the rural citizens. In Indian sub-continent, one of the major concerns is ensuring "rural citizen interface through inclusion" and role of ICT in addressing this concern is challenging. This is because of the fact that rural India constitutes 72 percent per cent of India's population who live in villages; 55 per cent villages don't have electricity in homes and 85 percent have no sanitation facilities. The per capita income of Indian villagers is INR 12,000, while the national average is INR 25,000 [rural poverty]. Thus appreciating the role of e-governance services as "central" to their livelihoods is a difficult proposition. However, e-governance services have the desired potential to transform this centrality through demonstration of its orchestrating capabilities through which services related to the rural citizen's demand could be rendered. This orchestration has remained a challenge because of ambiguous relationships among various stakeholders including government agencies who need to coordinate the information management imperatives (ADB, (2008)). There are many successful ICT initiatives in India oriented towards rural development with a focus to address some specific issues of rural citizens, thus forming "islands". These initiatives are mostly led by the government administration, non-governmental organizations (NGOs) and some are even in private sectors. National e-Governance Plan (NeGP) recognizes the vitality of some critical, but successful ICT initiatives for their inclusion as mission-mode projects for scaling up at national level. The aim is to provide a portfolio of services to the citizens integrated with e-governance backbone to install a good e-governance system without getting affected during scale up phase.

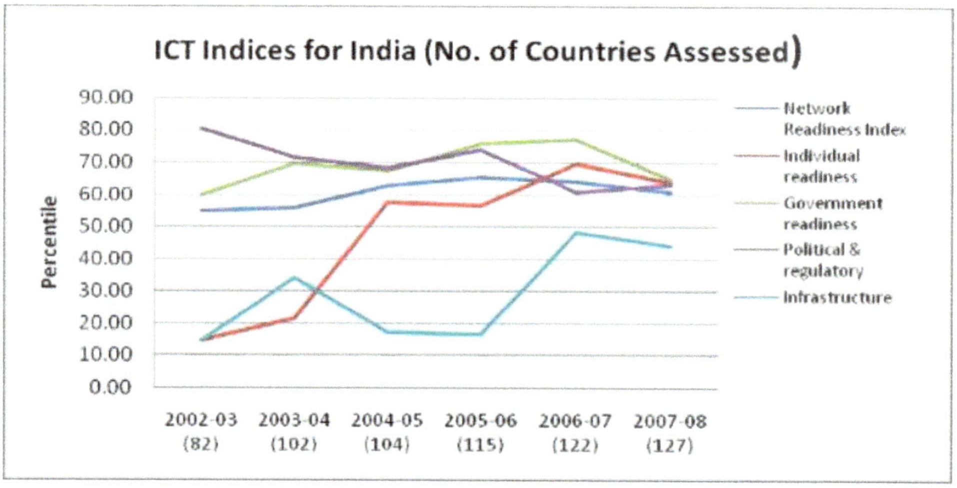

Figure 1. ICT Indices for India (Dutta et al, (2008); Kaul, (2008)).

Good e-governance efforts need useful ICT infrastructure, individual readiness, government readiness, support of political and regulatory systems and network readiness. Individual readiness in Indian context, is quite critical because of the rural citizens are oblivious of the e-governance initiatives which are yet to bring desired impact in the lives of these rural citizens. Global "e-readiness" exercises to assess the ICT enabled capacities of countries and the usage the infrastructure indicate this readiness as an important contributor. In India, this readiness is gradually increasing. In Figure 1 other ICT indices which predominantly influence Indian e-governance efforts are presented in global context. It reveals that ICT infrastructure and individual's orientation towards IT need more attention in order to hasten the process of implementing e-governance systems in the country (Chan, (2005); Converged services with local contents are critical contributors to a successful e-governance initiative. In India, this is much more important since rural citizens need these services under local conditions and on demand. This demands a suitable infrastructure with adequate rural penetration (infrastructure readiness), government's presence in the villages in digital form with adequate reengineering (government readiness), decentralized governance systems with adequate ICT support (political and regulatory readiness) and networking of agencies (network readiness) to facilitate converge services. In all these areas India needs improvement as per global standards.

UNDERSTANDING INDIAN E-GOVERNANCE ARCHITECTURE

Choosing a good ICT driven architecture, identifying scalable components and managing a sustainable relationship are basic tenets of ICT infrastructure set up and for understanding its readiness. Successful architecture advocates for addressing "views", "relationships" and "growth" among various components (Mishra, (2009)); Garlan & Shaw, (1994)) to meaningfully contribute to ICT enabled services without compromising desired services. Egovernance architectures are no exceptions since these are aimed at national level encompassing a diverse pool of stakeholders. In India national e-governance architecture is being planned with these objectives to formulate standards for e-governance initiatives (Mishra & Hiremath, (2006)). "Common Service Centres" under the auspices of NeGP and "Telecentres" with mandate of "Mission 2007" are critical attempts of government of India to scale up e-governance project implementation strategy. Such national scale up strategy bears relevance of an architectural treatment (Prabhu, (2004)).

In order to understand the rural e-governance architecture in India, two approaches are considered important in this paper. The first one is the Architecture itself which is essentially useful for understanding the services to be rendered to the stakeholders and the second, the service grid that may be made available through 'back end' that can provide theservices 'on demand'. These two approaches aim to discuss the underpinnings of the architectural issues for generating desired rural citizen centric services.

Most of the Indian e-governance services are now in the phases of consolidation and gradually coming out of the 'incubation' period. 'Integration' of 'information and services silos' is being networked through NeGP nationally. State data centres, national data centres and other related backbone for 'back end' netwrok and grid are being installed.

Diverse platforms are extensively used for development of applications, services with focus on local, regional and national languages. State level efforts are contributing to such situations. Open standards along with web 2.0 technologies and grid computing environment are being considered for implementation to enhance 'user services' (Prabhu, (2007)). However, provisioning of user independence, usability of services and even demanding the services are few challenges which have considerable impact on Indian egovernance efforts. In the 'development' parlance, this is more critical due to the fact that most of the 'users' belong to 'rural areas' and they lack basic infrastructure and facilities.

SOA based services therefore, are quite relevant in Indian context.

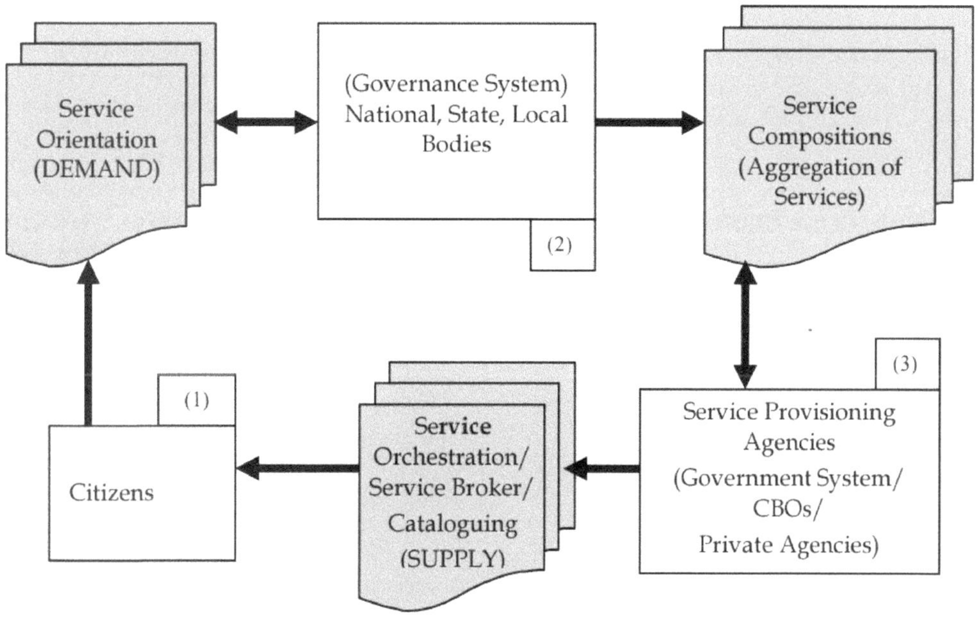

Figure 2. Service Orientation Framework of Indian E-Governance System

Service orientation is an essential component for Indian e-governance systems since 'desired services' need to be provided to the citizens. As per NeGP, 'service grids' are being developed through 'data centres' with an organised backbone. At this point of time, aggregation of service requirements is more critical for the e-governance to generate a broad-based pool. In Figure 2 a scenario of service orientation is presented. It is posited thatcitizens form the most critical element who are target recipients of services. In India, rural citizens form a major stakeholder in the e-governance system and their acceptance of the egovernance enable services would render the effort successful. As shown in (1) rural citizens are vulnerably placed to project their demand on services and receive them. Therefore, the architecture needs to capture their requirement appropriately. This is possible either through individual citizen collaboration or through collectively held institutions as legally framed through Indian governance systems. The later is quite strongly visible in the rural areas that interface with citizen as representatives with government administration. These bodies at local (panchayats, self-help groups, micro finance institutions etc.), district (district level PRI bodies, municipalities, corporations etc.), state (assembly) and central (parliament) levels as shown in (2) are empowered to aggregate the demand and facilitate provisioning of desired services. Even at individual level, right to information act (RTI Act) has been a powerful instrument to raise demand on e-governance systems being developed. As shown in (3), it is the government system who is the service provider to uphold governance system, to implement the desired interface with citizens and provide services on demand. Therefore, it is the responsibility of district, state and national government administration to orchestrate the services and provide them to the citizens.

This is possible through a SOA based model which would enable service orientation through citizen demands. Governance systems in India are organized at the grass root level to capture this citizen service orientation. However, this is most difficult task since most of the citizens reside in rural areas where 'digital divides' are quite strong (Heeks, 2003). Aggregated service demanded are the inputs for the 'service provisioning agencies' in the national network engaged for establishing the orchestrated link to manage the 'service brokering' facility and supply the services. This provides a scope for the citizens to receive the desired service through SOA based service model.

SOA principles and E-governance strategy

SOA principles draw strength from the benefits of well-practiced architectures in software engineering discipline like client-server, distributed (including component object (COM)/ distributed component object (DCOM) and Object-Oriented) architecture. SOA principles work closely with applications and enterprise with 'service-orientation', 'services' and 'service-oriented solution logics' (Erl, 2008). SOA promotes loosely coupled services which could be independent from each other, but are related in certain way to accomplish common tasks. SOA also encourages process orientation and includes organization and technology seamlessly. Analogous to business paradigm, where SOA principles have provided the intended impetus to reusability and productivity (Ravichandra et al., (2007)) egovernance oriented information systems demand intensive deployment and use of information technology (IT). Thus e-governance systems need agility, innovation and adaptable service oriented architectures which SOA could provide. SOA however, represents a paradigm shift at the architectural level to tackle integration requirements. Egovernance services require such treatment at all levels of deployment of infrastructure and other resources.

E-governance services are mostly regarded as 'enterprise' level services since it includes various 'stakeholders' in the process. Major stakeholders are 'citizens', 'government agencies', 'communities' and 'service provisioning agencies'. SOA based models help revolutionalise enterprise environment by leveraging web services technologies. 'IT-enabled service-orientation' provides the right impetus for a good architecure which can be possible through the SOA. Web-services driven SOA is fast gaining its status against traditional 'distributed architecure' environment. SOA builds on the strengths of 'application architecure' and 'enterprise architecure' and therefore, has potential to manage e-governance projects. Application architecures have evolved in Indian states disjointly and there are a mumber of mission mode projects evolving for scale up. This scale up exercise entails federating the application architecures and their 'reuse'. Enterprise driven solutions are part of the mission mode projects which aim at having 'national reach' and providing distributed environment for the services to reach the citizens. Indian citizens have varied demands with strong rurla-urban disparities and yet having a huge potential to have converged and unified services across the nation. This leads to an 'environment' conducive for encouraging individual 'service orientation' while providing 'standardised services' nationally. Indian villages cover large population to ignore and demands of this population vary depending on local, hosuhold and individual priorities, market conditions and national policies. In enterprise driven IT solutions like enterprise resource planning (ERP), SOA principles have helped in provided service orientation through which IT and organizations are finely blended. Despite rising complexities due to SOA applications, benefits are quite substantial in terms of integration, reusability and user orientation and SOA oriented solutions have provided effective support for business-process driven alignment. E-governance systems look for these strengths since the back end services need all these properties for an effective e-government service orientation. Besides, studies show that principles of "transaction cost theory" and "agency theory" which are well supported by conventional ERP based information systems have derived better results through SOA orientation in terms of their characteristics related to "specificity", "uncertainty", "strategic importance" and "frequency" (Bocke et al., 2009). All these attributes and principles of economic theories discussed above are foundations of e-governance information systems and therefore, there is a scope to induct SOA principles in those systems.

In order to formulate a strategy to have SOA oriented e-governance services, it is essential to study the concept of SOA. SOA is expected to provide 'universal service identifier' in the system so that desired service can be identified 'on demand' with least transaction time, transaction cost and independent of spatial constraints. Universal service identifier is expected to coordinate with service broker with service descriptions so as to mine the desired service from the warehouse. A typical architecure is presented in Figure 3.

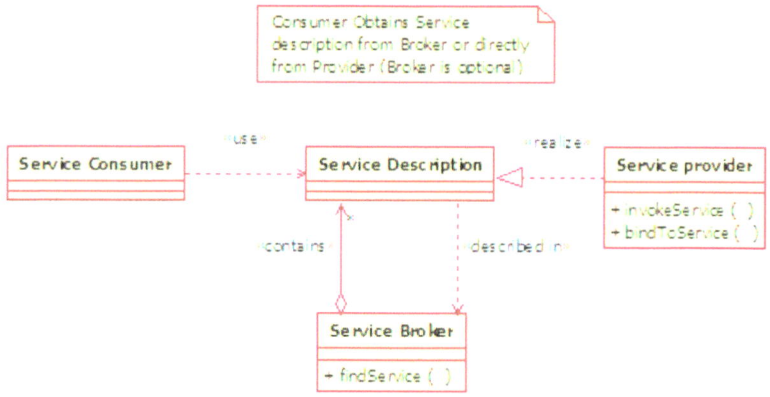

Figure 3. Conceptual Model of SOA (Arsanjani, 2004)

In Figure 3 the concept behind SOA describes the service orientation and relationship of various stakeholders who collaborate, orchestrate and provide services as desired. But an enterprise level SOA needs an elaborate treatment for collating all possible services with best practices, interaction among components and relationships. In order to capture the underpinnings of SOA architecture for detailed abstraction seven layers are presented and discussed in Figure 4 below.

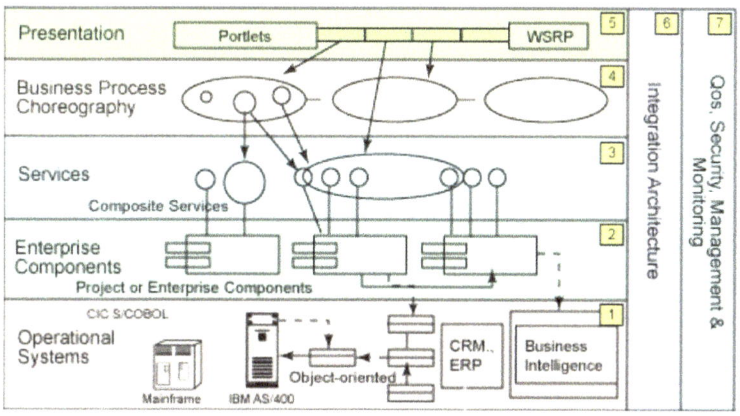

Figure 4. Abstracted SOA (Arsanjani, 2004)

Each of the seven layers is numbered and discussed with reference to Indian e-Governance SOA model. In Figure 3, it is suggested that each layer in SOA model, specific tasks are to be carried out with clear delivery mechanisms. Each layer should also relate to the other as per the demand of the enterprise in order to meet the overall objectives of the services rendered (Erl, 2008). In this model quality of service, monitoring of services and establishing security standards for citizen transactions are the most important contributors to maintain trust, transparency and inter-operability which major deliverables of Indian e-governance systems (Stayanaryana, 2004) .

PROPOSED ARCHITECTURE

As explained in section three, various service components of SOA can contribute to the Indian e-governance system in order to provided desired services. The components are 'citizen demand on services', 'service on demand aggregation', 'service-on-supply aggregation', 'service orchestrators' and 'service providers'. A seamless integration of all the services and service provisioning components need to collaborate effectively to focus on citizen centric services. Besides, capabilities of SOA can also be harnessed for garnering all the benefits that e-government systems could provide through effective integration of backend services networked nationally in a unified way.

In Table 1 below, the proposed deliveries of SOA based e-governance systems are discussed based on its layers. These layers are 'operational systems', 'enterprise component', 'services', 'business process composition', 'access', 'integration' and 'quality of services' as explained in Figure 3 in section three. Operating system is a major layer in governance architecture which provides the base for establishment of systems, procedures and interaction principles among all the stakeholders to derive the desired services targeted for overall development of the society. This layer therefore, demands IT orientation for better ambience for orchestration among all the stakeholders, and establishment of service brokerage. In layer two, enterprise component is established to extend support to the service provisioning. This is a critical layer which accounts for establishment of 'on demand' service portfolios, provisioning of infrastructure and their maintenance. SOA principles look for loosely coupled components in this layer so as to make them convenient for creation, deployment and use. Layer three is focussed on identification of services, their points of generation and aggregation of these services through layer two. Layer four calls for an integrated environment in which all service provisioning agencies collaborate to capture services demanded, analyze them and provide value added services through continued innovation. Layer five is the access layer in which citizens are expected to gain access to the desired services. This establishes user component based on user centred design principles and calls for greater usability of the user driven application interfaces. In layer six, integration services, components and user interfaces is managed for converged services which is reflected in layer seven through management of quality principles.

In Table 1 below, a SOA model is presented with specific contribution to e-governance scenario which could be mapped to Indian context. In the proposed model four layers of SOA architecture are presented with a view to contribute to a good SOA architecture as discussed in Figure 3. In Table 2 these layers are discussed. This simplification is done in order to apply the e-governance framework presented in Figure 2 which is represented in Figure 3 through UML.

The first layer (SOA-I) stage considers elicitation of 'citizen demand'. It is an independent activity in the SOA since citizens may any type of services and these services may be specific to local conditions. In second layer (SOA-II), demands are aggregated, composed and service-orientation is done through an agency at the local level. This layer in turn is expected to 'orchestrate' with layer-III (SOA-III) which carries all the 'services' available through service providers. Layer-III, all the 'service providers' and 'services' are orchestrated. In layer IV (SOA-IV), 'service agencies' are collaborated and in Indian context these are 'national government', 'state government' and 'NGO'. There are other service providers like corporate agencies and social trusts engaged and can be added to the process of aggregation.

Table 1. Probable SOA based Deliveries

Layer	Layer Description	Rationale	E-Governance (Indian Context)	SOA Component Proposed
1	Operational Systems	Legacy Systems, Business Intelligence of enterprise	Legacy systems have evolved for e-government systems as backend services. E-governance pilot projects are emerging in isolation and there is effort to identify, design and implement National Mission mode Projects.	Service Provisioning (Service Brokerage and Service Orchestration)
2	Enterprise Component	Maintain Quality of Services; Organize Service Level Agreements	State Data Centres, National Data Centres, Identification of Service Providers are in the agenda	Services Composition, Loosely Coupled
3	Services	Business Processes, Interfaces and Orchestration	State level Grids, Connectivity to Citizen services and Interfaces with Citizens	Service Providers (Service Composition, Aggregation, Orchestration)
4	Business Process Composition	Choreography, Business Integration	Government services and business services to converge; Government and Business process Re-engineering	Service Orchestration (Supply)
5	Access	User Interfaces	Citizen Interfaces	Services (Demand)
6	Integration	Intelligent interfaces, protocol mediation	Location specific contents	Services Composition, Services Composition and Choreopgraphy
7	Quality of Services	Monitor, Manage and maintain quality of service	e-governance standards at national government level, interoperability protocols	Service orchestration

Table 2. layers proposed

Layer Description	SOA Component Proposed
SOA-I	Service Demand
SOA-II	Service Aggregation, Orientation
SOA-III	Service Orchestration
SOA-IV	Service Agency Collaboration

The proposed model is sequenced and presented in Figure 5 through UML principles. UML provides a scope to generate solutions through business process modelling. E-governance processes provide such opportunities since these services are mostly component based and can be brokered through component objects. The UML generated model depicts the explanations made in section three through Figure 2. This model posits that SOA-I would capture demand of services raised either individually or collectively. It would take care of the point of raising demand on services, the latency and appropriateness. This "point of service (POS)" will generally be backed by appropriate technology to manage mode, medium and frequency, service components to be pulled by appropriate component technologies. In SOA-II, these services are collated for better management of information systems. This layer also manages the service provisioning agencies which could be called for active collaboration on demand. It provides the facility to add citizen demand as well. SOAIII generates the platform for addition of service providers and their services for orchestration. It relates to maintenance of databases for services, service providers related to government and non-government systems, business houses and entrepreneurs. This is mainly related to 'orchestration'. SOA-IV establishes the need for backend 'service-oriented bus' which would ensure detailed mapping of agencies their profiling, establishment of adequate infrastructure, computing grids and application layers for providing services as desired. Unified service provisioning facilities are created through this layer. This model attempts to provide cyclic treatment to "service demands" and "service supplies" which would provide the right input to the intermediary agencies to collaborate, orchestrate and add value to the services being generated.

Figure 5. Proposed SOA e-Governance Model (UML Based)

It may be noted here that Indian democracy provides limited autonomy to states which take part in the governance systems with relation to the state boundaries. State legislations are part of the state administration whereas the national level governance looks after central governance issues. Therefore, e-governance projects reflect traces of such dual administrative structure. In other words, there are concurrent attempts to provision citizen centric services taken by central and state authorities. Of late, central administration has deployed mission mode projects with states collaborating as part of NeGP (Chandrashekhar, 2006). NeGP also mandates for public-private-participation (PPP) based services for the citizens. Therefore, convergence of services is of prime importance so as to provide commercial approach to the services and establish sustainable and remunerative information service provisioning.

DISCUSSION OF TWO CASES

In this section two cases from India are presented and assessed through the model discussed in section three in Figure 4. This assessment provides insights to the SOA based approach to e-governance systems and their prospects to serve the citizens.

Case of national E-governance plan

National e-Governance Plan (NeGP) is getting implemented through 100,000 common service centres (CSC) in India (Misra, 2009). The entire project is being based on "Entrepreneurship Model" in which six villages would be covered by one CSC.

It is envisaged that the information backbone would extend services to these CSCs. The vision states "Make all Government services accessible to the common man in his locality, through common service delivery outlets and ensure efficiency, transparency & reliability of such services at affordable costs to realize the basic needs of the common man" (Misra, 2009). It considers "state level and national level mission mode projects" as critical success factors for the plan. In Figure 6 the approach of NeGP suggests an integrated environment and therefore, calls for a robust architecture.

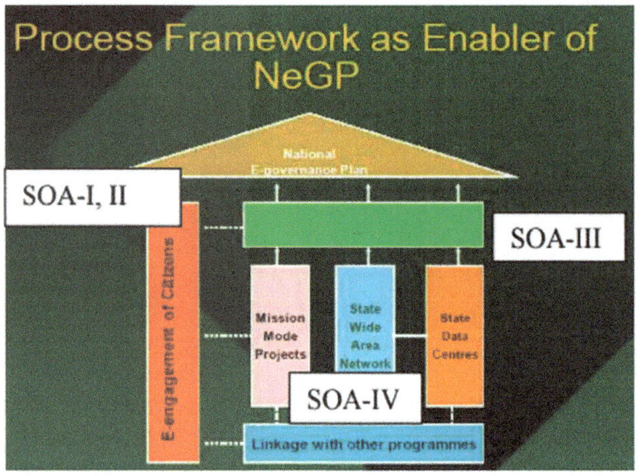

Figure- 6. CSC Implementation Approach (Mishra, 2007; EGovOnline, 2009)

NeGP infrastructure includes state level data centres, state wide area networks, and considers integration among various ICT enabled services. The Status of NeGP implementation programme is presented in figure 7 and Figure 8. As regards service oriented contents, NeGP recognises the scope for large-scale implementation of application under mission mode projects (MMPs) with emphasis on integrated services. Under NeGP, national level MMPs and state level MMPs are identified for implementation on scale-up mode as presented in Figure 7. Every interested state government is now under a state wide area network (SWAN). Each state is now in the process of having state data centres under the NeGP policy. This endeavour is part of state readiness exercise which is adapted mostly from the global information technology report framework published annually by the World Economic Forum. This assessment commencing in 2003 has provided insight to the performance of states which are placed in six categories: Least Achievers (L1), Below Average Achievers (L2), Average Achievers (L3), Expectants (L4), Aspiring Leaders (L5), and Leaders (L6). The latest rankings of the participating states are given in Figure 8.

Case of E-Gram1

E-Gram is a state level e-governance project initiated by state authorities in one of the states in India. The state has commissioned the project to provide services to citizens which include issuing of documents and certificates, application forms for various development and welfare schemes (like record of rights (land records), property registration, vehicle registration, driving license, health care, employment registration and passport). Commercial services include market rates, and distance learning opportunities. It has also helped 10,000 rural entrepreneurs in managing these e-gram centres on commission/incentive/salary basis. Gram Panchayats2 are empowered to manage the infrastructure deployed. Gram Panchayat can further offer services like; VSAT communication technology based broadband connectivity; free of cost communication between panchayats; common service centre facility for the villagers. Villagers can also take advantage of internet and cyber services through the establishment of these e-Gram services. This e- Gram would gradually also take other services under its ambit, like electricity and telephone bills, visa, e-Postal services. The technology partners involved in this e-Gram project are Airtel, Gilat, Cisco, IBM, Prodelin and Nokia Siemens Networks. E-Gram covers all 13,693 panchayats of the state (egovIndia, (2009)).

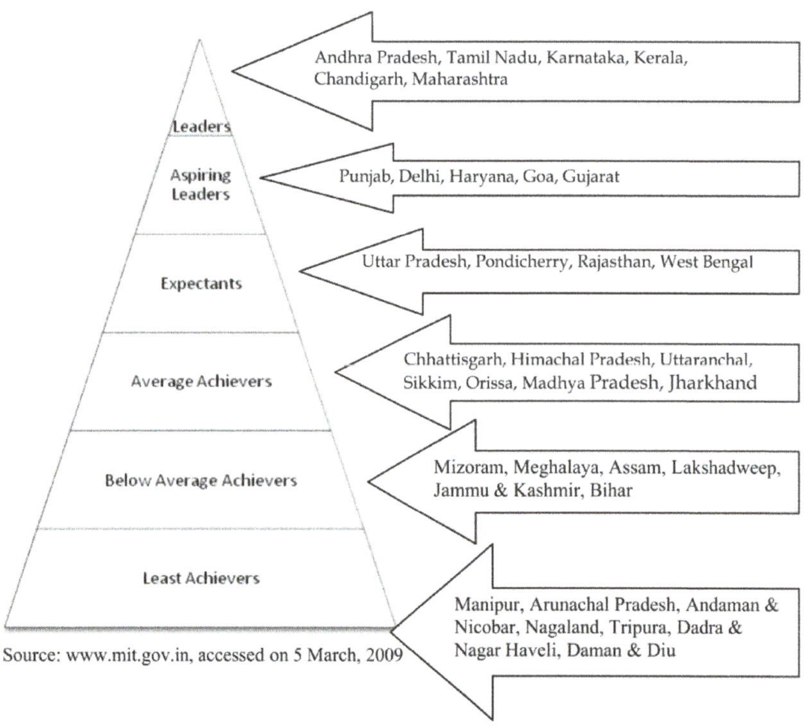

Figure 7. Status of NeGP

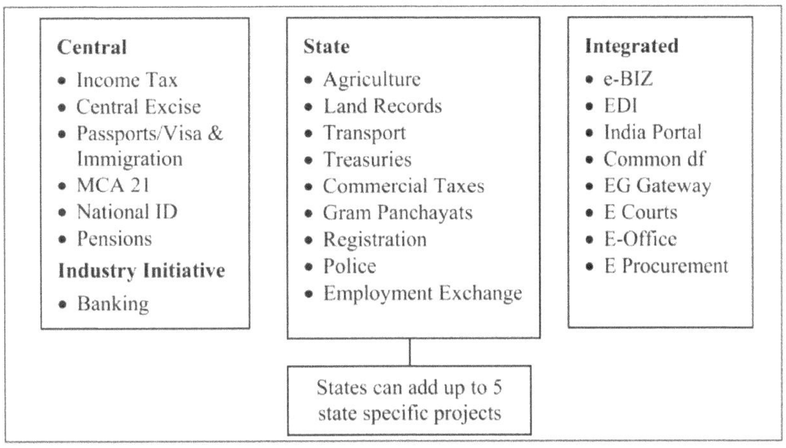

Figure 8. Status of NeGP driven Projects. Source: www.mit.gov.in, accessed on 5 March, 2009

Case Analysis

Two cases discussed in section 5.2 provide an insight to e-government scenarios in India. In the case of NeGP, a national level project covering all the willing states is driven by policy on e-governance. This project having a 'top-driven agenda' intends to deploy mission mode projects covering the entire nation. The next case on e-gram, a state sponsored project provides similar services to the citizens through panchayats and in addition, it extends state services which are otherwise not under the purview of national network under NeGP. The backend services are mostly driven from the state data centres and a backbone network funded through a NeGP. As per SOA model described in section 4 a comparative analyses of both the cases are presented for appreciation. In Table 3 the analyses are discussed.

Table 3. Case analyses

Layer	Layer Description	SOA Component Proposed	Case (NeGP)	Case (E-Gram)
1	Operational Systems	II,III	Available through Mission Mode Application Software (strong for SOA)	Disjoint Application (Weak in SOA)
2	Enterprise Component	IV	Available through Mission Mode Application Software (Strong in SOA)	Service Composition is localised to state government (Weak in SOA)
3	Services	IV	Common Service Centres are on entrepreneurship model. So, multiple services are available (Strong in SOA)	E-Gram is state sponsored. Panchayat is empowered to take decisions on management, not services (Weak in SOA)
4	Business Process Composition	III	Citizens are not included in planning (Weak in SOA)	Citizens are not included in planning (Weak in SOA)
5	Access	I,II	Access point is near to village. (Strong in SOA)	E-Gram is in Local Language and in the panchayat. (Strong in SOA)
6	Integration	III	Services of State Agencies and National Network do not converge (Weak in SOA)	Services of State Agencies and National Network do not converge (Weak in SOA)
7	Quality of Services	I	Broad based Citizen Demand is not planned and captured. (Weak in SOA)	Broad based Citizen Demand is not planned and captured. (Weak in SOA)

CONCLUSION

NeGP in India is policy driven project with an aim to spread ICT infrastructure in rural areas, provide converged services to rural citizens and establish the backend data centres to establish the linkage between governance systems. E-Gram initiative, in contrast, is a state sponsored service. SOA architecture based treatment to NeGP and e-Gram services reveal that there is a need to carefully conceptualize and to incorporate all the characteristics of SOA in order to provide citizen centric services. It is far more important that countries like India need to carefully articulate services with active collaboration of the citizens in order to provide good governance systems. In Table 2 it is discussed and noted that both the egovernance projects having sponsorship from national and state governments respectively, these projects lack effort in 'orchestrating', ''composing', 'choreographing', and making the services 'demand driven' from the view points of the citizens. SOA approaches provide a comprehensive view to such projects and provide the necessary tools and appropriate internet technologies to conceptualise, design, develop and implement e-governance services. This paper is carved out of an initial research work done in the areas of SOA for egovernance projects and there is a plan to take the research forward to implement SOA driven software engineering principles and evaluate e-governance efforts in India.

REFERENCES

1. Arsanjani, Ali, (2004), Service Oriented Modeling and Architecture, Web Service Centre of Excellence, IBM
2. Asian Development Bank (2008), Strategy 2020, The Long-Term Strategic Framework of the Asian Development Bank, 2008–2020, ISBN 978-971-561-680-5.
3. Benamou, N. (2006) Bringing e-Government Interoperability to Local Governments in Europe, egovInterop'06 Conference, Bordeaux, France.
4. Brocke, Jan Vom, Schenk, Bernd and Sonnenberg, Christian, (2009), Classification Criteria for Governing the Implementation Process of Service-Oriented ERP Systems – An Analysis Based on New Institutional Economics, Americas Conference on Information Systems(AMCIS 2009); Http://aisel.aisnet.org/amcis2009/316 accessed on 23.10.2009.
5. C S R Prabhu, (2007), Towards an E-Governance Grid for India (E-CGI): An Architectural Framework for Citizen Service Delivery, International Conference of E-Governance (ICEG 2007), Hyderabad, 29-30 December.
6. Chandrashekhar, R., (2006), Common Services Centres: A Strategic Cornerstone of NeGP, Workshop on Knowledge Centre Initiatives, Jaipur, April, 19.
7. Dutta, Soumitra, Lanvin Bruno and Paua, Fiona, (2008), The Global Information Technology Report, INSEAD, New York, Oxford University Press.
8. Egovonline,(2009), http://www.egovonline.net/news/news-details.asp?News=GujaratLaunches-e-Gram-Project&NewsID=15781, accessed on 27.02.2009
9. E-Readiness Assessment Report, (2008), Department of Information Technology, Ministry of Communication and Information Technology, Government of India, New Delhi.
10. Erl, Thomas, (2008), SOA Principles of Service Design, Pearson Education, Boston, ISBN-13: 9780132344821.
11. European Commission (2006), Revisiting E-Inclusion: From Vision to Action.
12. Garlan David and Shaw Mary, (1994), An Introduction to Software Architecture, Carnegie Mellon University Technical Report CMU-CS-94-166, January.
13. Heeks, Richard, (2005), ICTs and the MDGs: On the Wrong Track?, UK Development Studies Association conference Open University, Milton Keynes, 7-9 Sep
14. Jansen, Arlid, (2005), Assessing E-Governance Progress- Why and What, Department of egovernment studies, University of Oslo, Norway, http://www.afin.uio.no/om_enheten/folk/ansatte/jansen.html accessed on 11.07.2006
15. Kaul, Urvasi, (2008), Common Service Centres: Slow Progress, http://dqindia.ciol.commakesections.asp/08061901.asp accessed on 19.09.2008
16. Mishra, D.C., (2007), Select Aspects of Conceptual Foundations of E-Government, Clearing the Fog for Better Vision, International Conference of E-Governance (ICEG 2007), Hyderabad, 29-30 December
17. Misra, H. K., (2009), Citizen Centric Rural E-Governance for Development in India: An Architecture Based Approach, The 3rd International Multi Conference on Society, Cybernetics & Informatics (IMSCI 2009), July 10-13, 2009 - Orlando, Florida, USA.(Coming Up)
18. Misra, H. K., Hiremath, B. N., (2006), Citizen-led Participatory E-Governance Initiatives: An Architectural Perspective, IIM Lucknow, Metamorphosis,A Journal of Management Research, Special Issue on Public-Private Partnership:Issues and Strategeis, Vol.5 No. 2, pages 133 to 148.
19. National e-Governance Plan (NEGP) (2005), Ministry of IT, GoI, http://www.mit.gov.in/plan/gdecisions.asp accessed on 09-07-2006
20. Prabhu, C.S.R., (2004), "E-Governance: Concepts and Case Studies", Prentice-Hall of India, New Delhi, pp.10-25.
21. Rama Rao, T.P., Rao, Venkata, V., Bhatnagar, Subhas, and Satyanarayana, J, (2004), EGovernance Assessment Framework, EAF Ver-2.0, Department of Information Technology, Ministry of Communication and Information Technology, Government of India, New Delhi, May.
22. Ravichandran, T., Leong, Yi-Xing, Teo, Hock-Hai and Oh, Lin-Bin(2007), Service-Oriented Architecture and Organizational Integration: AN Empirical Study of IT-Enabled Sustained Competitive Advantage, International Conference on Information Systems (ICIS); http://aisel.aisnet.org/icis2007/92 accessed on 23.10.2009.
23. Riley, Thomas B., (2003), E-Governance Vs. E-Government, I4D, November, Vol.1-4, New Delhi.
24. Satyanarayana, J., (2004), e-Government, the Science of the Possible", Prentice-Hall of India, New Delhi, pp.8-22.

25. Simone Cecchini, and Christopher Scott, (2003), Can Information and Communications Technology applications contribute to poverty reduction? Lessons from rural India, Information Technology for Development 10 (2003), 73–84 73, IOS Press

26. WSIS, (2004), Partnership on Measuring ICT for Development, Project Document prepared on 23 June 2004 WSIS Thematic Meeting on Measuring the Information Society, Geneva, 7 to 9 February 2005.

Section IV - SOA Applications in the Public Sector

CHAPTER 15

A LIGHTWEIGHT SOA-BASED COLLABORATION FRAMEWORK FOR EUROPEAN PUBLIC SECTOR

Adomas Svirskas, Jelena Isačenkova and Refik Molva

INTRODUCTION

E-Business and e-Government solutions are becoming more and more widespread with constantly growing number of users depending on availability, accuracy and security of such e-Services. The users must be able to trust these services; otherwise they will be reluctant to embrace the new opportunities and will not be able to reap the potential benefits. In addition, the end users wish to use the e-services in the simplest way possible and to have them "on tap" 24x7 as other conventional utilities. For this to become possible, a robust interoperability fabric among the involved institutions needs to be established. This means having a lot of collaborative interactions invisible to the end-user (a business or an individual citizen) in order to fulfil the promise of e-Services. Such interactions become more complex when the organizations belong to different countries, act according different laws in different languages. This chapter presents the work among to create an efficient, secure and trusted interoperability framework for public sector agencies of European Union member countries.

In a simplified view, the administrations in Europe as a whole can be seen as a forest. Each tree is one specific administration of one member state (Fig. 1.). Each leaf is one particular service provided by this administration. E-Administration today mostly consists of providing services via IT tools and reducing the paper support via a user-friendly interface to the service. This is what we call "e-Administration in the small".

The real challenge is to enable smooth collaboration between the trees, i.e. between administrations of the same or of different member states. This is "e-Administration in the large" and reflects our understanding of collaborative e-Government systems. The R4eGov project (R4eGov, 2005), aims at providing the basic conceptual and technical framework for the first e-Administration in the large for Europe. R4eGov emphasises the basic control and security principles of:

- Local data ownership: each "leaf" uses data stores, in most cases local, to store its data. For example, civil status data (état civil), which records the birth, marriage, death of French citizens born in France are managed by each city.
- Local information access policies: data access is generally restricted to some personnel of the administration which operates the service. Access to some of the data, certainly not to the entire data stores, must be granted to personnel of other administrations, under controlled conditions. Data stores/bases in their entirety should never be displaced nor copied nor merged to permit e-Administration in the large.
- Local enforcement of organisational control and security policies, according to the local legislative acts

Citation: Adomas Svirskas, Jelena Isacenkova and Refik Molva (2010). A Lightweight SOA-based Collaboration Framework for European Public Sector, E-learning Experiences and Future, Safeeullah Soomro (Ed.), InTech, DOI: 10.5772/8818.

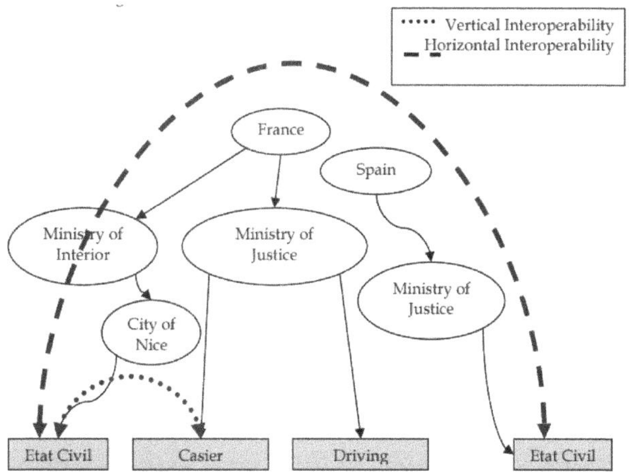

Figure 1. E-Government Forest and types of interoperability

A stepwise refinement approach focusing on progressive development and seamless deployment of collaborating, cross-organisational collaborative workflows is required as no single process model covering all European administrations will ever be created from scratch. To permit the progressive take-up of government process modelling, the environment must allow for incomplete and not fully formal descriptions, in addition to descriptions being developed separately with little concern for interoperability.

The R4eGov project takes into account the answers provided by existing bodies (eEurope eGovernment Subgroup, IDABC Management Committee , ADAE , etc), which debate on how to best grant access to private data owned by other Member States, while protecting privacy as requested in the constitution of the concerned Member State. To be practical, we address the problems raised by the case studies of the R4eGov project (such as Europol/Eurojust, Austrian government etc). We develop a collaborative interaction model of the European e-Administration, where the processes, the levels of control, security and timing requirements are described. This will constitute the top level picture of the European e-Government. Boxes at the bottom of Fig. 1 are examples of domains (Etat civil, Casier judiciaire, Driving offences) that have adopted IT and are examples of successful eAdministration applications. Today, exchanges between administrations of one country (such as, for example, between French Etat civil and Casier judiciaire) are being put in place with often little consideration for the need of mutual trust. Exchanges between states are possible but of little practical use. It is urgent to address these issues.

Thus, the three main objectives of the R4eGov project are:

- To gather and elicit the requirements for e-Administration in the large, on basis of which a concrete interoperation of web service enabled legacy public sector applications will be achieved using collaborative interactions.
- To provide the tools and methods for an e-Administration in the large from a technical and sociological perspective.
- To provide the required security and privacy for an e-Administration in the large, defining the appropriate methods and tools for control, security and privacy at the collaborative workflow and application layer.

One of the main results of this project is a reference framework and its proof-of-concept implementations based on several case-studies derived from the business requirements of the public administration organizations participating as partners in R4eGov project, such as Europol, Eurojust etc. The framework, thus, is quite generic and customizable to fit varying business needs.

Interactions among the participants of knowledge-intensive collaborations are often based on the Service Oriented Architecture (SOA) paradigm - the partners use each other's' services. Such collaborative on-demand interactions take various forms depending on various factors such as complexity, scope, duration of the interactions, level of formalization and the application domain. Within the scope of our work, the term collaborative denotes the type of interactions where the partners are peers, i.e. they do not have direct control over each other and communicate by exchanging mutually understandable messages among themselves.

The notion of peers is well suited to collaboration of the governments and other public service agencies of 27 European Union member countries - these organizations are independent, act according to the law of their respective countries yet have strong needs (and obligations) for interoperable interaction. For example in the Hague Programme (Hague, 2004), the European Council stated: "The mere fact that information crosses borders should no longer be relevant. With effect from 1 January 2008 the exchange of such information should be governed by conditions (...) with regard to the principle of availability, which means that, throughout the union, a law enforcement officer in one Member State who needs information in order to perform his duties can obtain from this from another Member State (...)". Currently, in European law enforcement domain work is underway to implement the principle of availability with respect to six categories of data: DNA, fingerprints, ballistics, vehicle registrations, telephone numbers and other communications data, and civil registers.

A MOTIVATING CASE STUDY FROM THE EUROPEAN E-GOVERNMENT FIELD

We have motivated our work, to a large extent, with a use case from the Europol (EP)/Eurojust (EJ) collaboration domain. These two agencies have been set up to help the EU member states co-operate in the fight against cross-border organised crime. Cooperation in criminal matters is a subject dealt with in the "third pillar" of the EU (Title VI of the Treaty of the European Union). Eurojust stands for the European Judicial Cooperation Unit whereas Europol refers to the European Police Office. Europol and Eurojust carry out very specific tasks in the context of the dialogue, mutual assistance, joint efforts and cooperation between the police, customs, immigration services and justice departments of the EU member states.

Europol became fully operational in 1999; Eurojust was set up by a Council Decision in 2002. Both agencies are based in The Hague, The Netherlands. Establishing a secure IT connection between Eurojust and Europol has been an objective shared by the two organisations for several years. Europol and Eurojust are two key elements of the European system of international collaboration within the areas of law enforcement and justice. Even though they differ considerably in the way they are organized, on how they operate and on their mandated areas, there is an overarching need to ensure smooth collaboration and effective information exchange between the two organizations.

In spite of the presence of legal basis for collaboration between the two organizations since 2002 (the Eurojust Decision and the Agreement between Eurojust and Europol of 9 June 2004), the complexity of the nature of the exchange (content, channels, sources, recipients, means, etc.), the compliance framework (legal basis, compliance and data protection rules) and the different implementation of policies and procedures in the 27 member states, have all limited the collaboration on cases to a small number.

From the technical point of view, it should be noted that both organisations already manage their information through computerised systems Europol's Overall Analysis System for Intelligence and Support (OASIS) and Eurojust Case Management System but these systems are currently separate.

Therefore, a structured approach on how to deal with the barriers to information exchange must be undertaken. While lines of communications at various levels already exist, these channels should be supported by computerised technical devices to allow the secure and swift exchange of information in the framework of the above legal instruments and the applicable data protection rules. In practical terms, it is necessary to follow an appropriate methodology to establish sound solution architecture and obtain/create ready-to-use tools (framework and software) in order to:

- Facilitate collaboration between Europol and Eurojust
- Improve the collaboration of the sources of Europol and Eurojust
- Get the tools and implement a practical viable solution

The creation of a framework (conceptual and practical, including tools) that allows dealing with the multiplicity of instances of technological and business rules, would allow for an identification of the barriers that impede international collaboration and for taking appropriate countermeasures on a technological or business level (including the change in legal framework) where necessary.

In order to illustrate the aforementioned issues, let's take a simple information exchange scenario depicted in the Fig. 1. The scenario involves four parties, each having their own independent administrative and security domains. All the parties should use some kind of Collaborative Workflow Management System (CWfMS) to better integrate and automate their collaboration processes.

Eurojust uses a Case Management System (CMS) to support the work of its prosecutors, but the CMS is not the only source of information. EJ depends on information provided by EP, which does the main investigation work. Furthermore, as EP is also a centre of collaboration of all member states of the European Union, it can request information on a suspect from a national investigation bureau.

This is what happens in the chosen scenario, which, roughly, consists of the following individual collaboration steps:

- An EJ case is created in the CMS
- During a meeting at EJ, it is decided that the National Member of state a (NMa) will request data from the Case Analysis bureau of her/his member state (MSCAa)
- NMa sends the request to the Europol Liaison Officer of her/his state (ELOa)
- ELOa contacts the Europol National Unit of her/his state (ENUa). ENUa contacts MSCAa and MSCAa sends back data to ENUa, which passes it on to ELOa
- ELOa retrieves additional data from the InfoEx system
- ELOa sends back both data sets to NMa.
- NMa updates the CMS with the data

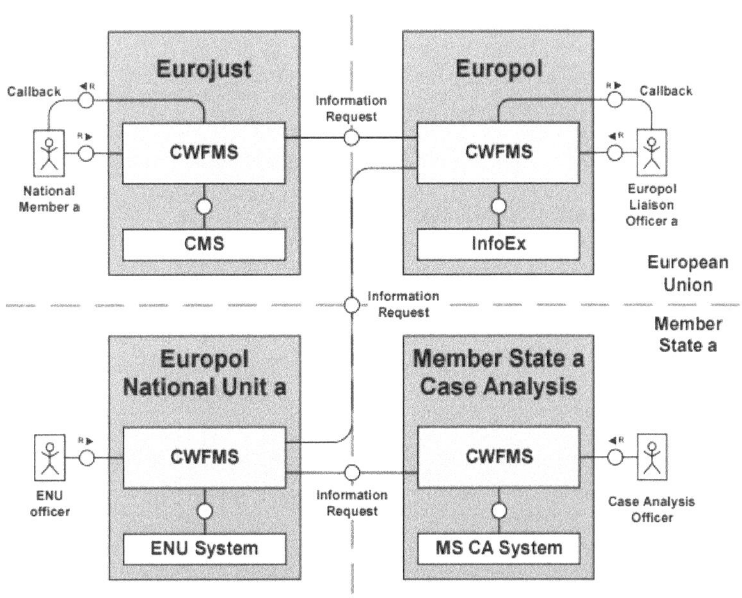

Figure 2. A sample information exchange scenario from EP/EJ case study

These steps, with some variation, are further depicted in more detailed and complex way in the Fig. 3, which is a real-world example of the issues to be dealt with. Furthermore, this simple scenario is only a very small part of the EP/EJ collaborative interaction needs and, in turn, the EP/EJ case study as whole is just a tiny (however important) bit in the overall European e-Government landscape.

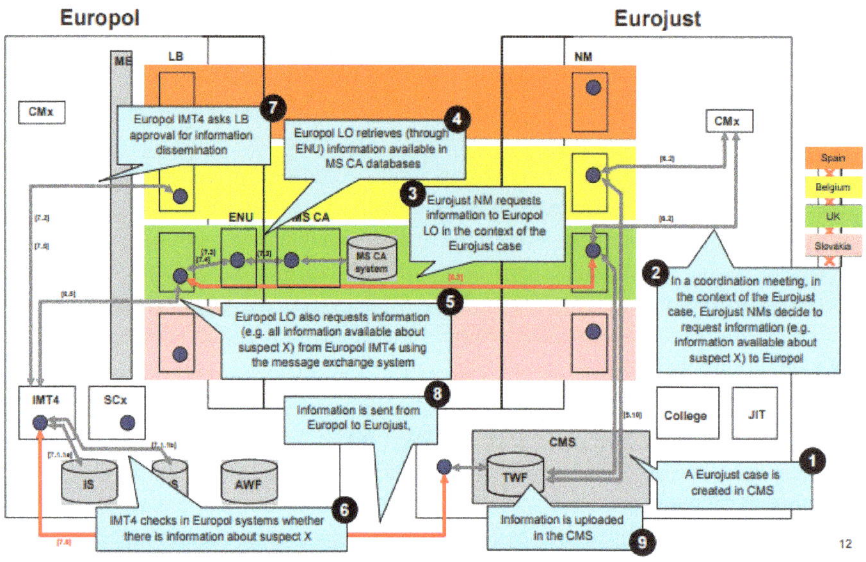

Figure 3. Interaction Flow - Exchange of information between Eurojust and Europol

It is obvious that the problem of pan-European interoperability among the public administration bodies is a very complex one and, of course, the R4eGov project is not the first effort trying to deal with it. In the following section we will outline the principles, which constitute the basis of our solution architecture and framework.

THE SOLUTION ARCHITECTURE

Before presenting the proposed solution, it is worth to discuss the architectural context in brief. Having studied the business requirements of public sector collaborative interactions (R4eGov case studies, 2007; eGovInterop Case Studies, 2006) and the current state of the art of possible implementation technology, we distinguish a few important factors, which determine the context of our solution architecture:

- A need for the public administration agencies (or their units) of the EU member countries to have standard ways for interconnecting and integrating their heterogeneous IS to ensure interoperability at shared information level.
- Independence of each agency and its operation according to the local legislative acts, regulations etc.
- Agencies being very protective of their data with regard to who can have access to it, what kind of "channels" the data can travel, who has seen the data etc.
- Enormous variety of the technical solutions being used by different agencies and countries
- Different countries and agencies are at very different levels of readiness to embrace e-Government collaborative interactions. The differences are found at legal, procedural, conceptual, cultural, technical, human skills levels.

These factors make a good case for using the service oriented (SOA) approach to integration of the information resources, i.e. each data source being exposed via well-defined interface, following the DaaS (data as a service) principle. The concept of data as a service (DaaS) suggests using service-oriented architecture (SOA) for accessing data "where it lives" - the actual platform on which the data resides doesn't make crucial difference for overall collaborative interaction among the partners. Thus, the key issues such as independence of the agencies and their differences become manageable – the agencies expose as much data as they possibly can and are willing to while the access to this data is granted only to the authorised parties.

The conceptual SOA approach

The architectural approach based on service and data virtualization is a sound practical foundation for implementing the data as a service concept in practice. Virtualization also allows uniform access to the software services exposed by the partners of collaborations. Virtualization and uniformity of services, provided by public administrations, are very important in order to have on-demand data aggregation, also referred to as enterprise mashups. This relatively new concept of Web 2.0 paradigm has already found its place in eGovernment: for example, the U.S. Department of Defense's lead intelligence agency is using wikis, blogs, RSS feeds and enterprise "mashups" to help its analysts collaborate better when sifting through data used to support military operations, (Havenstein, 2007).

In addition to this, the integration framework needs to be lightweight and reasonably simple, taking into account that the level of integration readiness varies greatly from agency to agency in different countries. Simplicity allows the agencies to start small, experience benefits of integration and collaborative interactions, then iteratively add new services, as needed. Such approach will lower the entrance barrier for the less-prepared partners and will increase the chance of successful adoption of the solution.

In our R4eGov solution architecture, service virtualization is implemented using the concept of application-level gateway - each participant of collaboration communicates with the peers via Web services based Interoperability (IOP) Gateway. That is, the real services within an agency participating in the interactions, are accessible by sending a request to well known address of the gateway and specifying what kind of resource is needed. Gateway redirects such request to the internal provider, access control rules permitting. This pattern is not a new concept (Schmidt, 2000; Svirskas, 2007) defines a gateway as a mediator that decouples cooperating peers throughout a network and allows them to interact without having direct dependencies on each other. We have chosen this pattern and the newest SOA-based technologies to implement a lightweight, flexible and efficient interoperability platform, which will be explained below.

Each participant, with rare exceptions, at different points of the interaction can find itself at either the sending or receiving end of the information (SOAP/XML messages). In other words, in this asynchronous mode of interaction each participant is capable to receive requests from outside (other participants) to access its internal resources (data, services) as well as to initiate the requests towards other participants (or respond to their requests).

The latter case means that the internal resources (legacy/back-end systems) of a participant issue requests to the outside of the participant domain. Thus we have requests coming in and the requests/data coming out for each given participant multiple times during an instance (a collaboration scenario or business protocol, choreography) of collaborative interaction.

Implementation Technology

echnically speaking, R4eGov SOA-based solution architecture primarily relies on Web services technology, including both the basic protocols/specifications such as SOAP, WSDL, HTTP/S and the more advanced ones - WS-Addressing, WS-ReliableMessaging, WSSecurity, WS-Trust etc. - collectively known as Web services advanced architecture (Web Services, WS Security). Web services are used for both inter-domain communication between the gateways and internal services, which may represent some newly developed functionality or serve as wrappers for legacy systems.

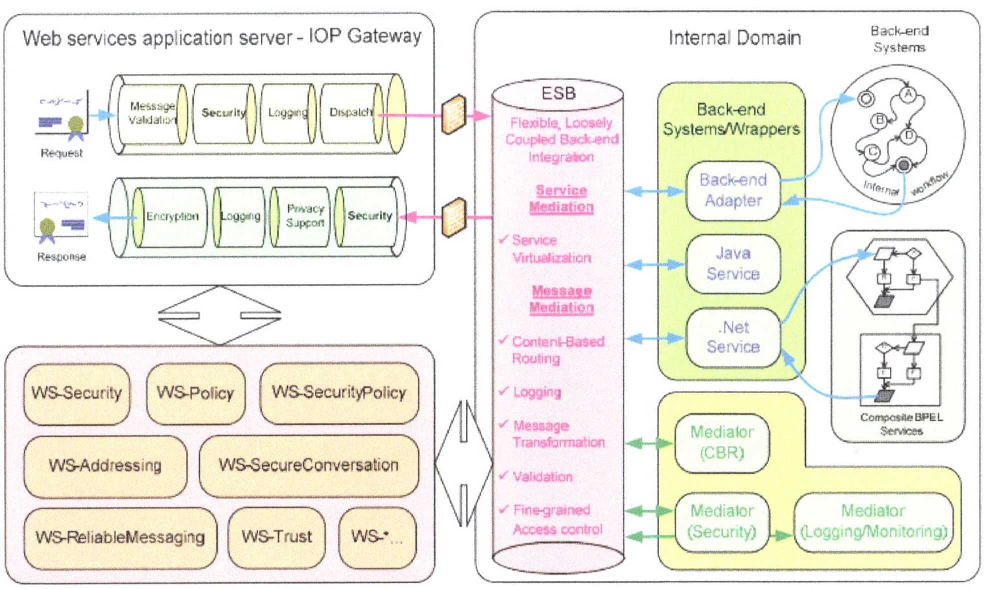

Figure 4. Architecture of collaborative interaction platform based on IOP gateways

It is quite clear, that implementing the IOP Gateway features, as depicted in Fig. 4., configuring gateway instances for operating in different environments and, in particular, ensuring appropriate security level, is not a trivial task - the gateway needs to map incoming messages to internal operations, support business rules, enact business protocols (choreographies), which govern collaborative interactions, enforce security policies, provide logging, and monitoring, at least.

To ensure manageability, adaptability and flexibility, functionality of the gateway needs to be decomposed and developed/deployed accordingly. Firstly, there is a need for modularity - each separate gateway function should be well-defined and of manageable scope. The R4eGov architecture (R4eGov), introduces the notion of extension module. Extension module is a software component that can be plugged into the execution environment and which fulfils a certain non-functional task in the context of collaborative workflows. In addition, this architecture need to support pluggability - the extension modules should be ready for deployment by changing gateway configuration; no extra coding should be involved for registering, un-registering, changing order of invocation and similar administrative tasks. This helps achieving flexibility, as it should be possible to compose modules into flows (pipelines) for sequential message processing, separately for outgoing and incoming messages, specifying necessary order of message processing.

Let's look how these principles are applied in R4eGov IOP Gateway architecture. The main functionality of the gateway – connecting inter-domain collaborative interactions with the internal services is achieved combining modern web services engines (Apache Axis2), which support pluggable message handler architecture, allowing to implement message processing chains in an elegant and efficient way. Furthermore, modern Enterprise Service Bus (ESB)- based mediation frameworks (Apache Synapse) support extensions called mediators, which facilitate such message processing functions as:

- Content-based routing
- Message transformation
- Logging

- Security support
- Message schema validation
- Load balancing and fail-over
- Quality of Service support
- Protocol (e. g. SOAP, REST, JMS) and presentation format (e.g. POX, JSON, XML) conversion
- ESB-based mediation framework can act like an intelligent yet lightweight and efficient application level router connecting the internal services providing access to the actual data with the external collaborative interactions. Such framework provides powerful means to define the rules according to which the messages are directed and handled.

As we can see, security-related extension modules can be implemented in two ways, depending on the context - they can be either Web services engine handlers or user-defined mediators in ESB mediation infrastructure. Such combination of Web service message processing handlers and ESB message mediators provides possibilities for composing very flexible chain of actions to be performed on a given message, which is crucial for IOP flexibility and usefulness. The implementations we have chosen, Apache Axis2 and Apache Synapse, packaged as WSO2 protocol stack (WSO2) are designed to work together, have solid developer and user base, which increases the chances of successful practical use.

SECURITY FEATURES OF THE R4EGOV FRAMEWORK

In a complex and heterogeneous ICT environment like the one R4eGov project faces, security requirements and expectations are often interpreted differently by different organizations and individuals, or simply specified in too-vague terms. For any security architecture related activity it is important to scope the area of security measures precisely, otherwise it is not possible to design and implement security solution in a timely and manageable manner. In short, our security/privacy solution addresses the following security concerns:

- Confidentiality of information items transferred between the IOP Gateways of collaborating organizations – implemented using Web services and XML security specifications (WS-Security, XML Encryption/Digital Signature).
- Authenticity of the information items being transferred between the organizations. This is implemented the same way as confidentiality.
- Role based access control to the resources offered by one organization to another. This is done by the target organization, based on the set of distributed roles.
- Role and identity based access control to the targets of partner organizations. This is done by the source organization, evaluating for each outgoing request whether the subject is entitled to be assigned a distributed (external) role in a particular collaboration and thus have an access right to a particular resource offered by target organization.
- Protecting privacy of the subjects in above authorization mechanisms by substituting their identity with pseudonyms. This way, the Personally Identifiable Information (PII) of the subjects remains within the boundaries of their "home" organization.

Apart from these general security concerns one of the frequent questions asked by the collaboration participants is whether their partners will apply adequate security measures to the data handed over to them. In a peer-to-peer collaborative environment, where data is transmitted among multiple partners it may happen, for example , that the transmitting authority applies higher security standards than the receiving authority, which consequently has to apply additional measures (which it does not usually apply to this type of information) in order to guarantee the same protection as the transmitting authority.

Alternatively, if we reverse the roles, both parties will simply need to apply their own security measures (and the security measures applied by the recipient of the information will actually be stricter than the ones applied by its owner). These requirements essentially mean that R4eGov solution will need to provide information protection policy harmonisation mechanisms. In our security architecture we address this issue by proposing the collaboration partners to share a common set of distributed roles. Inherently, the access control rights will be transferable across the domain boundaries and harmonisation of the security measures will be quite straightforward. The solution of distributed roles support based on (and extending) XACML (Lee & Luedeman, 2007). In order for this to happen there must be a level of trust established between the transmitter and the receiver. The former needs to be sure that the latter actually enforces the specified policies. There are several ways to establish such trust, for example implementing access control enforcement using trusted code – components and services. (Djordjevic et al. 2007) describe a method for combining software resource level security features offered by Web services technologies, with the hardware-based security mechanisms offered by Trusted Computing Platform and system virtualisation approaches. They propose a trust-based architecture for protecting the enforcement middleware deployed at the policy enforcement endpoints of web and grid services. Such approach can be used in conjunction with our distributed roles-based access control.

ORGANIZATION OF SECURITY MECHANISMS

Security mechanisms of such solution are not simple and cannot be implemented in one piece/concentrated in one place. It is commonly (with some variations) acknowledged, that these mechanisms need to be distributed and grouped according to their purpose.

We can distinguish the following main security tiers:

- Protection and threat prevention
- Access enablement: Identity and Access Management – IAM

The security mechanisms are distributed accordingly. In our security architecture the "protection and thread prevention" part spans not only network/transport layer security but also message (e.g. SOAP) layer security, delivery of messages between the gateways according to the confidentiality, authenticity and integrity requirements.

Similar security functionality distribution is also advocated by (Mozes, 2004), he distinguishes between the

SOAP intermediaries and security intermediaries in WS-based collaborative security architecture. The authentication (between the IOP gateways) and coarse-grained authorization can be performed at the system boundary (we put these functions into Web services engine message processing handlers), using any one of a variety of authentication mechanisms, such as conventional Web-access management techniques or one of the available federated identity solutions. This ensures that messages must pass a rigorous test before being allowed into the internal network. If service interfaces must be exposed to unauthenticated clients, messages must be subjected to a different test. In this case, schema-validation is a suitable test to prevent XML attacks. In both cases certain attacks remain a problem, e.g. Denial of Service (DoS) attacks. Gruschka & Luttenberger propose a mechanism to address the threats of DoS attacks (Gruschka & Luttenberger, 2006).

On the other hand, schema-validation, fine-grained authorization and other aspects of security policy can be enforced close to the application environment. This allocation of security services also supports an appropriate division of responsibilities between network administrators, who are responsible for the integrity of the internal network and who must have the controls necessary to do that, and application administrators, who are responsible for policy enforcement in the applications and who must have the controls necessary to do that. This functionality of our security solution resides in ESB mediators.

Protection and threat prevention part of our solution focuses on data authenticity, integrity and confidentiality, which actually means encryption and digital signatures. In the Web services domain, WS-Security, an OASIS standard, is an open format for signing and encrypting message parts (leveraging XML Digital Signature and XML Encryption protocols), for supplying credentials in the form of security tokens, and for securely passing those tokens in a message. The core standards in this group comprise WS-Security Core (SOAP Message Security) and several token profiles including UserName Token Profile, X.509 Token Profile, Kerberos Token Profile, and SAML Token Profile. The token profiles enable serializing credentials in a consistent manner across platforms, certainly one of the driving forces behind the adoption of WS-Security in the first place.

Access Control Mechanisms

One of the central questions in security solutions is that of access control. In a nutshell, access control is the process of mediating every request to data and services maintained by a system and determining whether the request should be granted or denied. Access control is meant to protect resources (i.e., data and services) against unauthorized disclosure (secrecy, confidentiality) and unauthorized changes (integrity), at the same time ensuring accessibility of the resources by authorized users whenever needed (availability). These aspects sometimes are mutually conflicting and balancing them requires a careful approach.

An important access control implementation principle of our security architecture is well coordinated operation usage of Policy Enforcement Points (PEP) and Policy Decision Point (PDP) – access control decision making is concentrated in a single place (dealing with a vulnerability of having a single point of failure is a separate issue) and accessed from several PEPs:

- Loose standards-based (XACML) coupling of PEP and PDP facilitates flexibility of potential deployment
- Policy management service supports the specification, interpretation and instantiation of different types of policies: access control & obligation (eventcondition-action, ECA).
- Policy deployment service supports distribution and deployment of policies for usage by PDP.

One of the apparent virtues of the XACML framework is its modularity. XACML specification explicitly acknowledges that PEPs can be implemented in a variety of ways and use the same PDP, essentially enabling authorization as a service. For instance, PEP may be part of a remote-access gateway, a part of a Web server or part of an email user-agent, etc. In our architecture we can foresee two types of PEP. Firstly, the incoming requests received by the IOP Gateway are processed by a chain of handlers, one of them serving as PEP and providing the initial crude screening of the request. This PEP acts as a "bouncer", performing fast "face control" and protecting the inner workings of the gateway from obviously unwelcome requests. The outgoing requests and responses are subject to inspection, outward access control and potential transformations, which are achieved by processing these outgoing messages by a chain of handlers controlling the outgoing flow. Once again, one of these handlers acts as a PEP and ensures enforcement of applicable policies.

Therefore, there is a need for a canonical form of the request and response handled by an XACML PDP. This canonical form is called the XACML context. Its syntax is defined in XML schema. The XACML-conformant PEPs may issue requests and receive responses in the form of an XACML context. But, where this is not the case, an intermediate step is required to convert between the request/response format understood by the PEP and the XACML context format understood by the PDP, as depicted in Fig . 5.

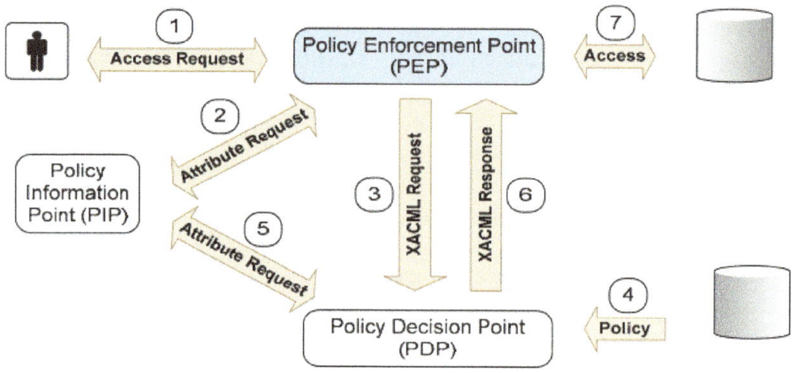

Figure 5. Typical XACML-based authorization process scheme

Assuming that integration of the IOP Gateway with the back-end systems of the participants of the collaborations is done using Enterprise Service Bus (ESB), certain functionality of modern ESB implementations can be leveraged to further secure the interactions. In particular, the feature of mediators, which can be set up to intercept the messages sent via ESB, can be used for installing additional PEPs for finer-grained access control to the resources. There can be additional PEPs implemented as required and installed at some points of the system, which can't be foreseen in advance due to the scale of integration. In addition, there can be legacy PEPs, which will need to enforce new and/or updated policies. Given the variety of PEPs, it is unrealistic to expect that all the PEPs in an enterprise do currently, or will in the future, issue decision requests to a PDP in a common format. Nevertheless, a particular policy may have to be enforced by multiple PEPs. It would be inefficient to force a policy writer to write the same policy several different ways in order to accommodate the format requirements of each sort of PEP.

The benefit of this approach is that policies may be written and analyzed independent of the specific environment in which they are to be enforced. The principle of separating the concerns of policy modelling/management from their enforcement environments/decision request formats is very important, as it allows to have consistent policy definition, verification and reasoning for all the requests/resources. XACML specification provides an abstraction-layer that insulates the policy-writer from the details of the application environment. As mentioned before, the canonical representation of a decision request and an authorization decision is called XACML context. Context handler is an entity, which converts decision requests in the native request format to the XACML canonical form and converts authorization decisions from the XACML canonical form to the native response format.

In multi-party interactions quite often is important to preserve privacy of the subjects (requestors), without compromising appropriate access control. Our contribution aims to solve this issue without a need to explicitly involve a third trusted party into the interactions. Privacy preservation is a complex task, affected by different kind of policies, defined by different parties:

- Access control policies govern access/release of data/ services managed by the party (as in traditional access control)
- Release policies govern release of properties/ credentials/PII of the party and specify under which conditions they can be disclosed
- Sanitization policies provide filtering functionalities on the response to be returned to the counterpart to avoid release of sensitive information related to the policy itself
- Data processing policies define how the PII will be (or should be) used and processed In our solution we will be using access control policies for fine-grained resource protection on the service provider side and properties/credentials release policies along with the sanitization policies on the requestor side.

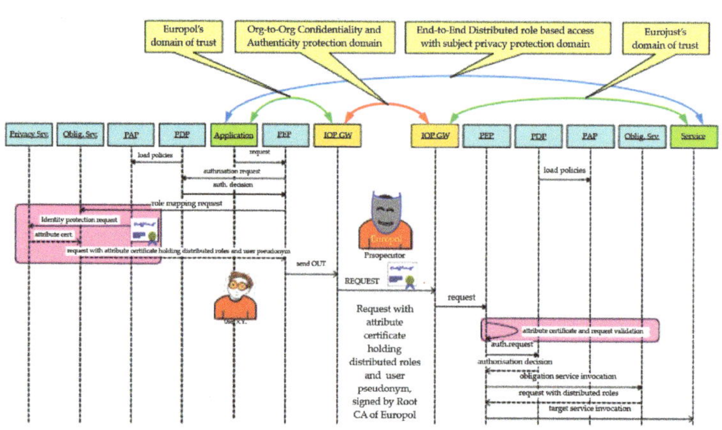

Figure 6. Typical XACML-based authorization process scheme

The traditional identity-based access control models where subjects and objects are usually identified by unique names are not always suitable due to privacy concerns. It is easy to foresee a need to protect subject's privacy in e-Government interactions, for example in judicial and/or law enforcement domain. Therefore, attributes other than identity are needed to determine the party's rights to access a resource. In this case access restrictions to the data/services should be expressed by policies specifying the attributes a subject has to possess to get access to the data/services. For example, a role or several roles (unless very explicit, such as top management) does not reveal person's PII. This is in line with rolebased access control principles. Fig. 6. illustrates privacy-preserving access control protocol of the R4eGov framework.

There are various ways to implement attribute based security tokens, one of them is to use digital certificates. Traditionally, a digital certificate has been mostly used as the identity certificate. An identity certificate is an electronic document used to recognize an individual, a server, or some other entity, and to connect that identity with a public key, thus solving key management issue. Another type of digital certificate is attribute certificate, which can be used in attribute-based access control mechanisms. An attribute certificate has a structure similar to an identity certificate but contains attributes that specify access control information associated with the certificate holder (e.g., group membership, role, security clearance).

CONCLUSIONS

The number of complex multi-domain/multi-country collaborations is constantly increasing, as the SOA concepts and supporting technologies are maturing. In order to gain acceptance, such solutions must be efficient, easy to use, secure and trusted. The work presented in this chapter aims to leverage the best implementations of standard and interoperable Web services specifications to provide a lightweight and modular framework for inter-organizational collaborative interactions. The concept of application-level gateway is implemented using pluggable extensions of Web services engine and further enhanced by using intelligent message processing based on Enterprise Service Bus and mediation techniques. This kind of virtualization allows achieving needed flexibility and security level providing standards based interoperability, data confidentiality, authenticity, integrity and role/policy based access control. These features, combined with the concept of Data as a Service (DaaS) enable the end users to have more power of creating ad-hoc enterprise data mash-ups, leverage benefits of enterprise social computing and gain additional opportunities when creating and reusing value-added knowledge.

A prototype of the described solution has been implemented using Apache and WSO2 Web services platform, WS-Security family of specifications. This prototype will be used to assess solution performance and suitability before moving towards enhancing choreographed interactions. A good case study for application of such compliance proof mechanism can be collaboration between public administrations of different EU Member States in legal/law enforcement domain (R4eGov case studies, 2007) where efficiency, security and trustworthiness of interaction steps is highly important. Further work is planned on privacy-preserving access control protocol, fine grained specifications of access entitlement and distributed authorization mechanisms.

ACKNOWLEDGEMENTS

The work presented here is partially funded by the European Commission under contract IST-2004-026650 through the project R4eGov (R4eGov). The authors would like to thank members of the organizations involved in R4eGov for their contribution: SAP Research Labs, University of Hamburg, Unisys Belgium, Europol, Eurojust, Austrian Bundeschancellor office, in particular.

REFERENCES

1. Apache Axis2, http://ws.apache.org/axis2 Apache Synapse, http://ws.apache.org/synapse Corporation, (2002). http://www.verisign.com/wss/architectureRoadmap.pdf eGovInterop Case Studies, 2006, http://www.egovinterop.net
2. Djordjevic, I.; Nair, K.S. & Dimitrakos, T. (2007). Virtualised Trusted Computing Platform for Adaptive Security Enforcement of Web Services Interactions. ICWS 2007, p.p. 615-622
3. Gruschka, N. & Luttenberger, N. (2006). Protecting Web Services from DoS Attacks by SOAP Message Validation
4. Hague Programme: strengthening freedom, security and justice in the European Union, 2004, http://www.libertysecurity.org/IMG/pdf/hague_programme_en.pdf
5. Havenstein, H. (2007). US Government Agency Embraces Web 2.0,
6. PCWorld, http://www.pcworld.com/article/id,129328-c,internetnetworking/article.html
7. Lee, H. & Luedeman, H. (2007). A Light-weighted Decentralized Authorization Model for Inter-domain Collaborations, ACM Workshop on Secure Web Services (SWS'07)
8. Moses, T. (2004). Security in Web services world", Entrust Inc. R4eGov,
9. R4eGov case studies (2007). EU IST FP6 project, http://www.r4egov.eu
10. Schmidt, D.C. (2000)."Applying a Pattern Language to Develop Applicationlevel Gateways," in Design Patterns in Communications (L. Rising, ed.), Cambridge University Press
11. Svirskas, A.; Wilson, M.D.; Roberts, B.; Ignatiadis, I. (2007). Adaptive Support of InterDomain Collaborative Protocols using Web Services and Software Agents, eds. O. Vasilecas, J. Eder, A. Caplinskas, Frontiers in Artificial Intelligence and Applications, IOS Press, Amsterdam Web Services, W3C, (2004). http://www.w3.org/TR/ws-arch/#technology WSO2 Web services Application Server, http://wso2.org/projects/wsas/java
12. WS Security: A Proposed Architecture and Roadmap, IBM Corporation & Microsoft
13. XACML, eXtensible Access Control Markup Language , OASIS Standard

CHAPTER 16 EDUCATIONAL MODELLING LANGUAGES AND SERVICE-ORIENTED LEARNING PROCESS ENGINES

Jorge Torres, César Cárdenas, Juan Manuel Dodero and Eduardo Juárez

INTRODUCTION

E-Learning Systems evolution (Torres et al., 2005) has offered an enhanced set of characteristics and flexibility to the learning process, starting from simple static Web contents, moving to the standardization of learning objects, and giving place to the creation of Educational Modelling Languages (EML) able to fully describe learning scenarios.

EMLs (Koper, 2001) represent an important approximation to integrate diverse educative aspects, allowing the design and implementation of spaces and activities supported by Information and Communication Technologies. With EMLs it is possible to integrate, under a learning process, personalized educative material for each student e.g. activities, services, resources, objectives, evaluations, profiles, promoting the active participation of the student with his learning process.

As EMLs evolve, design issues and more needs have been identified giving place to new desirable EML characteristics, such as pedagogical diversity, learning flow description, dynamic and unanticipated composition, separation of learning process and service, learning service availability and transaction support (Dodero et al., 2005).

To represent a learning environment under different complexity levels and mixing didactic techniques, it is necessary for the EML to be expressive enough to specify complex activity structures, dependences, rules, contents, roles, and participants, which can interact to achieve the learning objectives. These structures allow the building of learning flows.

At first, EMLs were thought only for E-Learning Systems containing all the resources the learning scenario will need to guarantee their availability. But as the employed resources evolved, such systems are not able to substitute them in an easy and transparent way, and furthermore, to provide a rich and diverse pedagogical experience for the learner, E-Learning Systems must implement a vast amount of applications e.g. Moodle [1] - forum, wiki, assignment, chat, choice, glossary, lesson, quiz, resource, survey, workshop and other modules; or LAMS [2] - chat, forum, multiple choice, noticeboard, notebook, question and answer, survey, voting and other activities, making even bigger the just mentioned issue. From a software architectural point-of-view, a service-oriented architecture (SOA) (Erl, 2004) provides an important approach in order to implement dynamically learning environments from diverse, distributed and heterogeneous learning resources and services, these can be hardly synchronized and coordinated through an EML specification. Furthermore, based upon SOA principles, Grid-Computing (Foster and Kesselman, 2003) offer a powerful environment to use of resources such as processing power, disk storage, applications and data, allowing the dynamic and unanticipated composition of distributed learning web services (Torres et al., 2008). These orchestration of web services and the long-lived nature of some learning activities, makes necessary for the execution engine to provide transactional support in order to guarantee the reliable execution of activities.

This chapter is organized as follows. Section two presents the four stage evolution of E-Learning Systems, outlining the interest in each stage, which moved from the focus on the

Citation: Jorge Torres, Cesar Cardenas, Juan Manuel Dodero and Eduardo Juarez (2010). Educational Modelling Languages and Service-Oriented Learning Process Engines, Advances in Learning Processes, Mary Beth Rosson (Ed.), InTech, DOI: 10.5772/8236.

development and deployment of Web contents of stage one, to the focus on Complex Learning Processes (CLP) in stage four. Section three presents an explanation of CLP, an educational perspective that combines different ways of learning and is focused on the participative role of the learner in the learning process. Section four presents the characteristics of EMLs and provides an overview of the three broadest languages: IMS LD, LAMS and LPCEL.

Section five presents the characteristics of the Learning Process Engine (LPE) and the following sections will discuss the ways the LPE must provide support for the EML characteristics, specifically for learning flow description, dynamic and unanticipated composition and transaction support. Section six shows the current EML design issues and then evaluates the learning flow expressiveness of current EMLs based on Workflow Control Patterns (WCP). Section seven provides a framework for the dynamic and unanticipated composition of learning services based on SOA and Grid-Computing principles. Section eight presents the importance of transactions along with Advanced Transaction Models (ATM), and then proposes a framework for the LPE to provide transactional support. Finally, in section nine we provide conclusions and further work.

EVOLUTION OF E-LEARNING SYSTEMS

E-Learning systems have been transcendental in the advance of traditional educational models. Learning technologies have evolved through different stages (Torres et al., 2005), each one with a meaningful progress for the design and display of pedagogical content, increasing functionality, semantic information and flexibility to support the different and complex pedagogical environments.

First Stage This stage is portrayed by the development and deployment of Web contents. Generally, they are simple applications (e.g. text les, HTML pages, and multimedia resources). The interest here is in the standardization of learning objects to be used in the learning process. Objects are simple instructional contents that can be deployed for learning (e.g. lessons, articles, task assignments, etc.). These objects lack of mechanisms to build learning processes, which are reduced to a sequential itinerary through contents.Second Stage In this stage the interest moves to the management, location and retrieval of contents. The way to deploy contents is improved and personalized according to the learner, as provided by IMS Learning Information Package Specification (LIP) (IMS, 2001). Technologies for the evaluation and tracking of the learner are developed, as IMS Question & Test Interoperability Specification (QTI) (IMS, 2004). Incipiently there is a chance for the exchange of learning resources among applications through interoperability facilities as IMS Content Packaging (IMS, 2003a). In the pedagogical domain, there is the possibility to design learning processes that are found on basic predefined structures with a sequential, hierarchical style. This is usually achieved by using IMS Simple Sequencing Specification (IMS, 2003c).Third Stage The search for greater flexibility and reusability is posed here. Interoperability architectures for learning management applications are introduced. A significant example is the Sharable Content Object Reference Model (SCORM) (ADL, 2004). Some initial efforts can be noticed to bring these technologies closer to a greater didactic flexibility. For instance, the proposal of Integrated E-Learning, developed by the Open University of the Netherlands, provides a vision of E-Learning Systems that support learning processes with pedagogical diversity. These interests are also approached by person-centred e-learning patterns. A step forward is taken from a pedagogical perspective, since it is possible to personalize contents and interactions of learners with their learning process, based upon scenarios, activities, roles and profiles, by using IMS-LD (IMS, 2003b). These structures can be predefined by the instructional designer prior to execution.Fourth Stage This stage focuses in Complex Learning Processes (CLP), which facilitate learning in rich and personalized pedagogical environments. We will explain this stage in the following section.

COMPLEX LEARNING PROCESS

A Complex Learning Process (CLP) (Dodero et al., 2005, Torres et al., 2006) is the result of the dynamic and unanticipated integration of mixed pedagogies and resources, and based upon the collaboration of instructors and learners, within a learning process (see Fig. 1). From a constructivist viewpoint, CLP recognize that learning is an active process, which is built upon experiences that are achieved by entwining contents, context, and educational objectives into a learning process. Such complexity depends on three main factors:

The complexity of the learning task per se, which is influenced by the multidisciplinary character of the subject of learning, the duration of the learning process, and the diversity of pedagogical approaches that may be applied.

The degree of autonomy of the learner, when it comes to selecting the learning targets, topics, and expected results.

The design and control of the process after the learning goals have been established. This responsibility can be shared among learners and the instructor, and consists in planning and selecting the activities and outcome products.

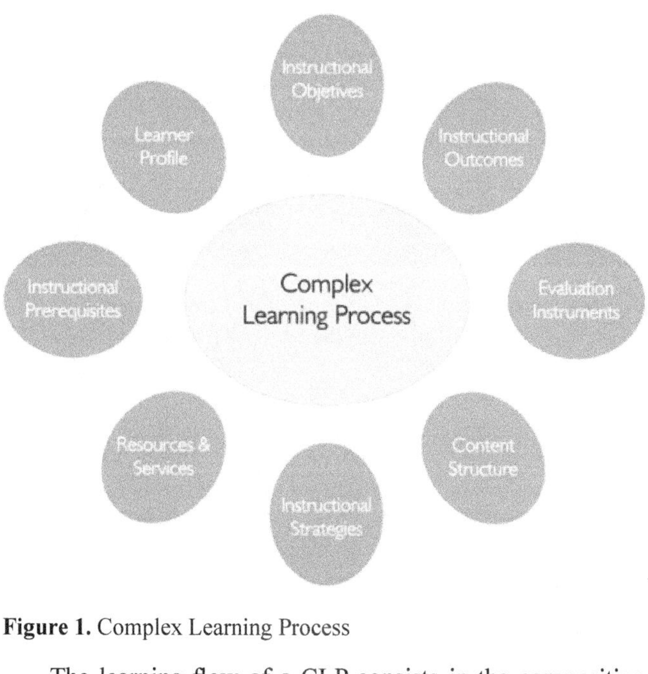

Figure 1. Complex Learning Process

The learning flow of a CLP consists in the composition of complex structures, which are formed by different building blocks (e.g. activities, resources, roles, dependences, restrictions, etc.). These elements interact in a complex and collaborative manner to achieve the learning objectives. Moreover, the composition of such structures cannot be fixed or programmed in design time, but on a dynamic and unanticipated basis. In some cases, the initial form of a CLP must be adapted and redened as the collaboration of learners and instructors changes. This is usually done in the run time, without missing the achieved state of the learning process.

These issues are not the only contributors to the complexity of a learning process. CLP assumes that the learning resources do not only appear as text, audio, lectures, animations, or documents, but they additionally invoke resources and services to be integrated in learning activities that the learner executes in different learning spaces (formal or informal). CLP allows learners' control over some learning activities (i.e. they can create activities). CLP incorporates different assessments techniques, like traditional tests, portfoliobased, outcome-based, self-assessment, and others. These principles are often identified as constructivist pedagogy and life-long learning.

The design of a CLP usually results in quite complex networks of learning (e.g. when a group of learners works together for projects development or problems solution). Activities of the network are executed by diverse roles who interlace their efforts to achieve the learning objectives.

EDUCATIONAL MODELLING LANGUAGES

Educational Modelling Languages (EML) (Koper, 2001, Rawlings et al., 2002) represent an important approximation to integrate diverse educative aspects, allowing the design and implementation of spaces and activities supported by Information and Communication Technologies. With EML it is possible to integrate, under a learning process, personalized educative material for each student v.gr. activities, resources, objectives, evaluations, profiles, promoting the active participation of the student with his learning process. Also, these languages are based in the creation of learning scenarios inside a Unit of Learning (UoL). The different elements implicated in the learning experience v.gr. Roles, objectives, results, activities, resources and services, are modeled in these units along with the organization mechanisms and coordination of the learning experience v.gr. activity structures, assignment of the activity structures to roles and rules which determine the material display. The temporal order in which the various learning activities unfold in a UoL is called learning flow (Koper & Tattersall, 2005).

Characteristics of Design, Execution and Control of EML

Koper (2001) defines a number of requirements for EMLs, which are: formalization, pedagogical flexibility, explicitly typed learning objects, completeness, reproducibility, personalization, medium neutrality, interoperability and sustainability, compatibility, reusability and life cycle. And due to the complexity levels and the vast didactic techniques, EMLs need to support Complex Learning Process (CLP) learning flows.

Fourth Stage Characterization of EMLS

In order to provide CLP support, new characteristics have been defined by (Dodero et al., 2005): (1) pedagogical diversity: EMLs must be able to guide the composition, execution and control of the learning process including various pedagogical mixings and levels of complexity; (2) learning flow description: EMLs need to be expressive enough to specify complex and dynamic structures (e.g. activities, dependences, rules, contents, roles, scenarios and participants); (3) dynamic and unanticipated composition: in some cases the initial specification of a learning process must be redefined and changed as of the collaboration and negotiation of learners and instructors, usually done in the run time, but the state of the learning process achieved at that point must not be missed; (4) separation of learning process and service: EMLs must contain detailed information to enable the dynamic and run-time access to the required services, i.e. semantic interoperability; (5) learning service availability and containment: suitable descriptions of resources and services are needed to maintain required availability that do not rely on self-containment, with the aim of not losing a chance for the further evolution, substitution and integration of other resources and services; and (6) transaction support: EMLs must be provided with operational transaction support to execute a learning process with the possibility to implement long-run activities.

A comparison of EMLs is presented in Fig. 2. As it can be seen, most EMLs do not have support for pedagogical aspects such as content cognitive structure, objectives, prerequisites and assessment, as well as the learning process and services. In this context, LAMS, the IMS Global Learning Consortium (http://www.imsglobal.org) Learning Design (IMS LD) specification and LPCEL are the broadest languages. The rest of the chapter will focus on these languages.

Implemented Elements	CDF	TeachML	LMML	PML	PALO	Xedu	LPCEL	IMS-LD	LAMS	E2ML
Metadata	+	±	+	±	+	+	+	+	±	±
Content	+	++	++	+	++	+	+	+	+	±
Content Structure	±	±	+	+	+	–	+	–	–	–
Content Cognitive Structure	±	+	+	+	+	+	+	–	–	–
Objectives	–	–	–	–	±	±	+	+	–	++
Prerequisites	–	–	–	–	±	±	+	+	–	+
Expected Results	–	–	–	–	–	±	+	+	–	+
Assessment	–	–	–	–	–	–	+	±	++	±
Learning Process										
Activity Sequence	–	–	–	–	+	+	+	+	+	+
Activity Parallelization	–	–	–	–	–	–	+	+	+	+
Optional Activity Parallelization	–	–	–	–	–	–	+	–	+	+
Conditions	–	–	–	–	–	–	+	+	+	+
Messages	–	–	–	–	–	–	+	+	+	–
Roles	–	–	–	–	–	–	+	+	+	+
Groups	–	–	–	–	–	–	+	–	+	–
Services										
Monitoring	–	–	–	–	–	–	+	+	+	–
Search	–	–	–	–	–	–	+	+	+	–
Communication	–	–	–	–	–	–	+	±	+	–
External Tools	–	–	–	–	–	–	+	±	–	–
Other Propietary Tools	–	–	–	–	–	–	+	–	+	±

Figure 2. Comparison of EMLs.

The IMS LD specification includes a language to describe learning experiences as UoLs, and provides a conceptual framework for the specification of learning process designs, which have to be afterwards deployed onto a computer-based execution engine. The LAMS approach has taken a step further by integrating design and execution of learning activities into the same LD language, design environment and execution engine. LPCEL (Learning Process Execution and Composition Language), provides a framework including the appropriate languages primitives to describe execution-aware learning designs, but still lacks of an implementation.

IMS Learning Design

IMS LD (Koper & Tattersall, 2005) borrows the theater metaphor to model a teaching-learning process. As illustrated in Fig. 2, the method part is where the top-level coordination of people and activities takes place. A play, as in a theatrical play, consists of acts, although there can be one-act plays. Acts run in sequence, with one starting when the previous act has finished, and the play ends with the completion of the last act. The transition from one act to another serves as a synchronization point for the multiple participants in a learning design, ensuring that they can all start the next act at the same time.

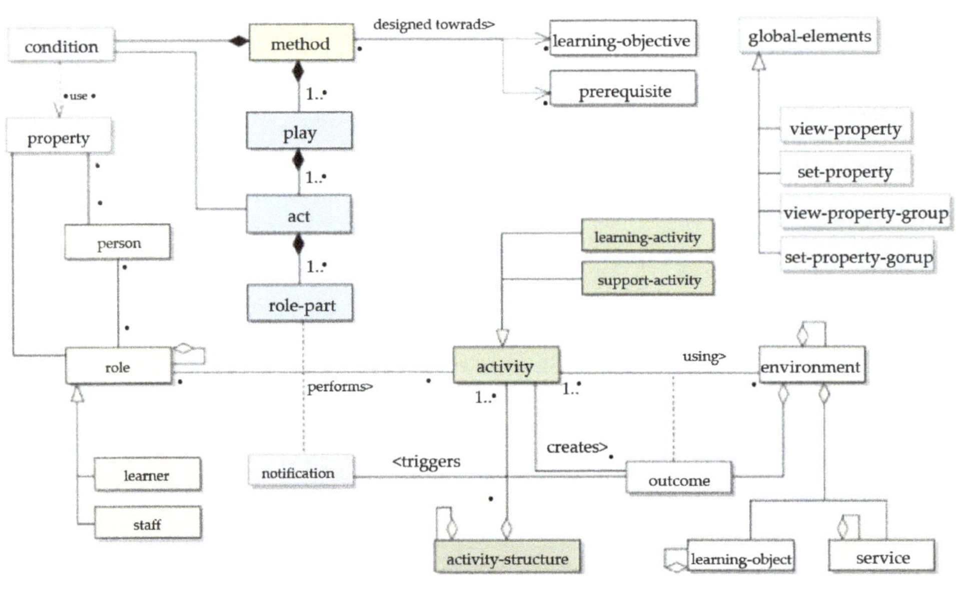

Figure 3. IMS LD Information Model (Koper & Tattersall, 2005)

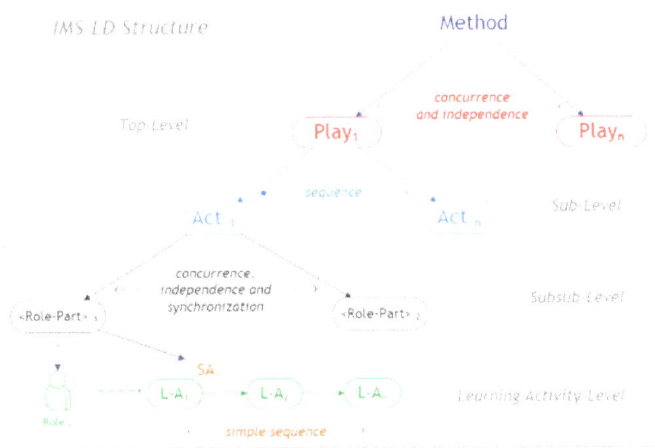

Figure 4. IMS LD Transactions (Torres et al., 2006)

An act is composed of activity, activity structure, and role-part. In every act, the role-part associates a role with an activity (i.e. learning activity, support activity or activity structure).

An activity is the basic learning unit and references to a physical learning material. It usually links to contents including plain text, hypertext, graphics, streaming media, and so on. This binding is accomplished through the environment tag for the sake of reusability.

The learning flow (Chen et al., 2005, Torres et al., 2006) of a UoL is generally represented by the nested structure of learning activities depicted in Fig. 3. An UoL is then organized as an activity tree, in which the top level method element puts together multiple concurrent and independent scenarios or plays. Inside a play, an act controls the synchronization of a scenario. A scenario, in turn, can include a number of acts that are executed sequentially. Acts may contain diverse role-parts, which are concurrent and independent, but synchronous. The learning activities of any activity structure under a role-part must be executed sequentially.

IMS LD implements collaboration between roles as the synchronized depiction of a number of activity lanes, which are portrayed independently as individual work for each role that participates in the collaboration. In this model, it is only possible to assign complete activity structures to specific roles, which cannot be changed or be dynamically associated to other activities. Fig. 4 represents the execution of a UoL instance along time.

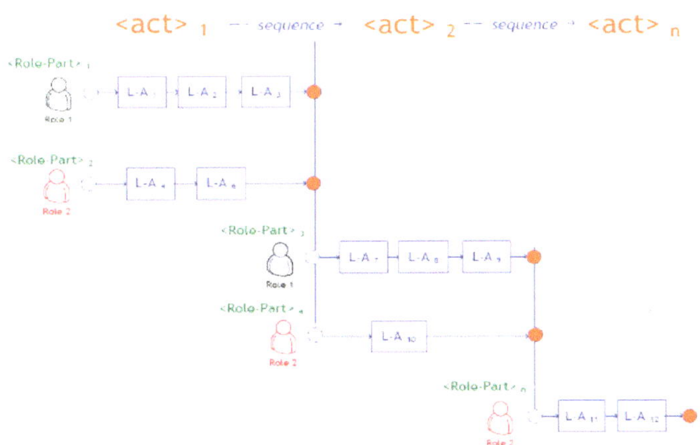

Figure 5. IMS LD Execution (Torres et al., 2006)

As a part of a research project at Massey University in New Zealand, Kim Hagen, Diana Hibbert and Kinshuk created Voyager, a prototype web-based learning management system, in compliance with the IMS LD specifications. Perceived benefits of such a system include the flexibility of the IMS LD model for different pedagogical approaches and differing levels of use. However, the educators who created the prototype LD found the theatre metaphor difficult to understand at first, and found it difficult to design a LD with multiple workflows and optional interactions. It was also difficult to model activities which are not done in a particular sequence, for example, learners completing an assessment activity may do it before or after attending class (another activity). For learners, the theatre metaphor introduces a new model which they must learn in order to learn the course content, increasing their cognitive load (Hagen et al., 2006).

LAMS

The Learning Activity Management System (LAMS) (Dalziel, 2003) is a software system capable to design, manage and deploy learning scenarios employing Internet based technologies. For that, LAMS integrates environments for user administration, student run-time delivery of sequences, teacher run-time monitoring of student sequences and, most importantly, teacher authoring/adaptation of sequences.

In LAMS, the learning design is centered in the design of a sequence of learning activities, which students need to carry out individually or in small groups to achieve the learning objectives. Each activity includes the tools and resources needed, such as: question and answer (with student answers shared with the group either anonymously or identified), polling (with total responses shared with the group), asynchronous discussion forum, synchronous chat, noticeboard (simple text content/instructions), resource presentation and sharing (URL/webpages/files), notebook/journal, assessment submission, MCQ and True/False (with options to display feedback, average class score and "high" score), and various combinations of tools, including "chat and scribe". In addition, a grouping tool allows any tool to run in either whole class or small group modes. The flexibility of the learning design indicates that many more collaborative tools can be developed to broaden the impact of the LAMS platform.

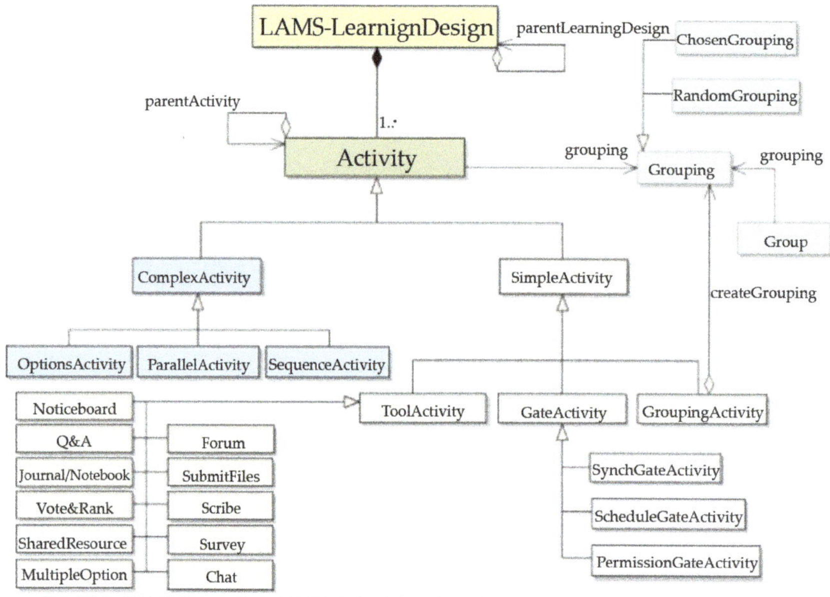

Figure 6. LAMS Learning Design Data Model

LAMS was inspired by IMS Learning Design. However, LAMS was not designed to be a reference implementation of the specification, but it is expected to be IMS Learning Design conformant as both LAMS and IMS LD evolve to address current IMS LD implementation challenges. Despite that LAMS does not propose an EML and its limited use of standards and specifications, the LAMS Learning Design Data Model presented in Fig. 5, suggests a practical orientation over some aspects barely boarded in current EMLs. Just to mention an example, LAMS maintains a special interest in learning design based in individual and collaborative activities; also an effort is made in the development of tools to facilitate the performing of such activities. And finally, LAMS incorporates some flexibility to design activity structures besides simple sequence of activities, such as, parallel activities, optional activities and synchronization mechanisms.

LPCEL

The Learning Process Composition and Execution Language (LPCEL) (Dodero et al., 2005, Torres et al., 2006) is a formal language that provides a containment framework of elements that can describe any design of a CLP. LPCEL is used to specify complex and dynamic activity structures, including roles, groups, dependences, restrictions, scenarios, contents, services, assessments and other resources, which interact to achieve a set of learning objectives. LPCEL allows re-designing the learning process in a dynamic and unanticipated fashion. LPCEL can be used to describe the execution of a learning process and to orchestrate the services and resources that are needed to carry it out. LPCEL can also integrate external applications and services into a learning process, so it becomes the core element of a service-oriented architecture that is thought to integrate, compose, and execute a CLP.

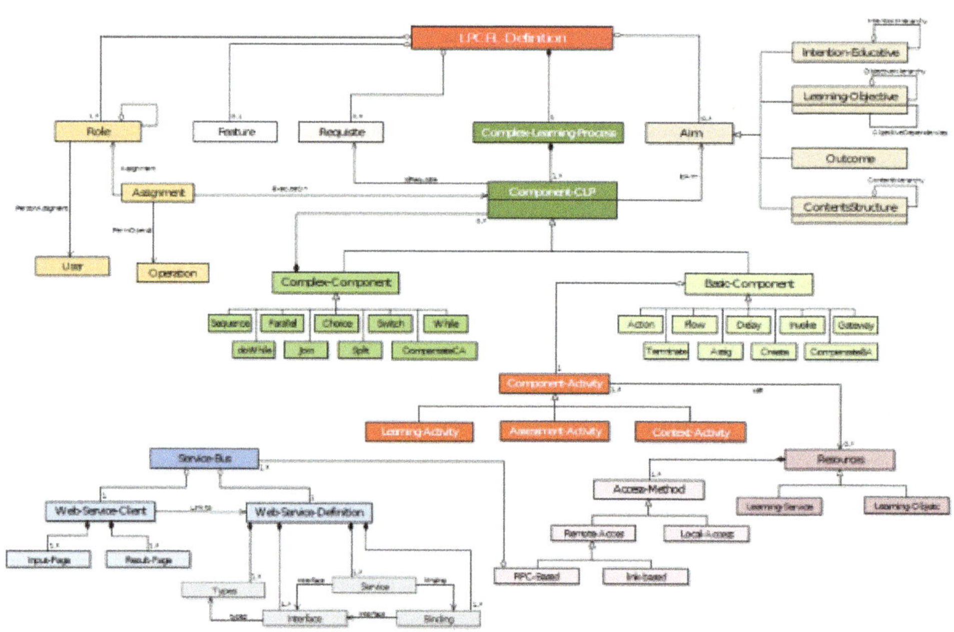

Figure 7. LPCEL Information Model

A conceptual overview of LPCEL is shown in Fig. 6. This model has four main groups of elements:

General information of the process, including prerequisites, learning objectives and/or outcomes, and general features.

The structure of the process, formed by complex activities, basic activities and roles.

The detailed activities that take part in the process, i.e. learning activities, assessment activities and context activities.

The resources and services that can be sought accessed, invoked, or composed by each activity.

The<lpcel-definition> element allows defining diverse <complexlearningprocess> to represents a CLP. Each one of these composed of one or several <component-clp> to design complex learning structures. A <complexcomponent> includes one or several <basic-component> and/or <complexcomponent>. Also it makes reference to a collection of elements to define learning flow (e.g. <complex-component>, <parallel>, <join>, <until>, <foreach>), including their relationships and a number of criteria to indicate the start and termination conditions of the <complex-component>. A <component-activity> contains a collection of elements to execute activities like <learningactivity>, <assessmentactivity> or <contextactivity>. Each basic activity (i.e. learning, assessment or context) can refer to different specifications of <resource> to be used in the activity. The <resource> can invoke local (i.e. <local-access>) or remote resources (<remote-access>) such as SCORM contents or remote applications (e.g. a project repository, virtual laboratories, simulators and collaborative tools, and design tools among others services). The <role> and <permission> are assigned to <componentactivity> and <complex-component> (i.e. role assignment). Moreover, the <aim-prerequisite> contain a sequence of elements for the definition of the <prerequisite>, <outcome> and <learning-objective> that can be assigned to complex and basic activities.

FOURTH GENERATION LEARNING PROCESS ENGINES

As seen in previous the section, EMLs are used to describe learning scenarios. But as in workflow management systems where the execution is in charge of the workflow engine (Hollingsworth, 1995), the Learning Process Engine (LPE) is the software responsible for (1) interpretation of the process definition; (2) control of process instances as creation, activation, suspension, termination; (3) navigation between process activities as sequential or parallel operations, deadline scheduling, interpretation of workflow relevant data and others; (4) sign-on and sign-off of specific participants; (5) identification of work items for user attention and an interface to support user interactions; (6) maintenance of learning flow control data and learning flow relevant data, passing learning flow relevant data to/from applications or users; (7) an interface to invoke external applications and services, and link any learning flow relevant data; and (8) supervisory actions for control, administration and audit purposes.

In workflows, many of these features are often handled by the means of implementing an Advanced Transaction Model(ATM) to ensure correctness and reliability. When this is the case they are called Transactional Workflows. In such a workflow, the process activities are mapped to constituent transactions of an advanced transaction supported by an ATM, and control flow is defined as dependencies between transactional steps. An extra control layer in terms of dependencies is added to ATM to provide functionality to the transactions running in large-scale distributed information systems environment. But it is necessary to remark transactional features form only a small part of a large-scale workflow application. Workflow requirements either exceed, or significantly differ from those of ATMs in terms of modelling, coordination and run-time requirements. So it is definitely useful to incorporate transactional semantics such as recovery, relaxed atomicity and isolation to ensure reliable workflow executions. Nevertheless, to view a workflow as an ATM, or to use existing ATMs to completely model workflows would be inappropriate (Worah and Sheth, 1997).

Fourth generation LPEs, must be able to support all the new EML characteristics mentioned in the previous section. The rest of the chapter will focus on the way LPEs should provide the support for these characteristics, focusing on: learning flow description, dynamic and unanticipated composition and transaction support.

LEARNING FLOW DESCRIPTION

EMLs such as IMS LD, LAMS and LPCEL can be used to describe a learning process, but they depict different degrees of expressiveness to represent learning flows. When working with UoLs, the design phase is fundamental because an UoL must be fully designed before it is delivered. The aspiration of this technology is to develop knowledge, abilities and competences employing instruction under several paradigms (Jochemes et al., 2004, Koper, 2003, Rosmalen et al., 2003).

Defining all activities and assign users at design time will result in a too rigid scheme that cannot be adapted to the concrete events coming out from executing the learning sequences. On the contrary, leaving all activities and task assignments to the run time, the result will be a more flexible scheme, but with no learning design at all. LAMS, IMS LD and LPCEL adopt a mixed approach. They allow defining some elements at design time, and letting other elements at run time. For instance, LAMS gates and grouping activities, or IMS LD Level B elements, are used to set up design-time solutions prepared to manage run-time issues, such as binding user groups to running activities. The LPCEL language, can manifest these execution-related issues emerged in a process-oriented Learning Design (Dodero and Torres, 2008).

Learning Process Design Issues

Learning process design issues to be considered during execution are:

(1) Composite Activities: When designing a learning process, pattern-based groups of activities that can be sequenced, selected and concurrently executed, are often needed. In IMS LD, activity-structures can be used, but they can be only sequenced or selected. If concurrent activities are needed, they can be defined at the play level. An alternative is defining different role-parts within the same act, which does not make sense when a single learner is executing the activities.

A third alternative is managing activities' completion status properties, but this is too burdensome when a large number of activities are considered. LAMS provides sequenced, parallel, and optional activities that comprise the complex activity type, which makes easier to describe such concurrent composite activities.

(2) Conditional Branching and Looping: The usual learning flow of activities must be branched sometimes, according to a special condition that often depends on the learner profile or the results of previously executed activities. Other times, remedial learning activities may require executing an activity or activity group an indefinite number of times, until the remediation condition is achieved by the learners. With IMS LD, to branch an activity an ad hoc property and a set of conditions must be defined to drive the learning flow through the branched activities. When LAMS is used, conditional branching is expressed through branching activities, which drive the learning flow depending on the teacher selection, grouping objects, or the output of previous tool-based activities.

(3) Parallel Branching on Users' Learning Flows: Sometimes is needed to fork the learning flow of one learner, a group of learners, or all learners, to define a branching of parallel but different activities, which are executed by different groups of learners. This is achieved in IMS LD by defining roles or properties plus conditions, but once the execution of an IMS LD run has started, the association of users to roles cannot change. On the contrary, LAMS provides a grouping activity type that permits expressing that association during run time. The combination of a LAMS branching activity with a grouping activity enables forking user groups on a set of activities during run time, without requiring defining additional properties and conditions.

(4) Synchronization points: Setting some synchronization points can be useful in a learning flow of activities, when parallel running activities must join on a given instant before proceeding with the following ones. The IMS LD specification states that plays always run concurrently, whilst acts always run in sequence. Synchronization points can be only marked on completion of the activities, according to user choices or time limits, or when a property is set. With LAMS, gate activities can be used to synchronize learning flows of activities, holding concrete semantics of concurrent access.

(5) Split running activities: A special case of learning flow synchronization occurs when two flows of activities (possibly run by different users) must synchronize in certain points along a number of iterations. IMS LD does not provide adequate primitives to describe this pattern. In LAMS gates and flows can be used to describe that complex structure, although it is not a straightforward learning design task.

Workflow Control Patterns

Workflow Control Patterns (WCP) (Russell et al., 2006) have been identified with the aim of delineating the fundamental requirements that arise during business process modelling on a recurring basis and to describe them in an imperative way. So far, 43 WCP have been identified and classified in Basic Control Flow, Advanced Branching and Synchronization, Multiple Instance, State Based, Cancelation and Force Completion, Iteration, Termination, Trigger and Disclaimer. A comprehensive description of a workflow process also requires consideration of the data perspective. With this in mind, another 40 patterns in the data perspective have been identified.

Learning flows range from basic activity structures such as sequence, parallel, loops, split and union; up to more complex structures such as multiple choices and multiple unions. In this section, an EML expressiveness evaluation will be presented focusing on 10 WCP including all the Basic Control Flow Patterns and some of the Advanced Branching and Synchronization and the Iteration Patterns, because of their capability to represent the most common learning scenarios.

Basic Control Flow patterns capture elementary aspects of process control, namely: (1) Sequence: an activity in a workflow process is enabled after the completion of a preceding activity in the same process; (2) Parallel Split: the divergence of a branch into two or more parallel branches each of which execute concurrently; (3) Synchronization: the convergence of two or more branches into a single subsequent branch such that the thread of control is passed to the subsequent branch when all input branches have been enabled; (4) Exclusive Choice: the divergence of a branch into two or more branches, such that when the incoming branch is enabled, the thread of control is immediately passed to precisely one of the outgoing branches based on the outcome of a logical expression associated with the branch; and (5) Simple Merge: the convergence of two or more branches into a single subsequent branch. Each time an incoming branch is enabled, results in the thread of control being passed to the subsequent branch.

Advanced Branching and Synchronization patterns characterize more complex branching and merging concepts. Although relatively commonplace in practice, these patterns are often not directly supported or even able to be represented in many commercial offerings. The patterns of this category included in the evaluation are: (1) Multi-Choice: the divergence of a branch into two or more branches, such that when the incoming branch is enabled, the thread of control is passed to one or more of the outgoing branches based on the outcome of distinct logical expressions associated with each of the branches; (2) Structured Synchronizing Merge: the convergence of two or more branches (which diverged earlier in the process at a uniquely identifiable point) into a single subsequent branch, such that the thread of control is passed to the subsequent branch when each active incoming branch has been enabled; (3) Multi-Merge: the convergence of two or more branches into a single subsequent branch. Each enablement of an incoming branch results in the thread of control being passed to the subsequent branch; and (4) Structured Discriminator: the convergence of two or more branches into a single subsequent branch following a corresponding divergence earlier in the process model. The thread of control is passed to the subsequent branch when the first incoming branch has been enabled. Subsequent times incoming branches that are enabled do not result in the thread of control being passed on. Finally the discriminator construct is reset when all incoming branches have been enabled.

Iteration patterns deal with capturing repetitive behavior in a workflow. Structured Loop is the Iteration pattern included in the evaluation, and it is described as the ability to execute an activity or sub-process repeatedly. The loop has either a pre-test or post-test condition associated with it that is either evaluated at the beginning or end of the loop to determine whether it should continue. The looping structure has a single entry and a single exit point.

Workflow Control Patterns and EML

Although WCP provide a good point of reference to design learning flows and evaluate the expressiveness of EMLs, it is important to differentiate between learning and workflows. In a learning environment the execution of a process activity does not guarantee that the objectives have been achieved, meanwhile in workflows, the execution of a process activity assures a state change. In other words, the completion of a learning activity does not assure new knowledge for the learner.

An EMLs learning flow expressiveness evaluation based on the WCP previously described is presented in Figure 8 IMS LD only has full support for the sequence pattern. A parallel split can be achieved by defining more than one play due to the concurrence and independence of them, but this will lead to a loss of sense of the script metaphor, because a play means a teaching-learning process and there will be many learning processes were pedagogically only one is supposed to be. Also there will be no synchronization for the plays later on. Also, IMS-LD provides the option to choose a number of activities. This does not mean the Exclusive Choice, Multi-Choice, Synchronization, Simple Merge, Multi-Merge or Structured Discriminator patterns are supported, because activities are then executed in a rigid sequence manner.

Workflow Control Pattern	IMS-LD	LAMS	LPCEL
Basic Control Flow			
1. Sequence	+	+	+
2. Parallel Split	±	±	+
3. Synchronization	–	±	+
4. Exclusive Choice	–	–	+
5. Simple Merge	–	±	+
Advanced Branching and Synchronization			
6. Multi-Choice	–	–	+
7. Structured Synchronizing Merge	–	–	+
8. Multi-Merge	–	–	+
9. Structured Discriminator	–	–	+
Iteration			
10. Structured Loop	–	–	+

Figure 8. EMLs learning flow expressiveness evaluation

In the LAMS Learning Design Data Model, full support for the Sequence pattern through "SequenceActivity" is provided. The Parallel Split, Synchronization and Simple Merge patterns are supported but limited to a set of activities already defined. The support for Synchronization and Simple Merge is provided by gateways such as "SynchGateActivity", "ScheduleGateActivity" and "PermissionGateActivity". A Parallel Split is achieved by the "ParallelActivity" element. The situation for the rest of the patterns, is the same as in IMS LD.

LPCEL, to define learning flow makes reference to a collection of <Complex-Component> elements such as <Sequence>, <Parallel>, <Choice>, <Switch>, <While>, <doWhile>, <Join>, <Split> and <CompensateCA>; and also to a collection of <Basic-Component> elements such as <Action>, <Flow>, <Delay>, <Invoke>, <Gateway>, <Terminate>, <Assig>, <Create> and <CompensateBA>; including their relationships and a number of criteria to indicate the start and termination conditions of the <Component-CLP>, providing support for a vast number of WCP including all the basic ones, as seen in fig. 8 but not limited only to them. These primitives allow LPCEL to support WCP, providing the necessary expressiveness to describe and guide the execution of a CLP.

DYNAMIC AND UNANTICIPATED COMPOSITION

Inside a CLP environment, there is a great variety of resources and services in which learners can access to achieve the learning objectives, some of them have a direct implication on learning itself learning services and resources; others allow to generate spaces for the development of collective competences community services and resources; and others show the activity students carry out in the learning environment context services and resources. Some examples for each category are: (1) Learning services and resources: Virtual labs, tutorials, simulators, educative contents, assessment systems, search systems, software with particular educative objectives e.g. programming environments, design environments, math and statistics tools, business games, and others. (2) Community services and resources: Collaborative tools, communication services, forums, distribution lists, coordination tools, shared agendas, repositories for group work or document management and others. (3) Context services and resources: Tutoring services, digital library services, university services, and others.

Some of these services may be recovered and deployed locally, and other may be executed in a distributed way, based in a Service-Oriented-Architecture (SOA) (Erl, 2004), also allowing the integration of new resources and services to the learning process.

GRID-Services within SOA

Grid networks consist in large-scale distributed systems that share physical heterogeneous resources (e.g. computing, storage, network components and equipment, sensors, etc.), and make possible the creation of virtual organizations (Foster and Kesselman, 2003). Furthermore, these capabilities enable powerful, flexible, pervasive, and cost-effective services to the users. Initially, Grid network services were focused on the "Anatomy" (e.g. computing power, data storage and network bandwidth), currently, it is recognized that for effective resource sharing and virtual communities support, the "Physiology" is also necessary A SOA approach.

In such a highly distributed community, the orchestration and management of numerous distributed hardware and software components presents a big challenge. Therefore, a service-oriented infrastructure was introduced to the resource management and provisioning mechanisms used to meet quality of service goals. Grid services come to serve this purpose; Grid services are essentially Web services with specific extensions or interfaces for use in Grids (Pankatrius and Vossen, 2003).

A Grid service meets a set of conventions for service lifetime management, inspection, and notification of changes in service states. Grid services provide for the controlled management of the distributed and often long-lived state commonly required in distributed applications.

Grid networks and services could help the learning to happen in different network domains and to enable high-performance experiments and applications to be used in learning experiences. Through the adoption of these technologies it is possible a wide-scale learning resource sharing in heterogeneous and geographically distributed environments, the implementation of learning organizations in which different actors (universities, teachers, learners) share a common target and are able to cooperate to get the same goal.

The integration of Grid services within the SOA framework provides more flexibility and make possible to leverage on the resources distributed across Grid networks in order to build the learning experience that best fit student requirements.

Web Applications and Services Enhanced Learning Architecture

LPCEL and the Web Applications and Services Enhanced Learning Architecture (see Fig. 7) are the first approach to the fourth stage of E-Learning Systems. In this proposed architecture, the learning scenario is designed with the Learning Process Editor and executed in the Learning Process Engine, which through semantic web services such as WSDL and WADL communicates with the Learning Services Bus where the Learning Web Services are plugged in. User interface must be Web 2.0-enabled and communication is made through an API WS-Access. Interoperability with other Learning Management Systems such as Moodle or LAMS can be achieved by Wrap ad-hocs.

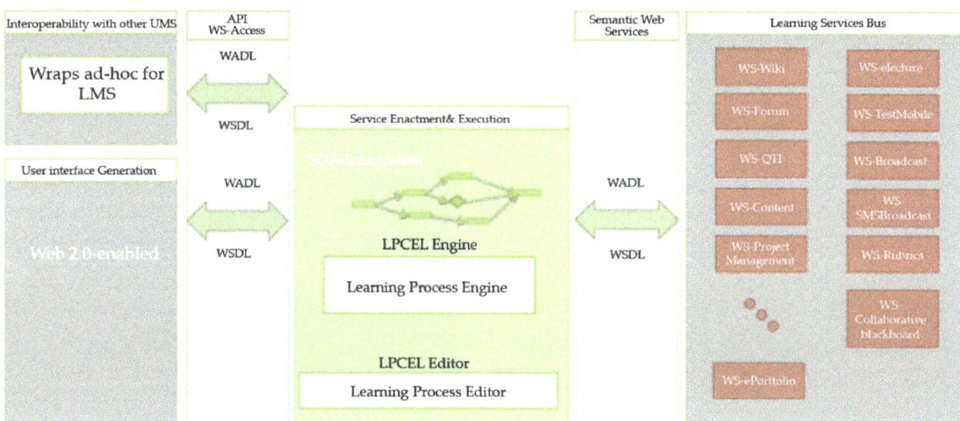

Figure 9. Web Applications and Services Enhanced Learning Architecture

TRANSACTIONAL SUPPORT

A transaction (Gray and Reuter, 1993) is a consistent and reliable computational unit, which executes from an initial consistent state and finishes its execution in a final consistent state, i.e. a transaction is a collection of actions which make a consistent transformation of the states of a system. To achieve this, transactions exhibit the ACID properties: (1) Atomiticity: A transaction is executed completely (commits) or the final effect is as it has never been executed (aborts); (2) Consistency: The code of the transaction should guarantee that if applied to a consistent state of the data it should bring the data to a new consistent state; (3) Isolation: The execution of concurrent transactions accessing common data should be equivalent to a serial execution of them; (4) Durability: The effects of a committed transaction should be preserved even in the advent of failures.

To guarantee the execution of a learning flow in EML engines, it is necessary for them to provide transaction support through Advanced Transaction Models(ATMs) to relax the basic ACID transaction properties. Nowadays, there are several ATMs summarized in (Elmagarmid, 1992) that could be suitable for the new generation of EML engines like Nested transactions, SAGAS, Open nested transactions, Flexible transactions, ConTracts, S-Transactions, the DOM Transaction Model and Multi-colored transactions. A comparison between these ATMs is made in Figure 10., showing the general purpose of each ATM, the ACID property they relax and a short description of them.

ATM	General purpose	Based on	Relaxed property	Short description
Nested transactions	Preserve all ACID properties for top level transactions		Durability on subtransactions	New transactions (subtransactions) can be started within another transaction yielding to a transaction tree structure.
SAGAS	Long-lived transactions		Isolation	Each subtransaction has associated a compensating transaction. A Saga commits if all its subtransactions also commit.
Open nested transactions	Long-lived activities	Nested transactions	Isolation	Open subtransactions externalise their results. If a transaction aborts, its committed open nested subtransactions are not automatically undone neither compensated.
Flexible transactions	Long-lived activities	Nested transactions	Atomicity and isolation	Two-level nested transactions with three kinds of transactions: compensatable, retriable and pivot.
ConTracts	Long-lived computations in non-standard applications like workflow and CAD		Isolation	Fault-tolerant execution of a sequence of actions (steps) according to a control flow description (script).
S-Transactions	Cooperation between organizations	Nested transactions	Isolation	Dynamically generated hierarchical distributed transactions. Sub-s-transactions commit as soon as they finish. A transaction decides on its result based on the results of its subtransactions.
The DOM Transaction Model	Long running activities and the execution of system-triggered activities	Nested transactions	Isolation	Nested transactions defined by the user or being the result from the firing of rules while executing a transaction. The subtransaction can be immediate, deferred or detached.
Multi-coloured transactions	Long-lived computations	Nested transactions	Atomicity	Increase the concurrency of nested transactions and allow partial results to became permanent. Three types of subtransactions: Subtransactions of a serializing action, glued actions and top-level independent actions.

Figure 10. Advanced Transactional Models

Advanced Transactional Models in a Complex Learning Process

So, why is this comparison made about the different ATMs? Because each learning activity is different and may require a certain ACID property not to be relaxed, or may have some specific requirements not suitable for every ATM. So it is not enough for the engine to have an ATM implemented, consequently the engine must support different ATMs so different learning activities may perform their transactions based on different ATM models. In general, the proposal is to manage three transactional levels (see Fig. 8) in a LPE:

Process: The general ATM used at the top level of the CLP, specifically on LPCEL, the <Complex-Learning-Process> element. An ATM focused on long-lived activities is suitable for this level.

Activity or subprocess: The most critical transactional level in terms of learning. By choosing the right ATM for each learning activity, a contribution to the achievement of the learning objectives which are the base of the CLP on LPCEL is made by the means of providing the right learning flow structure and behavior to the learner. Different ATMs can be used on different activities and structures, e.g. ConTracts may be used on the <Complex-Component> elements involving <Sequence>, <doWhile> and <While> elements or activities following a behaviorism approach, meanwhile S-Transactions can be used for <Complex-Component> elements with the <Switch> and <Split> elements or activities following a constructivism approach.

Resource: This level occurs at the <Resources> element on LPCEL. The main matter is about state and stateless services. With stateless services a simple transactional model with preserving all the ACID properties can be used, meanwhile with state services the transactional model to use is up to the kind of resource.

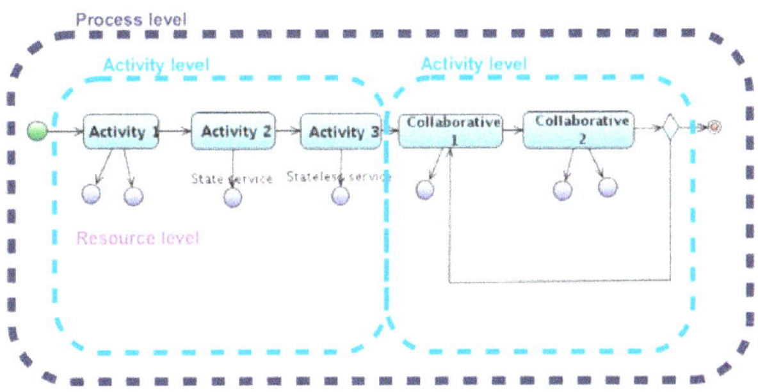

Figure 11. Transactional Levels for a Learning Process Engine

In other words, suppose Alice and Bob are enrolled in a course. The whole course can be viewed as transaction with many subtransactions (learning activities) and because the course would last a considerable amount of time, it is a long-lived activity with partial results where Open nested transactions can be used as the Process level ATM. But then, what happens when the professor wants his students to develop certain skills which can be better obtained through a behaviorism approach, where a sequence of tasks must be completed in a certain order until each task is fully completed in an everything or nothing

Basis? A ConTract ATM for the Activity level must be implemented for it. And then, when it is time for a collaborative activity with a constructivism approach, where Alice and Bob need to be working together with partial deliverables to achieve a certain objective, the S-Transactions model is more suitable. And finally, each task has associated resources to it; some of them could be simple stateless services which can be handled by the Activity level

ATM or perhaps by a simple transactional model with all the ACID properties, but others may need complex interaction with state services, if this is the case, a different ATM may be implemented depending on the kind of resource.

On learning flow activities, when a transaction fails can be because a software or hardware such as unavailability of resources, incorrect input formats, internal application failures and others; or also it could be because the learner did not achieved the learning objectives, even though the activity was completed, i.e. a grade below the minimum to pass a test, a correction of a stakeholder in a project, and others. So a LPE has to provide the ways to deal with learning flow compensation activities to achieve the learning objectives of each task.

CONCLUSION

The enhanced set of characteristics and flexibility offered by the e-learning systems evolution provides new and better ways to facilitate learning, particularly, the fourth stage service oriented approach. In this perspective, it is of high relevance to show our vision of a new generation of learning web services, which need to be integrated and executed by the participants in a pedagogical sense, *i.e.* participants may perform learning activities by consuming many different web services. Some services have already been developed by students, faculty and staff from the Tecnológico de Monterrey. The following are some examples:

WS-TestMobile: A web service implementation of the IMS Question and Test Interoperability Standard (IMS, 2004). WS-Rubrics: A web service for the elaboration and application of rubrics. WS-Qualitative Research: A web service to provide support for qualitative research techniques. WS-Wiki: A web service for the elaboration of wikis. WS-Collaborative Lecture: A web service to download lectures and make comments in a collaborative way. WS-Project Management: A web service interface for the Trac System [3] - . WS-Brainstorming: A web service to provide support for the brainstorming technique.

As web services, they can be consumed by different clients, *e.g.* web clients or even a mobile device client, allowing the participant not to be attached to a computer terminal. Also, services can be located in different places or even replicated for grid computing.

In most of cases, activities are not performed in an anarchic way. For that, it is necessary to employ EMLs able to orchestrate and drive the learning process of each participant. As an example, with these specific services and LPCEL, it is possible to design a learning scenario starting with a collaborative lecture and followed by a brainstorming of project ideas. Once the project is chosen, WS-Project Management, WS-Qualitative Research and WS-Wiki, could be used in parallel and in an iterative and collaborative way to do the project. When the project is finished and presented, it is evaluated through a rubric and a self-evaluation by employing WS-Rubrics and WS-Test Mobile.

Service-Oriented Learning Process Engines, represent a new generation of e-learning systems. From a technological and pedagogical perspective, it is relevant the study of ATMs in order to guarantee a reliable execution of a learning scenario. Finally, from a technological and communications perspective, SOA represents an opportunity for the implementation of these systems. Further work consists in testing the current developed web services in real scenarios.

REFERENCES

1. ADL 2004 ADL. SCORM: Content Aggregation Model (CAM) Version 1.3. Technical report, Advanced Distributed Learning (ADL), 2004.
2. M. Chen, C. Chen, Y. C. Cheng, C. Hsieh, 2005 On the development and implementation of a sequencing engine for IMS Learning Design specification. In Advanced Learning Technologies, 2005. ICALT 2005. Fifth IEEE International Conference on, 636 640 , 0-76952-338-2 2005, Kaohsiung, Taiwan.
3. J. R. Dalziel, 2003 Implementing Learning Design: The Learning Activity Management System (LAMS). In G. Crisp, D. Thiele, I. Scholten, S. Barker, and J. Baron, editors, Proceedings of the 20th Annual Conference of the Australasian Society for Computers in Learning in Tertiary Education (ASCILITE), 0-97517-020-1 Australia, December 2003.
4. J. M. Dodero, J. Torres, 2008 Awareness of execution in designing learning activities with LAMS and IMS LD. In European LAMS Conference 2008, 978-1-74138-287-7 Cadiz, Spain, June 2008.
5. J. M. Dodero, J. Torres, I. Aedo, P. Díaz, 2005 Beyond descriptive eml: Taking control of the execution of complex learning processes. In Simposio Pluridisciplinar sobre Diseño, Evaluación y Descripción de Contenidos Educativos Reutilizables (SPDECE), 8-49788-350-0 2005.
6. A. Elmagarmid, 1992 editor. Database Transaction Models for Advanced Applications. Morgan Kaufmann, 1-55860-214-3
7. T. Erl, 2004 Service-Oriented Architecture: A Field Guide to Integrating XML and Web Services. Prentice Hall PTR, 0-13142-898-5
8. I. Foster, C. Kesselman, 2003 The Grid 2: Blueprint for a New Computing Infrastructure. Morgan Kaufmann, 1-55860-933-4
9. J. Gray, A. Reuter, 1993 Transaction Processing: Concepts and Techniques. Morgan Kaufmann, 1-55860-190-2
10. K. Hagen, D. Hibbert, P. Kinshuk, 2006 Developing a learning management system based on the IMS Learning Design specification. In Advanced Learning Technologies, 2006. ICALT 2006. Sixth IEEE International Conference on, 420 424 , 0-76952-632-2 2006, Kerkrade, The Netherlands.
11. D. Hollingsworth, 1995 The workflow reference model-1 1. Specification TC001003 , Workflow Management Coalition, 2 Crown Walk, Winchester, Hampshire, UK, SO22 5XE, Jan 1995.
12. IMS 2001 IMS Learner Information Packaging Information Model Specification, Version 1.0 Final Specification. Technical report, IMS Global Learning Consortium, March 2001.
13. IMS 2003a IMS Content Packaging Information Model, Version 1.1.3 Final Specification. Technical report, IMS Global Learning Consortium, June 2003.

14. IMS 2003b IMS Learning Design Information Model, Version 1.0 Final Specification. Technical report, IMS Global Learning Consortium, January 2003.
15. IMS 2003c IMS Simple Sequencing Information and Behavior Model, Version 1.0 Final Specification. Technical report, IMS Global Learning Consortium, March 2003.
16. IMS 2004 IMS Question and Test Interoperability: Item Overview, Version 2.0 Public Draft. Technical report, IMS Global Learning Consortium, June 2004.
17. W. Jochemes, J. Van Merriënboer, R. Koper, 2004 An introduction to integrated e-learning. In Integrated E-Learning: Implications for pedagogy, technology & organization. Morgan Kaufmann, 0-41533-502-7 Mateo, CA.
18. R. Koper, 2001 Modeling units of study from a pedagogical perspective: the pedagogical metamodel behind eml. Technical report, Open University of the Netherlands, June 2001.
19. R. Koper, 2003 Chapter 6. In Learning technologies: An integrated domain model, 64 79 . RoutledgeFalmer, London.
20. R. Koper, C. Tattersall, 2005 Learning Design, A Handbook on Modelling and Delivering Networked Education and Training. Springer, 3-54022-814-4 Heidelberg New York.
21. V. Pankatrius, G. Vossen, 2003 Towards e-learning grids: Using grid computing in electronic learning. In IEEE Workshop on Knowledge Grid and Grid Intelligence, 4 15 , Halifax, New Scotia, Canada, 2003.
22. A. Rawlings, P. Van Rosmalen, R. Koper, M. Rodríguez-Artacho, P. Lefrere, 2002 Survey of Educational Modelling Languages. Technical report, CEN/ISSS WS/LT, September 2002.
23. P. Van Rosmalen, F. Brouns, C. Tattersall, H. Vogten, J. Van Bruggen, R. Koper, 2003 Towards an open framework for adaptive, agent-supported e-learning. In International Journal of Continuing Engineering Education and Life-Long Learning, 15 3-6 , 261 275 , 1560-4624.
24. N. Russell, A. H. M. Ter Hofstede, W. M. P. Van Der Aalst, N. Mulyar, 2006 Workflow Control-Flow patterns: A revised view. Technical report, BPM Center, 2006.
25. J. Torres, J. M. Dodero, I. Aedo, P. Días-Pérez, 2005 A characterization of composition and execution languages for complex learning processes. In Proceedings of the 4th IASTED International Conference on Web-Based Education (WBE 2005), 0-88986-480-2 Switzerland, February 2005.
26. J. Torres, J. M. Dodero, I. Aedo, P. Diaz, 2006 Designing the execution of learning activities in complex learning processes using LPCEL. In Advanced Learning Technologies, 2006. ICALT 2006. Sixth IEEE International Conference on, 415 419 , 0-76952-632-2 2006, Kerkrade, The Netherlands.
27. J. Torres, C. Cardenas, J. M. Dodero, I. Aedo, 2008 A grid-based architectural framework for composition and execution of complex learning processes. In Advanced Learning Technologies, 2008. ICALT 2008. Eighth IEEE International Conference on, 61 63 , 978-0-76953-167-0 July 2008, Santander, Cantabria, Spain.
28. D. Worah, A. Sheth, 1997 Transactions in Transactional Workflows. In Advanced Transaction Models and Architectures, Jajodia, S. & Kershberg, L., (Ed.), 3 45 . Kluwer Academic Publishers, 0-79239-880-7 MA, USA.

CHAPTER 17 SERVICES ORIENTED TECHNOLOGIES: A FOCUS ON THE FINANCIAL SERVICES SECTOR

Mazanai Musara

INTRODUCTION

Over the years, business and our daily lives have been bombarded with various forms on inventions and technology. The public adopted technology at an exceedingly fast rate and the world was transformed. In the 21st century, technology rules our daily lives. We assemble documents and reports on computers, use them for PowerPoint presentations, take laptops on the road and communicate via email and social networks, complete our banking transaction using cell phones and do online banking to mention just a few. The 21st century worker has the freedom to work from any place at any time, with always available access to information. Laptops, notebooks, wireless broadband, Smartphones and social networking have transformed the world into a global market. The shape of the business landscape took a different course because of the proliferation of technology. The financial services sector in South Africa is one of the sectors, where the impact of the information and connection era is highly felt and ever changing.

There is a growing recognition across financial service providers in South Africa that technology and innovation is the cornerstone for surviving in the 21st century economy. This is evident in almost all corporate messages in the banking sector. Therefore, the chapter focuses on technological innovations in the financial services sector. The chapter presents a theoretical review as well as the results of the empirical research that was conducted in South Africa. It is paramount as the starting point to shed light on the concept of technology and innovation in detail. Understanding the concept of technology in detail is paramount as a basis from which innovation can clearly be articulated. Innovation can be in the form of product innovation (that results in new products or services) or process innovation (that involves the introduction of new ways of performing tasks in an organisation).The following section begins with an explanation of the concept of technology and technological innovations.

Citation: Mazanai Musara (2012). Services Oriented Technologies: A Focus on the Financial Services Sector, Management of Technological Innovation in Developing and Developed Countries, Dr. HongYi Sun (Ed.), InTech, DOI: 10.5772/36362.

LITERATURE REVIEW AND CONCEPTS

The section will provide a concise discussion of the key concepts, key events and literature related to technological innovations with a particular focus on financial services sector. This is intended to shed light on the key issues related to technological innovations and their impact in the 21st century economy.

Technology and Technological Innovation

The term technology can be defined in many different ways depending on the context in which it is applied. For the purpose of this chapter, technology can be defined as, material objects or tools that are used by human beings such machines, hardware and utensils, in performing different activities (Bain, 1937). Technology furthermore, includes systems, methods of organisation and techniques used by the business. The term technology can be applied generally or to specific area, for example information technology (technologies use in obtaining, storing, retrieval and dissemination of information), medical technology (tools, machinery, utensils, etc, used by medical practitioners), state-of-art technology, etc. In the financial sector, technologies which are mainly going to be focused on in this chapter includes Automated Tellers Machines (ATMs), computer hardware and software, telephones and mobile phones, the internet, among others. Technological innovations have been attributed to contribute to the distribution channels in the financial services sector. Electronic Banking (E-Banking) is one of the most notable channels. E-Banking merges several different technologies such electronic fund transfer point of sale technologies, internet banking, cell phone banking, etc. Each of these evolved in different ways, but in recent years different groups and industries have recognized the importance of working together. Several technologies were invented with a particular aim to improving service delivery in the business sector. Of particular influence in the financial services sector is the information technology, the following section discuses information technology.

Information Technology

Information technology (IT) refers to hardware and software that are used to store, retrieve and manipulate information. IT comprises computer hardware and software as well as other telecommunication equipment such as telephones, fax machines and mobile communication devices to mention just a few (Jürgen, 2002). The introduction of telecommunications into bank markets dates back to 1846 when the telegraph reduced stock price differentials between New York and regional stock markets (Garbade and Silber, 1978). According to Leslie (2000), the most important IT applications had their origins in US governmentsponsored research in the first half of the twentieth century. Interactive IT applications would never have existed without a long and expensive gestation period in which computer power and telecommunication applications were devoted to help the US gain the initiative in science and technology. Indeed, the British experience with computer hardware development would tend to confirm the view of a defence-based technology push. The first stored-program computer in the world was developed in 1948 by academics (Freddie Williams and Tom Kilburn) at Manchester University (Anonymous, 1998).

In brief, early adoptions of telecommunications and computer applications had greatest impact in organised high value wholesale bank markets, that is, those activities that had traditionally been further away from volume transactions through retail bank branches (Anonymous, 1998). Banks absorbed the new technology on the back of a growing market for retail bank services, which expanded as middle income individuals became a growing proportion of the population. Information technology has enormous effects on the functioning of each and every enterprise operating in the 21st century economy. Jürgen (2002) argued that IT facilitates complementary innovation, enabling firms to increase output via the introduction of new processes and altering the competitive environment, thereby creating pressure for firms to adjust. Meeting these challenges require changes in the organisation of firms, for instance in the form of vertical disintegration, streamlining of managerial levels and more decentralised production, and a well-educated labor force able and motivated to exploit the opportunities offered by new technology.

Knowledge on the existence and importance of IT to an enterprise alone is not sufficient for the successful running and competitiveness of the enterprise in the market. The ability to develop new and unique ways of doing things is the key to success in the 21st century economy, which is characterised by rapid changes in technology. Hence, to be competitive in the market the enterprise should be innovative. The financial services sector in South Africa is bombarded with information technologies, a differentiation strategy by several banks.

Technological Innovation

Innovation involves using new knowledge to transform organizational processes or create commercially viable products and services. The sources of new knowledge may include the latest technology, the results of experiments, creative insights or competitive information. Innovation can be broadly defined as the process of creating new ideas and putting them into practice. It is the means by which creative ideas find their way into everyday practice in the form of new goods or services that satisfy consumers or as new systems or practices that help organisations to improve the produce of goods or services (Wood, Wallace, Zeffane, Schermerhorn, Hunt and Osborn, 2001:611).

Rogers (1998:2) defined innovation as a process of introducing new ideas to the firm which result in improved performance of the firm. He identified five types of innovation which are:

- Introduction of new products/services or a qualitative change in the existing product,
- Process innovation new to the industry,
- Opening of a new market,
- Development of new sources for raw materials and other inputs, and
- Changes in industrial organisation.

Innovation can be thought of in two contexts: product innovation and process innovation.

a. Product Innovation

Product innovation results in the creation of new or improved goods or services. Product innovation encompasses development of new products, changes in design of established products, or use of new materials or components in manufacture of established products (Wood et al., 2001). Product innovation can take one of the following ways:

- a modified version of an existing product range,
- a new model in the existing product range,
- a new product outside the existing range but in a similar field of technology,
- a totally new product in a new field of technology

b. Process Innovation

Innovation that results in better ways of doing things, which is new efficient and effective processes and structures, is called process innovation (Wood et al., 2001). Process innovation is aimed at improving the operations of the organisations. This includes increasing productivity, efficiency, safety at work and waste reduction to mention just but a few. Process innovation culminates in the production of high quality products at lower costs, thus process innovation can be viewed as instrumental to product innovation. Both product and process innovation are important in creating, communicating and delivering superior value to consumers. Technological innovations, which encompass both product innovation and process innovation, should be part of the organisation's culture to survive the competitive pressures of the 21st century economy.

Technological innovation comprise of product or process, continuous or discontinuous, radical or incremental innovations in the financial services sector leading to improved or new products. 'Radical' innovations refer to new products that result from advances in knowledge/technology. 'Incremental' innovations include improvement of process or product designs, with or without up gradation of machinery/ acquisition of new machinery. Two main aspects form the core of innovation namely invention and application. Invention is the process of discovery, while application is the act of use (Wood et al, 2001).

Thus;

Innovation = Invention + Application

Innovation should be viewed as a continuous process in an organisation if the organisation is to continue operating successfully.

Having laid out the major aspect of technology and innovation, the meaning of technological innovations becomes apparent. In this case technological innovations can be viewed in terms of the creation of new tools, machines and processes that are used by human beings in the quest to develop better goods or services, and better ways of doing things. According to Subrahmanya (2005) technological innovation is the transformation of an idea into a new or improved saleable product or operational process in industry or commerce. It is therefore important to examined technological innovations in relation to their deferential impact on the business landscape. The following section provides an overview of a few selected services oriented technologies that impact the financial services sector and business in South Africa.

An overview of Services Oriented Technologies in the Financial Services Sector

Technological innovations in the financial services sector appeared in the form of the introductions of automated tellers machines, the rise of internet banking, electronic cards, cell phone banking and various other customers tracking and accounts management software to mention just a few. In the financial services industry at large, the banking sector was one of the first to embrace rapid globalization and benefit significantly from Information Technology (IT) developments. Technological developments in the banking sector started in the 1950s with the installation of the first automated bookkeeping machine at banks. Automation in the banking sector became widespread over the next few decades as bankers quickly realized that much of the labour intensive information handling processes could be automated with the use of computers. The first Automated Tellers Machine (ATM) is purported to have been introduced in the USA in 1968 and it was only a cash dispenser (Jayamaha, 2008). The emergence of the ATM marked the beginning of self service banking as services provided by the bank teller could be performed on a 24-hour schedule and at the customers' convenience rather than during banking hours.

The following case study illustrates the way technology is shaping the financial services sector, in particular banking.

Partnering around technology to tackle poverty

The mobile money transfer service M-Pesa (M stands for "mobile", Pesa means "money" in Swahili) is one of the best examples of transformative power of partnerships. With the initial support of the UK Department for International Development (DfID) through matching a fund, the Kenyan mobile phone service provider Safaricom has created a service which allows users to make and receive payments, transfer money to other users and non-users, and deposit and withdraw money without needing to visit a bank.

By relying solely on the ubiquitous mobile phone, M-Pesa has significantly expanded financial access among Kenya's poor. By bringing the unbanked into the market, it has also created new markets for goods and services tailored to mobile banking. Already serving more than 14 million users in Kenya, this service is being replicated in other African countries including Rwanda, South Africa, Tanzania and Uganda.

Source: Adapted from: African Business, 45th year, No. 377. July 2011

These new technologies in the financial services sector introduced new ways of doing financial transactions and also, had made possible the introduction of other financial products or services. For example, in South Africa, technological innovations made it possible for Standard Bank to introduce the E-Plan (Electronic Plan – a card based transaction product that was introduced in 1994). Also a result of technological innovation is FNB's Smartsave suite of products – card-only account access, often with some savings or other features (such as funeral insurance) built in (Porteous and Hazelhurst 2004). ABSA also offers a Business Essentials package that includes QuickBooks Pro Bookkeeping which also assists in financial management.

Various transformations took place in the banking sector which resulted in new banking products, services and processes. Of notable importance is the introduction of online banking, card based banking and ATMs which played a significant role in increasing convenience to banking services by customers. A number of ATMs can be found in most of rural towns and townships as well as in major towns in South Africa. Also notable in the South African banking sector is the increasing use of electronic commerce (e-commerce). E-commerce is the sharing of business information, maintaining business relationships and conducting business transactions by means of telecommunication networks (Chaffey 2002). The increasing use of the internet and mobile phones has made possible the implementation of e-commerce.

The arrival and wide use of credit cards in the South African economy is also a notable consequence of technological innovations in the South African Banking Sector. Credit card alliances with non financial institutions have been common practices in South Africa. For example credit card alliances were noted in 2006 between Edgars and Standard Bank, Metropolitan and Mercantile Bank, Kulula and FNB and Virgin and ABSA and Voyager and Nedbank among others (Hawkins 2006). These alliances allow customers to do their trading transactions with these companies anywhere without having to go to the bank or the bank's ATM to make withdrawals, thus increasing easy access to funds for customer whenever on demand.

Apart from consumer intended technologies, technologies such as smart phones, notebooks, broadband access and social networking sites and applications among others, found a place in the day to day operations of businesses. For example, smart phones have increased productivity by enabling employees to work outside the confines of their offices by creating a new phenomenon in business that I would like to term, 'the mobile workforce". Besides being an integral part of our daily lives, smart phones play a critical role in businesses and smart phones are fast becoming a replacement for laptops and notebooks.

Furthermore, the use of social networking sites as marketing tools as well as connecting with customers is fast becoming common practice among several businesses in South Africa and elsewhere around the world. According to Intergr8 co-founder, Rob Sussman, an estimate of about 10% of the world population is on Facebook, with 50% active every second day. From a business perspective, Facebook allows you to build a substantially larger social network than one can build in an isolated non-networked geographically restricted environment. "I use Facebook to connect to the Intergr8 employees and customers for more direct personal communication" said Rob. The majority of companies in South Africa have Facebook pages where they can connect with customers anytime. Almost all banks in South Africa have Facebook pages where customers can "like" and express their views, raise their concerns and ask questions. Furthermore, banks also use this platform to communicate their corporate messages to their customers and potential customers.

The introduction and use of different technologies in the banking sector is mainly to create, communicate and deliver superior value to consumers with the major objective of being competitive in the market. A question will arise as to how consumers are viewing such a technology wave and whether it is beneficial to them. The next section will account for consumers' use of technology and their reactions to technological changes.

The use of Technology in the Services Sector

Technological innovations play an important role in increasing the competitiveness of the firm, particularly in the 21st century economy where advances in technology are a common phenomenon. Simple technologies in the financial services sector came in terms of the widespread issuing of magnetic stripe ATM cards and the phasing out of high cost manual methods of banking such as transacting at counters with savings books (Porteous and Hazelhurst 2004). A study by the research company, Gartner (2011), estimated that by 2014 more than three billion of the world's adult population will be able to transact electronically via mobile and internet technology. Gartner (2011) revealed that two trends are emerging that will drastically change the future of the world's trading economy, viz; (i) the rapid rise of the adoption of mobile and internet technology in emerging economies; and (ii) advance in mobile payment, commerce and banking. These trends exhibit the shape of our technological era. Also contributory to the banking sector is the increasing use of cell phones. World Bank analysts have suggested that mobile commerce, (the use cell phone in doing trading transactions) and electronic finance are apparent in developing countries as connectivity levels and reliability increases. They predicted that this trend will allow developing countries to leapfrog in the development of their financial systems. For South Africa, 2006 was projected as the take off year for online banking (Porteous and Hazelhurst, 2004).

Herferman (2001) asserted that the retail banking sector has witnessed rapid process technology, where new technology has altered the way key tasks are performed. In his study in the UK, the number of ATMs in services has risen from 568 in 1975 to 15208 in 1995, a trend he said was also observed in all industrialized countries.

In another study, Berger (2003:143) identified the changes in the use of selected banking technologies, indicating a significant growth in the use of new information technologies (IT) and financial technology. To this extent, the role of technology in the banking sector and financial services sector at large need to be examined critically, as the information and communication technologies (ICT) is changing the banking sector operations and efficiency The benefits accruing from the introduction of new technologies in the banking sector determines greatly the reactions of consumers to these technologies. In that light these chapters highlight some of the perceptions about new technologies by both consumers and the corporate.

RESEARCH METHODOLOGY AND DESIGN

The empirical study was approached from the perspective of a formal research design through the definition of the study population, the incorporation of suitable measuring instrument and reliable techniques for data analysis as stipulated in Cooper and Schindler (2008). The empirical research for the study was conducted in two ways; a pilot study and the main survey. The measuring instrument was designed to measure the influence to technological innovations in the financial services sector. Following the design of the initial questionnaire, a pilot study on 20 respondents was conducted. The result of the pilot study and a discussion with a panel of experts led to the initial questionnaire being revised accordingly taking into consideration all the flaws identified in the process. The questionnaire was later administered to 613 respondents which consisted of financial services sector customers as well as members of the general public in the Eastern Cape province of South Africa. Following rigorous follow-ups on respondent a response rate of 65.7% was achieved.

Figure 3.1 below illustrated the percentage respondents by age who participated in the survey. The majority of the respondents (27%) were between the ages 26-35 and the least number of respondents was from the ages of more 65.

Furthermore, to supplement the results of the questionnaire survey, interviews were conducted with banking sector officials. Fifteen employees from banks were interviewed and they were from Standard Bank, First National Bank, ABSA, NedBank and Capitec Bank.

RESULTS AND DISCUSSIONS

This section presents the results of the study that was conducted in the Eastern Cape Province of South Africa. A discussion of the results, linking them to previous studies was also incorporated in this section.

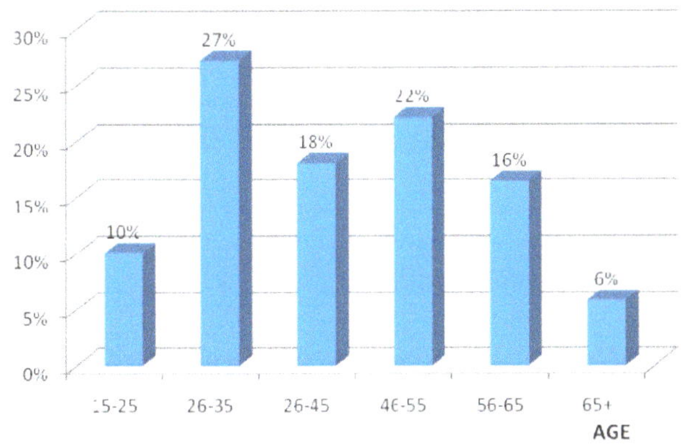

Figure 3.1. Percentage respondents by Age

Perceptions about Services Oriented Technology

Customer Perceptions

There is a mixed reaction by consumers about the ever changing technological advances. In a study conducted in South Africa, the results reviewed that adult population is not so pleased by rapid changing technological advances. 86% of the adult population (65 or more years old) interviewed argued that technological advances are becoming a burden on their part and in several cases they need a technological savvy or well up individual to assist them in making certain transactions using technology. The reaction was markedly different from that of the younger population with more than 73% viewing technology as a must have necessity to function effectively. Arguments raised include the fact that the use of technology, particularly for business purposes is funny and more convenient.

While the introduction of new technology into the banking sector come with several benefits to the organisation and consumers, the reactions of different groups of people to such changes are different. Some consumers see technological changes as a threat to their old ways of doing things (they have inertia), while other groups of consumers see it as opening doors to learning new things and ways of doing things.

The results of the study further suggested that many people perceive new technologies as a "push" by banks. In this study, 63% of SA adults agreed that banks force them to use new technology due to circumstantial reasons. However a closer analysis of the results suggested that it is not technology per se that is a problem but rather how it is applied. Two thirds of people, rich as well as poor, prefer face to face service to an ATM, a third of the elderly claim to avoid banking machines as much as possible. However 75% of poorer and 83% of the richer people say they are prepared to learn new technology. The rapid acceptance of cell phones across the population is an indication of an ability to learn new technology if the benefit are substantially enough. These results corroborates with findings presented by Porteous and Hazelhurst (2004).

The fact that businesses exist to serve consumers any action should have a customer focus in mind. Business must ensure that their new technologies are received positively by consumers or ensure a thorough market assessment before investing in some sophisticated technologies which may make the consumer worse off.

Corporate Perceptions

The impression that we get from the business sector is that technology is a 'necessary evil', something that every enterprise operating in the 21st century economy must embrace in order to improve and maintain its competitiveness. An analysis of the banking sector in South Africa revealed that every bank is striving to stand out with a unique technological innovation that distinguishes it from competitors. In every corporate message, every bank is trying to convey the message that, 'We are leaders in technology and we give you the best value for money'. This message is evident in the adverts by FNB, ABSA, NedBank, Capitec and standard Bank among others.

Furthermore, too often businesses use technology as motivating tools for their employees. Social networking sites like Facebook, Twitter, Myspace and Skype are viewed as tools to boast the employees' moral during their spare times. However, the overuse of such will reduce productivity if employees use company time and resources to pursue their social needs. Using social media can be overwhelming but employees need not be carried away. However, employees can use sites that best fit their goals, market and personality for personal branding purposes. Spending time on social networking promoting yourself online can yield powerful positive results, however you need to be consistent in both promoting your image and your efforts.

If employees approach the social media with a plan and a specific focus of providing and sharing useful information while interacting with fans, friends, family and followers, it can be an effective and even fun part of your marketing mix. Overall, businesses view technological innovations as a tool that must be embraced and be kept improving to remain competitive in the ever-changing market.

Costs and benefits of Technological Innovations in the Financial Services Sector

Technological innovations have had major contributions in improving the efficiency of the financial services sector. Of particular note is the fact that technological innovations have reduced significantly the cost of transacting and this will benefit both the bank and the consumer. The use of ATMs, Credit cards, internet banking, among other recent advances in technology in the South African Banking Sector, has seen substantially decreases in the cost of doing banking transactions. The new channels for delivery of banking products and services, such as through the internet, ATMs and cell phone banking, have the advantage for customers of longer hours of service and more efficient and cheaper means of delivering the products (Reixach 2001).

Changes in ways of transacting from the recent advance of information and communications technology are not limited to improving the efficiency of traditional businesses but are also enabling the development of new instruments in specific fields. A good example is the development of a new supply channel for financial services, namely the internet, which has made it possible to establish extensive and low-cost financial networking (Hayami, 2000). To this end, information and communications technology has enabled the more diversified and convenient provision of financial services, including via the internet and ATM networks. These will significantly reduce costs compared to old ways of doing banking transactions, which require face to face-over the counter transactions associated with huge travelling costs for customers to bank branches.

Furthermore, IT innovation affects the competitive position of firms both through production efficiency and changes in the goods markets. Firms that are competitive in the modern market are those that are able to create, develop and implement new and better ways of carrying out tasks. This calls for all the firms to be innovative in order for them to be competitive in the marketplace. Technological innovations enable firms to increase output via the introduction of new processes and altering the competitive environment, thereby creating pressure for firms to adjust (Jürgen et al 2002).

Technological innovations have undoubtedly introduced enormous benefits to banks, particularly in terms of productivity increases, cost reduction through labour saving and increased profitability. The use of new technology has increased outputs and reduced costs as both technological capital investments and technology human resources have a positive relationship to productivity (Jayamaha 2008). Consumers should be awarded the chance to enjoy the full benefits derived from the use of latest technological advances. This would increase banks' competitiveness through differentiation and customer service improvement, reduced transaction costs, better risk avoidance, and maintaining a stable customer base and market share (Jayamaha 2008).

Despite the wide spectrum of benefits identified from the introduction and use of technological innovations in the banking sector, there are some social and economic problems associated with technological innovations some of which have enormous consequences to the society and the nation at large if left unattended.

One of the problems brought in by technological innovations is their strain on the budgets of the banks. Most of the banks' resources are being channelled towards advancing and coping with rapid changes in technology. Apart from personal costs, technology is the biggest item in the budget of the bank, and is the fastest growing one (Reixach 2001). If not managed with caution, emphasis may be put on pursuing technological advancement while compromising other activities which are important to the success of the enterprise.

Technological innovations, particularly in information and communication technology (ICT) have resulted in globalisation of businesses and business operations. Under such conditions, competitive pressures are likely to intensify in many parts of the economy and increasingly affect previously sheltered sectors such as energy, transport, communication and distribution. The result is an increased pressure to adjust and could lead to transition problems in economies which are insufficiently able to change, a common problem of most African economies (Reixach 2001).

To the society, technological innovations, if not managed properly may result in such problems as pollution and unethical behaviours. For example the use of short message services (SMS) had been an instrument in conveying malicious information and images among teenagers which lead to moral decay.

Furthermore, the advances in technology also mean that consumers must learn how to use such technologies. Such learning should furthermore be fast to be up to date with the fast changing technologies. Slow learners and the elders who have inertia may be frustrated with such demands leading to psychological problems on consumers. More importantly, technological innovations have significant effects on service quality, efficiency and profitability.

Technological Innovations vs Services Quality

Studies have shown that among consumers, service quality and experience is the most spoken about topic, followed by a great product or service which is closely related to something "astonishing". Customer service should focus on understanding and meeting the needs of customers effectively. According to Accenture (2007) the customer service levels in South Africa leaves a lot to be desired. South Africa is rated as one of the worst countries globally in terms of customer service, with a service maturity rating of 6%. Compared to the leader, Singapore with a rating of 89%, there is a need for improvement in customer service in South Africa. This outstandingly poor customer service in the country, however provide a fantastic opportunity for all business owners who want to gain a competitive advantage by tapping into exceptional customer service offering. Providing the best customer service is the best, if not the only solution to gain customer satisfaction, customer retention and creating customer value. Technological innovations plays a significant role is delivering quality customer service. Effective and prompt modes of communication, instant feedback and customer tracking solutions are all ingredients of an excellent customer service package. This has been enabled by the advent of the latest information and communication technologies.

A study into on the banking sector in South Africa revealed that consumers (88.5%) are satisfied with the level of communication they get from banks about their accounts information and in terms of how quick their complaints are addressed due to advanced technologies. Consumer however indicated their displeasure with some bad systems in a few banks. The study revealed that an estimated 80% of the aggrieved customers' problems with technology are caused by bad systems. It became apparent that most of the service problems customers' encounter in trying to do business occurs as a result bad delivery systems, which are out of date, too complex or just customer unfriendly.

Taking for instance, most dysfunctional systems include telephone technology that are characterised by features like call director or voice-mail systems with frustratingly lengthy menu options, or caller holder features that attempt to entertain customers with sometimes annoying music. In several cases some businesses even interrupt the entertainment with an occasional commercial message. Imagine an aggrieved customer on the other end of the line. To aggravate the problem, imagine when a customer finally reaches a real person, too often to find that the person is a company's newly appointed secretary with little knowledge of the company's product and no authority to solve the customer's problem. Such technologies cost companies millions in lost customers due to poor management of technology. It is therefore paramount to ensure that a smooth and efficient management system of technology is embraced in every aspects involving direct contact with customers and elsewhere in the services chain.

Technological Innovations vs Efficiency

Efficiency is a general term in economics that describes how well a system is performing in generating the maximum output for given inputs with the available technology. Efficiency is improved if more output is generated without changing the level of inputs, or in other words, the amount of "friction" or "waste" is reduced. The idea of efficiency broadly refers to the fact of using limited resources in the best possible way (Caruana, 2003). Qayyum and Khan (2007) defined efficiency as the ratio output per unit input in which case they suggested that efficiency is decomposed into two components namely, allocative (economic) efficiency and technical efficiency.

Efficiency relates the cost incurred compared to the product obtained. In general terms, the idea of efficiency broadly refers to the fact of using limited resources in the best possible way. In other words, an economic system is efficient if it does not waste its resources, in such a way that it minimises individuals' well-being (Caruana, 2003).

A system can be called economically efficient if no one can be made better off without making someone else worse off. The most output is obtained from a given amount of inputs and when production proceeds at the lowest possible per unit cost. Efficiency introduces an additional factor to an enterprise, namely risk. Thus in every effort to improve efficiency, the risk factor should be taken into account. This idea factors in significant constraints and makes it necessary to focus on improved efficiency as a balanced process in which attention must be paid to a series of management elements that should not be taken for granted in cost-cutting drives. For example, no clear efficiency gain is achieved if it is done at the expense of increasing operational risk (Caruana, 2003). Operational risk refers to the risk of loss resulting from inadequate or failed internal processes, people and systems, or from external events. The definition includes legal risk, which is the risk of loss resulting from failure to comply with laws as well as prudent ethical standards and contractual obligations (Anon 2003).

These definitions of efficiency are not exactly equivalent. However, they all encompass the idea that nothing more can be achieved given the resources available. Thus efficiency is achieved through making the best use of the available resources. Measures of technical output efficiency include estimates of banks' scale efficiency. Scale efficiency refers to banks or branches achieving an optimum size for producing financial services and thereby, ensuring operation at the minimum point of the average cost curve. There is a negative relationship between bank branch size and branch efficiency (Oster and Antioch 1995). Some of the strategies adopted by banks includes re-engineering its processes (through identifying key business activities that can either be streamlined or eliminated), improving the skills of its labour force through training and increasing the use of technology. Over time, the net effect of these initiatives will result in significant improvements in branch efficiency and elimination of the negative relationship between branch size and efficiency (Oster and Antioch 1995).

Furthermore, the increased competition resulting from financial deregulation may provide impetus for the achievement of further technical output efficiencies through scale economies. Economies of scale are achieved when a bank recognises that the cost of producing a range of outputs is less than the cost of producing them independently (Oster and Antioch 1995). To measure the efficiencies of the banks the major interest is in Xefficiency, which shows whether banks use their inputs efficiently or not (Schure and Wagenvoort, 1999). To customers efficiency is perceived in the sense of the bank completing transactions in the shortest possible time thus minimising the amount spent by customers to complete transactions.

In the financial services sector at large, the concept of efficiency can be thought of in terms of how well a bank employs its resources relative to the existing production possibilities frontier (or, in other words, relative to the current 'best practice') how an institution simultaneously minimises costs and maximises revenue, based on an existing level of production technology (Oster and Antioch 1995). Investment in technology is an important mechanism for attaining greater efficiency. This is because technological development allows processes to be undertaken more easily, simultaneously eliminating certain time and labour-intensive tasks so that operating cost cuts are achieved.

In addition the capacity to process massive amounts of data efficiently in real time allows for better risk management and also for services better tailored to client needs. However, efforts to improve efficiency must be compatible with the challenges posed by new technologies (Caruana, 2003). In that light, the costs of new technologies should not outweigh the benefits associated with these technologies. Thus a thorough cost-benefit analysis is important in making decisions regarding new technologies. In other words it is imperative that when employing a new technology that the anticipated benefits should outweigh the anticipated costs. Technical efficiency correlates directly to overall company efficiency, this means if a business spends wisely on information technology it will reap the rewards in sales and customer service improvements and ultimately improved profitability.

A detailed account on the determined measurement of efficiency in the South African banking sector is the one provided by Mboweni (2004). According to him, the efficiency of the banking sector can be determined by expressing operating expenses as a percentage of total income.

"Currently, the international benchmark for efficiency is 60 per cent. In the past, South African banks were able to keep this ratio below or close to the international benchmark. The ratio, however, has increased from 60.2 per cent in 1999 to 67 per cent in 2002. The high volatility in efficiency in 2002 indicates that the South African banking sector was indeed experiencing problems with profitability in the first six months of 2002. This deterioration was confirmed by the return on equity of 5.4 per cent (smoothed over 12-months) and the return on assets of 0.4 per cent (smoothed over 12- months) as at the end of June 2002. Since 2002, however, the efficiency ratio has improved and, as at the end of October 2004, the efficiency of the banking sector was 65.2 per cent. By the end of October 2004, the return on equity and the return on assets of the banking sector had similarly improved" (Mboweni 2004).

The historical account of the efficiency of the South African Banking sector above shows a growing trend. This is an indication of various new approaches to service delivery which improve efficiency, most notably advance in new technologies. Looking at the efficiency trend in the South African banking sector, a possibility for further improvements is there if new approaches to improving efficiency are sought.

In a study of the banking sector in South Africa on the view of consumers regarding the improvement of efficiency of the banking sector in the past ten years, 92% of the respondents agreed that the efficiency of the banking sector has improved in the past ten years due to improvement in technology. Only 2% disagree of the fact that the efficiency of the banking sector has improved while 6% neither agree nor disagree.

The perceived improvement was attributed to continued improvements in technologies used in banks. The perceptions of respondents on ATMs, online banking and cell phone banking on their contributions to efficiency and cost reductions were also sought. These also receive a positive response with 53% of the respondents indicating that ATMs are cost effective, 77% of the respondents agreeing that online banking and cell phone banking are cost effective.

Technological Innovations vs Profitability

Approaches to increasing efficiency in every venture are aimed at ultimately increasing profitability. This objective is tantamount to that of the firm namely wealth creation for the owners. Thus it is critical to address the link between technological innovations, efficiency improvement and ultimately profitability.

Several studies revealed a positive relationship between efficiency and profitability, that is, the higher the efficiency, the greater the profitability. However in a study carried out by Abbaso˘glu, Aysan and Gunes, (2007) it appears that there is no clear relationship between efficiency and profitability. In their study of the Turkish banking sector, the results indicated that there is no significant evidence from the data that efficiency affects profitability. In the study which took the return on assets into account, foreign banks were found to be significantly more profitable than domestic banks. While the least efficient banks turned out to be foreign with the exception of a few, being foreign increases banks' profitability. This result shows us that foreign banks are less efficient but more profitable compared to the domestic banks. Hence, there is no clear evidence that there is a positive relationship between efficiency and profitability (Abbaso˘glu, Aysan and Gunes, 2007).

Increasing profitability is one of the fundamental objectives of any business operating as a going concern. To achieve increased profitability, the business should aim at reducing costs in the best way possible. The use of advanced and up to date technological innovations is instrumental in this regard. The major focus on improving efficiency is to reduce the costs of producing a desired level of output. Strategies and actions to minimise costs are paramount in the bid to reduce the firm's expenses and this leads to increased profitability of the venture. In the banking sector it is important that the bank be able to employ the most cost effective approaches to complete every transaction. A study on the banking sector in South Africa revealed that 75% of the respondents agree that technological innovations resulted in cost savings. Sixty five percent (65%) of the respondents agreed that cell phone banking is helping in reducing costs of banking. Among the reasons cited included cheapness of cell phone banking, no costs of travelling to the bank and the convenience of cell phone banking (customers can do their transaction anywhere, anytime). 35% of the respondents were of the opinion that cell phone banking does not help in reducing banking costs for customers. The reason for their argument ranged from the need for airtime, the need for cell phones with access to internet (that is, a phone with GPRS) which are expensive and the fact that some transaction are simply not feasible using cell phone banking.

Linking Efficiency to Profitability

Approaches to increasing efficiency in every venture are aimed at ultimately increasing profitability. This objective is tantamount to that of the firm namely wealth creation for the owners. Thus it is critical to address the link between efficiency improvement and profitability. Soteriou and Zenios, (1997) suggested a joint analysis of operational efficiency and profitability as shown in Fig 1. In the analysis bank branches were categorised into four categories similar to the Boston Consultants Group (BCG) matrix, namely stars, dogs, sleepers and cows.

Sleepers are those branches that are highly profitable, while they are inefficient. Hence, their profitability can be further increased if they are awakened and improve their operational efficiency. Stars are the branches that match their superior operational efficiency with profitability, while cows are lagging in profits and a major reason for this is their operational inefficiency. Finally, for the dogs it was concluded from the analysis that enhancement of their profitability can not come from improvements in operations, since they are already efficient on the operational side (Soteriou and Zenios, 1999). The analysis revealed a positive relationship between efficiency and profitability, that is, the higher the efficiency of a bank branch the greater the profitability. However in a study carried out by Abbaso˘glu, Aysan and Gunes, (2007) it appears that there is no clear relationship between efficiency and profitability. In their study of the Turkish banking sector, the results indicated that there is no significant evidence from the data that efficiency affects profitability. In the study which took the return on assets into account, foreign banks were found to be significantly more profitable than domestic banks. While the least efficient banks turned out to be foreign with the exception of a few, being foreign increases banks' profitability. This result shows us that foreign banks are less efficient but more profitable compared to the domestic banks. Hence, there is no clear evidence that there is a positive relationship between efficiency and profitability (Abbaso˘glu, Aysan and Gunes, 2007).

Increasing profitability is one of the fundamental objectives of any business operating as a going concern. To achieve increased profitability, the business should aim at reducing costs in the best way possible. Thus the use of advanced technologies to improve efficiency and cut costs should the focal strategy to remain competitive in the 21st century economy.

CONCLUSION

Overall, the analysis leads to the conclusion that technological innovations have changed the business landscape of the 21st century. The majority of the respondents interviewed showed positive responses with respect to the improvement of efficiency and cost reductions as a result of the use of advanced technological innovations in the financial services sector.

From the above discussion, it can be noted that the importance of technological innovations in the financial services sector reign supreme for the success of banks operating in the 21st century economy. It is important to lay a foundation to understanding the concept of technology and technological innovations. Understanding the concept of technology in detail is paramount as a basis for which innovation (the creation, introduction and use of new ideas and tools) can take root. Innovation can be in the form of product innovation (that results in new products or services) or process innovation (that involves the introduction of new ways of performing tasks in an organisation).

More contributory to the new developments in the banking sector is the innovation in information technology (hardware and software that are used to store, retrieve, and process and communicate information). This has been discussed in this chapter. Furthermore the acceptance, use and reactions of consumers to new technologies in the financial services sector had been discussed. Finally, the contributions of technological innovations to the banking sector as well as to consumer had been alluded to in this chapter. It can be deduced from the contributions of new technology that, technological innovations has resulted in reduced transaction costs for both the customers and banks, as well as improved efficiency in the banking sector.

REFERENCES

1. Abbaso˘glu, O. F., Aysan, A. F and Gunes, A., (2007). Concentration, Competition, Efficiency and Profitability of the Turkish Banking Sector in the Post-Crises Period [Online: available http://mpra.ub.uni-muenchen.de/5494/ MPRA Paper No. 5494, posted 07. November 2007 / 04:45, Accessed April 17, 2008.
2. Abhiman, D., Subhash, C. R. and Ashok, N., (2007). Labour-use efficiency in Indian banking: A branch-level analysis, Omega 37 (2009) pp 411 – 425 [Online: available at www.sciencedirect.com accessed April 17, 2008)]
3. Anon (2003). Supervisory Guidance on Operational Risk Advanced Measurement Approaches for Regulatory Capital.
4. Bain, R. (1937). Technology and State Government. American Sociological review Vol. 2 No. 6 p. 860-865.
5. Caruana, J. (2003). Savings banks - Efficiency and an ongoing commitment to society. Efficiency of financial institutions [Online: available at www.bis.org, Accessed April 17, 2008].
6. Chaffey, D., (2004). E-Business and E-commerce Management 2nd Edition, Essex: Pearson Education Limited.
7. Halkos, G. E. and Salamouris, D. S., (1999). Efficiency measures of the Greek Banking Sector: A non-parametric approach for the period 1997-1999. University of Thessaly, Department of Economics, Discussion paper series 01/04
8. Hawkins, P., (2006). South African banking landscape: Introduction & Background, Greenside: FEAsibility Pty Ltd
9. Hayami, M., (2000). The impact of innovation in information and communications technology on financial systems [On-line]. Available: www.bis.org [accessed April 3, 2008].
10. Jayamaha, R, (2008). Impact of IT in the Banking Sector [On-line]. Available: www.bis.org [accessed February 7, 2008].
11. Jürgen, S., (2002). IT innovations and financing patterns: implications for the financial system [On-line]. Available: www.bis.org [accessed April 3, 2008].
12. Mboweni, T. T, (2004). The South African banking sector - an overview of the past 10 years [Online: available at www.bis.org, Accessed April 17, 2008].
13. Oster, A. and Antioch, L., (1995). Measuring Productivity in the Australian Banking Sector [online: available at http://www.rba.gov.au/PublicationsandResearch/Conferences/1995/OsterAntio ch.pdf Accessed (May 26, 2008).
14. Porteous, D. and Hazelhurst, E. (2004). Banking on Change: Democratizing Finance in South Africa, 1994-2004 and beyond, Cape Town: Double Story Books
15. Qayyum, A. And Khan, S., (2007). X-efficiency, Scale Economies, Technological Progress and Competition: A Case of Banking Sector in Pakistan. Islamabad Pakistan Institute of Development
16. Reixach, A., (2001). The effect of information and Communication technologies on the Banking Sector and Payment System, University de Girona
17. Rogers, M., (1998). The Definition and Measurement of Innovation, Melbourne Institute Working Paper No. 10/98
18. Schatzberg, E. (2006). Technik Comes to America: Changing meanings of Technology before 1930. Technology and Culture, Vol. 47, No, 3 pp. 486-512.
19. Schure, P. and Wagenvoort, R.(1999). Economies of Scale and Efficiency in European Banking: New Evidence, European Investment Bank Economics and Financial Report, 1999.
20. Soteriou, A. and Zenios, S. A. (1999). Operations, Quality, and Profitability in the Provision of Banking Services. Management Science, Vol. 45, No. 9, Performance of Financial Institutions, (Sep., 1999), pp. 1221-1238
21. Subrahmanya, M. H., (2005). Pattern of technological innovations in small enterprises: a comparative perspective of Bangalore (India) and Northeast England (UK). Technovation 25, pp 269-280 [online]
22. Wallace J., Zeffane R. M., Schermerhorn, J. R., Hunt J. G., and Osborn R. N., (2001). Organisational Behaviour: A global Perspective 2nd Edition, Milton: John Wiley & Sons Inc.

INDEX